Women, Gender and Disaster

WOMEN, GENDER AND DISASTER

Global Issues and Initiatives

Edited By

Elaine Enarson
P. G. Dhar Chakrabarti

Los Angeles I London I New Delhi
Singapore I Washington DC I Melbourne

First published in 2009
Paperback edition published in 2015 by

SAGE Publications India Pvt Ltd
B1/I-1 Mohan Cooperative Industrial Area
Mathura Road, New Delhi 110 044, India
www.sagepub.in

SAGE Publications Inc
2455 Teller Road
Thousand Oaks, California 91320, USA

SAGE Publications Ltd
1 Oliver's Yard, 55 City Road
London EC1Y 1SP, United Kingdom

SAGE Publications Asia-Pacific Pte Ltd
3 Church Street
#10-04 Samsung Hub
Singapore 049483

Published by Vivek Mehra for SAGE Publications India Pvt Ltd, typeset in 10.5/12.5pt Adobe Garamond by Star Compugraphics Private Limited, Delhi.

Library of Congress Cataloging-in-Publication Data

Women, gender and disaster: global issues and initiatives/edited by Elaine Enarson and P. G. Dhar Chakrabarti.
   p. cm.
Includes bibliographical references and index.
   1. Disasters—Social aspects. 2. Emergency management. 3. Women—Social conditions. 4. Sex role. I. Enarson, Elaine, 1949– II. Chakrabarti, P. G. Dhar.

HV553.W63   363.34'8082—dc22   2009   2009031291

ISBN: 978-93-515-0239-5 (PB)

The SAGE Team: Rekha Natarajan, Jayshree Kewalramani, Sanjeev Kumar Sharma and Trinankur Banerjee

Dedication

In recognition of their pioneering work with and on behalf of grassroots women striving to reduce the risk of future disasters, all book royalties will be donated to the international network of Grassroots Organizations Operating Together in Sisterhood (GROOTS) to support the Disaster Watch project. To learn more, please visit their website http://www. disasterwatch.net/index.html

Contents

————•✦•————

Part Four: Gender-sensitive Disaster Risk Reduction

List of Tables, Figures and Boxes

———•✦•———

List of Tables

List of Figures

List of Boxes

Foreword

———— • ✦ • ————

Disasters have been on the rise and are predicted to increase in frequency and intensity due to climate change, rapid urbanisation and environmental degradation. When facing this challenging future of storms, floods and droughts, the active participation of all sections of society—particularly women—is crucial for building the resilience and well-being of all communities and nations. Disasters affect women and men differently, and due to deep-seated gender inequalities, women are at greater risk of suffering from disasters. But discrimination against women does not only accentuate women's vulnerabilities during disasters—it also wastes women's potential as sources of resilience.

Women's roles in securing water, food and shelter, during and after disasters, have been well documented. Yet women are still marginalised in decision making on disaster issues, even as they often hold vital social knowledge and vast untapped capacity for reducing community risk. *Women, Gender and Disaster: Global Issues and Initiatives* reflects both women's and men's needs and concerns and shows why gendered perspectives need to be integrated into the risk and disaster management process. This book brings a wide-ranging, cross-cultural and grass-roots perspective to the two essential parts of disaster management: disaster response and disaster risk reduction, including case studies on how women are taking disaster matters in their own hands. It not only highlights challenges that must still be overcome but also provides recommendations for achieving equal participation of women in decision making and approaches for integrating a gender perspective into disaster reduction strategies.

For example, practical issues such as gathering sex-differentiated data to address the gender division of labour and power in disaster planning are important tools for change. The overarching analysis of this volume makes it clear that without gender equality, sustainable development is not possible.

We can and should use the cross-cultural insights shared in this book as a tool to increase our knowledge and understand gender vulnerabilities and capacities. The key role women play in disaster risk reduction has been clear to the UN International Strategy for Disaster Reduction (UNISDR) since its inception. This is reflected in the *Hyogo Framework for Action 2005–2015: Building the Resilience of Nations and Communities to Disasters*, which calls for a gender perspective in all disaster risk management policies, plans and decision-making processes. The UNISDR Secretariat encourages governments, local authorities, international agencies, civil society and non-governmental organisations to use this publication to help make disaster risk reduction a movement founded on the specific needs, roles and potential of women, men, boys and girls.

Sálvano Briceño, Director
Secretariat of the United Nations International Strategy
for Disaster Reduction (UNISDR), Geneva

Preface

—— • ✦ • ——

Risk is a part of the human condition, and we live with an eye to the ground and a will to self-protection—women no less (and perhaps more) than men, and people of all ages, abilities, life conditions and cultures. Indeed, the historic inequalities we carry forward into the 21st century— inequalities in health, income, education, welfare, political voice and violence in war and in our homes—have made women risk managers extraordinaire. Women's survival and coping skills, their interpersonal networks and intimate care of the most vulnerable among us and certainly their knowledge of environmental resources and ecosystems are all life-saving in a flood or earthquake. This knowledge protects our families and communities as much or more than the risk maps we create, levees we build or technological information systems we develop.

Many readers of this volume will know, as we do from our respective positions in academia and government, that gender in disasters is more salient in the management of disaster risk than ever before. Why is this? Part of the answer lies in the simple facts of rising social vulnerability: When extreme poverty increases, more women than men are plunged into extreme poverty. When lands are degraded, small landholders like women are most affected. An ageing population is a feminising one, and a society with more people living alone or rearing families alone has more single mothers and widows. Globalisation and urbanisation increase migration, bringing million more women to risky environments on the fringes of urban life. The list goes on.

Part of the readiness now to examine gender may lie in the public face of disaster, as the mass media and independent media alike frame suffering and loss as female. The enormous tragedies of just the past five years (earthquakes in Pakistan and China, wild storms and floods in the United States, Burma and Indian Ocean states) are made real to outsiders through the grief of women and children. Moreover, the transformation of the lives of men and boys in the aftermath was never more evident than in the period following the 2004 tsunami. Certainly, gender is more salient now because of women's political mobilisation around issues such as the avoidable harm inflicted upon their families, livelihoods and neighbourhoods.

The need for an inclusive and holistic approach to vulnerability reduction and resilience building has never been more urgent, and the effectiveness of gender approaches never more evident to mainstream disaster experts. This is still most true with respect to impact and emergency response but the momentum today is towards an understanding of women as risk managers whose contributions to preparedness, mitigation, emergency relief and sustainable recovery are indispensable. This builds on and goes beyond the decade-old campaign of the International Decade for Natural Disaster Reduction to highlight 'women and children as keys to prevention'.

The Social Construction of Gendered Risk Analysis and Practice

The pioneering meeting of women in emergency management in Costa Rica and the early gathering in Multan, Pakistan, in 1993 sparked numerous subsequent gatherings, consultations, workshops and conferences (eight global conferences at last count). The constant refrain woven throughout these proceedings is for more gender-sensitive policy and practice, including both women and men. But the stronger message is for women's leadership at the grass-roots, the development and use of women's capacities and resources and approaches to disaster, linking both vulnerability and capacity to specific contexts and times. Women's lives are as complex and contingent as men's, and our gendered bodies, personalities, roles, organisations and politics are but one part of the social kaleidoscope.

The new approach to gender that we see on the horizon also emphasises the contradictions in women's lives and their different and sometimes divergent needs and interests in disaster contexts. Do female relief workers necessarily 'get it' or respect the culturally specific gender relations they see in the wake of disasters? Do women always act as stewards of the land to reduce emissions or protect forests, for example? No, and nor do women by definition suffer more than men in disasters or always take proactive action in a crisis. In fact, the conclusion to be drawn from the disasters of the past two decades is much simpler: sex and gender are never automatically the primary social facts on the ground nor are these ever in play in isolation from other facts of life. But gender is also never irrelevant and must always be examined and reflected in practice, for men and boys as much as women and girls.

But we do not do this very well yet. In a review of over 100 published articles (English and Spanish) written directly on research questions related to gender and disaster, Enarson and Meyreles (2004) identified two parallel and sometimes divergent analytic streams. Writers from the world's most affluent societies still tend to focus on the individual woman and her socially constructed vulnerabilities, especially those that are psychological and that develop in the wake of discrete disaster events. In contrast, writers based in less affluent countries describe gender relationally, taking into account how differently women and men earn their livelihoods or move in and out of the household and public spheres. They write more on the construction of risk than the management of discrete events. Surely, all angles of vision are needed to address this complex subject. But the global patterns of risk evident in our era of global warming manifestly threaten most of all the girls and women of the global South. Theirs is the knowledge we must capitalise upon to walk a different path and put human safety and freedom first. This is the most pressing knowledge transfer challenge today.

Like our readers, we know that substantial barriers exist to a gender-equitable approach to disaster mitigation, preparedness, relief and recovery; even more so when we confront entrenched male dominance as a root cause of social vulnerability. But, at the turn of the 21st century, we also note the counter trends: a new community of practice is emerging based on converging interests, inter-organisational coalitions and inter-personal networks of all kinds. Gender and disaster specialists, activists, advocates and practitioners no longer work in isolation. There are new initiatives (for example, grass-roots women's groups partnering for prevention, response and recovery), new networks (for example, the Gender and Disaster Network [GDN] and Gender and Climate Change Network), new resources (for example, the Gender and

Disaster Sourcebook and the Inter-Agency Standing Committee [IASC] Gender Handbook) and new institutional initiatives (for example, pre-positioned gender expert teams active in the aftermath of disasters). In the wake of the enormous tragedy in the Indian Ocean and other losses, women's groups, large and small, are organising as never before to reduce hazards, rebuild sustainable communities for women and their families and protect women's fundamental human rights. The International Strategy for Disaster Reduction and its partners are also taking on gender mainstreaming more holistically than ever before.

The Organisation of this Book

The authors whose research and experience are represented here write on a very solid foundation that has grown rapidly since the publication of *The Gendered Terrain of Disaster: Through Women's Eyes* (Enarson and Morrow 1998), including rich analysis by practitioners and advocates (for example, Ariyabandu and Wickramasinghe 2004; Bradshaw 2001); the extraordinary achievements of the women's groups partnering through Disaster Watch around the world (Disaster Watch 2007); the first and second special editions on gender from the *International Journal of Mass Emergencies and Disasters* (Morrow and Phillips 1999; Phillips and Morrow 2008); special editions of the Oxfam journal *Gender and Development* (for example, Clifton and Gell 2001; Masika 2002); papers contributed to the Ankara conference (UN DAW 2001) and to the Honolulu workshop (Gender Equality and Disaster Risk Reduction Workshop 2004); past contributors to *The Gendered Terrain of Disaster: Through Women's Eyes*, and many others whose current research and observations from the field can be accessed through the Gender and Disaster Network (GDN).

Grounded in this new work, we selected writing that illuminates different aspects of reducing risk in the new century. Readers will find wonderfully diverse discussions of what this means for women, men and disaster risk management. In the first part, we set the stage by offering some foundational analysis of gender and disaster risk reduction for readers who may not be familiar with this terrain. Other readers may want to jump ahead to the second part, in which we move to specific challenges and the responses they elicit. Part three carries this perspective forward but focuses more closely on specific initiatives undertaken by women's groups to reduce risk. In the final part, theoretical and operational concerns in gender mainstreaming of disaster risk management are examined. Here, contributors identify specific strategies and outcomes and offer a variety of models, resources and action guides for implementing more general commitments to gender equity in disaster risk reduction.

We offer this book as a testament to what is possible. We hope it is a book that will be read and used. With apologies for blind spots imposed by language, oversight or space constraints, we give sincere thanks to all who made this book possible, including our publisher and reviewers. To our colleagues who have much to say but not enough time to stop and write, we say—stop and write, we need to learn from you. May the next book come soon.

Elaine Enarson

References

Ariyabandu, M. and W. Wickramasinghe. 2004. *Gender Dimensions in Disaster Management: A Guide for South Asia*. Colombo, Sri Lanka: ITDG South Asia.

Bradshaw, S. 2001. *Dangerous Liaisons: Women, Men and Hurricane Mitch*. Managua, Nicaragua: Fundacion Puntos de Encuentro.

Clifton, D. and F. Gell (eds). 2001. 'Humanitarian Work', *Gender and Development*, 9(3): 8–18.

Disaster Watch. 2007. *Archived Materials*. Available online at http://www.disasterwatch. net/ (Accessed on 8 June 2009).

Enarson, E. and Lourdes Meyreles. 2004. 'International Perspectives on Gender and Disaster: Differences and Possibilities', *International Journal of Sociology and Social Policy*, 14(10): 49–92.

Enarson, E. and B. H. Morrow (eds). 1998. *The Gendered Terrain of Disaster: Through Women's Eyes*. Westport, CT: Greenwood Publications.

Gender Equality and Disaster Risk Reduction Workshop. 2004. Proceedings available online at http://www.ssri.hawaii.edu/research/GDWwebsite/pages/proceeding. html.

Masika, R. (ed.). 2002. 'Climate Change', *Gender and Development*, 10(2).

Morrow, B. H. and B. Phillips (eds). 1999. 'Women and Disasters', *International Journal of Mass Emergencies and Disasters*, 17(1).

Phillips, B. and B. H. Morrow (eds). 2008. *Women and Disasters: From Theory to Practice*. Bloomington, IN: Xlibris Books.

UN Division for the Advancement of Women (UN DAW). 2001. Gender Equality, Environmental Management and Natural Disaster Mitigation. Expert Working Group Meeting in Ankara, Turkey. Proceedings available online at www.un.org/ womenwatch/daw/csw/env_manage/documents.html (Accessed on 8 June 2009).

PART ONE

Understanding Gender Relations in Disaster

The four opening chapters of this book initiate our journey by focusing on the concepts of gender and the role of both men and women in disaster risk reduction.

Madhavi Malalgoda Ariyabandu focuses on the concept of gender and its difference from sex or sexuality. She discusses the relationship of both gender and sex with caste, class, age, ability and other aspects of human life and states that gender mainstreaming in disaster risk reduction can be short-circuited by simple confusion about terminology, and the world view and politics they convey. The author sets the stage for dialogue by explaining the central ideas that come into play whenever we speak of 'gender and disaster'. The author quotes examples to show how sex and gender relations in societies invariably augment the vulnerability of women in disasters. The needs of women are generally overlooked in the relief and recovery processes and their capacities and skills are not used as a resource in emergency management and planning. This not only results in denial of benefits to women but also worsens their social and economic status.

Helena Molin Valdés sketches the outlines of the linkages between sustainable development and gender relations with respect to hazards and disasters. The author drives home the point that disasters are unresolved problems of development in which gender and development patterns play a large role and thereby increase the risk for all. Hazards and disasters are no more 'gender blind' than the economic, political, social and environmental development decisions that produce them. The gender dimension is not optional—it is a central dimension of all of our efforts to develop more sustainable and safe ways of organising life on the planet.

Both women and men are put in harm's way through risky development choices and both have much to offer in the struggle to change course. The author has illustrated various case studies where women, who are generally marginalised, have acted as agents of change. The need of the hour is to ensure gender equality in disaster reduction policies and measures by promoting women to be increasingly involved in roles such as leadership, management and decision making, as well as recognising women's position in their community and the larger society.

Prafulla Mishra shares his experience as a researcher and also a relief worker in some of the world's most hazardous places by highlighting how the term gender has become synonymous with 'women', thereby neglecting the issues related to men in the process of disaster risk reduction. What needs to be understood is that men and masculinity are issues not only for humanitarian relief workers but also for feminist theory as well as gender and women's studies. The self-organisation of men around gender difference and gender inequalities is at the cutting edge of all future dialogue in this era. The author emphasises the point that experiences of men need to be shared and listened to, along with involving them in the engendering process. There is also a need for men to understand their own masculinity and the way it plays out in society and at family levels. Moreover, engaging them as agents of change, rather than barriers to change, would help to push gender-based boundaries based on the exclusive involvement of women only.

Finally, Cheryl L. Anderson traces the genesis, structure and process of the international workshop on Gender Equality and Disaster Risk Reduction organised by the Social Science Research Institute of the University of Hawaii in August 2004. Nearly 100 participants from twenty-eight countries deliberated on the themes of *(a)* capacity building in women's groups, *(b)* communication, training and education strategies to reduce risks, *(c)* using science and technology differently, *(d)* new partnerships and collaborations, *(e)* changing organisational culture and structure and *(f)* research for social action and adopted a set of recommendations, which formed the basis of the Honolulu Call to Action. This was probably the first important document that provided a systematic framework for mainstreaming gender-fair practices in disaster management in international and national programmes. One direct fall out of this document was the formal recognition of the importance of gender in disaster risk reduction in the Hyogo Framework for Action adopted at the World Conference on Disaster Reduction in Kobe in January 2005. Another outcome was the recognition of the Gender and Disaster Network as a delegation at the Global Platform for Disaster Risk Reduction in Geneva in June 2007.

1

Sex, Gender and Gender Relations in Disasters

—————•✦•—————

Madhavi Malalgoda Ariyabandu

The effects and impacts of disasters, the individual and institutional response, differ for men and women. These differences arise from a combination of factors and their dynamic inter-relationships. Some of the key factors include biological, sexual and socio-cultural factors which are reflected in gender relations in communities and societies. These are reviewed in turn in the discussion in this chapter.

Gender Perspectives in Disasters

Gender issues are not manifestations of disaster-related crisis situations, but are prevalent in society, operational and visible in daily life at the level of the individual, family, community and society at large and reflected institutionally as well as in social and cultural norms. Gender aspects within the social and community organisation lead to substantial differences in how men and women of all age groups experience and deal with disasters before, during and in the aftermath. The social interactions between men and women in society result in socially constructed roles, responsibilities and identities for men, women, girls and boys. Gender relations in society are broadly reflected in *gendered identities*: a combination of physical and behavioural characteristics which set apart boys from girls, men from women; *perceptions*: views as to how they are differentiated in their roles as men and women; *attitudes*: actions guided by the perceptions and *status*: the place occupied by men and women in family, community and society. Gender relations come into effect in all spheres of life: personal, social, economic and political; they are not equitable and almost always unfavourable and prejudiced towards girls and women. Gender relations have evolved in such a way, resulting in women occupying a subordinate status within family, community and society; and within the same class or caste category women have less power to effect change in comparison to their male counterparts.

Women and men of varying age groups have different life experiences and skills owing to gendered identities, roles and responsibilities. This is key to understanding gender-based differences in disaster impact, response and recovery. It is widely observed, researched and documented that women belonging to different social classes, races, ethnic and age groups are more vulnerable than their male counterparts of the same social class/group before, during and after disasters (Box 1.1).

Box 1.1   Vulnerable among the Vulnerable

Gender-based social, economic, religious and cultural constructs marginalise women across all community groups irrespective of class, caste, economic standing, status, ethnicity, age, and so on. Gendered marginalisation is manifested in terms of levels of poverty, where among the worlds poor more than 60 per cent are women. Women have less ownership of assets and property and they earn less—women all over the world are paid less than men for equal work. Also, women are less skilled and have fewer opportunities to develop skills and have fewer decision-making possibilities within the family and in public sphere. They face greater risk of sexual abuse, domestic and other forms of violence and are often dominated by male members in the family. In essence, women and girls are economically and socially weaker in comparison to men and boys and hold a subordinated status within respective communities, leading to gender-based inequalities and vulnerabilities. Thus, women within the vulnerable populations can be categorised as 'Vulnerable within the vulnerable'.

Source: Ariyabandu, M. M. and D. Foenseka. 2006. 'Do Disasters Discriminate?' in Duryog Nivaran (ed.), *South Asia Network for Disaster Mitigation: Tackling the Tides and Tremors*, pp. 23–40. South Asia Disaster Report 2005, Islamabad.

Gender-based prejudices and divisions in many societies mainly affect girls and women and as these are based on views of them as physically and emotionally weak, inferior in comparison to men and boys, dependent, subordinate and a burden to family such gender-based perceptions form the nature of interactions at personal, family and institutional levels and contribute towards the formulation of gendered attitudes leading to observations, decisions and actions within family and society, as well as in the formal institutions of different kinds including the state. In crisis, these pre-established views are extended to girls and women to identify them as passive and incapacitated victims who are in need of rescue and help.

These perceptions mask and undermine the skills and capabilities of women as individuals and as a group, and they are subjected to social and institutional inequalities. Gendered inequalities are observed with respect to enjoyment of human rights, social, political and economic status, ownership of assets, exposure to sexual and other forms of violence, in 'normal times' as well as different phases of disaster cycle.

Analysis of real situations clearly indicates that although women are often more vulnerable to disasters than men owing to social relations, expectations and conventional gender responsibilities, they are not just the 'helpless victims', as often represented. Women have valuable knowledge and experience in managing and coping with disasters, often formed by living with regular, seasonal disaster cycles and managing the associated risks. Research conducted in five South Asian countries on varying hazards and disasters highlights the gender division of labour in each different phase of the disaster cycle, where women and men perform distinct functions in preparing for and recovering from disasters (Ariyabandu and Wickramasinghe 2004). As a result, both sexes develop specific skills and capabilities, which are often complementary for survival and recovery from disasters. In many communities, women outnumber men in taking an active part in community disaster initiatives—both in leadership roles and at the grass-roots. Yet, in larger, more formal emergency planning organisations, women are scarcely represented, and they are markedly absent from decision-making positions. This appears to be true for both developed and developing countries (Enarson and Morrow 1998).

The strengths and capabilities of women are often ignored in policy decisions and in all formal arrangements related to mitigation and recovery, as has been amply demonstrated in the aftermath of all recent major disasters. This leads to wastage of valuable human resources, creates dependency situations and it reinforces the existing socially and economically imbalanced relationships. This dichotomy is the crux of gender issue and needs to be addressed by both development and the disaster managers.

In the chaos of the disaster situations, when existing family, community and institutional security and protection breaks down, generally prevailing gender-based disparities surface to a greater degree, putting already vulnerable groups at higher risk. The following are some of the gender-based factors which put girls and women at higher risk in disasters (Ariyabandu and Wickramasinghe 2004):

1. Limitations in mobility, segregation, social restrictions which require women and girls to be accompanied by males.
2. Less access to warning information and poor ability to respond.
3. Greater risk of sexual and domestic violence, sexual abuse.
4. Childbirth and pregnancy-related factors.
5. Higher illiteracy rates, lower levels of schooling and training.
6. Socially assigned role of caring for the young, elderly and the sick within the family.

Implications of Gender Factors for Men in Disaster Situations

Gendered identities lead to the concepts of masculinity and femininity, through which men are expected to be physically and emotionally strong and capacitated, be in control and be able to provide economic and physical security to the family. In crisis, the male identity as the provider is challenged when displacement occurs and livelihood opportunities are lost. Also, there are hardly any avenues to deal with the emotional stress since the formal aspects of psychosocial support tend to bypass men, since they are expected to be strong, to be able to face the crisis in a 'manly' manner. While there may be specific interventions to support widows and female-headed households, the concerns of widowers who are left with the responsibility of raising young families are often not addressed. The gender-based social conditioning does not give men and boys space to develop the skills of domestic chores and care giving. Thus, gender-based social expectations largely isolate men in the aftermath of disasters, leaving them to deal with their own loss and grief. The gaps in coping capacities of men in such circumstances can victimise them. It is observed that alcohol consumption and violent tendencies among men increase in the aftermath of disasters, as they adopt these 'coping mechanisms' to deal with loss and trauma.

Biological Factors

The biological/sexual differences between men and women make significant variations in how they individually behave, relate and respond in the disaster cycle. These differences also have implications in the social and institutional patterns of the response. In terms of the socio-cultural aspects, there are processes which make the experience of girls and women quite different from that of boys and men. The sexual differences are mainly related to the biological reproductive function. The social extension of reproductive function has implications for both men and women, but with significant differences for each sex. In looking at the position of women vis-à-vis men in terms of the reproductive function, child bearing and early nurturing functions that are specific to women are extended to a range of social and cultural values, processes and systems. The biological reproductive function itself makes women more vulnerable before, during and in the disaster aftermath as compared to men.

The pre-puberty, puberty, pregnancy and lactating periods often require specific medical, psychological and nursing care and protection. The social aspects of reproductive functions provide the required physical and psychological support and protection in culturally specific manners. The culture of protection of women, young girls and children in the pre-disaster (normal) situations by family and social networks breaks down in the disaster, and both men and women are not familiar or prepared for the new situation. In the new scenario where all individuals are vulnerable, including men and boys, it is the women and young girls who are at the highest risk of rape, assault, sexual violence and trafficking, while young boys, too, can be victims of sexual assault and trafficking. There are observations that people become more aggressive in the stressful circumstances presented by disasters, and it is women and children who become easy victims of such aggression, manifested in the forms of domestic violence, assault and rape. Consequently, it is women who bear the brunt of unwanted pregnancy, psychological trauma of rape and sexual assault, while both men and women run the risk of STDs and AIDS.

Numerous such cases were reported during the Asia tsunami. In Sri Lanka, there were reports of rape in the immediate rescue stages (Fisher unpublished): 'within hours of the tsunami having devastated entire coastal regions of Sri Lanka, tsunami-affected women were subjected to rape and physical and sexual abuse'. There is the reported incidence of a 17-year-old girl who was gang-raped hours after being washed ashore, left orphaned and homeless (Senanayake 2005) and of a 17-year-old whose grandfather tried to sexually assault her in a relief centre (Associated Press 2005). In Chennai, Pattinapakkam Srinivasapuram, a 15-year-old girl was raped and murdered, while she was asleep along with all the other tsunami-affected fisher folks (APWLD 2005: 12).

Biological Aspects in the Emergency Response

Displacement in the disaster aftermath presents different scenarios for women and men, although both have been impacted and uprooted from home. The biological aspects demand certain specific needs of women that must be met: that is, the sanitation and privacy associated with menstruation, pregnancy and lactation, as well as dealing with the social and cultural norms attached to menstruation and childbirth.

In some cultures, menstruating women are separated from the rest of the household, as they are considered unclean; therefore, they do not engage in their regular household work such as cooking and cleaning. Young girls who menstruate for the first time go through complex and elaborate cultural rituals, keeping them in seclusion for days or weeks before they are bathed and integrated within the regular routine of a household.

In emergency response, the sanitary and privacy needs are often neglected even by the most experienced relief and response agencies. In Aceh, Indonesia, in the camps of displaced people, the lack of closed bathrooms forced women to go unwashed for weeks which affected their reproductive health. There were no separate toilets for women and men, making women feel insecure (APWLD 2005: 8). Similar situations were observed in other tsunami-affected countries.

In the camps where management committees were largely male domi-nated, women's health, reproductive care and privacy needs were largely ignored. There have also been instances in Sri Lanka where women were harassed in matters of public distribution of sanitary items. The prevailing socio-cultural norms do not encourage women requesting sanitary wear and contraceptives from male camp leaders (APWLD 2005: 19).

In the first disaster response phase following Hurricane Mitch, with the exception of Nicaragua, information on the affected population was not disaggregated by sex, and relief efforts did not incorporate a gender perspective. This was evident in the inadequacy of addressing women's reproductive health needs: no provisions were made for menstrual and other reproductive health needs in the shelters (Buvinic et al. 1999).

In post-tsunami Aceh, no special care was provided to pregnant women. There were cases of miscarriages and premature births, and others continuing their pregnancies under conditions of severe deprivation (APWLD 2005: 7). Premature babies and low breast milk production were indicative of the levels of stress and malnutrition mothers were facing. Women were giving birth in unsanitary conditions without medical assistance, some in the open air in the rain. In Tamil Nadu, the needs of displaced women who were lactating and those who were pregnant were not adequately addressed by the state (APWLD 2005: 9). It is reported that no treatment was given to women who suffered from breast milk clotting (after losing their babies) at the camps.

Gender Issues in Survival in Disasters

Disasters are windows that showcase the prevailing gender-based inequalities in society. Women were as much as 80 per cent of the dead in some parts of Indonesia, India and Sri Lanka following the tsunami. In five villages in Aceh's Lampu'uk sub-district, according to the women's group Flower Aceh only 40 of the 750 total survivors from a population of 5,500 were women (APWLD 2005). Statistics are similar in other affected communities in the province. According to Oxfam (2005: 4), in four villages in Aceh Besar district, male survivors outnumber the females by a ratio of 3:1. In four villages in North Aceh, the female death toll made up 70 per cent of all fatalities. In Kuala Cangkoy, 80 per cent of the dead were female (APWLD 2005). In the Ampara district in Sri Lanka, 66 per cent of the deaths were those of women (Ariyabandu 2006). This outcome of more female deaths in the 2004 tsunami is a reflection of gendered factors such as *(a)* gendered skill development: most women from the above mentioned countries are not allowed to learn the skills such as swimming and climbing; *(b)* cumbersome female attire: ankle length cloths, saree, salwar kameez make swift moves with the successive tsunami waves impossible and *(c)* women's efforts to carry children and elders who needed help for safety, which made their own survival more difficult.

There are also cases of the social and cultural behaviour expectations of women having implications in the survival. In Bangladesh, without proper protection and observance of *purdah*, women do not respond to cyclone warnings and move to safety: the risk of being socially stigmatised for breaking the socio-cultural norms takes precedence over the risk of cyclone.

Hurricane Mitch, too, demonstrated these worldwide gender differences in health conditions. Mortality was higher among males, but women reported more health problems, both physical and psychological. In El Salvador, women accounted for 52.7 per cent of a total of 8,423 people seeking pre-hospital care and 54.5 per cent of a total of 448 people seeking hospital care. There was also a significant increase in reproductive tract infections (Gomáriz 1999).

Gender Issues in Recovery

Disaster recovery processes clearly demonstrate the gender equity biases in participation, access and rights, mirroring the pre-disaster status. Under normal circumstances, women are less represented in leadership and decision-making positions at formal, public levels, as their domain is largely identified within the home and family. This is largely to do with social attitudes, accepted norms and prevailing patterns in the gender division of labour, which continue into disaster recovery. The intensification of women's multiple roles and the invisibility of their contribution in emergency management and recovery were clearly observed post-tsunami (Ariyabandu 2006) and post-Katrina New Orleans (Enarson 2005). In relief camps, women and girls were often seen taking responsibility for dependents and the needy—taking care of families, children and the elderly. As in regular situations, it was their job to secure firewood, ensure meals for the family and take responsibility for family nutrition and welfare.

In Aceh, Indonesia women were not involved in the governance of the camps and were excluded from the negotiation processes with aid organisations and government institutions that provide supplies

(APWLD 2005: 8). In Sri Lanka, women's participation at different levels of recovery planning and management remained at a low level, despite a range of committees appointed to consult stakeholders. While in the districts in the South, women's participation reached up to 40 per cent in some instances, in the East where the socio-cultural traditions are relatively more conservative it was less than 10 per cent. A large majority of the camps in Sri Lanka, where nearly 250,000 of the displaced lived, were managed almost entirely by teams of men, with the exception of occasional women members in the teams. Similarly in Pakistan, it was observed that in Azad Jammu and Kashmir and North Western Frontier Province, women were not involved in camp management, especially in the camps run by religious organisations (Rural Development Policy Institute Islamabad 2006).

Observers from the Asia Pacific Forum on Women, Law and Development (APWLD) note the clear lack of consultation with women and their roles in rebuilding and sustaining their own families as well as their communities. Women were not adequately consulted in relocation decisions, or house design, even though their knowledge and experience within the community make their ideas need-based and practical. Displaced women mentioned a severe lack of avenues for expressing their concerns during the various stages of recovery planning.

Downplaying of women's knowledge, skills and capabilities, deployment of women in unskilled manual work and poor attentiveness to women's livelihood options in recovery planning were commonplace in the Asia tsunami, Kashmir earthquake and Hurricane Katrina recovery processes. This gap has manifold implications: first, it does not take into account women's knowledge about the family's nutritional, emotional and other basic needs, which is of utmost importance in the camp situations. Second, it denies women the opportunity to contribute to, learn about or respond to a demanding situation with their knowledge and skills. Marginalisation of women in this manner has implications for their strategic needs, with respect to denied opportunities for participation, learning and leadership.

Access to recovery assistance, as well as gaps in legal literacy, particularly in relation to the issues of land and house ownership was highlighted as a concern for both men and women, and particularly for women in the post-tsunami recovery process of Sri Lanka (Human Rights Commission in Sri Lanka 2005: 49). The severe gaps observed in women's direct access to emergency relief were attributable to the 'head of the household' basis for relief planning and distribution. In the socio-cultural set-up in Sri Lanka, it is almost always the father or the husband who is registered as the head of the household in official population statistics. All the government relief distribution schemes were operated on this basis, thus bypassing women and denying them direct access. This approach reinforced women's position of dependency within the family and society.

Gender-based inequities within the existing property and inheritance laws were also highlighted in the tsunami rebuilding procedures. The gaps in existing law, legal literacy and the lack of support and advice leading to issues of land and house ownership for women were clearly evident. Women in Aceh in Indonesia and India do not have ownership rights to land which is registered to their husband and father's names as women are not recognised as head of household (APWLD 2005: 4). According to the Government of Sri Lanka resettlement programmes and regulations, the ownership of new houses/property can only be single, which rules out joint ownership by husband and wife. It showed a strong tendency for the registration of new property for those who lost houses to be in the name of the head of the household, even if the lost house was in the name of the woman, thus denying women the right to ownership (Box 1.2).

Similarly, in South Florida, low-income women such as public housing residents, migrant workers and battered women were particularly hard hit by Hurricane Andrew and were slow to recover. Two years after the hurricane, those still struggling to get housing were the poorest of the poor, mostly minority women (Enarson and Morrow 1998). Indications are that unless specific measures are implemented, female-headed households may also be among the last to recover in the wake of Hurricane Mitch (Buvinic et al. 1999).

Box 1.2   Key Gender Issues in Disasters

- Women and men are vulnerable to disasters in different ways due to social and economic reasons.
- Due to pre-existing gendered relations, within the same social group/class women are poorer and more vulnerable in comparison to men of the same category.
- Impacts of disasters are different on men and women—in terms of survival, death, injury, trauma and recovery.

(Box 1.2 Continued)

(Box 1.2 Continued)

- Needs and priorities of women and men in different stages of the disaster cycle are different (biological, family, social and cultural).
- Gender-based prejudices view women as weak, passive, incapacitated victims in need of rescue in crisis situations, although in reality women of different age groups play an active role.
- Gender-based identities view men as strong and capable who require least assistance.
- Due to gendered identities, women's vulnerabilities get highlighted, capacities and skills get masked.
- Due to gendered identities, vulnerabilities of men are not visible and not recognised.
- Women and men have different skills and capacities resulting from gender-based roles and responsibilities and gender-based division of labour.

Source: Ariyabandu, M. M. and M. Wickramasinghe. 2004. *Gender Dimensions in Disaster Management: A Guide for South Asia,* p. 176. Colombo: ITDG South Asia.

Concluding Notes

Gender 'neutral' actions in the disaster cycle in effect are not neutral, but force women into situations of distress, humiliation, increased risk of being victims of violence and reduced access to opportunities and options which are available to their male counterparts. As the recent disaster events demonstrate, approaches which are gender insensitive have proven to be barriers in effectively reaching the affected, often barring women from getting direct access to relief and recovery—whether it is food rations or shelter for resettlement—and denying them opportunities to participate and contribute with their knowledge and experience. Such interventions not only put women under extra pressure but also limit their engagement in areas such as recovery planning and management and long-term disaster risk reduction, where their opinions and points of view are valid and relevant.

Such actions worsen women's social status and economic position, reinforce women's subordinated position in society and bypass the opportunity offered by the recovery process for social change. These clearly are outcomes of continuation and extension of existing socially inequitable gender relations. Therefore, awareness must be increased of these significant inequalities, imbalances and discriminatory practices in pre-disaster situations that render women of all age groups more vulnerable to disasters.

Inaccurate gender assumptions by policy makers and practitioners, and insensitivity to women's issues and gender perspective in development planning and disaster risk reduction means that interventions fall short of reaching both the development and the disaster reduction goals. Therefore, gender inclusiveness in policies, strategies, plans and programmes is vital in order to empower nations and communities to successfully build the resilience to face the challenges posed by disasters.

References

Ariyabandu, M. M. 2006. 'Gender Issues in Post-tsunami Recovery Case of Sri Lanka', *Earthquake Spectra,* The Professional Journal of the Earthquake Engineering Research Institute, USA, 22(S3): S759–75.

Ariyabandu, M. M. and D. Foenseka. 2006. 'Do Disasters Discriminate?' in Duryog Nivaran (ed.), *South Asia Network for Disaster Mitigation: Tackling the Tides and Tremors*, pp. 23–40. South Asia Disaster Report 2005, Islamabad.

Ariyabandu, M. M. and M. Wickramasinghe. 2004. *Gender Dimensions in Disaster Management: A Guide for South Asia*, p. 176. Colombo: ITDG South Asia.

Asia Pacific Forum on Women, Law and Development (APWLD). 2005. 'Why Are Women More Vulnerable during Disasters?' in *Violations of Women's Human Rights Concerns in the Tsunami Aftermath*. Available online at http://www.apwld.org/pdf/tsunami_report_Oct2005.pdf (Accessed in October 2005).

Associated Press. 2005. 'Fears of Rape Haunt Women in Lankan Tsunami Relief Camps', *Lanka Newspapers*. Available online at http://www.lankanewspapers.com/news/2005/1/151.html (Accessed on 5 February 2005).

Buvinic, M., M. Bertrand, R. Grynspan, and G. Truitt. 1999. *Hurricane Mitch: Women's Needs and Contributions*, p. 19. Technical Paper Series. Washington, DC: Sustainable Development Department, Inter-American Development Bank.

Enarson, Elaine. 2005. 'Women and Girls Last? Averting the Second Post-Katrina Disaster'. Available online at http://www.gdnonline.org/ (Accessed in September 2005).

Enarson, Elaine and Betty Hearn Morrow. 1998. *The Gendered Terrain of Disaster: Through Women's Eyes*. Westport, CT: Greenwood Publications.

Fisher, Sarah. Unpublished. *Gender-based Violence in Sri Lanka in the Aftermath of the 2004 Tsunami Crisis: The Role of International Organisations and International NGOs in Prevention and Response to Gender-based Violence*. Ph.D. Dissertation submitted to the University of Leeds, Institute of Politics and International Studies, United Kingdom in 2005.

Gomáriz, Enrique. 1999. 'Género y Desastres: Introducción Conceptualy Análisis de Situación', Working Document, Inter-American Development Bank (IDB).

Human Rights Commission in Sri Lanka. 2005. *Report of the Women's Division: Disaster Relief Monitoring Unit.* Colombo.

Oxfam. 2005. *The Tsunami's Impact on Woman, Oxfam International Briefing,* p. 17. Novib: Oxfam Netherlands.

Rural Development Policy Institute Islamabad. 2006. 'Field Observations post-2005. Earthquake in Azad Jammu and Kashmir and North Western Frontier Province, Pakistan', Field Notes.

Senanayake, S. 2005. 'Officials Probe Child Rape in Sri Lanka', 1 January. Available online at http://apnews.myway.com/article/20050101/D87BFNJG0.html

2

A Gender Perspective on Disaster Risk Reduction

———•✦•———

Helena Molin Valdés

A gender approach in disaster risk reduction is built on the understanding that both women and men are part of the same society, which as we know, does not mean that we have the same rights, education and options—neither in 'normal' times nor when a disaster strikes. Examples from recent tsunami-stricken South Asia, Central America, India and the Pacific show that women can act as agents of change. Several studies do confirm, however, that most of the time women are affected much worse than men when a disaster strikes and receive fewer benefits when recovery begins. Therefore, we already need to address the specific concerns of women when designing disaster risk reduction policies and measures.

'The Hyogo Framework for Action 2005–2015: Building the Resilience of Nations and Communities to Disasters', adopted by 168 governments in January 2005, at the World Conference on Disaster Reduction in Japan, provides a clear commitment that can guide policy makers and the community at large to engage more systematically in reducing risk to disasters. 'The Hyogo Framework for Action' puts disaster risk reduction into the context of sustainable development planning, programming and poverty reduction strategies and provides an opportunity for these issues to be addressed in emergency preparedness and recovery programmes. It reaffirms the approach of the 23rd special session of the General Assembly ('Women 2000: Gender Equality, Development and Peace for the Twenty-first Century'), stating that as part of the cross-cutting principles: 'A gender perspective should be integrated into all disaster risk management policies, plans and decision-making processes, including those related to risk assessment, early warning, information management, and education and training.'

Disaster reduction policies and measures need to be implemented with a twofold aim: to enable societies to be resilient to natural hazards, while ensuring that development efforts decrease the vulnerability to these hazards. Sustainable development is not possible without taking into account multi-hazard risk assessments in planning daily life, and as such is an issue that impacts on the lives of both women and men. Given that the magnitudes of disasters are partially influenced by the political, economic and socio-cultural contexts, mainstreaming gender into disaster reduction policies and measures translates into identifying the ways in which women and men are positioned in society. This enables the mapping of not only the ways in which the lives of women and men may be negatively impacted but also the ways in which they can contribute to disaster reduction efforts.

In other words, cultural patterns that structure the lives of women and men must also be clearly understood and differing needs, roles and social power in different social and cultural contexts need to be taken into account. Men are usually seen as primary income generators while women's economic activities, often the mainstay of the household economy, are less visible. Women carry the primary responsibility for the care of children, the elderly, the disabled and the ill whose mobility and survival in disasters may be limited. Gender-specific dependencies and vulnerabilities based on reproductive differences are relevant in disasters, as is the respective ability of women and men to participate fully in household, community and national decision making about hazards and risks.

Disasters: Increased Impact

During the past decade, natural hazards, such as earthquakes, landslides, droughts, floods, tropical storms, wild fires and volcanic eruptions, resulted in significant losses in terms of human lives and livelihoods, the destruction of economic and social infrastructure, as well as environmental damages. No systematic sex disaggregated data are available, but anecdotal evidence suggests that women are typically the most affected by disasters, which was certainly the case during the tsunami. Also, women were highly overrepresented among the 120,000 killed in the 1991 cyclone in Bangladesh (Chowdhury et al. 1993) and in more recent events, because cultural norms constrained their access to emergency warnings and cyclone shelters.

A study carried out by the WHO Collaborating Centre for Research on Epidemiology of Disasters (CRED) in Tamil Nadu, India, during 2005–06 found that young children, the elderly and women between 15 and 50 years of age had the highest risk of death during the tsunami.

> Swimming ability appeared to be a significant protective factor against mortality and it is likely that more women would have survived the tsunami if they had known how to swim. As expected, individuals from fishing families and from households located less than 200 meters to the sea had a much higher mortality risk than others. Although the two factors were closely linked, the most influential risk factor was the proximity of an individual's dwelling to the sea. (Guha-Sapir et al. 2006)

The results of this study suggest that the vulnerability of coastal populations could be reduced in a number of ways. Promoting and providing swimming lessons among women and girls is likely to reduce their risk in flood disasters. While the relocation of entire fishing communities away from the coast may not be feasible, improvements in local housing and other infrastructure could strengthen the resiliency of such populations in the future, as could the investment in multi-purpose emergency shelters. Early warning systems are likely to be beneficial, with careful consideration of message dissemination methods to ensure their effectiveness. These should be developed with a gender-sensitive approach in conjunction with community disaster preparedness and awareness programmes.

Gender relations are part of the social and cultural context that shape a community's ability to anticipate, prepare for, survive, cope with and recover from disasters. The loss of women's home-based workspaces, supplies and equipment can have serious repercussions for the household economy. However, these losses are rarely documented. 'The women who lost all their belongings and their life-long savings in India, after the recurrent floods during the monsoons, have not been able to compensate their losses decades later', says Madhavi Malalgoda Ariyabandu, Programme Manager for Disaster Mitigation of the ITDG South Asia, based in Sri Lanka (cited in Enarson 2004):

> This situation has threatened their security within the family relationship. Children (both girls and boys) drop out of school. Young girls whose families lost their savings and jewellery during the floods, which were to provide their dowry in marriage, either lost the opportunity, or had to delay getting married. This has serious implications for their social status, psychology and survival.

In both rural and urban households hit by Hurricane Mitch in Central America in 1998, significant increases were reported in rates of female-led households, which doubled by some accounts. A year after the devastating storm, Honduran relief workers reported that half the sheltered households were headed solely by women; in Nicaragua, 40 per cent of the households were run by women (Delaney and Shrader 2000).

Women: Agents of Change

Nevertheless, women are not only victims but also agents of change. Furthermore, women and men, working together, can identify those hazards that threaten their homes and livelihoods and work together to build safer communities. Some examples illustrate how this can be done.

Gender-sensitive Risk Assessment Model in the Caribbean

Women's community-based organisations in the Dominican Republic and St Lucia participated in an exploratory project to map risk in their communities, including the daily disasters that affect low-income women's lives and the hurricanes, landslides and fires to which they are exposed. With training in basic research methods, the community women conducted interviews, recorded life histories, developed photo essays and drew risk maps to assess their own strengths and the dangers they face. This information was then compiled into Community Vulnerability Profiles to be used by community leaders and shared with local emergency managers. A set of practical guidelines was developed to help women's and other community groups conduct research to assess risk (Enarson et al. 2003).

Women as Agents of Change for Disaster Risk Reduction

Springing from a spontaneous demonstration against indiscriminate deforestation in 1976, women's civil society movement in India (Action for Disaster Reduction and Inclusive Development Dasholi Gram Swaraj Mandal) began to lead development initiatives by addressing environmental issues through a disaster risk reduction perspective. This local environmental movement was founded by women, due to their key role as natural resource managers and close relationship with the forest as a resource. This movement is an expression of the central role women play in environmental and natural resource management in many agricultural communities. After winning respect from communities with their activism, women were increasingly able to position themselves as community leaders and disaster risk reduction activists in their own right. Local women have worked with men to effectively change the ecological profile of the area by preventing deforestation and recharging water resources. This has reduced the risk of flooding and landslides from extreme weather events—disasters which are likely to be exacerbated by climate change (UNISDR 2008: 39).

Reducing Women's Risk, Capitalising on Window of Opportunity after Hurricane Mitch

Several studies show that increased violence against women is often a secondary effect of post-disaster stress all over the world. The Honduran non-governmental organisation (NGO) Puntos de Encuentro conducted a major household survey, participated in a social audit, launched public education campaigns and developed workshops on women and re-construction after Hurricane Mitch in Nicaragua. To mitigate possible violence against women in the aftermath, Puntos de Encuentro integrated anti-violence education directly into post-disaster recovery work. Working through various media outlets, they developed a community education campaign with a key message: 'Violence against women is one disaster that men can prevent'. 'This workshop not only enabled participants to work through the emotional difficulty of post-traumatic stress but also helped them understand the need for transforming gender roles in their community,' one observer recalled. Puntos de Encuentro's work has been used as a model for capitalising on the window of opportunity to challenge structural inequalities that undermine community solidarity in the face of disaster (Delaney and Shrader 2000).

Reducing Social Vulnerabilities and Providing Skills Training for Disaster Preparedness

An experience from the Tsunami Response Programme, Andaman and Nicobar Islands led by Action Aid International in partnership with Disaster Emergency Committee showcases that it is possible to build women's resilience to disasters by empowering them as participants in community decision making. This was achieved through a Participatory Vulnerability Analysis that gave women space for awareness raising, sharing experiences, skills training and forming participatory women's group and community groups. It shows that even in cultural contexts where women have very little public role, women can be supported to take a much more important role in reducing disaster risk and in helping their entire communities adapt to climate change. Disaster preparedness training such as learning to swim and increasing disaster recovery capacity through financial management, fishing and water management have been ways that these women have been able to adapt to the predicted increased risk of flooding, soil salination and changing rainfall patterns (UNISDR 2008: 34).

Early Warnings and Getting the Message Across—Overcoming the Barriers

Gender-sensitive messages and means of dissemination are key elements to communicating life-saving early warnings that are 'people-centred'. Cheryl L. Anderson, from the University of Hawaii, gives an example from Hawaii, where women participated as community:

> During the 1997–98 El Niño event there were three locations out of seven in our study that had a few women who participated on the ENSO (Pacific El Niño Southern Oscillation) task forces to mitigate drought. These women were responsible for developing public education and awareness programmes in which information was spread from village-to-village and public service announcements were broadcast on radios and television. In addition, a campaign to treat water before drinking helped reduce the recorded incidence of diarrhoeal disease. (Enarson 2001)

Understanding the Scope of Disaster and Risk Reduction

The United Nations adopted an International Strategy for Disaster Reduction (ISDR) in 2000, as a partnership with governments, UN Agencies, regional bodies, civil society and communities, to further pursue increased awareness and public commitment to vulnerability and risk reduction, expanded partnership and networking, as well as research and implementation on hazards, risk and specific disaster reduction measures. Disaster reduction, as envisioned within the ISDR framework, aims to build disaster resilient societies and communities to withstand natural hazards and related technological and environmental disasters and reduce environmental, human, economic and social losses.

It is important to stress that gender equality in disaster reduction policies and measures requires promoting women to have increasing roles in leadership, management and decision making, as well as recognising women's position in their community and the larger society. Since disaster reduction activities are part of development, they are linked to promoting the general welfare of societies, without increasing the risk to hazards.

The initially cited 'Hyogo Framework for Action', promoted and facilitated by the ISDR system, represents a solid commitment and benchmark in how to move forward to substantially reduce disaster losses. Its principles, three strategic goals and five priority areas of action, with key activities and decisions on follow-up and implementation arrangements, indicate the way forward for states and regional and international organisations. Systematic reports on progress will be prepared by the ISDR secretariat. Let us make sure that these actions and reports are gender sensitive (Table 2.1)!

Table 2.1 Gender Equality in Disasters

SIX PRINCIPLES FOR ENGENDERED RELIEF AND RECONSTRUCTION

1. Think Big

Gender equality and risk reduction principles must guide all aspects of disaster mitigation, response and reconstruction. The 'window of opportunity' for change and political organisation closes very quickly. Plan now to:

- respond in ways that empower women and local communities
- take practical steps to empower women, among others

(*Table 2.1 Continued*)

(*Table 2.1 Continued*)

- rebuild in ways that address the root causes of vulnerability, including gender and social inequalities
- create meaningful opportunities for women's participation and leadership
- fully engage local women in hazard mitigation and vulnerability assessment projects
- ensure that women benefit from economic recovery and income support programmes; for example, access, fair wages, non-traditional skills training, childcare/social support
- give priority to social services, children's support systems, women's centres, women's 'corners' in camps and other safe spaces

- consult fully with women in the design and operation of emergency shelter
- deed newly constructed houses in both names
- include women in housing design as well as construction
- promote land rights for women
- provide income-generation projects that build non-traditional skills
- fund women's groups to monitor disaster recovery projects

2. Get the Facts

Gender analysis is not optional or divisive but imperative to direct aid and plan for full and equitable recovery. Nothing in disaster work is 'gender neutral'. Plan now to:

- collect and solicit gender-specific data
- train and employ women in community-based assessment and follow-up research
- tap women's knowledge of environmental resources and community complexity
- identify and assess sex-specific needs, for example, for home-based women workers, men's mental health, displaced and migrating women versus men

- track the (explicit/implicit) gender budgeting of relief and response funds
- track the distribution of goods, services, opportunities to women and men
- assess the short and long-term impacts on women/men of all disaster initiatives
- monitor change over time and in different contexts

3. Work with Grass-roots Women

Women's community organisations have insight, information, experience, networks and resources vital to increasing disaster resilience. Work with and develop the capacities of existing women's groups such as:

- women's groups experienced in disasters
- women and development NGOs;
- women's environmental action groups
- advocacy groups with a focus on girls and women, for example, peace activists

- women's neighbourhood groups
- faith-based and service organisations
- professional women, for example, educators, scientists, emergency managers

(*Table 2.1 Continued*)

(*Table 2.1 Continued*)

4. Resist Stereotypes

Base all initiatives on knowledge of difference and specific cultural, economic, political and sexual contexts, not on false generalities:

- women survivors are vital first responders and rebuilders, not passive victims
- mothers, grandmothers and other women are vital to children's survival and recovery but women's needs may differ from children's
- not all women are mothers or live with men
- women-led households are not necessarily the poorest or most vulnerable
- women are not economic dependents but producers, community workers, earners
- gender norms put boys and men at risk too, for example, mental health, risk taking, accidents

- targeting women for services is not always effective or desirable but can produce backlash or violence
- marginalised women (for example, undocumented, HIV/AIDS, low caste, indigenous, sex workers) have unique perspectives and capacities
- no 'one-size' fits all: culturally specific needs and desires must be respected, for example, women's traditional religious practices, clothing, personal hygiene, privacy norms

5. Take a Human Rights Approach

Democratic and participatory initiatives serve women and girls the best. Women and men alike must be assured of the conditions of life needed to enjoy their fundamental human rights, as well as simply survive. Girls and women in crisis are at increased risk of:

- sexual harassment and rape
- abuse by intimate partners, for example, in the months and year following a major disaster
- exploitation by traffickers, for example, into domestic, agricultural and sex work
- erosion or loss of existing land rights

- early/forced marriage
- forced migration
- reduced or lost access to reproductive health care services
- male control over economic recovery resources

6. Respect and Develop the Capacities of Women

Avoid overburdening women with already heavy workloads and family responsibilities likely to increase. Try and:

- identify and support women's contributions to informal early warning systems, school and home preparedness, community solidarity, socio-emotional recovery, extended family care
- materially compensate the time, energy and skill of grass-roots women who are able and willing to partner with disaster organisations

- provide childcare, transportation and other support as needed to enable women's full and equal participation in planning a more disaster resilient future

Source: Enarson, Elaine. 2005. Gender and Disaster Network. Available online: http://
www.gdnonline.org/resources/genderbroadsheet.doc (19.06.2009).

Acknowledgements

The original version of this chapter appeared in *@local.glob. Disaster Risk Reduction: A Call to Action*, Issue 3, 2006. The ISDR Secretariat (UNISDR) collaborated with the United Nations Division for the Advancement of Women in the organisation of an expert meeting on *Environmental Management and the Mitigation of Natural Disasters: A Gender Perspective* held in Ankara, Turkey, 6–9 November 2001, including the holding of an online debate, moderated by Elaine Enarson, expert in gender and disasters. Many of the experiences reflected in this chapter are based on these discussions and from continued dialogue at the Commission on the Status of Women of the UN (2004 and 2005) and within the Gender and Disaster Network. For more information, contact the ISDR Secretariat isdr@un.org or visit the ISDR website at http://www.unisdr.org. See the flagship publication: *Living with Risk: A Global Review of Disaster Reduction Initiatives* (2004) at the ISDR website.

References

Chowdhury, A. Mushtaque, Abbas U. Bhuyia, A. Yusuf Choudhury and Rita Sen. 1993. 'The Bangladesh Cyclone of 1991: Why so Many People Died', *Disasters*, 17(4): 291–304.

Delaney, P. and E. Shrader. 2000. *Gender and Post-disaster Reconstruction: The Case of Hurricane Mitch in Honduras and Nicaragua*. LCSPG/LAC Gender Team, The World Bank. Available online at http://www.gdnonline.org/resources/reviewdraft. doc (Accessed on 21 September 2007).

Enarson, E. 2001. *Gender Equality, Environmental Management, and Natural Disaster Mitigation*. A report from the online conference conducted by the Division for the Advancement of Women. Available online at http://www.un.org/womenwatch/daw/csw/env_manage/documents/BP2-2001Nov16.pdf (Downloaded on 07.11.2008).

———. 2004. 'Gender Matters: Talking Points on Gender Equality and Disaster Risk Reduction'. Available online at http://www.gdnonline.org/resources/gendermatters-talkingpoints-ee04.doc (Accessed on 19 June 2009).

———. 2005. 'Gender and Disaster Network'. Available online at http://www.gdnonline.org/resources/genderbroadsheet.doc (Accessed on 19 June 2009).

Enarson, E., L. Meyreles, B. Hearn Morrow, A. Mullings and J. Soares. 2003. *Working with Women at Risk: Practical Guidelines for Assessing Local Disaster Risk*. Florida: International Hurricane Research Centre, Florida International University. Available online at http://www.ihrc.fiu.edu/lssr/workingwithwomen.pdf (Accessed on 21 September 2007).

Guha-Sapir, D., L. V. Parry, O. Degomme, P. C. Joshi and J. P.Saulina Arnold. 2006. *Risk Factors for Mortality and Injury: Post-tsunami Epidemiological Findings from Tamil Nadu*. Brussels: CRED. Available online at http://www.em-dat.net/documents/Publication/RiskFactorsMortalityInjury.pdf (Accessed on 21 September 2007).

United Nations International Strategy for Disaster Reduction (UNISDR). 2008. *Gender Perspectives: Integrating Disaster Risk Reduction into Climate Change Adaptation Good Practices and Lessons Learned.* Available online at http://www.unisdr.org/eng/about_isdr/isdr-publications/17-Gender_Perspectives_Integrating_DRR_CC/Gender_Perspectives_Integrating_DRR_CC_Good%20Practices.pdf ((Accessed on 19 June 2009).

3

Let's Share the Stage: Involving Men in Gender Equality and Disaster Risk Reduction

———•✦•———

Prafulla Mishra

A female colleague in a disaster relief agency, very active and passionate about gender issues, once wondered,

> Why can't men just wait while the focus is on women? After all, women have been neglected for long and a great deal still needs to be done before they can even match men's power and control. This is just another male ploy to regain attention; it will diffuse the focus.

Here, I examine some of the issues involving the participation of men and boys in gender equity initiatives related to the Darfur conflict (Sudan), flood-affected areas of eastern and north-eastern India, and the south Indian tsunami, all areas with which I am personally most familiar. In each of these emergencies, the humanitarian community reached out in significant ways to support the survivors. While the contexts, scale and nature of interventions were very different, there was remarkable similarity in the approach to gender equity in the family and community: that is, with a focus on gender as 'women'.

Men and Disasters: Breaking the Stereotypes

The differential vulnerability of women and men to disasters is now well established (see Briceño 2002; Enarson 2001; Mishra et al. 2004). Women's vulnerability compounded by their social inequality and lack of access and control over economic and political resources is understood. For example, most of those killed by the Indian Ocean tsunami across India, Indonesia and Sri Lanka were women; their increased vulnerability was due to factors such as livelihood roles, being on the beaches while the men were away at sea when the waves hit the coast and not having physical survival skills, swimming or tree climbing (Oxfam 2005). The focus of most post-disaster damage and vulnerability assessments, therefore, is rightfully on the issues that affect women.

Yet, there is a strong need for broadening the approach to issues involving men and boys. Disasters impact men through the loss of family, neighbours, assets, livelihoods and income, and the ensuing loss of social power. There is emotional trauma, particularly for single men and widowers who are looked down upon. Despite uncertainties, men continue to be responsible for the family income; protecting remaining assets, safeguarding family members against natural elements and violence and participating in post-disaster community activities like repairing broken roads or clearing debris. Men's community engagement is not always evident to casual visitors. In the tsunami-affected villages of south India, it may seem that the men were just sitting idly while the women on their own were carrying out the excessive work of organising the remaining household assets around the temporary shelters, cooking, fetching water, cleaning debris and so forth. Many men would go out early in the morning, to the village common place, sit in groups and talk. Pictures of these men reinforced the stereotype of men not working hard, simply gossiping.

These supposedly idle men, however, were involved in planning various activities and meeting with large numbers of aid groups, the media and government officials; the men had to plan the distribution of all relief goods, making sure to be fair to all; prepare and customise beneficiary lists according to the needs and stipulations of aid organisations and the varied needs of different groups: fishing gear for fishermen, religious support for families, education for adolescent girls, housing and health care for families and the high health care costs of the elderly. Responsibilities among the villagers had to be designated (for writing applications, repairing boats, meeting with district officials, and so on). The men also discussed new issues concerning the village, conflicts between families and longer term plans for the community. Some villages were situated very close to the sea and governments were interested in moving them inland, which would cut off access to the sea, affecting communities whose sole livelihood depended on the sea. Although men dominated such planning and decision making, their apparent physical inactivity did not indicate lack of engagement in critical aspects of family and community recovery.

Portraying men as pampered and lazy patriarchs, self-centred, ignorant, promiscuous and violent drunkards is common (Jolly 2004; White 1997). Indeed, men are situated higher on the ladder of gender hierarchy, but there is a need to recognise that power and privilege are determined by a complex array of factors such as age, economic class and social norms. Boys and men are also constrained by current gender stereotypes regarding male roles and masculinity which makes it difficult for men to be different. The male socialisation process and social expectations lead to personal insecurities due to a perceived failure to make the masculine grade. Even the threat of such failure is enough to generate emotional tension and internal conflict expressed through fear, isolation, anger, self-punishment, self-hatred and aggression in many men, particularly young men (Women's Commission for Refugee Women and Children 2005).

Vivid pictures of crying and inconsolable women affected by disasters are common and there is no denying the pain and suffering that they face. However, the equally painful experiences of men are not often reflected in mainstream media or agency reports. Travelling in the tsunami-hit south Indian areas in the immediate aftermath, I came across a group of men sitting together and mourning their dead, crying their hearts out. As the majority of the village was grieving, I noticed that some men apparently found it very unusual that men would sit together to cry: someone commented that they were crying to get their photographs in the newspapers.

Not all men may agree with traditional gender relations embedded in culture and faith. A traditional male leader, a sheikh from Darfur once shared his thoughts with me on the widely accepted view of outsiders that his community has oppressive norms that do not allow women freedom of movement or participation in community decision making. He said that although many of the men in the community had conflicting ideas, they felt that they were expected to abide by this unequal and oppressive power relation. No one individual or a minority group could challenge it without retaliation from the rest of the community and from religious leaders and even possible humiliation or punishment of the women and girls themselves. In his view, unless the entire community shared similar views, oppressive relationships would not change, and to achieve this, he recommended intensive education and awareness. While this may appear to simply excuse oppressive norms, the fact that male leaders are at least willing to be engaged in any discussion and awareness in this regard was what I found interesting and welcoming. Unfortunately, not many agencies are coming forward to engage with men.

Disasters/war conflicts change the demography of a place, age and sex ratios in unpredictable ways. This makes it necessary for women or men to step out of conventional roles. Women in the post-cyclone situation in Orissa, India (Krishna forthcoming), took on men's roles. The increased political participation of women in Rwanda seems to be attributable in part to the change in the sex ratios (about 70 per cent women and girls after the 1994 genocide) because of the massacres of the men, or their leaving the country. Women in this context took up many non-traditional roles (Powley 2004). There would be similar changes in men's role in another context. Visiting the Shimelba refugee camp in the northern Tigray region of Ethiopia, I was immediately struck with the fact that men were performing almost all the domestic chores that women would normally do: such as cleaning clothes, collecting water, cooking food, cleaning houses, and so on. The Eritrean refugees (Kunama tribe) in the camp had only 14 per cent women of decision-making age (ages 18–59 years) as compared to 59 per cent of men in the same age bracket. The roles and responsibilities had to change.

Opportunities for Change

Disasters are seen to be levellers, changing old gender norms and creating new power dynamics. Governments and humanitarian organisations increasingly implement projects that help to create ownership for women, including them in discussions and creating space for them to help influence larger community decisions in the aftermath of disasters. The conventional 'women in development' approach underlined women's participation in mainstream development, with very little attention on men. The 'gender and development' approach, on the other hand, rightfully focuses on understanding and changing existing gender relations between men and women as the true focus of transformation.

Towards this end, how to include men in discussions and processes around gender has emerged as a key discussion and research topic, in recent years, and in the practice of many development practitioners, UN agencies and international aid and development organisations. The UN Division for the Advancement of Women, for example, organised an Expert Group Meeting on 'The Role of Men and Boys in Achieving Gender Equality' (see Flood 2006; Kaufman 2003; Sweetman 1997). Discussions have centred on notions of social cohesion and mutual cooperation as critical factors in truly ensuring women's participation and gender equity (Chant and Gutmann 2000). At the 48th session of the UN Commission on the Status of Women (2004), participating governments agreed to address the role of men and boys in achieving gender equality. The governments, UN bodies and civil society stakeholders were urged to promote action at all levels in fields such as education, health services, training, media and the workplace to develop and strengthen the contribution of men and boys to attain gender equality (UNDAW 2003). There is considerable experience behind the argument that including men and boys in this movement is a 'win–win' situation that can further and hasten the process of building gender equity at all levels. However, there remain significant challenges to this as well and these are apparent in the context of disasters.

Listening to Men

In a discussion in Darfur (November 2006) on including gender issues in humanitarian programmes in Darfur, the conversation shifted to the experiences of an all-male group of seven, most aged between 28 and 45 years, and all employed as mid-level or senior managers in non-governmental humanitarian organisations. All had practical experience working on gender issues, used gender-sensitive language and were able to share individual learnings, including how they felt within their own organisations when trying to discuss gender issues. It was quite revealing to listen in as they spoke about the need for gender equity in their work and in their organisations, and the barriers they faced.

These men did not all agree on everything and there were some contradictions but, in general, the feeling was one of helplessness that they were just not being listened to. Seven specific concerns were voiced:

1. Male staff members talking about gender issues are mostly not taken as seriously as a woman talking about gender. Within organisations, staff positions in gender programmes are predominantly held by women. Being gender sensitive is not enough: 'You have to be a woman to feel the experience of women' is a view many subscribe to and believe.

2. Incorporating gender dimensions in programmes focuses excessively towards women and there is considerable challenge in including men because there is not enough commitment from organisations and the idea that has not yet 'caught on' enough to convince donors and staff at headquarters.

3. As the focus is so much on working intensively with women, there is simply not enough experience engaging with men, which is more challenging. The men in the local communities simply would not accept the gender perspective of agency staff but would repulse, confront, debate and argue. Not many staff are willing to spend the time going through that route and having their 'ego bruised'. On the other hand, working with women is easier as they listen and show enthusiasm.

4. Women's participation and consultation with them at community level is needed and there is a certain satisfaction in being able to do that. Consultations with male sheikhs and other male leaders, however, do not get the aid workers' attention, mainly because the mindset is that gender sensitivity is synonymous with focusing on women. Consultations with men are done simply because there is no other way to work in the community without first securing their permission.

5. While aid agencies are keen to engage with women and try to ensure quality consultations with them about programmes (ranging from the location of a latrine to the best way to distribute supplies), consultations with men are oddly very 'dry and routine' and do not get into programming details. Women gain some power in

decision making and determine the nature of relief work, leaving men feeling 'used' by agencies who want only to secure their consent. Yet, women do not make the final decisions and men can readily find reasons to bar them from important areas of decision making. This reduces women's participation to tokenism and furthers male dominance. Many of the decisions taken by women are again ratified through the men and many times overturned.

6. There is little challenge to stereotypes in agency work towards gender equity. For instance, vocational skill-building programmes for men are predominantly sanitary work, carpentry and motor engine repair, whereas women are trained in weaving, dress making and food processing. This only reinforces the role stereotypes and results in lost opportunities for changing stereotypical roles in a socially fluid time when social norms are more dynamic.

7. Interventions related to reproductive health focus excessively on women. Not many agencies are able to carry out effective outreach programmes that make people aware that reproductive health requires the participation and understanding of both men and women. Separate clinics for women is a norm; however, there is no equivalent private space for men who are somehow considered immune from the embarrassment of discussing intimate details of sexual or reproductive health.

In a different context, at workshop on gender equality and disaster risk reduction in Honolulu, Hawaii (Anderson and Enarson 2004), male participants echoed the same feelings of not being heard. The participants were from 28 countries and represented international, regional, national and community-based organisations, academic and research organisations and UN agencies. At a breakaway group discussion session, which I attended, the majority of those attending were male; the focus shifted to the interest and commitment of men in furthering genuine gender equity. The group identified the current practice of centring discussions on identifying and mitigating women's disaster vulnerabilities as a problem, an approach it was felt would be limiting in the long run. The men in the group went on to call attention to the need for all stakeholders to identify and engage with men and boys in equal measure so as to build a true gender equity agenda. The major points raised were that men needed to advocate for gender equality, deliver gender mainstreaming messages to other men, be full partners in gender-sensitivity trainings, as leaders they would need be committed to achieving gender equity results within their own organisations, confront gender stereotyping and create opportunities for personal and institutional transformation and recognise that women have considerable personal knowledge and skills in coping with disasters, and that more women need to be trained to be first responders. Tools and methodologies were needed to sensitise and empower men to implement gender equality.

Engaging Men in the 'Engendering Process'

There is a great need for increased engagement of men in the movement to engender disaster relief and development work. Creating opportunities for a larger inclusive social process in which the concerns identified here can be considered will result in greater understanding of the underlying issues as well as action to address them. It will also promote long-lasting changes in attitudes, beliefs and practices by men as well as women, and increase the potential for new partnerships between men and women on an equal footing, based on common understanding and experiences. Men's feelings must be understood and not dismissed, if they are to be effectively engaged in a positive way.

While it is imperative to use gender-sensitive approaches in post-emergency assessments, the tools must measure the impact on, and vulnerability of, both women and men. Gender training should be carried out with men and by men to help them challenge the norms and practices that enable them to assume dominant roles in their society. The specific needs of boys and men are as important as those of girls and women in post-emergency programmes. Identifying and disseminating the effective messages that raise the salience of these concerns is important (Ruxton 2004) and must be done in a culturally sensitive way that is non-threatening. The equal participation of men and women would help ensure concerted community action to prepare and put in place efficient contingency plans that reach all people. Societies and families can function most effectively if there is equitable cooperation between men and women. This needs to be understood and underlined in all programmes that aim to bring about gender equity. Changing societal norms and value systems can only be achieved if men and women challenge them and take steps at different levels to overcome existing inequities.

Disasters severely stress all social dynamics including gender relations in the family and society, but provide a real opportunity for change by engaging men and women equally. However, this clearly requires that men better understand their own masculinity and how it plays out in the family and society. Unfortunately, not many men are exposed to analyses of their own socialisation process, and their behaviour and practices towards women do not reflect an understanding of the social construction of gender roles and identities. In addition, disaster situations victimise both women and men, unlike the everyday crisis which certainly affects women more than men. Therefore, disasters provide an opportunity for engaging with men also, which may not be so easy to do in 'normal' circumstances. Engaging with men as agents of change rather than barriers to change would help push conventional boundaries. To effect lasting change we must identify positive role models within the community, use the real-life experiences of men in disasters and in other times of their lives, identify effective entry point activities for men and boys and design and implement programmes that address underlying gender inequities.

These recommendations are put forward to ensure that change agents pursue a more balanced agenda that will promote lasting change, including fundamentally different relationships between men and women. These steps must be taken with caution, care and empathy for the gender-related constraints and opportunities in the lives of men as much as women.

Acknowledgements

I would like to thank Elaine Enarson, Shaheen Nilofer (UNICEF, India programme) and Amanya Michael Ebye (Currently Regional Director, Middle East Programme, International Rescue Committee) for their support and insights. Suman (Oxfam GB, India programme) and Sumi Krishna (Independent Consultant) provided valuable feedback and I am grateful for the same.

Bibliography

Anderson, Cheryl and Elaine Enarson. 2004. 'Proceedings of the Gender Equality and Disaster Risk Reduction Workshop, 10–12 August 2004.' Honolulu: University of Hawaii Social Science Research Institute and the East–West Center. Available online at http://www.ssri.hawaii.edu/research/GDWwebsite/pages/exec_summary.html (Accessed on 11 November 2008).

Briceño, Sávano. 2002. 'Environmental Management and Mitigation of Natural Disasters: A Gender Perspective', statement at the UN Commission on the Status of Women (46th session) panel discussion on Environmental Management and Mitigation of Natural Disasters: A Gender Perspective. Available online, through DAW, at http://www.un.org/womenwatch/daw/csw/csw46/panel-briceno.pdf (Accessed in August 2009).

Chant, S. and M. Gutmann. 2000. 'Mainstreaming Men into Gender and Development: Development Debates, Reflections and Experiences', Oxfam Working Papers. Oxford: Oxfam.

Enarson, Elaine. 2001. *Gender Equality, Environmental Management and Natural Disaster Mitigation.* A report from the online conference conducted by the UN Division for the Advancement of Women (November). Available online at www.un.org/women watch/daw/csw/env_manage/documents.html (Accessed in March 2007).

Flood, M. 2006. *The Men's Bibliography.* Available online at http://www.mensbiblio. xyonline.net/ (Accessed in March 2007).

Jolly, S. (ed.). 2004. 'Special Issue: Gender Myths', in *In Brief Bulletin*, September 2004. BRIDGE. Available online at http://www.bridge.ids.ac.uk/dgb-myths.htm (Accessed in March 2007).

Kaufman, M. 2003. 'The AIM Framework: Addressing and Involving Men and Boys to Promote Gender Equality and End Gender Discrimination and Violence', paper prepared for UNICEF. Available online at http://www.michaelkaufman. com/wp-content/uploads/2009/01/kaufman-the-aim-framework.pdf (Accessed 10 August 2009).

Krishna, Sumi. Forthcoming. *Genderscapes: Revisioning Natural Resource Management.* New Delhi: Zubaan. Extract from Chapter 2 (Personal Communication, Prafulla Mishra, 2000).

Mishra, Prafulla, Shaheen Nilofer and Sumananjali Mohanty. 2004. 'Gender and Disasters; Coping with Drought and Floods in Orissa', in Sumi Krishna (ed.), *Livelihood & Gender: Equity in Community Resource Management*, pp. 226–47. New Delhi: Sage Publications.

Oxfam. 2005. 'The Tsunami's Impact on Women', *Briefing Note*, March 2005. Available online at http://www.oxfam.org.uk/what_we_do/issues/conflict_disasters/downloads/ bn_tsunami_women.pdf (Accessed in January 2007).

Powley, Elizabeth. 2004. 'Strengthening Governance: The Role of Women in Rwanda's Transition—A Summary', in United Nations Office of the Special Adviser on Gender Issues And Advancement of Women (OSAGI), Expert Group Meeting on 'Enhancing Women's Participation in Electoral Processes in Post-conflict Countries', Glen Cove, 19–22 January. Available online at http://www.un.org/womenwatch/osagi/meetings/ 2004/EGMelectoral/EP5-Powley.PDF (Accessed in March 2007).

Ruxton, S. 2004. *Gender Equality and Men: Learning from Practice.* London: Oxfam GB.

Sweetman, C. 1997. *Gender in Development Organisations.* London: Oxfam GB.

UN Commission on the Status of Women. 2004. 'The Role of Men and Boys in Achieving Equality,' UN Commission on the Status of Women, Division for Advancement of

Women, Department of Economic and Social Affairs, 48th session, 1–12 March. Available online at http://www.un.org/womenwatch/daw/egm/men-boys2003/Connell-bp.pdf (Accessed on 10 August 2009).

UNDAW. 2003. *The Role of Men and Boys in Achieving Gender Equality*. A report from expert group meeting organised by UNDAW in collaboration with the ILO, the joint UN programme on HIV/AIDS and UNDP held in Brasilia, Brazil, 21–24 October. Available online at http://www.ashanet.org/focusgroups/sanctuary/articles/Connell-bp.pdf (Accessed in February 2007).

White, S. 1997. 'Men, Masculinities and Politics of Development', *Gender and Development*, 5(2): 14–22.

Women's Commission for Refugee Women and Children. 2005. *Masculinities: Male Roles and Male Involvement in the Promotion of Gender Equality—A Resource Packet*. New York: Women's Commission for Refugee Women and Children.

4

Organising for Risk Reduction: The Honolulu Call to Action

———•✦•———

Cheryl L. Anderson

In early August 2004, almost 100 participants from twenty-eight countries gathered in Honolulu for the International Gender Equality and Disaster Risk Reduction Workshop hosted by the University of Hawaii Social Science Research Institute and the East-West Center with support from the US Office of Foreign Disaster Assistance and others. Disaster risk managers, policy makers, development and gender specialists, emergency managers, humanitarian relief workers, academics, activists and community members from around the world came together to strategise ways to incorporate gender equality in disaster risk reduction activities. The workshop provided a forum for learning about gender and disaster connections from various perspectives. Participants travelled vast distances to share their knowledge, experience and insight.

The workshop participants proposed actions related to six specific themes, as well as a series of general recommendations for ensuring that actions become implemented in international, regional, national and local disaster risk management agendas. An online coordinating group began looking at the workshop recommendations to (*a*) draft a 'Call to Action' for participants, their agencies and the broader disaster risk reduction community; *(b)* develop a platform for action to be presented in Kobe, Japan, at the world conference on Disaster Risk Reduction in January 2005 and *(c)* provide recommendations for a group that would actively review the status of gender mainstreaming risk reduction strategies. In addition, a follow-up meeting was held involving a small international writing team that would go on to develop the Gender and Disaster Sourcebook, an online compilation of case studies, training materials, good practices, policy guidelines and other materials.

The voluntary coordinating group began meeting online the week following the workshop. The use of the internet enabled input from individuals representing non-governmental, grass-roots and research organisations globally in preparation of the Honolulu Call to Action— a series of recommendations and implementation strategies, resulting from the workshop. Participants included men and women based in India, Bangladesh, Australia, Cook Islands, Sri Lanka, Honduras, Canada, Nicaragua, Dominican Republic and the United States. Using the results of the workshop working group discussions, the coordinating group formulated the Call to Action that advocates using gender analysis and social equity in risk reduction policies and measures.

The Gender Equality and Disaster Risk Reduction Workshop

In the process of planning the workshop, the conveners asked the practical question, 'Why another conference?' It was important to consider this in asking participants to spend precious time and resources to meet in Honolulu. The disaster risk management community concerned with gender issues met both formally in a number of workshops and virtually through the Gender and Disaster Network (GDN). As the community grew, it was essential to interact periodically to build momentum and gain support in taking action towards engendering disaster risk management.

The 'decade of disasters' vividly demonstrated that catastrophic social events are gendered and that there is a corresponding need for global approaches that consider gender to reduce disasters. Since gender relations structure the lives of both women and men, with differences through the life cycle and across cultures, the work of reducing risk should not fall to men alone. In many parts of the world, women have organised effectively to reduce the risk of natural, human-induced and technological disasters, but these efforts are neither well-known nor integrated into mainstream disaster risk reduction programmes. The full and equal participation of women and men is needed to mitigate hazards, reduce social vulnerabilities and rebuild more sustainable, just and disaster-resilient communities.

In 2000, founding members of the GDN hosted a conference called 'Reaching Women and Children in Disaster'. Recommendations from the workshop encouraged gender awareness in the development of projects and improved the networking capabilities of participants. Recommended actions developed from past conferences in Costa Rica, Australia, Canada, Pakistan and the United States also urged increasing gender awareness in disaster risk reduction, as did the Expert Working Group consultation conducted in November 2002 in Ankara, Turkey, by the United Nations Division for the Advancement of Women and the International Strategy for Disaster Reduction (Secretariat for ISDR 2001). Proceedings from these events with more information about sponsors, participants and goals can be accessed through the website of the Hawaii workshop (see Anderson and Enarson 2004).

The results of these previous workshops stressed that mainstreaming gender equality is urgently needed, but implementation of basic changes in education, policy and practice is lacking in most parts of the world, especially with respect to mitigation and the reduction of social vulnerability.

The intent of the Honolulu workshop was to push towards developing strategies to implement these recommendations. Even though we understand gender issues better after more than a decade of research and lessons about women's disaster vulnerabilities and capacities, gender equality goals have not yet been well integrated at the planning, implementation and evaluation levels in either the private or the public sectors of most nations and regions. Opportunities for gender-fair practices and policies in community-based risk reduction efforts are often overlooked just as they are in government initiatives, and these gaps make a real difference in long-term outcomes. With attention to previous work and recommendations, the Honolulu workshop tried to find a place for considering the next steps towards implementation.

The workshop organised plenary discussions and six breakout discussion sessions. The six sessions included the following:

1. Building Capacity in Women's and Community Groups
2. Communication, Training and Education Strategies to Reduce Risk
3. Using Science and Technology Differently
4. New Partnerships and Collaborations
5. Changing Organisational Culture and Structure
6. Research for Social Action

In each of these sessions, participants reviewed a series of questions about the current state of affairs within a topic with regard to gender and risk reduction. Participants evaluated resources, funding and needs for improving risk reduction in these areas. The recommendations became part of the workshop documents and formed the basis for the Honolulu Call to Action.

Honolulu Workshop Recommendations

Workshop participants proposed overarching recommendations to increase gender mainstreaming and incorporate gender-fair practices in disaster risk management in international and national programmes, including actions to (Participants of the Gender Equality and Disaster Risk Reduction Workshop 2004):

1. Guarantee representation of grass-roots and wider civil society organisations by providing resources and access to information.
2. Incorporate gender and risk reduction analysis as a compulsory element for all development projects.
3. Ensure that dynamics of disaster risk, gender and environmental analyses are considered in an integrated manner.
4. Highlight gaps in millennium development goals in terms of disaster risk reduction and gender.

Participants of the Gender Equality and Disaster Risk Reduction Workshop, Honolulu 2004, recognised that we all have spheres of influence and varying expertise. Women and men both acknowledged and advocated their specific roles in ensuring gender equality. In an effort to pursue disaster risk reduction in activities, participants agreed to review proposals and policies in disaster management and incorporate gender as an integral part of policies and programmes, with specific attention for the background documents leading to the World Conference on Disaster Reduction (WCDR) in Kobe. The participants stressed the importance of taking the core message of the workshop into suggested actions in the organisations where they had influence and to use this in building alliances and collaborations to promote regional, national and international platforms that influenced the Kobe discussions and outcomes. Workshop participants discussed forming an advocacy and advisory group to monitor policy commitments made by our governments and international actors, though follow-up on this action was limited to input into the Kobe Workshop without developing this formal advocacy group.

As of 2008, the participants had accomplished many of the recommendations in their own organisations, although the pace has been slow. The importance of gender in disaster risk reduction was recognised formally in the documents following the Kobe WCDR, primarily the Hyogo Framework for Action (United Nations ISDR 2005; see document online at http://www.preventionweb.net/globalplatform/first-session/docs/Background_docs/HFA_Eng.pdf) and in the document titled, 'Words Into Action' (United Nations 2007a: 5). The ISDR has tried to build on the fourth recommendation (mentioned earlier) by developing a network of advisors with gender expertise to better inform the actions to implement the Hyogo Framework.

Men's Advocacy for Gender Equity

During the Honolulu Workshop, several men began thinking about the first day's discussions (see Prafulla Mishra's chapter in this volume). They listened to stories of inequity and realised challenges women facing in particular in areas of risk reduction. Men participating in the workshop realised that *men* controlled most of the leadership positions in the formal risk reduction sector—in governmental agencies, academia and response organisations. Without men advocating for social equity and diversity in these positions, women faced organisational obstacles.

The men attending the workshop held an impromptu meeting following lunch on the second day to briefly discuss their roles in promoting gender equality in disaster risk reduction. The men proposed the following statements of advocacy that were incorporated into the final workshop report:

1. Men need to advocate for gender equality.
2. Men need to deliver gender mainstreaming messages to other men.
3. Men need to be full partners in gender sensitivity training.
4. Men as leaders need to be committed to bringing gender equity results within their own organisations.
5. Men need to confront gender stereotyping and create opportunities for personal and institutional transformation.
6. Men need to recognise that women have lots of personal knowledge and skills in coping with disasters, and that more women need to be trained as first responders.
7. Tools and methodologies are needed to sensitise and empower men to implement gender equality.
8. A separate workshop on men's role in gender equality/gender mainstreaming is needed, and sessions should be held at upcoming meetings, such as the National Hazards Research Workshop, Sociology, Disaster Mitigation and other forums.
9. The GDN should be used to share ideas, tools and best practices.

Even though most participants saw this advocacy statement as an achievement of the workshop, they recognised that this type of advocacy should be the norm; yet, most participants had not witnessed this type of demonstration of support for gender equity in previous workshops on risk reduction.

Opportunities at the WCDR

The WCDR in Kobe, Japan, in January 2005 provided the first forum for integrating gender as a cross-cutting issue. According to the discussions and recommendations of the Honolulu Workshop, promoting gender equality must occur at many levels and in many fora before we see real change and implementation of strategies. The WCDR provided an opportunity to share the results of the Honolulu Workshop. This included distributing the Honolulu Call to Action as well as influencing language through national and non-governmental delegations.

Participants in the post-workshop voluntary coordinating group examined the language in WCDR background documents and recommended areas where gender considerations should be incorporated into disaster reduction strategies. These recommendations were made through the national delegates attending the WCDR. By working through national delegations, the workshop participants had the ability to ensure that the recommendations reflected local cultural and social considerations along with gender equity.

Individuals from the workshop continued to promote the concepts of improving gender equality in their organisations. The Call to Action appeals to the participants in their spheres of influence and extends into the local and national organisations. By working on multiple levels throughout the world, the hope is that gender issues will be better understood in disaster risk management, that organisations and institutions will develop gender equity and that gender-fair practices will be implemented globally.

The Honolulu Call to Action

The Call to Action was envisioned as a way to engage participants in pursuing their good ideas and implementing suggested strategies following the workshop. By engaging a voluntary coordinating group to develop the call, the workshop results became realised through a number of actions pursued by participants both in and beyond the scopes of their everyday lives.

The general elements of the Call to Action reiterate workshop recommendations, which emphasise the importance of gender equality and social equity in disaster risk reduction:

1. Include gender issues and social equity in assessment, design and implementation and monitoring as a compulsory element for all development projects.
2. Ensure that dynamics of disaster risk, gender, social equity and environmental analyses are considered in an integrated manner.
3. Highlight gaps in the millennium development goals in terms of disaster risk reduction and gender.

4. Guarantee representation of grass roots and wider civil society organisations by ensuring that they receive adequate resources to be active participants.

The Call to Action further focuses on recommended actions of the working groups. These appear much more issue specific, but may still be cross-cutting as the recommendations establish a list of best practices.

For building capacity in women's groups and community-based organisations, the participants recommended that programmes and projects *(a)* involve community at all levels, *(b)* ensure equitable power in partnerships, *(c)* ensure resources and funding and *(d)* address root causes of vulnerability.

In efforts to improve communication, training and education, the participants recommended that they should *(a)* improve formal and informal curriculum standards, *(b)* develop gender-sensitive policies, programmes and laws, *(c)* improve management, leadership skills and decision making with gender awareness, *(d)* ensure access to information, *(e)* educate the media, *(f)* mainstream a gender perspective in educational and training initiatives using non-governmental organisations and non-traditional institutions, *(g)* establish and strengthen cross-cutting initiatives and mainstream gender in corporate society and *(h)* encourage the employment of women in key positions in disaster management organisations.

To increase gender perspectives in science and technology for risk reduction, participants recognised that they should *(a)* promote participatory action research in science and technology through a paradigm shift that infuses participatory research and gender in all aspects of risk reduction, *(b)* recognise expertise from many different backgrounds, *(c)* continue to focus on recruiting and retaining women in the fields of science and technology, *(d)* promote ethical scientific and research awareness in disaster risk reduction and *(e)* enhance efforts to share lessons from science and technology in different communities, regions and disciplines and build on lessons learnt from successes and failures in risk reduction.

To recognise the specific challenges in engendering complex emergencies, participants recommended that they needed to *(a)* promote recruitment and retention of experienced men and women in the field, *(b)* create institutional memory that promotes dealing with specific gender issues on the ground in complex humanitarian emergencies, *(c)* undertake gender training activities and improve gender awareness with a view towards long-term implementation, *(d)* engage in civil–military interaction and interface training and *(e)* develop mechanisms for accountability, funding and evaluation to pursue long-term improvement in gender awareness.

In order to improve the capability and response of organisational structures, participants recommended that they should *(a)* develop legislation ensuring that disaster risk reduction is gender sensitive and addresses social equity, *(b)* ensure that gender issues and social equity become part of disaster risk reduction agendas at international and national levels, *(c)* develop a global legal framework for ensuring risk reduction is gender sensitive, *(d)* improve structural arguments in national governments, local governments and non-governmental organisations that link gender, social equity and risk reduction, *(e)* institute a Global Fund for Gender-specific Disaster Risk Reduction (GDRR) (in all phases of disaster management) with national commitment and membership prerequisites to ensure resource allocation and *(f)* establish mechanisms for gathering and distributing information related to gender mainstreaming in disaster risk management.

For ensuring that there are increased participatory approaches towards disaster risk reduction, participants called one another to *(a)* develop a gender-focused ethical framework, *(b)* ensure accountability to gender guidelines and frameworks in risk reduction, *(c)* fund research that addresses vulnerability and *(d)* develop indicators for gender analyses in participatory approaches.

After the Call to Action

In the years since the Honolulu Workshop, many of the recommendations have been pursued through international, national and regional activities. The Honolulu Workshop and resulting Call to Action became part of an ongoing process to increase gender awareness in risk reduction efforts. Efforts have since extended into background documents and dialogue of the Global Platform for Disaster Risk Reduction (GP-DRR) in Geneva, Switzerland, in June 2007 (UNISDR 2007), in setting a strategy for implementing the Hyogo Framework for Action.

At the Global Platform, the GDN was recognised as a delegation. As such, the head of the delegation, Dr Maureen Fordham, was invited to submit an oral and written statement in the conference. The statement appears in Box 4.1.

Box 4.1   GDN Statement to the Global Platform for Disaster Risk Reduction, Geneva, Switzerland, 5–7 June 2007. Oral and Written Statements Submitted by Dr Maureen Fordham, Head of the GDN Delegation

Building disaster resilience effectively and equitably requires the recognition and participation of all members of nations and communities. The GDN would wish to identify explicitly the particular needs and capacities of women and girls, alongside those of men and boys. We call upon governments as well as regional, international and non-governmental organisations to clearly recognise gender within the Hyogo Priority Actions as follows:

- Ensure that disaster risk reduction is a national and local priority which explicitly recognises gender as a cross-cutting concern requiring attention throughout response, recovery, rehabilitation, preparedness and mitigation phases of disaster reduction planning.
- Identify, assess and monitor disaster risks and enhance early warning. Recognising that the daily routines and social conditions of women and men, girls and boys place them differently at risk and engage them in different networks of communication.
- Use knowledge, innovation and education to build a culture of safety and resilience at all levels and for all members of nations and communities, based on a solid knowledge base of gender-disaggregated data, tools and information.
- Reduce the underlying risk factors which result in differential levels and occasions of vulnerability and endangerment and shape the capacities and resources of women and men to minimise harm.
- Strengthen disaster preparedness for effective response at all levels by promoting the inclusion of women in disaster-related professions where they are under-represented, and actively engage with grass-roots women's groups—scaling up their effective solutions through partnerships—to enhance resilience in families and communities.

That concludes the statement from the GDN. Thank you.

By appearing as a delegation, the GDN members intervened in high-level dialogue, side meetings and organised workshops, which ensured advocacy for gender equity in more detailed areas and discussions throughout the GP-DRR. GDN participants highlighted the demand for gender-disaggregated data and the need to use gendered divisions of labour in disaster risk assessment and reduction measures. GDN members requested monitoring implementation of gender-sensitive policies to demonstrate the ways that these policies and programmes would improve risk reduction strategies. As nations begin to implement the Hyogo Framework for Action, it is hoped that they will incorporate gender-sensitive measures to reduce risk.

The Global Platform provided another opportunity to engage in the process of analysing disaster risk using a gender perspective. Participation in the platform by GDN and many other community-based grass-roots organisations will help to institutionalise the understanding of gender equity in disaster risk reduction (see UN 2007b on good practice). Ongoing work at regional levels in the upcoming years will hopefully demonstrate the importance of gender equity during the next global platform in 2009. Each step forward leaves a vital track for those that follow.

Acknowledgements

This chapter reflects the work of many conference participants and members of the GDN. Readers will find links to prior conference proceedings through the website of the Hawaii workshop: www.ssri.hawaii.edu/research/GDWwebsite (Background, Lessons Learned), as well as the original Call to Action http://www.ssri.hawaii.edu/research/GDWwebsite/pdf/HonoluluCall_111504.pdf.

References

Anderson, Cheryl and Elaine Enarson. 2004. Proceedings of the Gender Equality and Disaster Risk Reduction Workshop, University of Hawaii Social Science Research Institute and the East-West Center, Honolulu, 10–12 August. Available online at http://www.ssri.hawaii.edu/research/GDWwebsite/pages/exec_summary.html (Downloaded on 11.11.2008).

Gender and Disaster Sourcebook. Available online at http://www.gdnonline.org/sourcebook.php (Downloaded on 11.11.2008).

Gender and Disaster Network (GDN). Available online at www.gdnonline.org (Downloaded on 11.11.2008).

Participants of the Gender Equality and Disaster Risk Reduction Workshop. 2004. 'Honolulu Call to Action', November, University of Hawaii Social Science Research Institute and the East-West Center, Honolulu. Available online at http://www.ssri.hawaii.edu/research/GDWwebsite/pdf/HonoluluCall_111504.pdf (Downloaded on 11.11.2008).

Secretariat for the International Strategy for Disaster Reduction (ISDR). 2001. 'Environmental Management and the Mitigation of Natural Disasters: A Gender Perspective',

Expert Group Meeting, Ankara, Turkey, 6–9 November. Available online at http://www.un.org/womenwatch/daw/csw/env_manage/index.html (Accessed on 11 November 2008).

United Nations. 2007a. 'Words into Actions: A Guide for Implementing the Hyogo Framework'. Geneva, Switzerland: United Nations Secretariat of the International Strategy for Disaster Reduction (UNISDR). Available online at http://www.preventionweb. net/globalplatform/first-session/docs/Background_docs/Words_into_Action.pdf (Accessed on 11 November 2008).

———. 2007b. *Gender Perspective: Working Together for Disaster Risk Reduction*. Geneva, Switzerland: United Nations International Strategy on Disaster Reduction. Available online at http://www.unisdr.org/eng/about_isdr/isdr-publications/09-gender-good-practices/gender-good-practices.pdf (Accessed on 11 November 2008).

United Nations International Strategy for Disaster Reduction (UNISDR). 2005. *Hyogo Framework for Action, Building the Resilience of Nations to Disasters, 2005–2015*. Kobe, Japan: World Conference on Disaster Reduction, 18–22 January. Available online at http://www.preventionweb.net/globalplatform/first-session/docs/Background_docs/ HFA_Eng.pdf (Accessed on 11 November 2008).

———. 2007. *Global Platform for Disaster Risk Reduction*. First Session, 5–7 June. Geneva, Switzerland. Available online at http://www.preventionweb.net/english/hyogo/GP/ (Accessed on 11 November 2008).

PART TWO

Gendered Challenges and Responses in Disasters

The second part of the book includes nine chapters which illustrate the experiences, responses and challenges faced by women and men in dealing with various natural and human-made hazards and disasters in different parts of the world. While the chapters in this part cover familiar terrain, they also raise new questions and demonstrate the varied ways in which women have responded to these challenges.

Manjari Mehta draws attention to the unique geophysical aspects of mountains which render highlands highly vulnerable to natural hazards. The isolation and inaccessibility of these areas pose a major challenge to the delivery of timely and effective relief to the disaster-affected populace. The author quotes varied examples from India, Nepal and Pakistan to support the cause of working with more vulnerable communities, including women, in order to empower them with information and skill to strengthen their resilience in emergencies by understanding their vulnerabilities and building their capacities.

Sarah Bradshaw and Brian Linnekar explore the extent to which gendered roles and relationships were transformed in the aftermath of Hurricane Mitch in Nicaragua. The reconstruction activities reinforced gender stereotypes by using women as a means to deliver resources to household, thereby focusing on practical gender needs and overlooking strategic gender needs. The authors conclude that reconstruction after a disaster needs to follow a correct path; otherwise, it has a negative impact on women's health, safety, material and emotional well-being.

Samia Galal Saad talks about gendered roles in the Arab world and what this means for women's management of natural resources. Education and exposure to the world outside have enabled women to assume significant roles within and outside household, yet women have suffered more during floods and drought in the area. The author invites consideration of the difference that geography, culture and politics make in women's exposure to hazards and disasters, the normative expectations of women and men and the ways in which women become involved or wish to be involved in disaster risk reduction.

Rosalind Houghton takes up the issue of domestic violence during the Whakatane floods of New Zealand in July 2004. Her chapter is based on interviews with eight professionals working with the governmental, non-governmental, indigenous and faith-based agencies that were on the front line after the floods. Various factors like financial stress, substance abuse, low level of social support from flood-affected agencies, closed childcare facilities and overcrowding were the factors that augmented domestic violence. The author recommends addressing policy gaps for mitigating such violence after disaster.

Lori Peek and Alice Fothergill examine the gendered nature of parenting in response to Hurricane Katrina. The parents had to deal with several challenges including family separation, lack of availability of childcare facilities, problems of shelter, and so on. The decisions regarding evacuation, relocation and childcare were generally taken by mothers, while fathers were more involved in disaster planning and response activities. The recommendations that flow from this chapter include utilisation of mothers' role as decision makers, acknowledging familial conflict and providing support for stressed parents.

Masai, Kuzunishi and Kondo recount the experiences of women in the Great Hanshin-Awaji Earthquake which claimed 6,434 lives and injured 43,000 in the Hyogo prefecture of Japan. Gender inequality surfaced in the aftermath of the disaster, as the rights of women were disrespected and women suffered more severe and lasting consequences. The authors discuss the issues of evacuation, shelter and pre- and post-earthquake housing conditions as key factors contributing to the vulnerability of women and advocate programmes which consider the needs of women and utilise their capacities to rebuild their neighbourhood.

Azra Talat Sayeed presents a critique of the relief and rehabilitation services offered by the Government of Pakistan in the aftermath of Kashmir earthquake in 2005 by highlighting the vulnerabilities of women in patriarchal social relations. This was clearly visible in the shoddy conditions of women in the temporary shelters, difficulties they faced in accessing relief and the bias against women in providing housing, death and medical compensation.

Simone Reinsch depicts the stress experienced by women in the Canadian province of Alberta. Bovine encephalitis affected the central nervous system of the cattle and this resulted in cancellation of export orders and lowering of the prices of beef. Varied factors like patriarchal relations, lack of involvement of women in the economics of farming, concern for the well-being of their children and a sense of powerlessness to influence governmental policies were some of the reasons cited by the women for their increased stress. The author recommends community development as well as empowerment of women as keys to mitigate the stress of the Canadian women.

This part concludes with a chapter about bio-hazard response. Tracey L. O'Sullivan and Carol A. Amaratunga present a case study of Severe Acute Respiratory Syndrome (SARS) outbreak in Canada in 2003. Nearly half of the 251 confirmed cases were female health care workers who became infected as a result of occupational exposure. They were put to test both professionally and socially as they were stigmatised as possible vectors of transmission, which created psychosocial stress among them. The authors advocate gender sensitivity in health care settings by providing organisational and societal recognition for public health care workers for their contribution to society.

5

Reducing Disaster Risk through Community Resilience in the Himalayas

———•✦•———

Manjari Mehta

In early October 2005, an earthquake devastated wide swathes of heavily populated areas of Kashmir on both sides of the Line of Control, primarily in Pakistan and to a lesser extent in India. At such high altitudes, in an inhospitable terrain and at the start of the harsh winter season, the devastation was staggering, especially in Pakistan where some 73,000 people were killed, at least as many injured and several million left homeless (Mathers 2006). It was a brutal reminder to both the Indian and Pakistani governments about the poor state of disaster management preparedness, and also drew attention to the unique challenges mountain environments pose in providing timely disaster relief to communities living in scattered and isolated villages and hamlets.

Despite the tremendous publicity and public outpouring of support for the millions affected by the environmental devastation and human misery that followed from it, what remained largely hidden to the public were the ways in which the experience of the earthquake itself, the subsequent learning to live with its effects and encounters with the humanitarian and relief efforts, were heavily gendered and often had very different impacts on women as opposed to men. Moreover, it created new categories of vulnerability that included orphans, widows and the disabled whose needs were often not fully acknowledged by relief and rehabilitation efforts (IUCN 2006).

I have three goals in this brief chapter. First, I shall draw attention to how the unique geophysical aspects of mountains render highlands highly vulnerable to natural hazards and how aspects of isolation and inaccessibility pose major challenges to the delivery of timely and effective relief to disaster-stricken communities. The discussion focuses on the Hindu Kush–Himalayan region (hereafter HKH) which extends some 3,500 km from Afghanistan in the west to Myanmar (including alphabetically, Bangladesh–the Chittagong Hill Tracts–Bhutan, China–the Tibet Autonomous Region–India, Nepal and Pakistan) in the east and sustains over 150 million people.

Second, I show how people's vulnerabilities to disaster risk, here as elsewhere, are shaped and exacerbated by pre-existing social stratification and gender inequalities. Third, I argue for the importance of working with communities in order to empower them with information and skills to strengthen their resilience in times of crisis. This process of empowerment demands an acknowledgement of how and why certain categories of people (women, the very young, the aged and the disabled) are more vulnerable than others, and the recognition that all members of communities, whatever their ages, gender or abilities, have something to contribute to ensure that a hazard need not necessarily turn into a disaster (see Figure 5.1).

Reducing Vulnerability to Natural Hazards: A Global Development Priority

It is now a well established fact that since the 1990s there has been an alarming increase both in the incidence and in the scope of natural disasters (Sudmeier-Rieux et al. 2006; WHO 2002). While it is the large-scale 'spectacular' ones like the Asian tsunami of 2004, Hurricane Katrina and the Kashmir earthquake of 2005 that inevitably capture the media's attention and the bulk of the global donor and humanitarian community's

Figure 5.1   Key Watersheds of the Hindu Kush–Himalayan Region

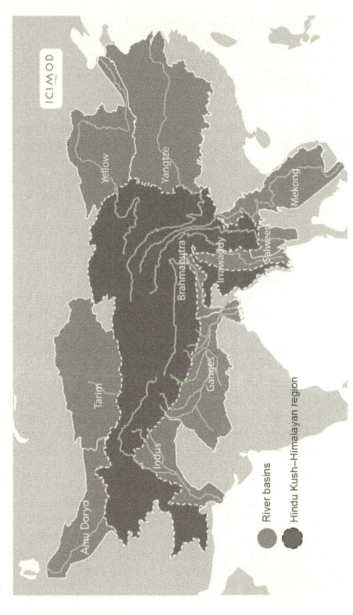

Source: International Centre for Integrated Mountain Development (ICIMOD), Kathmandu, Nepal.

resources, the ongoing 'small-scale' and often 'invisible' ones extract no less enormous costs because they occur on a regular basis (or are simply not seen as sufficiently 'dramatic'), devastating local populations and their livelihoods and destroying untold economic, social and environmental assets (UN General Assembly 2006).

The greatest costs in terms of lives and assets lost are felt most strongly in low-income countries, which are estimated to be four times more likely to be affected by natural disasters than richer ones, countries which typically have the least capacity to respond to natural hazards and whose priorities for money spent on disaster relief and management ideally need to be directed towards sustainable development initiatives (Abramovitz 2001; WHO 2002, 2005). Heavily populated and socially vulnerable Asia has been especially affected, accounting for 70 per cent of all lives lost over a period from the mid-1980s to the late 1990s (Abramovitz 2001: 9). In the past decade (1994–2004), 91 per cent of those reported affected lived in Asia (World Bank 2004).

It is against this backdrop that the first years of the new century have witnessed a growing commitment at global policy levels to minimising vulnerability to natural hazards. An important paradigm shift in thinking about and responding to disasters now acknowledges that the social and economic costs of disasters are not only holding back the processes of sustainable development but are also major obstacles to achieving the Millennium Development Goals. Contemporary thinking now places hazard and vulnerability reduction within the broader context of the development process, focusing as much on longer term development needs as on obvious short-term, life-saving goals (United Nations 2004). The Hyogo Framework for Action (2005–15), which provides the central framework for informing country-level risk reduction and post-disaster recovery and rehabilitation processes, also calls for a gender perspective to be integrated into all disaster reduction management plans, policies and decision-making processes (ISDR 2005: 4) Despite this, there remains a disturbing gap between the acknowledged need for gender sensitivity and a more socially inclusive approach in the field of disaster risk reduction and what is happening on the ground, with the many gender and socially differentiated impacts of disasters often continuing to be overlooked by governments, relief and rehabilitation agencies, and many non-governmental organisations (Chew and Ramdas 2005: 1).

Mountains and Natural Hazards

Mountains are by definition fragile, susceptible to a wide range of naturally occurring geophysical hazards ranging from glacial lake outbursts, volcanic eruptions, seismic activities, floods and flash floods, avalanches and land and giant rock slides. The geologically young Hindu Kush–Himalayas, home to some of the world's major river systems, including the Ganges and Brahmaputra, is in this respect particularly susceptible due to unstable geological formations, fragile soil structures and an enormous range of extreme altitudes which result in steep, undulating terrain and extremes of climatic variability. While the earthquake in Kashmir is one of the more graphic instances, the interplay of man-made interventions with climatic and geophysical conditions also contributes to the intensity of natural hazards. In recent decades, the expansion of agriculture onto increasingly steep and marginal lands, deforestation, dam and road construction and infrastructural development to support a growing tourism industry have reconfigured and made the mountain landscape more fragile. This has rendered communities increasingly vulnerable to the risks of natural hazards, land and rock slides being amongst the most common disasters with the changing climatic patterns affecting predictability and also undercutting true and tried hazard reduction activities (Murshid 2006).

Why all this should matter begins to fall into place when we appreciate the importance that mountain agro-ecologies constitute, not only for the people who live in them but also for lowland populations. Mountains cover as much as a quarter of the earth's landscape and are home to about 12 per cent of the world's population with another 14 per cent living in close proximity to them. In addition, they are vital global sources of water with as much as 80 per cent of fresh water sources originating in the highlands, and provide a range of essential food supplies, timber and energy to as much as half the world's population (Murshid 2006). Socio-politically, mountain communities the world over are also among the most vulnerable of the world's populations, facing a host of 'inequalities of opportunities' relative to their lowland brethren (Kollmair 2007). This explains why in many areas of the world, mountains are home to many of the world's most deep-seated and intractable conflicts. The HKH is home to a disproportionate number of socio-economically and ethnically marginalised as well as politically disenfranchised communities, a majority of whom—even in this globalised age—live on the edges of state systems inadequately served by government and market services. Compared even to the often minimal standards of other lowland areas of their countries, all but the most accessible regions have little or no infrastructure, from passable roads, electricity and adequate access to the means of communication, and very poor access to health, sanitation, education and water facilities. Against this broader context, one begins to appreciate how and why mountain dwellers are highly vulnerable to disruptive hazards, and why the spillover effects of disaster events in the mountains potentially reach far beyond their geographic boundaries.

The Kashmir earthquake vividly demonstrated how the convergence of these factors stymied the best intentioned relief and rehabilitation efforts at moments when they were most required. Physical isolation, exacerbated by roadblocks, inclement weather and freezing temperatures prevented timely distribution of assistance. There were also instances in which political bias affected ethnically and politically marginalised communities' access to relief and rehabilitation facilities in an equitable way (IFRC 2006; IUCN 2006; Oxfam 2006).

Gendered Worlds, Gendered Risks

While catastrophic natural events obviously pose a threat to and affect everyone caught in their proximity, both the risks to and the impacts of disasters are disproportionately carried by those who are already socio-economically and physically disadvantaged by virtue of age (the elderly, infants and children), condition (the disabled, ailing, women who are pregnant or lactating) and gender (Mehta 2007). Though not invariably, this last category typically refers to women and girls. Context and culture also play a large role in determining outcomes, and there is evidence that often it is men who may even suffer higher mortality and morbidity rates (Bradshaw 2004; Twigg 2004). Nevertheless, a considerable body of evidence highlights the extent to which gender relations place women in socially, economically and politically marginalised positions vis-à-vis men that serve as a limiting 'pre-condition' of people's ability to anticipate, prepare for, survive, cope with and recover from disasters. The mere fact of being a boy or man, a girl or woman, often makes all the difference to whether an individual is killed or manages to survive and, if surviving, the degree and kind of access she or he has to aid and rehabilitation (Enarson 2001a, 2001b; IFRC 2005, 2006; Yoner et al. 2005).

While gender is not necessarily always the primary measure of vulnerability, it tends to cross-cut other dimensions of it; for instance: *(a)* infants and the very young are dependent on caregivers who are typically women; thus, the precarious situation of mothers has far-reaching and often deadly consequences on their children; *(b)* in many parts of South Asia, girl children have less access to food, education and medical attention compared to their brothers and carry a larger burden of domestic work which tends to be exacerbated in times of crisis; *(c)* older women are considerably more socio-economically vulnerable and socially isolated than older men and *(d)* disabled women of all ages are more at risk than their male counterparts of not having familial support.

Despite the socio-cultural diversity in the HKH, the broad tendency is for women to have considerably less access than men to productive resources and decision-making processes. Asymmetrical access to resources at the household level is manifested by their disproportionate rates of poor health and nutritional status, lower levels of literacy and education and higher morbidity/mortality rates relative to males (Gurung 1999). In certain cultural contexts, categories of women such as widows, female heads of households, the disabled, girl orphans and others who fail to fit conventional ideas of women can also find themselves without adequate social supports; in times of crisis, this can translate into social exclusion, destitution and even death. Women's subordinate status relative to men is also validated by culture and religion. Too often understood as beyond the pale of criticism, especially by 'outsiders', these injunctions may include limitations placed on women's mobility and their ability to autonomously participate in decision making around issues that address their needs. In crises, women's limited agency can also prevent them from taking steps that could save not only their lives but also that of their dependents. It is important to explore empirically the suggestion that women had lower mortality rates in the 2006 Kashmir earthquake in areas where *purdah* (seclusion) norms were less rigorously observed and women could move more freely in public.[1]

---

[1] Farid Ahmad, personal communication, International Centre for Integrated Mountain Development, Kathmandu, Nepal, 2006.

But local cultural mores alone are not the source of women's vulnerabilities. Erroneous assumptions, prejudices, biases and plain ignorance permeating official thinking also result in women facing a host of discriminatory and exploitative situations in post-disaster situations. Lessons from the field have long illustrated how typically women's specific health and sanitary needs are not addressed in disaster response efforts (Byrne and Baden 1997; Chew and Ramdas 2005; WHO 2002): their rights as individuals are overlooked, their leadership roles and knowledge are not adequately recognised and often their pressing needs for personal security are ignored (Enarson 2006; IFRC 2006).

As in other South Asian disasters, many of these issues played out in the Kashmir earthquake. Women's higher death rates have been attributed to them being more likely to be inside dwellings which were susceptible to collapsing; many had only limited independent access to health care in the absence of gender-sensitive health facilities and personnel in a socio-cultural context where it is inappropriate for male health practitioners to attend to women. Moreover, limited mobility made it hard for widows, single women and women heads of households to get to relief camps outside their local areas or to deal with male relief workers and women felt insecure living in tents which did not provide adequate sense of protection and were often located at considerable distances from latrines (IUCN 2006).

Developing Community Resilience: Women and Men Equally as Part of the Solution

Natural hazards in the HKH are unique and diversified, affecting the lives of millions of people every year. As a result, communities have had little choice but to learn to adapt to the seasonal (and occasionally daily) threats of hazards. Here, the inconveniences of being cut off from the outside world for weeks or months is simply part of the texture of what it means to make one's home in the mountains (Dekens 2007a). This reality is very much in evidence as the 2009 monsoon season, despite being less than optimal, wreaks havoc throughout South Asia, with mountain areas already witnessing a heavy toll in terms of lives lost, people displaced and homes damaged or washed down fragile slopes.

The details of this devastation of roads, animal herds, 100-year-old orchards and other sources of local livelihoods are, as noted earlier, typically underreported in the media. Either the obvious losses are not deemed sufficiently high or heavy rains breach embankments and flooded lands and roads do not permit media access, or simply because these losses are taken for granted as part of the annually recurring monsoon experience the destruction is minimised. One result is that the intensity and impact of most natural disasters in mountain areas, coupled with inaccessibility, do not readily permit speedy rescue and relief efforts. Insufficient understanding of vulnerabilities caused by gender and other dimensions of social exclusion also results in oversights. The question, then, is what can be done?

Strategies that develop and strengthen women's capacity in hazard reduction and disaster response acknowledge that they, along with men, are key social actors in developing more hazard-resilient communities. Examples from around the world illustrate how, in conjunction with civil society organisations, as members of formal groups and informally, local communities generally and women particularly are 'first responders', often at the forefront in participating in disaster risk activities (Enarson 2001b; IFRC 2004; Twigg 2004; Yoner et al. 2005). This has vital implications in contexts where for various reasons local and national-level disaster response efforts are less than adequate.

Throughout the region, community-based organisations are developing innovative ways of addressing issues of social exclusion in order to contribute to populations' abilities to deal with hazards. The following examples indicate how useful it is to provide adults and children with the necessary information and skills so that they can strengthen their individual and household capacity to meet the challenges that emerge in crises, be more resilient in the face of recurring hazards and possibly even help to ensure that a hazard need not necessarily turn into a disaster.

Good Practice: Community Preparedness in Nepal

In the plains of southern Nepal, known as the Terai, various local project partners, funded by the European Commission's Disaster Preparedness ECHO programme (DIPECHO), are working to develop the resilience of community members of all ages and genders through a range of activities, including contingency planning and mitigation workshops, evacuation drills and classroom discussions. In this socially conservative region where women are not encouraged to take on public roles, initiatives stress the importance of bringing about greater parity between the genders, both adults and children.

One way of ensuring women's participation at trainings has been to hold single-gender demonstrations in women's own villages and limit their length, a factor much appreciated in a situation where women suffer from 'time poverty'. In the company of people with whom they are familiar, women feel comfortable about talking, asking questions and actively participating. Other community training tactics that have helped to bring women out include the provisioning of childcare and stalls for children so that women have greater freedom to visit those stalls of particular interest to them and be able to take advantage of skills training courses. School contingency planning processes, discussions and competitions have also demonstrated how gender issues can be addressed in simple, non-confrontational and yet effective ways. One strategy is to make it mandatory for girl students to become actively involved and take leadership roles, with the result that many young girls are now 'coming out of their shells' and even dominating their male classmates.

Asked why the first-aid trainings were so popular (for both sexes), one woman replied that while women had always thought of first-aid as prestigious and challenging work which only men could do, they now realised that women could do it too. In the same programme, evacuation drills which emphasised participation of the most vulnerable groups have witnessed high turnout rates from women, children and historically socially excluded groups who typically remain under-represented or overlooked in conventional programmes. Feedback sessions revealed that both women and men now recognise that by becoming more organised and coordinated they have the tools to respond more effectively and quickly to future hazards.

Trainers realised that they had not paid sufficient attention to the specific needs faced by pregnant women, and women's participation in evacuation drills was limited due to the cultural belief that these activities might endanger the pregnancy. This helped to highlight how, in actual flood situations, cultural norms could negatively inform people's responses and have subsequently encouraged the community to engage in group discussions about how to elicit greater involvement by women. One example that has emerged is the role of community radio in helping to illustrate, and even challenge, beliefs that place some people at risk more than others.

Good Practice: Targeted Community-based Mitigation in Northern India

Another instance comes from a mountain district in the northern Indian state of Uttarakhand where the Sri Bhuvaneshwari Mahila Ashram (SBMA), with support from Plan International, has built on its deep roots in local village communities and long tradition of working specifically with women and children to develop disaster mitigation programmes. The focus of its work is orienting the entire community to address hazardous situations, placing special emphasis on the needs of very small children, pregnant women and the elderly. Its adolescent empowerment programme trains girls in specialised rescue, relief and first-aid training, skills that have in the past been put into practice after cloudbursts and which helped the community to quickly move back to some semblance of normality. Women's groups (*mahila mandal dals*) have also mobilised their members to get involved: during the same cloudburst disaster, when heavy rains continued from early evening until late into the night. Almost 900 women from nearby villages were engaged in rescue and relief work helping to clear away mud, recovering bodies and providing counselling to the most affected families. One such group from a badly affected area immediately began working to reconstruct village paths, working for almost two days in order to create temporary footpaths.

Good Practice: Training Women and Men in Northern Pakistan

The Kashmir earthquake demonstrated how essential it is for successful rescue and relief initiatives to involve both women and men. One such instance is illustrated by the work being done by Focus Humanitarian Assistance (FHA), an international non-governmental organisation which works in the mountainous district of Chitral in northern Pakistan. Operating under the philosophy that communities in high altitudes have to live with risk, FHA's work focuses on providing basic information and skills needed to protect lives and property in an effective and timely fashion. In this socio-culturally conservative region, emphasis has been placed on the training of women volunteers alongside men. Their prevention, mitigation and preparedness initiatives emphasise the raising of awareness about hazards and their impacts, introducing preventive measures to help reduce impacts and building the capacity and skills of community volunteers. These include emergency response training in first-aid, fire-fighting, light search and rescue, community-based disaster assessment, evacuation techniques, the handling of mass casualties and hazard identification and assessment. It has also set in place formal community mobilisation systems by working through community institutions to respond to emergencies and to help in the stockpiling of resources (including first-aid boxes, tents, blankets, crowbars, torches, helmets, ropes, hammers, and so on) in preparation for crises.

Over the past few years, local volunteers have responded to over 300 emergencies, managing to evacuate thousands of people before the onset of the disasters. During heavy snowfall in Chitral in April 2007 and floods and mudflows due to the glacial break-up at the end of June, local volunteers could issue warnings in advance that allowed people to evacuate before damaging landslides and avalanches hit local villages. In June, ice blocked the main river and caused enormous damage to embankments and bridges, but collaborative efforts among local volunteers and the police force helped to open alternative paths that helped people to escape.

Good Practice: Community-driven Gender-sensitive Watershed Management in North-western India

A final example comes from Hamirpur district in the Shivalik range in the north-western Indian state of Himachal Pradesh where, in 2000, People's Science Institute (hereafter PSI), a non-profit public interest research and development organisation began working with local communities in five watersheds in order to address water-related needs in a way that would also fulfil basic needs for food, fodder, fuelwood and livelihoods (Mehta 2005). Unlike the rapid onset disasters discussed earlier, this region faces the slow onset variety, with communities who have for decades lived with acute seasonal water scarcity due to diminishing rainfall aggravated by poor state-level water management. Central to PSI's participatory and community-driven approach was the centrality of women's involvement in any water-related activity. Here, however, fieldworkers faced an enormous challenge since this is a region where seclusion norms prevailed to such an extent that, at that time, women were veiled, did not speak to non-kin men and lacked a formal voice in village affairs. Painstaking work within communities was required in order to persuade people that in order to address their needs, everyone's input (including women and lower castes) would be essential, a process which took 3 years of institution and capacity building to achieve. Because water is a 'women's issue', women's groups began to take the initiative to clean and rebuild old wells and other water sources and, subsequently, some even applied—successfully—to local development bodies for loans to construct new ones. Today, while water remains a precious commodity, many once water-deprived areas are now water adequate, and a growing number of communities are engaging in practices designed to conserve and harvest water resources.

Villagers agree that moving forward is only possible with the cooperation of both women and men, and they have a new understanding of what their relationship to the development process can be. This model is also important in that it offers a viable way of linking disaster preparedness with a broader vision of sustainable development, a key element of the Hyogo Framework.

Past Lessons and Future Strategies

Disasters have been likened to magnifying glasses that bring into sharp relief the social fault lines of a society, identifying those with and without the resources and abilities to minimise their vulnerabilities and to protect themselves (Schwoebel and Menon 2004). The preceding section illuminates some of the valuable community-level work being done throughout the HKH to lessen these impacts. A number of lessons emerge. First, disaster risk reduction work that takes into account the needs and energies of both women and men not only contributes to more equitable responses in times of crisis but also helps to ensure that human and material resources are used as efficiently as possible. This is especially vital in the socially conservative regions that prevail in many parts of the HKH. Second, effective engagement entails developing working relationships with local bodies (for example, village councils, schools and other relevant institutions) and building a community-centred approach that includes everyone, especially the socially excluded. Third, 'tradition' and 'culture' are not immutable: some of the most successful disaster preparedness and management work has been achieved because of the willingness of people to envisage new gender relations and to have the courage to see that these can, at their very best, work to everyone's benefit. Finally, disaster preparedness that is part of a wider vision of sustainable development, and that draws on local collective action has the potential to put down deep roots.

The challenge is that these instances are small-scale, tend to be geographically scattered and, because of lack of adequate communication among Disaster Prevention and Mitigation (DP/M) practitioners, remain largely unknown to those who shape disaster risk reduction policies. It is, however, becoming imperative that conventional models of mountain development and DP/M approaches acknowledge local energies and knowledge in helping people to survive catastrophes and reduce risk. DP/M practitioners must begin to think outside the boxes that have informed the field: first, the notion that in times of crisis gender and other social and cultural vulnerabilities are ill-affordable luxuries and, second, that technical responses need to be privileged over those that combine technologies with social inputs. After all, 'mitigation is not a technical accomplishment but a social process' (Fordham 2000).

Two other barriers need to be acknowledged and reduced. The first is the idea that 'the community' exists as a homogeneous entity: to the contrary, and especially in the HKH, class, caste, ethnicity, religion and other aspects of social identification play critical roles in shaping people's abilities, needs and interests in often very dissimilar and conflicting ways. Second, following from the first, is the need to see the manner in which intra-household dynamics influence how issues of gender and generation structure people's access to resources and their ability to make decisions that could play a vital role in saving lives. Both underscore what is by now well acknowledged: that participatory techniques should be consciously sensitive to issues of gender and social inclusion, or risk simply reinforces the *status quo* (Action Aid International 2005). Vulnerability assessments, too, must recognise the potentially valuable role that local knowledge can play in risk reducing activities and in highlighting the capabilities of all community members (Dekens 2007a, 2007b). This is crucial, for while regional and national governments may eventually provide financial and other relief to the people in affected areas, the immediate and most effective relief is typically generated from within the community, very often by women as well as men who possess a keen knowledge of community members and their needs.

Building capacities obviously take time. The challenge lies in finding ways to scale up best practices and disseminate them to a range of other institutional actors, and to promote ongoing dialogues across different groups with a particular emphasis on bringing government and field personnel together in order to ensure that local-level initiatives and learning experiences find meaningful expression in DP/M policies and actions. Related to this is the need to develop innovative and flexible strategies that enable socially excluded people, both women and men, to participate in training programmes and contribute in other ways to develop local resilience to hazards. Perhaps the biggest challenge lies in translating the rhetoric of gender mainstreaming and social inclusion into reality. These goals can only be adequately achieved if there is a concerted political willingness to shift the terms of the conversation about what is possible and put it into practice.

Gender can make the difference between life and death. Working with women and men, young and old, to build community resilience has been found to pay enormous dividends. There can be no single blueprint for how to develop and practice gender-sensitive and socially inclusive methodologies; these will have to evolve on a case-by-case basis, and through trial and error. However, with the prediction of ever-increasing natural hazards and their attendant high social and economic costs, the people of these fragile majestic mountains demand nothing less.

Acknowledgements

I am grateful to a number of people who provided information on the good practice examples cited in the chapter. Christina Chan, CARE-DIPECHO project coordinator, Kathmandu, Nepal (via email); Syed Harir Shah, FHA, Chitral, Pakistan (via email); M. M. Doval, SBMA, Anjanisain, Tehri Garhwal, India (via email) and Dipesh Sinha, All India Disaster Mitigation Institute, Ahmedabad, India.

References

Abramovitz, Janet. 2001. 'Unnatural Disasters', Worldwatch Paper 158, Worldwatch Institute. Available online at http://www.worldwatch.org/node/832 (Accessed on 19 June 2007).

Action Aid International. 2005. *Participatory Vulnerability Analysis: A Step-by-Step Guide for Field Staff.* London: Action Aid International. Available online at http://www.swan.ac.uk/cds/pdffiles/Chiwakaworkingpaper.pdf (Accessed on 19 June 2007).

Bradshaw, Sarah. 2004. *Socioeconomic Impacts of Natural Disasters: A Gender Analysis.* United Nations, Sustainable Development and Human Settlements Division, Women and Development Unit. Available online at http://www.eclac.org/.../xml/3/15433/P15433.xml&xsl=/deype/tpl/p9f.xsl&base=/mexico/tpl/top-bottom.xslt (Accessed on 19 June 2009).

Byrne, B. and S. Baden 1997. *Gender, Emergencies and Humanitarian Assistance.* Report No. 33 (Commissioned by the WID Desk, European Commission, Directorate General for Development), BRIDGE, Institute of Development Studies, Sussex University, Brighton, UK. Available online at http://www.earthscape.org/r1/ES2_6863/6863.pdf (Accessed on 19 June 2009).

Chew, Lin and Kavita Ramdas. 2005. *Caught in the Storm: The Impact of Natural Disasters on Women.* The Global Fund for Women. Available online at http://www.cohintl.org/02projects/_docs/_srilanka/disaster-report.pdf (Accessed on 19 June 2007).

Dekens, Julie. 2007a. *Herders of Chitral—the Lost Messengers: Local Knowledge on Disaster Preparedness in Chitral District, Pakistan.* International Centre for Integrated Development (Kathmandu, Nepal) and DIPECHO, European Commission Humanitarian Aid (ECHO). Available online at http://www.disasterpreparedness.icimod.org/articles.php?id=7 (Accessed on 19 June 2009).

———. 2007b. *The Snake and the River Don't Run Straight: Local Knowledge on Disaster Preparedness in the Eastern Terai of Nepal.* International Centre for Integrated Development (Kathmandu, Nepal) and DIPECHO, European Commission Humanitarian Aid (ECHO). Available online at http://www.disasterpreparedness.icimod.org/articles.php?id=7 (Accessed on 19 June 2009).

Enarson, Elaine. 2001a. *Gender Equality, Environmental Management and Natural Disaster Mitigation.* Report from the online conference conducted by the Division for the Advancement of Women, International Strategy for Disaster Reduction (ISDR). Available online at http://www.erc.gr/English/d&scrn/murciapapers/session2/Enarson_Meyreles_II_Original.pdf (Accessed on 19 June 2009).

———. 2001b. *We Want Work: Rural Women in the Gujarat Drought and Earthquake.* National Hazards Research and Applications Information Centre, University of Colorado. Available online at http://www.colorado.edu/hazards/research/qr/qr135/qr135.html (Accessed on 19 June 2009).

———. 2006. *Violence against Women in Disasters.* Gender and Disaster Network. Available online at http://www.gdnonline.org/resources (Accessed on 19 June 2009).

Fordham, Maureen. 2000. 'The Place of Gender in Earthquake Vulnerability and Mitigation'. Available online at http://www.iiasa.ac.at/Research/RMS/july2000/Papers/fordham0208.pdf (Accessed on 19 June 2009).

Gurung, Jeannette (ed.). 1999. *Searching for Women's Voices in the Hindu Kush–Himalayas.* Kathmandu, Nepal: International Centre for Integrated Mountain Development.

International Federation of Red Cross and Red Crescent Societies (IFRC). 2004. *World Disasters Report: Focus on Community Resilience.* Sterling, VA: Kumarian Press, Inc. Available online at http: www.uat.ifrc.org/PUBLICAT/wdr2006/index.asp (Accessed on 19 June 2009).

———. 2005. *World Disasters Report: Focus on Information in Disasters.* Sterling, VA: Kumarian Press, Inc. and London: Eurospan. Available online at http://www.ifrc.org/publicat/wdr2005/ (Accessed on 19 June 2009).

———. 2006. *World Disasters Report: Focus on Neglected Crises.* Sterling, VA: Kumarian Press, Inc. Available online at http://www.uat.ifrc.org/PUBLICAT/wdr2006/index.asp (Accessed on 19 June 2007).

ISDR. 2005. *The Hyogo Framework for Action, 2005–2015.* Geneva: Secretariat of the International Strategy for Disaster Reduction, United Nations. Available online at http://www.unisdr.org/eng/hfa/hfa.htm (Accessed on 19 June 2007).

IUCN with Khwendo Kor (Sisters' Home) Women and Children's Development Programme. 2006. *Hearing Their Voices: The Women and Children in the Earthquake Affected Areas of Pakistan.* Pakistan: IUCN Country Office.

Kollmair, Michael. 2007. 'Greater Voice for All Mountain People in the Himalayan Region', *Sustainable Mountain Development,* International Centre for Integrated Development, Kathmandu, Nepal. Volume 52 (Spring). Available online at http://www.icimod.org/uploads/newsletter/nl52/ (Accessed on 19 June 2009).

Mathers, Nick. 2006. 'Humanitarian Principal Framework for the Success of any Emergency Response', *Emergency Response Challenges in Mountainous Terrain,* Asian Disaster Preparedness Centre (ADPC), Volume 12 (2, April–June). Available online at www.adpc.net/v2007/IKM/ASIAN%20DISASTER%20MANAGEMENT%20NEWS/Default-NEWS.asp (Accessed on 19 June 2009).

Mehta, Manjari. 2005. 'An Assessment of Community Mobilising and Village-level Institutions in Five Watersheds in Hamirpur District, Himachal Pradesh', People's Science Institute, Dehradun, Uttaranchal. Available online at http://www.peoplessscienceinstitute.com/resource/pubs/pubs intro.html (Accessed on 5 August 2009).

———. 2007. *Gender Matters: Lessons for Disaster Risk Reduction in South Asia.* International Centre for Integrated Development, Kathmandu, Nepal and DIPECHO, European Commission Humanitarian Aid (ECHO). Available online at http://www.disasterpreparedness.icimod.org/articles.php?id=7 (Accessed on 19 June 2009).

Murshid, Zubair. 2006. 'Improving Disaster Response in Mountain Regions', *Emergency Response Challenges in Mountainous Terrain,* Asian Disaster Preparedness Centre (ADPC), Volume 12 (2, April–June). Available online at http://www.adpc.net/v2007/IKM/ASIAN%20DISASTER%20MANAGEMENT%20NEWS/Default-NEWS.asp (Accessed on 19 June 2009).

Oxfam. 2006. 'Keeping Recovery on Course: Challenges Facing the Pakistan Earthquake Response One Year on', Oxfam briefing note, Oxfam International, Oxford, UK. Available online at www.oxfam.org/en/policy/briefingnotes/bn0610_pakistan_earthquake_oneyear (Accessed on 19 June 2009).

Schwoebel, Mary Hope and Geeta Menon (CEDPA). 2004. *Mainstreaming Gender in Disaster Management Support Project*. A report submitted to USAID, India. Available online at www.gdnonline.org/sourcebook/chapt/sec_view.php?id=7.2 (Accessed on 19 June 2009).

Sudmeier-Rieux, K., H. Masundire and S. Rietbergen (eds). 2006. *Ecosystems, Livelihoods and Disasters: An Integrated Approach to Disaster Risk Management*. IUCN, Ecosystem Management Series No. 4. Gland, Switzerland: IUCN. Available online at www.iucn.org/themes/CEM/documents/publications/ (Accessed on 19 June 2009).

Twigg, John. 2004. 'Disaster Risk Reduction: Mitigation and Preparedness in Development and Emergency Programming', *Good Practice Review*, No. 9. London: Overseas Development Humanitarian Practice Network.

United Nations General Assembly. 2006. *Implementation of the International Strategy for Disaster Reduction*, A report of the Secretary–General. Available online at www.unisdr.org/ (Accessed on 19 June 2009).

United Nations. 2004. *Women 2000 and Beyond—Making Risky Environments Safer*. Division for the Advancement of Women, Department of Economic and Social Affairs. Available online at http://www.un.org/womenwatch/daw/public/W2000andBeyond.html (Accessed on 19 June 2009).

World Bank. 2004. *World Development Report: Making Services Work For Poor People*. Washington D.C. Available online at http://web.worldbank.org/external/default/main?menuPK=477704&pagePK=64167702&piPK=64167676&theSitePK=477688 (Accessed on 19 June 2009).

World Health Organisation (WHO). 2002. *Gender and Health in Disasters*. Geneva: World Health Organisation. Available online at http://www.who.int/gender/other_health/disasters/en/- 19k (Accessed on 19 June 2009).

———. 2005. *Gender Considerations in Disaster Assessment*. Geneva: World Health Organisation. Available online at http://www.who.int/gender/other_health/disasters/en/ (Accessed on 19 June 2009).

Yoner, Ayse with Sengul Akcar and Prema Gopalan. 2005. *Women's Participation in Disaster Relief and Recovery*. SEEDS. Available online at www.popcouncil.org/pdfs/seeds/Seeds22.pdf (Accessed on 19 June 2009).

6

Gender Perspectives on Disaster Reconstruction in Nicaragua: Reconstructing Roles and Relations?

————— • ✦ • —————

Sarah Bradshaw and Brian Linneker

When Hurricane Mitch hit Central America in October 1998, the increasing inequalities and vulnerabilities associated with over ten years of neo-liberal policies were brought into sharp focus, provoking one of the worst disasters in over 200 years. The disaster affected almost 3.5 million people with the greatest impacts in Honduras and Nicaragua. It was estimated that 18,000 people died or disappeared with financial losses estimated at over US$ 6 billion (CEPAL 1999).

In Nicaragua alone, over 870,000 people were affected and over 3,000 died (Linneker et al. 1998). Nicaragua is the poorest country in the region with three-quarters of the population living on less than US$ 2 per day (Oxfam 1998). A large part of the population lost their homes, land and means of survival with the damages principally affecting the poorest sectors living in vulnerable areas, exposed to flooding, landslides and in fragile housing.

While there is little evidence to suggest that the general level of damage suffered as a result of Hurricane Mitch varied significantly by sex, evidence does suggest that relief and reconstruction projects favoured women and children (Bradshaw 2004a; CIET International 1999a, 1999b; Delaney and Shrader 2000; ECA 2000). This apparent focus on women makes Nicaragua an interesting case study to explore questions concerning the extent to which gender roles and relations can be transformed in the aftermath of a large-scale disaster.

One positive outcome in Nicaragua of the hurricane was the formation of the Civil Co-ordinator for Emergency and Reconstruction (CCER). A coalition of 350 national non-governmental organisations (NGOs) and other expressions of civil society, the CCER emerged out of the co-ordinated practical response to the hurricane by non-governmental actors. However, it very quickly assumed an advocacy role and became a key actor attempting to influence the reconstruction processes in the country (Bradshaw 2002; Bradshaw et al. 2002). In February 1999, the CCER undertook a large-scale social survey (social audit) of some 10,500 households in sixty-one of the worst affected municipalities, seeking people's opinions about the relief operations and the damages they suffered. In September of the same year, a second social audit focused on reconstruction efforts and involved 6,000 households in forty-eight of the municipalities affected (see CIET International 1999a, 1999b).

The social audit was supplemented by a more in-depth study of four communities undertaken in July 1999 by the Nicaraguan feminist NGO Puntos de Encuentro. The study utilised questionnaires, semi-structured interviews and focus group discussion to investigate the potential changes in gender roles and relations in both the public and the private spheres after Hurricane Mitch (Bradshaw 2001a). While focused on women, in two of the four communities, questionnaires and semi-structured interviews were also undertaken with the male partners of the women interviewed.

This chapter provides a gendered analysis of post-Mitch reconstruction efforts in Nicaragua drawing on the findings of the social audits and the in-depth community study, in which both the authors participated. It focuses on the role of women in reconstruction, their participation in reconstruction projects and in individual household responses in order to explore the possibilities for transforming gender roles and relations through reconstruction.

Reconstruction for Transformation

Anderson and Woodrow (1998) have suggested that disaster responses too often have not contributed to long-term development and, worse, may actually subvert or undermine it. At the very least, social, economic and political vulnerabilities are often reconstructed after a disaster, thus reproducing the conditions for a repeat disaster (Wisner et al. 2005). However, it is also largely accepted that events such as Hurricane Mitch do provide an opportunity to transform society, to use the devastation in order to 'build back better', both physically and socially. This notion has become ingrained among practitioners and politicians alike, as reflected in the titles of the reconstruction plans produced by the region's governments post-Mitch, such as 'Transforming El Salvador to Reduce its Vulnerabilities' and slogans such as 'The Government Invites You to Reconstruct and Transform Nicaragua Together'.

The idea that opportunities for transformation exist after a disaster is largely based on the profound changes that such an event may produce in the lives of the people involved (Byrne with Baden 1995; CAW 1998). It may also be related to the fact that disasters tend to reveal existing national, regional and global power structures, as well as power relations within intimate relations (Enarson and Morrow 1998: 2). This helps explain why gender roles and relations have become a focus of many post-disaster interventions. However, little evidence exists to support the idea that profound changes can be brought about in women's relative position and situation in society by such events.

The idea that gendered change may occur rests on a number of inter-related assumptions. First, that as women often have to assume non-stereotypical gender roles in the wake of such events, such as rescue, repair and construction, attitudes around women's capabilities may be changed. Similarly, coping strategies adopted by households in response to an event may force women to take on new roles, including income-generating activities. Women's involvement in income-generating activities in turn is often seen as a key means to improve their position within the household; in particular, their ability to participate in decision-making processes around the use of household resources. The physical absence of a male partner after an event, through death, migration or desertion, may also lead to women assuming decision-making roles within the home and *de jure* or *de facto* headship of the household. Reconstruction initiatives that encourage the participation of women in wider community projects or provide resources to women are often seen as a means to build on these existing processes to bring about lasting changes in gender roles and relations.

Gendered Reconstruction Initiatives

The results of the social audit a year after Mitch highlight how reconstruction in Nicaragua, to the extent that it had taken place at all, had occurred largely via national and international NGOs. Government initiatives had been few, and largely centred on large-scale transport infrastructure projects. Indeed, to the question, 'What is the most important thing the government has done in the reconstruction process?' Sixty per cent of those interviewed in the September social audit replied, 'Nothing'. The social audit findings also highlighted that it is not just resources received that have an impact on well-being but that the nature of the organisation that provides these resources; in particular, if resources are received from governmental or NGOs also influences perceptions of well-being (Linneker 2002). The initiatives of NGOs are the focus of discussion here.

Majority of the national NGOs in Nicaragua were involved in the reconstruction process, and although a number of them did not radically alter their activities, others modified their programmes to include, for example, reconstruction of damaged housing (Bradshaw 2001b, 2002). Women's groups in particular were active in reconstruction projects and the wider women's movement was a key actor in advocating for a more people-centred reconstruction process. The involvement of national NGOs in the reconstruction process was facilitated, and in some cases fuelled by, an influx of money from international organisations. The need for those reconstruction projects financed by international donors to include a gender component meant gendered NGOs and consultants were in great demand as an efficient mechanism by which to understand women's needs and interests, often taking the place of direct dialogue with the women affected and grass-roots women's groups (Bradshaw and Linneker 2003).

What is meant by a gender perspective also became an issue post-Mitch and highlights the need to critically evaluate gendered projects rather than assume that inclusion of gender is automatically a good thing. Gender is increasingly popular among development actors and for example, the World Bank (2001) now has a strategy for 'Engendering Development' while the UN promotes its aim of 'gender mainstreaming' through various initiatives, including the inclusion of 'gender equality and women's empowerment' as one of the Millennium Development Goals (MDGs). However, the gender perspective of the World Bank, which promotes gender equality as an efficient means to bring wider economic growth gains, stands in contrast to those who see equity as a goal in itself (Chant 2003a; Jackson 1996). Similarly, the MDGs have been critiqued for mainstreaming gender by pushing gendered rights to the margins, as demonstrated by the exclusion of sexual and reproductive rights and gender-based violence from the goals (Bradshaw 2004b; WICEJ 2004).

The gender perspective of some organisations post-Mitch similarly demands closer examination. The comments of a representative of one well-known agency working in post-Mitch reconstruction are informative in this context. She noted how the agency had 'positively discriminated towards women' by giving 'some of the resources to rehabilitate liveli-hoods' to the women. When asked about men's reaction, she commented that men had accepted the focus once they saw that the project supported the household economy noting how, 'the women have their cows and the men are drinking the milk' (Bradshaw 2001a, 2001b). Such 'gendered' projects target women as the most efficient mechanism by which to provide resources to the household or to facilitate women's fulfilment of a 'practical' gender need stemming from their position within the gen-dered division of labour (Molyneux 1985; Moser 1989). Defining needs such as access to a supply of clean water, health, food or other essentials as 'women's needs' reinforces gender stereotypes of women as mothers and carers, and does not call into question the conditions that construct women in these roles or their consequences.

In contrast, 'strategic' gender needs and interests are formulated on the basis of an analysis of women's subordination in society and call into question the nature of the relationship between men and women while aiming at changing women's situation and position. It is perhaps easier to think of strategic gender needs as the changes necessary for reducing inequality between men and women. Although usually assumed to have a greater transformative capacity, projects geared to promoting strategic gender needs also have limitations post-disaster. In Nicaragua, a women's organisation that had for a number of years been working to promote strategic gender interests by providing workshops and consciousness raising activities to those women that came to them to get small loans, found their activities difficult to promote in the post-Mitch context. While more women were seeking credit out of necessity, training was not their priority. As a representative of the organisation noted, 'Their priority is survival, being in business, looking for a penny to live off, and no matter how interesting it [the training] might be, it will always be last on the scale of priorities.'

Gender Issues in the Targeting of Reconstruction

As noted earlier, the need for a gender focus in the reconstruction process was generally accepted by both national and international NGOs. This often translated into the inclusion of women as 'beneficiaries' of resources or those who were to 'participate' in the activities. Notions of participation have more recently come under scrutiny and participation has been critiqued as the 'new tyranny' (Cooke and Kothari 2002; Cornwall 2001; McGee 2002). The post-Mitch experience highlights some of the concerns around ideas of participation.

In the four communities studied, the majority of women thought it was women who had participated most in reconstruction. Over half of the women interviewed thought women were participating more than men in reconstruction, however, only a quarter felt that it was women who benefited most from this participation and most women perceived 'the family', especially children, to be the main beneficiaries of their participation. The reconstruction projects seem to have responded to women's practical needs that focus on the family and as such tend to reinforce stereotypical gender roles rather than redress them.

Among women, female heads in particular were targeted in reconstruction projects. The focus on female heads may be taken as a positive intervention given the rather marginal if not marginalised position of female heads in many societies and their supposed 'vulnerable' position, not least their economic position. However, this notion of female heads as the 'poorest of the poor' is a contested notion which is often promoted by policy makers but not consistently supported by research (Chant 2003b, 2004).

Studies suggest that female heads were not only active participants in reconstruction projects post-Mitch (female heads reported the highest levels of participation) but also direct beneficiaries of key resources. For example, higher proportions of female than male-headed households received help with housing and among those with agricultural land similar proportions of female heads as male heads received help to restore their livelihood (CIET International 1999b).

In terms of housing, while female heads appear to have 'participated' more in material terms (that is, received more) fewer female than male heads felt that their opinion had been taken into account about where to build new housing, and even fewer in terms of how to build new housing. Similarly, while similar proportions of female heads as male heads received help in order to sow their land after Mitch, fewer female heads actually did sow. Women were less likely than men to receive cash or agricultural training, and more likely to receive inputs such as seeds. As women often have to rely on male labour to complete crucial agricultural tasks, this lack of cash to pay day labourers may help to explain women's lower capacity to sow the land and why more female than male farmers continued to live from donations a year after Mitch.

In general, the proportion of women in productive activities declined post-Mitch, both in absolute numbers and relative to men's reported employment in income-generating activities. However, unlike men, who tend to continue to report their occupation as 'farmers' even when they were not working in the land or actively engaged in agriculture, women may be less likely to identify themselves through a productive activity unless they are actively engaged in it, reverting instead to describing themselves as 'not working' or the label 'housewife'. This self-identification is important as it may lead to a misrepresentation of who is and who is not actually 'working' after an event and hence affect post-disaster assistance that misrepresents the economic needs of women and men.

Differences in employment patterns were apparent between women and also between different types of households. Compared to female heads, more women with a male partner ceased to perform productive activities post-Mitch. However, while female heads were forced by necessity to seek some form of income-generating activity, many may have struggled to do so. The social audit suggests that a year after Mitch only 47 per cent of female-headed households had a more or less regular income source, compared to 63 per cent of male-headed units. Fewer women with a male partner continued to earn incomes or sought alternative sources of income with many 'returning' to the home post-Mitch. Rather than a transformation and diversification of gender roles, then, this suggests that one impact of Mitch was the reinforcement of 'traditional' female roles and women's increased economic dependency on men, specifically among those living within 'traditional' household structures before the hurricane.

In contrast to declines in employment or income-generating activities among women, participation rates among women in community-based projects and programmes increased after Hurricane Mitch, rising from under a quarter to over half of the women interviewed in the in-depth study in the four communities. The lowest levels of participation were recorded among young women living with a male partner, while the highest levels of participation were recorded among female heads of household. This is perhaps not surprising since other indicators suggest young women have less personal freedom in general, a situation that appeared to worsen after Mitch (Bradshaw 2001a, 2002). In contrast, women heads are assumed to have to take on the dual responsibilities attached to the role of male head and female partner. The fact that female heads appear to have been actively targeted in reconstruction also suggests that the workloads of women heads may have doubled as they undertook productive work and also increased their community work through their participation in reconstruction activities. In contrast, women with male partners may have swapped one role for another.

It is not clear if women were able to take on an active role in reconstruction because they had lost income-generating opportunities, or if the need to participate in reconstruction meant women were effectively unable to continue with income-generating activities. While there may be a trade-off between work and participation, the two activities are not viewed equally. Analysis from the social audit suggests that even among those involved in 'Food for Work' programmes their activities were often not perceived of as 'work' and as such the resources received may be defined more as 'donations' than earnings. This may be linked to the fact that the resources received were 'in-kind', not in cash. This may have important consequences for those involved in the programmes and their position in the household and their wider community.

Reconstructing Gender Roles and Relations within Households

While communities were isolated in the immediate aftermath of Mitch due to damaged infrastructure, reports suggest that men and women worked together to evacuate people, move belongings and later to clear the roads for safe passage. However, even when women and men worked together, men still often saw women only as 'helping' them and women's tasks were seen as distinct from those of men. Women's activities that did not directly complement or help men appear to have been given lesser value. Moreover, over time memories may be lost and as one woman noted only one year after the event 'men recognised our contribution at the time. Some have now forgotten' (Bradshaw 2001b).

The notion of the relative contribution that each person makes is important for determining an individual's status and for establishing claims or entitlements to resources. Sen's (1987, 1990) cooperative–conflict model of household functioning highlights how ideas of relative contribution influence each individual's bargaining power within the household and their ability to make decisions over how available resources are used. The in-depth community study sought to explore ideas around contribution and decision making, asking women about their ideas of who made the most important contribution to the household, before and after Mitch.

Perceptions of contribution are complex to analyse and are based on more than just monetary valuations, being dependent also on social norms and individual characteristics, such as levels of self-esteem (Agarwal 1997). Nonetheless, the literature suggests that income generation and the amount of money brought to the household strongly influence perceptions of contribution and in turn influence relative bargaining power within households. Perceptions of contribution are also relative. A woman in a male-headed household may well devalue her own contribution in comparison with that of her male partner, especially if hers is non-monetary. This is compounded by the fact that men's perceptions may influence those of women. Women heads of household may be assumed to be free from such influence and thus have a greater recognition of their own contribution to the household.

In the pre-hurricane context, the majority of women with no male partners did name themselves as the person who made the most important contribution to the household and the key decision maker. However, the presence of an adult son in a female-headed household makes a differ-ence, as women often name their sons as the heads of households, thus granting them real or imagined power. The research suggests that, after Mitch, fewer women heads of household valued their own contribution to the household as being the most important, despite the fact that they continued to seek productive work and also participated more than married women in the reconstruction process. It may be that resources obtained by women through reconstruction projects are valued less highly than those gained through their own income-generating activities or those of male relatives.

In contrast, in male-headed households, although there were fewer women partners with productive work following Mitch, more stated that it was they who made the most important contribution to the household and fewer said that it was the man alone who took the decisions. Par-ticipation in reconstruction may help explain this also, and involvement in reconstruction did appear to influence women's perception of their ability to participate in decision making in the home alongside (not instead of) men. However, when the male partners of some of the women involved in the study were questioned, it was found that in only 55 per cent of the households did men and women's views of who makes decisions coincide. For example, of the men interviewed who said that they alone took the decisions in the household, over a third (37 per cent) of their wives had reported that decisions were taken jointly. In contrast to women, men do not appear to value women's activities if these activities are not perceived to be 'work' and if the resources women bring to the household are in-kind rather than cash. Less than 10 per cent of men who said that their partner did not work (although it can be assumed she was working in the house) recognised the woman as making any contribution to the household.

It appears that women's perception of who is making a contribution to the household and who is involved in decision making does not necessarily reflect (men's) reality. The difference of opinion could also represent a possible point of conflict within the household—more pronounced after Mitch than before given the changes in women's roles and their perceptions of the value of their role.

When asked about the levels of conflict, or 'strong discussions' within households in the community where they live, there was a tendency for respondents to suggest an increase post-Mitch. However, overall, the findings around violence were inconclusive and perceptions of violence did not appear to be related in any significant manner to any of the key reconstruction variables, including reporting emotional affect and the need for counselling (Bradshaw 2001b, 2002). The in-depth study did find that more of those who thought there had been problems with reconstruction projects also thought conflict within the home, between couples, had increased and more also thought that violence against women in the community had increased post-Mitch. However, while conflict or 'strong discussions' within households were seen to increase post-Mitch, the research shows no direct relation between perceptions of conflict in couples and perceptions of increased violence. This suggests the mechanisms by which violence is being transmitted in situations of crisis and reconstruction warrant further research.

Conclusions

The evidence from Nicaragua appears to suggest that involving women in reconstruction initiatives is not sufficient to bring about changes in their position or situation. While the post-disaster context requires a practical response to meet very real needs, using women as an efficient means to deliver resources to households may reinforce rather than restructure gender roles and relations. Moreover, even if women feel their situation has changed, their male partners may not share this view. How involvement in reconstruction projects is viewed by those who are involved and those who are not and what this means for notions of contribution, value and decision making remain areas that are little studied. The wider impact on households of the processes set up by a large-scale disaster, including relations between men and women, conflict and violence, similarly remains an area yet to be fully explored.

One thing clearly suggested by this research is that getting reconstruction wrong may adversely affect women's position and situation in the home, their emotional well-being as well as their material well-being. A key lesson from the experience of Hurricane Mitch in Nicaragua, therefore, is that short-term practical benefits from relief and reconstruction may bring longer term strategic costs for the women involved.

Acknowledgements

The authors would like to thank all those in the CCER and Puntos de Encuentro who were involved in the studies cited here. Many thanks to International Cooperation for Development/Progression UK for their continued support.

References

Agarwal, B. 1997. '"Bargaining" and Gender Relations: Within and Beyond the Household', *Feminist Economics*, 3(1): 1–51.

Anderson, M. and P. Woodrow. 1998. *Rising from the Ashes: Development Strategies in Times of Disaster*, 2nd edition. London: IT Press.

Bradshaw, S. 2001a. *Dangerous Liaisons: Women, Men and Hurricane Mitch* (*Relaciones Peligrosas: Mujeres, Hombres y el Mitch*). Bilingual publication. Managua, Nicaragua: Puntos de Encuentro.

———. 2001b. 'Reconstructing Roles and Relations: Women's Participation in Reconstruction in Post-Mitch Nicaragua', *Gender and Development*, 9(3): 79–87. Reprinted in Caroline Sweetman (ed.), *Gender, Development and Humanitarian Work*, pp. 79–87. Oxford: Oxfam.

———. 2002. 'Exploring the Gender Dimensions of Reconstruction Processes Post-hurricane Mitch', *Journal of International Development*, 14(6): 871–79.

———. 2004a. *Socio-economic Impacts of Natural Disasters: A Gender Analysis*. United Nations Economic Commission for Latin America and the Caribbean (ECLAC) Serie Manuales 32.

———. 2004b. 'On the Margins and the Mainstream: Engendering the Disasters Agenda', Paper presented at the Gender Equality and Risk Reduction Conference, Honolulu, Hawaii, August 2004.

Bradshaw, S. and B. Linneker. 2003. *Challenging Women's Poverty: Perspectives on Gender and Poverty Reduction Strategies from Nicaragua and Honduras*. CIIR-ICD Briefing. London: CIIR-ICD.

Bradshaw, S., B. Linneker and R. Zuniga. 2002. 'Social Roles and Spatial Relations of NGOs and Civil Society', in Cathy McIlwaine and Katie Willis (eds), *Challenges and Change in Middle America: Perspectives on Development in Mexico, Central America and the Caribbean*, pp. 243–69. Harlow, England: Pearson Education.

Byrne, B. with S. Baden. 1995. *Gender, Emergencies and Humanitarian Assistance*. BRIDGE Report 33, IDS.

CAW. 1998. *Weaving Gender in Disaster and Refugee Assistance*. Commission on the Advancement of Women.

CEPAL. 1999. Evaluación de los Daños Ocasionados por el Huracán Mitch, 1998; Sus Implicaciones para el Desarrollo Económico, Social y el Medio Ambiente. (LC/MEX/L.375). CEPAL (United Nations Economic Commission for Latin America and the Caribbean), Sede Subregional de la CEPAL en México D.F., 18 de Mayo.

Chant, S. 2003a. 'The "Engendering" of Poverty Analysis in Developing Regions: Progress since the United Nations Decade for Women, and Priorities for the Future Strategies', LSE Gender Institute New Working Paper Series, Issue 11.

———. 2003b. 'Female Household Headship and the Feminisation of Poverty: Facts, Fictions and Forward Strategies', LSE Gender Institute New Working Paper Series, Issue 9.

———. 2004. 'Dangerous Equations? How Female-headed Households Became the Poorest of the Poor: Causes, Consequences and Cautions', *IDS Bulletin*, 35(4): 19–26.

CIET International. 1999a. *Principales Resultados de la Auditoría Social para la Emergencia y la Reconstrucción—Fase 1*. Managua, Nicaragua: Civil Coordinator for Emergency and Reconstruction.

———. 1999b. *Principales Resultados de la Auditoría Social para la Emergencia y la Reconstrucción—Fase 2*. Managua, Nicaragua: Civil Coordinator for Emergency and Reconstruction.

Cooke, B. and U. Kothari (eds). 2002. *Participation: The New Tyranny?* London: Zed Books.

Cornwall, A. 2001. 'Making a Difference? Getting Serious about Gender and Participatory Development', IDS Discussion Paper, 378.

Delaney, P. L. and E. Shrader. 2000. 'Gender and Post-disaster Reconstruction: The Case of Hurricane Mitch in Honduras and Nicaragua', Decision review draft presented to the World Bank.

ECA. 2000. *Independent Evaluation of Expenditure of DEC Central American Hurricane Appeal Funds*. San Jose, Costa Rica: ECA.

Enarson, E. and B. Morrow. 1998. 'Why Gender, Why Women?' in E. Enarson and B. Morrow (eds), *The Gendered Terrain of Disasters*, pp. 1–8. Westport, CT: Praeger.

Jackson, C. 1996. 'Rescuing Gender from the Poverty Trap', *World Development*, 24(3): 489–504.

Linneker, B. 2002. 'Gendered Comparisons of the Capital Influences on the Well-being of Women and Households Experiencing Poverty in Nicaragua', Social Audit III Working Paper, Coordinadora Civil para la Emergencia y la Reconstrucción (CCER), Managua, Nicaragua.

Linneker B., J. M. Quintanilla and R. E. H Zúniga. 1998. *Evaluación Crítica del Impacto del Huracán Mitch en Nicaragua*. Managua, Nicaragua: Coordinadora Civil para la Emergencia y la Reconstrucción (CCER).

McGee, R. 2002. 'Participating in Development', in U. Kothari and M. Minogue (eds), *Development Theory and Practice: Critical Perspectives*, pp. 92–116. Houndmills, Basingstoke: Palgrave.

Molyneux, M. 1985. 'Mobilisation without Emancipation? Women's Interests, the State and Revolution in Nicaragua', *Feminist Studies*, 11: 2.

Moser, C. 1989. 'Gender Planning in the Third World: Meeting Practical and Strategic Gender Needs', *World Development*, 19(11): 1799–825.

Oxfam. 1998. 'Debt Relief for Nicaragua: Breaking Out of the Poverty Trap', Policy Paper. UK: Oxfam.

Sen, Amartya. 1987. 'Gender and Co-operative Conflicts', World Institute for Development Economics Research, Working Paper 18, Helsinki.

Sen, Amartya. 1990. 'Gender and Cooperative Conflicts', in Irene Tinker (ed.), *Persistent Inequalities: Women and World* Development, pp. 123–49. New York: Oxford University Press.

WICEJ. 2004. *Seeking Accountability on Women's Human Rights: Women Debate the Millennium Development Goals.* Women's International Coalition for Economic Just-ice. Available online at http://www.wicej.addr.com/mdg/index.html (Accessed on 17 June 2009).

Wisner, Ben, Piers Blaikie, Terry Cannon and Ian Davis. 2005. *At Risk: Natural Hazards, People's Vulnerability and Disasters.* London and New York: Routledge.

World Bank. 2001. *Engendering Development.* Available online at www.worldbank.org/gender/prr/ (Accessed on 17 June 2009).

7

Environmental Management and Disaster Mitigation: Middle Eastern Gender Perspective

•✦•

Samia Galal Saad

The Middle East region extends over Africa and Asia from the Arabian Gulf in the east to the Atlantic Ocean in the west. Due to massive population growth, the resulting need for more intensive agriculture and improper management of very limited water resources, the region is suffering from a scarcity of fresh water (ESCWA 2005). In addition, the region is experiencing an increasing food security gap between agriculture, livestock, fish and marine productivity, steadily increasing population demands and high desertification rates. Water policies vary between countries which creates potential political unrest between upstream and downstream users.

Oil-rich gulf countries have managed to desalinate seawater to meet their escalating water needs. They also rely on groundwater in most of the remote human settlements. Countries like Egypt, Lebanon, Syria, Iraq and Sudan rely mainly on river water passing by their territory and originating from neighbouring countries with greater rain-fed areas and groundwater-irrigated lands. Other countries in the region, such as

Jordan, Libya, Tunisia, Algeria and Morocco, are rain-fed and depend on surface and groundwater as much as it is available.

The region encompasses variable topographic features, from desert plains to mountains and river valleys. Mountainous regions and their adjacent valleys suffer from unpredicted flash floods, which create massive soil erosion, landslides and destruction to any human settlements established in their natural conduits. Flash floods occur 20 or 50 years apart and people may forget about these events during the long periods of drought.

Prolonged dry seasons due to climate change have resulted in extensive loss of the forest and natural green cover; in addition, cutting trees to accommodate agriculture developments and expansion of urban settlements is currently practised in Syria, Lebanon and Morocco. Dry weather also increases forest fires with losses in human properties as well as biodiversity. This loss of green cover has led to noticeable desertification and loss of fertile soil to the sea and rivers, increasing the impacts of floods. The absence of green cover enhances the rainwater velocity leading to severe flood flushing power with more destruction, loss of property and land fertility. Desertification also impacts livestock rearing, reducing the economic asset women usually depend upon in needy days.

The region also suffers from an increasing number of natural disasters from drought, flash floods, earthquakes, landsliding, desertification, floods and the implications of escalating high temperatures due to climate change. Earthquakes occur in the region and their implications are very severe, as the building and planning codes have not integrated this type of natural disaster into their regulations due to their infrequent nature and the tendency to forget about them. Tornadoes and typhoons are not common in the region as the climate tends to be more settled with little variability throughout the year. Volcanoes are not recorded.

Gender Issues in the Arab Region

Women in the region are climbing the ladders of education and participation in planning, execution and evaluation of development projects (Moghadam 2007; World Bank 2004). They are also increasing in numbers as professional engineers, medical doctors and service providers, as well as decision makers in different governmental and non-governmental organisations (NGOs). Although their presence in the cabinet of ministers, parliament, advisory political councils and administrative local councils is still very low, they have managed to increase their acceptance by the people at the community level in the different countries of the region.

In Egypt, Lebanon, Syria, Tunisia and Jordan, for example, women's contribution to development is becoming more and more recognised, and they are also receiving political support from the First Ladies in these countries. Saudi women are now involved in trade and business, utilising the internet and telecommunication technologies which suit their secluded culture and traditions. Saudi women are also participating in postgraduate, graduate and undergraduate female education at female-segregated universities. They are handling services, including banking and medical care centres designed for Saudi women. Workforce statistics calculate female participation in the workforce based on paid work, but women's contributions are actually much higher if the non-paid workforce is accounted for, especially in the agricultural and the private family sectors.

Women's power in controlling family decisions should not be neglected, although men in the region, due to cultural stereotypes and stigmas, may not acknowledge this role. Women in the region are playing very strong and dependable roles in natural disasters in addition to their daily life chores. The problem lies with the mass media which has hindered community perception of women in these heroic roles, while always portraying men as heroes and saviours. Women who take on roles in securing water, food, medical care and shelter during and after the disaster rarely receive attention. Despite this, women have never felt that they should neglect these primary roles because they are not valued or appreciated. On the contrary, they always seek ways to improve their performance.

Involving more women in the mass media has created a growing tendency to focus on those invisible roles. Television camera women and female programme producers in the Egyptian television currently give more attention to analysing the roles of men and women in any situation in the dramas and melodramas they broadcast. Emergencies due to natural or man-made disasters are no exception. Gender-balanced roles seem to satisfy most of the audiences in Egypt. The Egyptian television production is highly accepted in almost all countries in the region, and their gender-balanced perception is now conveyed to other Middle Eastern countries.

Women as Managers of Natural Resources

Historical inscriptions record the survival management strategies of women living in the desert and mountain periphery areas seeking to obtain safe drinking water and safe temporary shelter in cases of limited food after drought, flash floods and other natural disasters. Through stories transmitted from mother to daughter, they learnt how to conserve food, keep water in leather and pottery containers and grow plants that conserve water in their tissue to the benefit of the animals that consume them. They also respected the natural bio-diversity of their surrounding environment. Their conservative means of survival did not create any garbage and solid waste problem because everything was derived from nature and returned to nature.

Changing patterns of life due to the discovery of petroleum and increasing community wealth and educational status have helped them to adopt new imported lifestyles; however, women have tended to forget their former techniques of conservation. Efforts are now directed towards informing women and men in the region that adopting new styles of life does not mean neglecting traditional conservative attitudes. The rich and poor countries in the region, with respect to agriculture, industry, services and trade, are now adopting conservation methodologies and approaches. Even new technology development integrates the conservative consumption of energy, water and raw materials.

Currently, the knowledge that Middle Eastern women possess of sustainable lifestyles is increasing due to their increased education and exposure to the outer world through the various mass media channels. Information dissemination by television, the internet and radios have facilitated the transfer of massive information to women under any cultural or social barriers. Increasing the number of women who have access to television and radio has helped most of the illiterate women learn new ideas about how to conserve water resources, ensure food security and clean energy sources and gain new skills for income generation to alleviate their poverty. Yet, there is still a dire need to secure those resources for many women in the region, especially with increasing economic sanctions, wars, escalating population and urbanisation, desertification and uneven distribution of wealth between people of different social status in the community.

Exposure to increasing environmental pollutants in urban and rural areas is an added burden on most women's productive and reproductive health. Female participation in agriculture constitutes up to 75 per cent of the total agriculture workforce in Egypt and several other countries with agriculture-based economies. Exposure to agrochemicals is one of the areas of danger seldom mentioned, and there is little consideration of the need to inform farmers regarding their occupational health and safety or the proper management of those chemicals. Female farmers are exposed to those chemicals while removing weeds, removing infected leaves for pest control and harvesting sprayed crops, vegetables and fruits, as the safe period between spraying and harvesting may not be observed.

Living with such daily stresses does not leave much time or energy for these women to think of preparedness actions. Yet, talking to groups of women in different countries always reveals how interested they are to adopt any measures intended to secure their families' health and safety.

Gender Issues in Disasters

In the Middle Eastern culture, it is shameful for men not to actively participate in controlling the impacts of natural disasters. Women tend to secure their families' household assets, which are basic for their survival after the disaster. Men will try to protect their amenities by voluntarily building dykes, in case of flood warnings, and reinforcing their houses and rescuing those under the rubble of demolished houses, in case of earthquakes. Women, children and the elderly, especially mothers, are assisted in moving to secure places. Elderly mothers are always given the best care of all people because of strong religious beliefs to do so. After the disaster, the sheltered areas offer men easier access to food, medicine, refuge and water relief given by donors and governments. Gender differences tend to disappear temporarily during and immediately after the disaster. Once the community settles after the disaster, women tend to suffer greater consequences than men as they can lose their privacy and income generating activity, with little mobility to seek other jobs as they are always tied to their families. With men abandoning the family more and more, women suffer the burden of single-headed household responsibilities with no source of money or family support. With the demolition of schools, more girls than boys are forced to drop education, as most likely they will be placed in distant schools, which they cannot easily access. The same applies to health care, as it will be much harder for women to travel long distances with their children or family members to seek medical treatment and preventive care.

Women are hit the most by the stress of limited water quantity and quality. Even in urban cities where water distribution systems supply water to most houses, the low water pressure in the system, resulting from limited supply, extends the working household hours to late night in order for modern washing machines and bath heaters to access the higher water pressure available at night. Informing the women in the community about the risks and the devastating implications of neglecting the government precautions in their communities could ensure that the majority of these natural disasters' consequences are avoided. Better information dissemination will also help the government to secure proper land use through better planning in urban and agriculture areas. Informing communities about the statistics of natural disasters and the locations of vulnerable areas is important for mitigation measures to be adopted by the community. But the mass media in most of the countries in this region does not place the necessary emphasis on natural disasters or their management, including mitigation or preparedness activities.

Poor men and women are the ones who suffer the most from the implications of natural disasters as they tend to live and produce in the low-cost lands, neglected by the governmental planning due to known vulnerabilities to natural disasters. Women usually receive the severest economic hit due to their restricted mobility. But women are seldom involved in community training on methods to manage natural disasters that can hit any vulnerable community. As a result, they are left to behave according to their survival instincts, which could be heroic or dangerous and fatal. The problem is further aggravated, as the governmental agencies do not spread the word about the risks encountered in those vulnerable areas. In addition, these agencies have no governance to prevent people from engaging in such dangerous living, as they do not offer them a safer alternative. Lack of maps covering all areas of the countries, with clear identification of vulnerable areas, could be behind the lack of knowledge in governmental agencies about those areas. Due to limited resources, most governments do not offer affordable alternatives to those with limited resources to live in places that are less prone to natural disasters. Women, being the poorest of the poor, find themselves residing in those high-risk areas.

Barriers to Including Women in Risk Management

Natural disaster managing councils are present in some countries of the region but their role needs more recognition and better integration into the policies of the countries to ensure the best preventive and preparedness actions. Women's participation in these councils is nearly non-existent. Consequently, more involvement is needed from men and women at both the governmental and the non-governmental levels.

Integration of methods of prevention of natural disasters and impact minimisation is currently practiced through the preparation of an environmental impact assessment (EIA) for all new projects. Most countries in the region adopt this technique as a valid tool for avoiding hazardous areas, such as flash floods passages, areas prone to landslides and dams built over river channels to control floods. Through the implementation of engineering design features, the effects of natural disasters can be minimised, if not avoided. This can be achieved during the planning and the construction phases of the projects.

The problems which both men and women in any country face regarding active participation in the management and mitigation of natural disasters can be summarised as:

1. Some governmental bodies, other than civil defence authorities, may not consider mitigation and preparedness principles at the country level while determining different land uses. As a result, more women and men could suffer severe economic and socio-economic impacts of natural disasters.
2. As natural disasters occur at unpredicted times and frequencies, decision makers as well as community members underestimate their vulnerability.
3. Lack of information dissemination regarding those areas especially vulnerable to natural disasters causes increased economic and socio-economic impacts.
4. Community members are not informed of the proper preparedness actions they should adopt in the case of disasters.
5. Women are even less informed about natural disasters and their management or mitigation. Lack of education and less involvement in development and the decision-making process in all domains create in women a lack of awareness about likely locations of

natural disasters, mitigation and environmental management or preparedness actions.

6. Funds are not budgeted to mobilise communities to face any unexpected disaster and reduce its toll on men and women, especially in developing countries. All mitigation measures combating the physical damages of disasters require extra finances to be invested in order to integrate these measures into the construction phases of projects. When country resources are limited, those measures tend to be forgotten or neglected.

7. Mass media channels place the least emphasis on natural disaster mitigation, management and preparedness actions to be adopted by the community. In turn, this limits the access of illiterate women to information, even more than in the case of men.

What Can be Done?

The Middle East represents a wide spectrum of hazards, risks and vulnerabilities. Historically, women in the region have mastered conservation of natural resources and proper management of their environment. Although their role is not properly understood due to gender bias in the mass media, it is now being recognised, and more governmental and non-governmental agencies are seeking women's participation. Increasing levels of education and involvement in male-dominated professions are enhancing their credibility as decision-making partners. There is a need to take advantage of these winds of changes by formulation of policy guidelines that would mainstream disaster risk reduction in development and at the same time mainstream gender relations in disaster risk reduction. Policy directions should include awareness campaigns targeting women that use a wide range of media to reach women with different literacy levels, and that reflect women's local traditions and environmental knowledge. Risk assessments should include information about women's livelihoods, social power, family roles and other considerations. Preparedness campaigns should reflect knowledge of the roles women play in the family and community.

Environmental deterioration leading to the occurrence of frequent disasters can be minimised through sustainable development approaches. Men and women should be involved in the planning and execution of projects related to development, and in implementing proper mitigation measures to avoid the devastating impacts of natural disasters. The role of civil society is growing steadily all over the countries of the region. More women are participating in NGOs, as they tend to function away from the cumbersome rules and regulations of the government. Women's NGOs can play a very important role in information dissemination by involving more women in disaster preparedness and avoidance measures. They can empower women decision makers to integrate these dimensions into their decision-making processes, as well as lobby for others to support these decisions by integrating the environmental dimension into their plans and actions, thereby insuring sustainable development.

Through participation in the process of EIA public hearings on new development projects, NGOs can create pressure to prevent natural disasters and their effects by the integration of mitigation engineering measures. NGO participation in EIA evaluations can also ensure proper urban planning, which avoids risky areas. International UN organisations and donor agencies play a key role in empowering women in the region to get involved in developmental issues and supporting their participation in sustainable development. These agencies need to work collaboratively on issues like natural disaster management and involve and consult local women experts and women's environmental and community groups to integrate gender into all their programmes and projects. Although they have raised awareness about the integration of the gender dimension, there is still a lot to be done to integrate both gender and environmental dimensions into sustainable development. Sustainable development has to be seen as one of the very important mitigation tools for natural disasters.

Acknowledgements

This chapter was adapted from the original version presented at the UN Division for the Advancement of Women, Expert Group Meeting on 'Environmental Management and the Mitigation of Natural Disasters: A Gender Perspective', 6–9 November 2001 in Ankara, Turkey. All original papers from the meeting are available online at http://www. un.org/womenwatch/daw/csw/env_manage/documents/EP3-2001Oct22.pdf

References

Economic and Social Commission For Western Asia (ESCWA). 2005. *ESCWA Water Development Report 1: Vulnerability of the Region to Socio-economic Drought*. New York: United Nations.

Moghadam, M. (ed.). 2007. *From Patriarchy to Empowerment: Women's Participation, Movements, and Rights in the Middle East, North Africa, and South Asia*. Syracuse: Syracuse University Press.

World Bank. 2004. *Gender and Development in the Middle East and North Africa: Women in the Public Sphere*. Washington, DC: The World Bank.

8

'Everything Became a Struggle, Absolute Struggle': Post-flood Increases in Domestic Violence in New Zealand

———•✦•———

Rosalind Houghton

Every year New Zealand experiences many potentially damaging natural hazard events as a consequence of its location on the western margin of the Pacific Ocean. Floods, earthquakes, landslides and even volcanic eruptions are becoming more and more common; and numerous studies have been completed on the level of public awareness, preparedness and perception of national hazards (Leonard, Johnston and Paton 2004; Leonard, Kelman and Johnston 2004; Walton et al. 2004). However, little research has been done on the day-to-day realities faced by those who have recently experienced an event and particularly little on the specific experiences of women.

Hazard events can have a multitude of downstream effects. If mild, these can provide distraction or even entertainment and potentially no significant disruption to everyday life. At the other end of the spectrum, a declared national disaster can completely disrupt everyday life leading to evacuation, perhaps even families being deprived of belongings, food, sanitation and privacy, and potentially also lead to permanent migration.

The gravity of impact does vary with each family and even with each individual, but a number of common patterns have been identifed by researchers (Wisner et al. 2004). For example, some international studies show an increase in the rate of domestic violence in affected areas (Enarson 1999; Fothergill 1999; Wilson et al. 1999; also see Fisher in this volume). This correlation is yet to be established for New Zealand and is the topic of this chapter. I report in this chapter a study conducted on possible changes in domestic violence reporting the wake of major flooding, as reported by organisations involved with families affected by abuse.

Gender Stratification, Control and Domestic Violence in Disasters

Disasters bring to light aspects of life that are relatively hidden in everyday life. Gender stratification is one of the social structures that become more apparent following disasters. It can take different forms and has different relevance in disasters across societies. In societies where gender roles and norms are strongly enforced or ascribed to, and where gender inequalities raise daily survival issues for women, disasters can have very serious and even fatal consequences for women. An example is the Indian Ocean 2004 tsunami in Sri Lanka where 91 per cent of adults killed were women (Abeyesekera 2006: 5). This is not to ignore ethnic, age and class stratifications that cut across gender and compound inequalities derived from gender stratification. However, as a feminist researcher, my focus is primarily on gender. All stratification is reinforced and reflected through access to resources, including education, health, food and shelter. This lack of access is then amplified in disasters (Fordham 1998).

In New Zealand, gender stratification is clearly evident in the domestic violence statistics compiled annually by both government and non-government agencies. Data from the national Family Courts indicate that the great majority (91 per cent) of applications for protection orders in 2004 were requested by women (Bartlett 2006). Domestic violence was found to affect one in three New Zealand women in their lifetime in another study involving both rural and urban residents (Fanslow and

Robinson 2004: 28). Further, half of all female homicides reported in 2004 were related to some form of family violence (Ministry of Justice 2005). These and other figures have put domestic and family violence on the political agenda, and many government initiatives now exist to attempt to reduce these high rates of domestic and family violence.

The definition of domestic violence used most widely by researchers and practitioners in New Zealand (and used here) is that adopted by the *Te Rito Family Violence Prevention Strategy* (Ministry of Social Development 2002). In this document, domestic violence is defined as 'a broad range of controlling behaviours, commonly of a physical, sexual, and/or psychological nature which typically involve fear, intimidation and emotional deprivation' (Ministry of Social Development 2002: 8). This definition highlights that domestic violence is not just physical violence but fundamentally about the control of another individual.

While 'stress' is often cited as the cause of abuse, and post-disaster stress in turn in disaster contexts, this is more likely a rationale or aggravating factor than a cogent explanation of why this stress leads to violence against spouses and not others, such as colleagues and friends. Umberson et al. (1998) emphasise loss of control in an abuser's life as a key factor in the intensity of domestic violence. They argue in the case of loss of job or the end of a relationship, when abusers fear they are losing control of their environment, they tighten the level of control at home, an analysis easily transposed to circumstances following a disaster. Disasters can destroy homes or render them uninhabitable, can impact on the employment of both abuser and victim through business and road closures and, if schools and other services are closed, throw daily routines into upheaval. Further, during disasters, families often become heavily reliant on external support agencies for even the most basic resources and this can cause a feeling of hopelessness and embarrassment (Fothergill 2003). Individuals to whom a high degree of personal and interpersonal control is important may seek to regain the feeling of control through violence or the threat of violence to retain their control over their 'domain'—their family. This could mean, for example, that domestic violence changes from psychological and economic abuse to physical assaults for the first time, or that current violence becomes more intense.

The Whakatane Flood: Case Study of Agency Responses to Domestic Violence

While there is a sound theoretical arguement that levels of reported domestic violence will increase after a disaster, few studies have been conducted after disaster events and none previously in New Zealand. As part of ongoing postgraduate work, a case study was undertaken on the events following the July 2004 floods in Whakatane, a town of some 30,000 people on the east coast of New Zealand's North Island. On 18 July 2004, the Whakatane district and surrounding region were hit by a high-intensity rainstorm. This rain caused a breach in the river levees and many land slips around the district. The river plains and most of the coastal lands were flooded.

The flooding closed off all access roads to Whakatane for two days and a state of emergency was declared for a two-week period following the initial flooding. Awatapu, the urban area most seriously affected, is a neighbourhood partially surrounded by a lagoon which flooded. Many residents of the 300 houses evacuated were put into the local hall which, in this predominantly Maori community, was the local Maori community centre (Marae) or the War memorial hall; or went to stay with extended family. In some cases, up to three different families stayed together in three bedroom homes for months after the event. Two years after the event, the local municipal council acknowledged the delay in repairs which continues as of this writing, 3 years later. In particular, the case study showed interesting organisational issues which I now discuss.

Study Design and Method

To explore the implications of this evacuation and displacement, I conducted interviews with eight professionals working in the area of domestic violence who were on the front lines after the flood and thus in the best position to assess any changes in violence levels and identify any common characteristics of post-flood clients. Tape-recorded interviews lasting approximately an hour were conducted in August 2005. Eight agencies participated in the study, representing diverse roles in the response and recovery phases of the flooding. Some specifically dealt with domestic violence while other agencies worked more generally with flood-affected families providing health services, stress counselling, food, furniture and other services. This research design was selected to contribute new data on this important subject as no organisational data collection procedures were then in place to track possible changes in reported domestic violence related to the flood and its aftermath.

New Zealand provides a good site for this research as it has a centralised government, with a single police force and single layer of government. There is also a group of agencies who are consistently present and active in most communities in New Zealand, in addition to area-specific agencies, which also allows for future comparative analysis.

Organisations included in this analysis represent governmental agencies with statutory rights and obligations, non-government secular and Christian agencies and an indigenous social support agency. Their activities before, during and after the flooding varied.

Government Responsibilities and Flood Responses

The New Zealand Police is the nation's law enforcement agency. Following the flooding, the police had a role in evacuating people from houses that flooded, and responding to normal callouts, including incidents of domestic violence. The police work closely with non-government agencies such as Women's Refuge and Victim Support on domestic violence cases. Child, Youth and Family (CYF) is a government body responsible for people aged 0–17 years. It, too, had a civil responsibility to respond immediately in both the response and recovery phases and specifically to coordinate counselling for youths aged 17 and under. However, following this event, they extended their scope to counselling support and coordination for all affected by the flood. Work and Income New Zealand is a government agency that provides financial support to welfare recipients and beneficiaries. This agency also has a civil responsibility to act immediately after a civil defence emergency is declared. Its responsibilities included the financial support of all those affected by flooding until such time as adequate housing was found.

Non-governmental Areas of Responsibility and Flood Responses

Victim Support is a national organisation that works closely with the New Zealand Police, giving support and information to all victims of crime and trauma to help them restore their lives. Their work can involve being called to the scene of an incident or referrals after the fact. They also work with Women's Refuge, which deals directly with victims of domestic violence, both those who seek them out and through referrals from the Police. It provides support, accommodation, advice, advocacy and any other service women need to get back on their feet when working on or leaving an abusive relationship. The indigenous Ngati Awa Social and Health Services (NASH) is a non-governmental agency that provides a myriad of social and health services to Whakatane residents, particularly Maori who are affiliated to the Ngati Awa iwi (tribe), including wellness checks for babies and counselling support. The James Family Trust is a faith-based domestic violence agency that offers one-on-one support as well as education programmes. During the event, they worked under the wing of CYF to provide social work services for families during the flood response. Later, in the recovery phase, they began to make home visits to ensure that families had adequate housing, financial assistance, accurate information and other needs met with. Finally, the Salvation Army, too, provided support and guidance as well as operating a church. They sponsored a mobile team that visited different districts as well as a stationery team of professionals responsible for furniture, food and other household items. They also provided an accommodation site for those who needed more support such as the elderly, disabled or others who did not wish to stay in the Town Hall which was used for emergency shelter.

These eight agencies each had a unique perspective on domestic violence. Some were on the front line of domestic violence work, interacting with victims of domestic violence very soon after, or in some cases during, the reported incident. Other agencies can become involved after a woman was referred by another agency up to a week after the actual incident. Two of the agencies participating in the study (Salvation Army and NASH) did not specifically deal with victims of domestic violence but instead worked with the broader social impacts of the flooding.

Agency Impacts and Responses to Domestic Violence

As might be expected, agencies working in the trenches of domestic violence response reported more significant changes to their caseloads than agencies more removed from the domestic violence work in the wake of the flood. Women's Refuge experienced a tripling of its workload beginning immediately after the flood. This placed pressure on Women's Refuge's already scarce resources, and lead to the safe house being so overcrowded (including families housed in the garage of the safe house) that some were instead taken home for safety to the houses of staff. During the peak of the flood, each worker had at least three families staying in their homes with them in addition to caring for displaced families in the safe home as part of their regular duties.

Work and Income New Zealand also experienced a tripling in their domestic violence work. At the time of the flooding, the agency had one liaison officer employed to work with women from the Women's Refuge who were seeking financial help. This generally involved one half-hour slot every week for the liaison officer prior to the flooding but staff member reported that this became a full-time position after the flood, in terms of increased workload and the challenges of responding to more complicated flood-related needs.

Both the New Zealand Police and Victim Support reported a doubling in the number of callouts. Fourteen callouts for family violence were recorded in June by the police and twenty-nine a month later following the flood. This higher level continued through to September. As Sergeant Neil Peterson of the New Zealand Police confirmed this in his own experience saying, 'We normally average five a week, that's just in Whakatane, and that jumped to about ten a week. So we had a marked increase after the event in July in cases that our front line cops were attending.'

The James Family Trust also reported an increased workload, specifically a doubling in the numbers of those wanting to participate in a programme educating women about violence and how it affects them. The increased demand lasted for two to three months and resulted in the creation of a waiting list for the programme where none had been needed before. Once cleared, the waiting list has not been reactivated which also implies that the demand was a direct result of post-flood conditions.

While the staff of agencies cited earlier reported doubling and tripling of their workload, others such as CYF did not. It is important to note that theirs is a much higher response threshold than other agencies receiving referrals only after three police callouts to the same family (and only when children are present) have been reported. The Salvation Army and NASH did not deal with domestic violence directly; yet, staff reported that they were aware of the increased workload in the primary agencies responding to domestic violence. Two professionals also stated that they knew of specific cases of domestic violence occurring either at the War memorial hall or at the Marae, both of which housed flood evacuees.

Explaining Flood-related Abuse: Agency Perspectives

If reported so, interviewees were asked what factors they felt played a role in this increase in reported violence following the flood. The primary reason cited was *financial stress* as the flood impacted heavily on people's financial situation, including lost possession, houses and earnings; some businesses were closed in the town and other employees were unable to work because childcare facilities were closed. Lack of insurance was often cited as nearly nine out of ten respondents to a mail survey conducted by the Whakatane District Council (454 of 509) lacked insurance for the contents of their homes. All agencies reported that the majority of women with whom they dealt lacked insurance and they felt the pressure this put on families was a contributing factor. Many of the factors mentioned were consistent with existing studies' findings.

Their poor financial and support situation led many women to return to abusive households. Women's Refuge staff suggested that 85 per cent of those who had come to them returned to their partners following the flood; of these, half subsequently returned to Women's Refuge. While this pattern of behaviour (leaving and returning from shelter) also occurs in non-disaster times, it was noted that many women were returning to these relationships only because of their dire situation following the flood.

Nonetheless, it is important to note that every agency dealt with people across the demographic spectra, all ethnicities, ages, incomes and education levels; none were specific to one demographic group. While financial strain was noted as a major factor by the agencies dealing with victims of domestic violence, after the Whakatane floods, women from all socio-economic groups approached agencies for help, suggesting that financial pressure was not the sole cause of the increases in domestic violence reporting.

Substance abuse, like stress, is often cited as a causal factor in domestic violence but all those interviewed stressed that, while there had been alcohol present in some cases, this was not the main reason for the violence, confirming the pattern noted in other studies of domestic violence (Farris and Fenaughty 2002: 343; Kaufman and Straus 1987; Raskin and Chen 2002). Focusing on addiction, or misuse of drugs or alcohol, like stress, sidesteps the question of why abuse, if any, is directed against intimate partners or children rather than friends or co-workers and why those who abuse are often able to function well in the public sphere.

Staff also reported a number of structural factors such that *communication lines* were not always open between, and within, agencies. This meant that contradictory information was distributed which made a frustrating process more so. Getting mixed messages and not knowing how to fulfil the requirements for attaining food parcels or bedding or any other essential items added more stress to the situation rather than mitigating it.

A reduced level of social support from agencies was also cited. When Women's Refuge was asked when the violence returned to a 'normal' level, the answer was that it did not. The Refuge staff noted that there had been a second surge in reporting when the other social service agencies withdrew from the community two or three months after the flood. Women's Refuge explained that the rise in clients coming to them in November on the heels of two relatively quiet months seemed linked to the reduced capacity of other agencies involved in the aftermath of the floods. As this domestic violence advocate explains:

> The services that were present at the beginning of the flood dissipated rapidly—within about two months from the July floods, by September or October, those services ... had retracted ... The council went into committee which didn't provide services. So community agencies were left with very little support and hence I think the numbers grew as well.

Closed childcare facilities were clearly a contributing factor in increased stress. As part of the civil defence emergency, all schools and childcare facilities were closed. Parents were left with children while trying to sort out the future of their house, possessions and, for farmers, livestock. Had the parents been relieved for at least a few hours a day during the first weeks, when still in a state of emergency, they might have been better able to re-group and get on with the work at hand without the additional concern of entertaining and watching out for the physical safety of children.

Finally, overcrowded housing was a major issue for many families as many people moved in with extended family for what they thought would be a short amount of time (a month at the most) and wound up staying for a year or longer. Many of these families were living in government housing at the time of flooding and had very few options for alternative accommodation while waiting for the repairs to be made. Coupled with rents that increased dramatically, rising from an average of US$ 145–US$ 170 a week to US$ 180–US$ 220; this meant that poorer families were left living with extended family for long periods of time.

Policy Gaps and Recommendations

Given the high level of awareness of domestic violence more generally in New Zealand, one would expect that there would be a high degree of responsiveness to any increased domestic violence reporting after disasters (Wilson et al. 1999: 120). However, this was not the case in Whakatane in 2004. Agencies reported increase in service demand due to flood-related domestic violence and were themselves both directly and negatively impacted by the flood. This was especially true of Women's Refuge. With the tripling in their client numbers, the staff sought to obtain a second safe house but this proved impossible for a number of reasons. Staff reported how poorly supported they themselves felt throughout the event though they recognised the importance of their efforts, especially when personally housing women and children displaced by domestic violence. However, in some regards, the Refuge was fortunate as the safe house had only minor water damage. There was no back-up plan for service continuity, and had the shelter been damaged beyond use even more vulnerable women and children would have been at even greater risk as their options were bleak—to public shelters where their abuser was likely to be, or back to the abuser's residence. This is consistent with what Enarson (1999) found, disaster planning is not a priority for agencies like Women's Refuge as resources are already stretched thin and so are focused on the immediate challenges, not mid- or long-term ones.

Three levels of overarching policy govern civil defence and emergency management practices (national, regional and local), with the intent that these be integrated and operated under similar structures across all phases of disasters, from readiness to recovery. For Whakatane, plans exist for the Whakatane district (local), the Bay of Plenty region and the national response, but no mention is made of the need to plan how to respond to cases of domestic violence, or how to protect the Women's Refuge.

Women's Refuge staff also noted that during the July flooding, no seat was 'reserved' for them on the Welfare Taskforce Committee. Only after local police highlighted the problem were they included.

Women's Refuge had a good working relationship with the police, and so the issue of domestic violence was eventually brought to the attention of both the media and the Civil Defence Welfare group. Well-established pre-flood relationships proved essential in drawing attention to women's increased risk of violence after the flood; conversely, without strong allies, the agency was not able to successfully locate and operate a second safe house at a time of critical need.

A common thread reported in this research was financial stress as a factor related to increased demand for services for victims of domestic violence after the flood. However, this was compounded by structural constraints that led to a lack of awareness of domestic violence as a potential outcome of the flooding. This gap is a clear flaw in national, regional and local emergency management planning and policy intended to ensure that no individual 'falls through the cracks' in the aftermath of any disaster in New Zealand.

Conclusions

Further research into changes in reported domestic violence following natural hazard events in New Zealand should be a priority for emergency management planning as policy is only relevant if it accurately reflects the needs and resources of local residents. This study demonstrated the potential need for New Zealand emergency management policy and planning to incorporate provisions for mitigating any possible increases in domestic violence. A study examining different communities which have, at different times, experienced different hazard events would prove fruitful.

Clearly, the root causes of abuse are deep and complex. Perhaps the reality is that focusing on resourcing and supporting agencies likely to engage with victims of domestic violence in times of disaster is what emergency managers can reasonably achieve. But, at present, emergency managers seem simply not to know about the increased need to address violence as a factor in flood response and recovery. Though some planners and responders are becoming more aware, domestic violence is still not explicitly stated in any emergency management policy. If not recognised as a problem, violence against women cannot be anticipated and mitigated and thus will continue in future disasters. *We can do better than this!*

Acknowledgements

Thanks to the interviewees who all gave so generously their time and wisdom, my parents and sister, Sandra Grey, Sara Williams, David Johnston, Ann Dostine, Raewyn Good and Elaine Enarson—all of whom gave such a wealth of support.

References

Abeyesekera, S. 2006. *Tsunami Aftermath: Violation of Women's Human Rights in Sri Lanka.* Thailand: APWLD.

Bartlett, E. 2006. *Family Court Report 2004.* Wellington: Ministry of Justice.

Enarson, E. 1999. 'Violence against Women in Disasters: A Study of Domestic Violence Programs in the United States and Canada', *Violence against Women*, 5(7): 742–68.

Fanslow, J. and E. Robinson. 2004. 'Violence against Women in New Zealand: Prevalence and Health Consequences', *The New Zealand Medical Journal*, 117: 1–12.

Farris, C. A. and A. M. Fenaughty. 2002. 'Social Isolation and Domestic Violence among Female Drug Users', *American Journal of Drug and Alcohol Abuse*, 28(2): 339–52.

Fordham, M. H. 1998. 'Making Women Visible in Disasters: Problematising the Private Domain', *Disasters*, 22(2): 126–43.

Fothergill, A. 1999. 'An Exploratory Study of Woman Battering in the Grand Forks Flood Disaster: Implications for Community Responses and Policies', *International Journal of Mass Emergencies and Disasters*, 17(1): 79–98.

———. 2003. 'The Stigma of Charity: Gender, Class, and Disaster Assistance', *Sociological Quarterly*, 44(4): 659–80.

Kaufman Kantor, G. and M. A. Straus. 1987. 'The "Drunken Bum" Theory of Wife Beating', *Social Problems*, 34(3): 213–30.

Leonard, G. S., I. Kelman and D. M. Johnston. 2004. *Residential Impacts, Perceptions and Preparedness Related to the Lower Hutt City February 2004 Flooding: Preliminary Results.* Institute of Geological and Nuclear Sciences Science Report, pp. 38–50.

Leonard, G. S., D. M. Johnston and D. Paton. 2004. *'Analysis of Te Anau Residents' Impacts, Awareness and Preparedness Following the 2003 Fiordland Earthquake*, Institute of Geological and Nuclear Sciences Science Report, pp. 37–57.

Ministry of Justice. 2005. *Family Violence Death Review*, p. 24. Wellington: Ministry of Justice.

Ministry of Social Development. 2002. *Te Rito Family Violence Prevention Strategy*. Wellington: Ministry of Social Development.

Raskin White, H. and P.-H. Chen. 2002. 'Problem Drinking and Intimate Partner Violence', *Journal of Studies on Alcohol*, 63(2): 205–14.

Umberson, D., K. Anderson, J. Glick and A. Shapiro. 1998. 'Domestic Violence, Personal Control, and Gender', *Journal of Marriage and the Family*, 60(2): 442–52.

Walton, M., D. Johnston, G. Leonard, W. Gray, R. Bell and D. Paton. 2004. *The Waikato Weather Bomb: Understanding the Impact*. New Zealand Institute of Economic Research Inc.

Wilson, J.,B. D. Phillips and D. M. Neal. 1999. 'Domestic Violence after Disasters', in E. Enarson and B. H. Morrow (eds), *The Gendered Terrain of Disaster: Through Women's Eyes*, pp. 115–22. Connecticut, London: Praeger.

Wisner, B., P. Blaikie, T. Cannon and I. Davis. 2004. *At Risk: Natural Hazards, People's Vulnerability and Disasters*, 2nd edition. London: Routledge.

9

Parenting in the Wake of Disaster: Mothers and Fathers Respond to Hurricane Katrina

———•✦•———

Lori Peek and Alice Fothergill

Although scientists and professionals had long warned of the dangers to New Orleans and the Gulf Coast of a slow-moving hurricane, few were prepared for the enormity of the devastation caused by Hurricane Katrina. The physical destruction and economic losses wrought by the storm, which impacted over 90,000 square miles, were immense by any measure. More than 300,000 homes were destroyed or made unlivable and over 150,000 businesses were severely impacted (White House 2006). Entire communities were wiped out by the floodwaters and fierce winds. Estimates suggest that the total damage may exceed US$ 200 billion, making it the costliest disaster in the history of United States (Cutter et al. 2006). Over 1,800 people are known to have lost their lives as a result of the storm, and as in all disasters of this magnitude, the ongoing human suffering has been severe. More than a million people were displaced from their homes and communities, and hundreds of thousands will likely never return. Lives and relationships were disrupted, family members were separated from one another, and a significant number of Katrina survivors have reported a decline in their physical health or deterioration in their mental health since the storm (Kaiser Family Foundation 2007).

After Hurricane Katrina made landfall, the media began to broadcast heart-wrenching images of young children crying in their mothers' arms, photos of babies in squalid conditions in the Superdome and dramatic footage of children and youth being rescued from rooftops by helicopters and from the floodwaters in boats. Mental health experts, in particular, expressed concern regarding how 'Katrina's Kids' would be affected in both the short and the long term. Soon after the storm, as with other large-scale disasters, pamphlets, websites and scholarly reports were circulated that offered suggestions for how parents could help children cope with the catastrophe.

It is obvious that parents are essential in caring for children in emergency situations and in the aftermath of disaster. Infants and very young children are totally reliant on adults for support and protection. Older children and adolescents depend, to varying degrees, on their parents and other caregivers for material and emotional support during and following a disaster. Parents face enormous challenges as they care for their children in a disaster, and mothers and fathers in less developed, or emerging, societies may face even greater obstacles in keeping their children safe in a disaster aftermath. Yet very little has been written explicitly about the experiences of mothers and fathers—either as individuals or as partners—in post-disaster contexts.

With the understanding that parenting is a gendered endeavour, this chapter focuses on the responses of mothers and fathers to Hurricane Katrina. We begin by reviewing the literature available on parenting in disasters. Then we briefly discuss the approach and methods that were used for this research. Next, we explore the various responsibilities that mothers and fathers assumed and examine some of the challenges and stresses created within families by this crisis experience. The chapter concludes with a set of policy recommendations.

Parenting in Disasters

Most of our knowledge of the roles and responsibilities of parents in emergency contexts has emerged from research conducted on women's experiences in the aftermath of disasters. Much of this work explores how the division of labour at home, particularly regarding caregiving roles and responsibilities, may increase women's pre-disaster vulnerability and place additional burdens on women during recovery (Enarson et al. 2006). In the United States and in most other societies around the world, the everyday and immediate responsibilities of parenting and caring for dependents are assigned to women. Thus, it is not surprising that during times of disaster, much of the responsibility for preparedness actions, evacuation decisions and sheltering fall on mothers (Enarson and Scanlon 1999).

Although their focus was not exclusively on parents, the analysis conducted by Alway et al. (1998) sheds light on different, but vital, roles that both mothers and fathers played in Hurricane Andrew. Moreover, their research shows that gendered roles and identities that women and men asserted before and after the disaster were shaped not only by personal interactions but also by institutional arrangements. Specifically, the pressures and expectations of paid employment often pushed fathers in the direction of the provider role (which subsequently meant that, generally speaking, men were not involved in hurricane preparations because they were required to work), while mothers were often pulled into the home-maker role because of the lack of reliable childcare and the fact that their schedules were typically more flexible or their incomes more expendable.

In his work on the Buffalo Creek Disaster, Erikson (1976) offers accounts of various things that parents did for their children in the aftermath of the devastating flood. For example, one father had to re-peatedly reassure his young son that the family was not going to drown. A mother talked of how she would hold her son and daughter in the middle of the night because they would wake up screaming and crying in fear of another storm. Erikson acknowledges that it can be very difficult for parents who are emotionally distraught themselves to fulfil all of their children's needs.

Even less is known about the lived experiences of those heading single-parent families and how they cope during times of extreme crisis. These households are typically headed by women, poorer than other families, among those most affected and often excluded in the recovery and relief process altogether (Morrow and Enarson 1996; Moser with Antezana 2001; Scanlon 1998). Moreover, women of colour who head so many of these families at risk are especially vulnerable to poverty and the deleterious impacts of disaster (Enarson and Fordham 2004; Jones-DeWeever and Hartmann 2006).

There is still much to be learned about those who care for children during times of disaster and the ways in which being mothers and fathers is central to their disaster experience. In this chapter, we explore the following questions: *(a)* Who took care of children in the aftermath of Katrina? *(b)* How did personal and social factors influence the caretaking responsibilities of mothers and fathers as caregivers? and *(c)* What challenges did mothers and fathers face during and following the storm?

Research Methods and Participants

We travelled to Louisiana in October 2005 and gathered interview and observational data on children's experiences in the storm, what adults were doing to lessen children's vulnerability and what children were doing for themselves and others to reduce the disaster impacts (see Fothergill and Peek 2006; Peek and Fothergill 2006). In May 2007, February 2008 and April 2008, we returned to Louisiana to follow-up on our initial research findings regarding children's experiences.

Data were collected using a combination of qualitative methods, including informal interviews, formal semi-structured interviews, focus groups and participant observation. We interviewed mothers and fathers from single-parent and two-parent families, grandparents and other extended family members, volunteer and professional childcare providers, school administrators, teachers, mental health service providers, social workers, disaster case managers, religious leaders and evacuee shelter coordinators. While we also interviewed children and youth in their classrooms and homes, in this chapter we draw on the data gathered from adults.

Over the two-and-a-half-year period of this research, we interviewed 51 women and 13 men. More women than men were interviewed because they are the majority of those who work in a professional capacity with children on a daily basis (for example, elementary school teachers, day-care providers, social workers); they also dominated among families headed by a single parent (just one family in our sample was headed by a father), and women more often agreed to speak with us. The adult sample included 26 African–American respondents, 34 Whites, two South Asian–Americans and two Lebanese–Americans. We visited schools, day-care centres and communities that were low income, working-class, middle-class and upper middle-class.

The average formal, tape-recorded interview lasted approximately an hour. We also spent many hours speaking informally with adults and children, running errands and sharing lunches and dinners. In the months between our field work visits to Louisiana, we communicated with research participants through telephone calls, email messages and cards and letters.

We gathered observational data at various locations and events in Baton Rouge, Lafayette, Metairie, New Iberia, New Orleans and Scott, Louisiana. In the aftermath of the storm, we observed shelter operations at a large mass shelter in Lafayette and at a much smaller shelter in a Baptist Church in Baton Rouge. We visited a food and clothing distribution centre for hurricane evacuees in Lafayette and the Welcome Home Center in New Orleans. We conducted interviews and observations at a private day-care centre and two childcare centres located in shelters. We met with students and teachers at six schools (including a temporary school established for Katrina evacuees in New Iberia, a public elementary school in Baton Rouge, a private Catholic school in Metairie, a charter school in New Orleans and two public schools that reopened in 2005 and 2006 in New Orleans). We also spent afternoons and evenings with families in Federal Emergency Management Agency (FEMA) trailer sites in Baton Rouge and Scott and in flood-damaged homes in New Orleans.

Mothers and Fathers in the Initial Crisis

The data included in this chapter represent a range of experiences that shed light on the complex and varied roles that mothers and fathers of different backgrounds play during times of disaster.

Evacuation

All the mothers and fathers in our study who were able to leave before Katrina struck said that they evacuated because they had children, which confirms earlier studies that have shown that adults with children are more likely to respond to disaster warning and evacuation messages than people without children (see Dash and Gladwin 2007). For some parents, these decisions were made together but, for many of the families in our study, mothers had to make decisions about their evacuation with little or no input from the children's fathers. This was true both for mothers who were married as well as those who headed up single-parent households. Prior research on hurricane evacuation has also shown that women are more likely to plan actively for evacuation and to make the final evacuation decision for their household (Bateman and Edwards 2002; Enarson and Morrow 1997; Gladwin and Peacock 1997).

In addition to deciding to evacuate, parents had to make plans of where to go, determine what to take with them and explain the situation to children. All parents spoke of how they had to assess quickly how bad the storm would be in order to decide what to bring and what to move to safer areas, so there was a range of responses depending on their views of the storm. Many of the mothers evacuated with their children while the children's fathers stayed behind, often because of work responsibilities or because the fathers wanted to stay longer at their homes. Other mothers evacuated without any coordination with the children's fathers, some of whom had been out of their children's lives for some time. For example, Debra, an African–American single mother, evacuated with her 11 year-old daughter to a hospital where she worked because she had no other options. She and her daughter, Cierra, eventually had to be rescued by a helicopter as the floodwaters began to rise in New Orleans. Deidre, an African–American single mother who was unemployed and homeless prior to the storm, had a dangerous, nerve-shattering evacuation with her 11-year-old son and infant baby girl in the middle of the storm.

Other women were responsible for both their children and their elderly parents, placing an even larger burden on them. For example, Sharlene, a White, middle-class woman, was responsible for four generations: she had to coordinate the evacuation of her elderly parents, her husband, her children and one young grandchild. They evacuated 2 days before the storm and stayed in the home of another family member.

Relocation

Soon after Katrina made landfall, families realised that what they believed would be a temporary evacuation would likely become a longer term or permanent relocation. As with the evacuation, many of the mothers were responsible for their children during the relocation. We found women were primarily responsible for the well-being of children in shelters or in host homes with extended family or friends.

For the mothers who were responsible for multiple generations during the relocation period, caring for older parents and children often became stressful and overwhelming. Sharlene, who evacuated with four generations, struggled to find chemotherapy treatments for her sick mother and heart medication for her father during the initial stages of relocation. Because of the stress caused by the evacuation and relocation, Beth, a White woman, had to ask her brother to care for their elderly mother who was very sick with emphysema and passed away less than a month after the hurricane. Beth told us:

> She was bouncing in and out of the hospital a lot. It was pretty stressful at home with that going on. So I thought, 'I cannot handle having Mom here as well, having all these kids and the dogs and just the whole evacuation stress.' And worrying that Mom was gonna crash at any moment. So I called my brother and said, 'It's your turn.'

Many mothers discussed the importance of enrolling their child in a good school and having them settled. Frank, a school social worker, told us that parents often had trouble with their children adjusting to new schools, especially children with behavioural problems or learning disabilities. He stated that parents typically did not have their child's Individualised Educational Plan (IEP) paperwork, and other parents with children with various behaviour and emotional disorders did not have their child's medication, all of which made their transition to a new school more difficult. In response to these and other challenges, several mothers who all evacuated to one town worked to put together a small new school for their children (see Fothergill and Peek 2006). Past research has also found that mothers organise around school issues in disaster aftermaths (Enarson 2001).

Care Work

Other case studies of disaster have found a clear division of labour between women and men in terms of care work, with women taking responsibility for re-establishing familial and social life (Enarson 2000, 2001; Fothergill 2004). Similarly, in our research, we found a division of labour between the unpaid care work of mothers and fathers. As with past research, our data show that post-disaster carework was performed primarily by women, including mothers, grandmothers, aunts and older sisters. This was true in both single-parent and two-parent families.

Before the storm, several of the unmarried mothers in our study lived on their own with their children, but maintained contact and relationships with the fathers of their children. Mothering became much more difficult and complicated for these women after Katrina, largely due to the separation from fathers and extended family networks. While a few of the single mothers spoke of 'absent fathers', most informed us that their children's fathers had played important roles in their children's lives before the disaster. In fact, many of the single mothers reported that even though they did not live together, these fathers still spent time with their children and shared in at least some parental duties. However, during the evacuation, mothers took care of the children and in the aftermath of the storm, the fathers and other extended family members often ended up in different cities or even different states. This left single mothers in a very difficult situation as they attempted to find adequate shelter, work and offer more attention to their children after the crisis.

Some fathers and other men also took care of children and the elderly. For example, Luke, who was no longer in a relationship with his son's mother, made arrangements so that he and his ex-partner would each spend equal amounts of time with their son. This meant that they had to drive between New Orleans and Houston twice a week, but they both were committed to ensuring that their son stayed in a more stable and safe environment. Sometimes, men were doing other work for the family while the women took care of the children. An African–American mother, Christie, for example, went with her husband and two young children to their damaged home in New Orleans immediately after the storm; while her husband started gutting the inside, she took care of the children outside. Other fathers stayed behind for their jobs or to secure the home, while the women relocated with the children. One father, Kanwal, asked his wife, Shashi, to stay in Lafayette with their two children so that they would not have to see their flooded home.

Parenting in the Aftermath of the Storm

Families in the Gulf Coast endured immense and debilitating material and financial loss in Hurricane Katrina. Many also lost long-established networks of neighbours, family and friends. In this section, we examine some of the specific challenges that parents faced when Hurricane Katrina struck.

Family Separation

Often, families that had lived near each other for generations were scattered in cities and states across the country. Parents had to soothe young children who desperately wished to see beloved grandparents, cousins or aunts and uncles. Mothers and fathers were often separated in evacuation and relocation, and most often children lived with their mothers. In addition, mothers spoke of how their children were also emotionally and geographically close to their fathers' extended families, and that familial support system too was lost. As noted previously, a number of fathers did not live with their children before the storm, but they were still very much part of their children's lives. In fact, some fathers saw their children daily despite being estranged from their children's mother and not providing much or any financial support.

The separation of family in evacuation and relocation was an emotional loss, but it was also the loss of a larger support system. These families had many needs as evacuees that could no longer be met by family. Various individuals and agencies assisted and worked as advocates for families that needed community assistance. Again, we found that women were primarily responsible for finding programmes, agencies, services, schools and childcare for their families, and that they were appreciative of any assistance. Some individual women made an enormous difference in the lives of women and children in the disaster aftermath. For example, at a Baptist Church shelter in Baton Rouge, the pastor's wife was the director of the shelter and a fierce and protective advocate for every person in her shelter. With the resources of her church and its congregation, her networks in the community and her hard work and determination, she was able to provide every adult with a job in the church, every child with free childcare in the church day-care centre and every individual or family with housing in a FEMA mobile home when the shelter closed.

Lack of Childcare

With the separation of these close networks, post-storm childcare became a significant challenge. In addition, day-care centres were destroyed in New Orleans and centres in evacuation towns were full. For families in shelters, childcare programmes with volunteer caregivers offered free childcare during certain hours of the day. This was a tremendous help to parents, as it gave them a much needed break to meet with disaster recovery officials, shower or take a quick rest. However, childcare centres in the shelters often only took young children between certain ages, such as 2 to 8-year-olds, and thus those with infants or older children often had fewer options for help with their children.

During non-disaster times, most private day care is unaffordable and often has long waiting lists, and this problem was exacerbated in Louisiana in the aftermath of Katrina (Reckdahl 2007). Even parents with more financial resources lamented the lack of high quality, available childcare in their new communities and some received spots in day-care centres or nursery schools only because of the influence of a relative whose child was already in care there. The director of a day-care centre in Lafayette explained to us that the state of Louisiana would not allow them to give childcare assistance funds to displaced families that did not have employment in the city of Lafayette. This rule prohibited many low-income families who were out of work after Katrina from enrolling and only further exacerbated the many financial struggles of evacuees.

Issues with Shelters and Host Homes

In the large mass shelters, mothers struggled to find quiet places to nurse or put young children down for naps, worried about safety when their children went to the restrooms and were frustrated by rigid rules imposed by shelter managers. We were told, for example, that they could not have baby-food jars because rumours about crime made the volunteers fear that the glass jars would be used as weapons. Parents of children with special needs often faced the greatest challenges, as described here by a day-care director who worked as a volunteer in the Cajundome shelter in Lafayette:

> This one woman had been in the Superdome with her autistic son, who was 18…. She said she had to change his diaper, and the women wouldn't let her in the women's room, 'cause he was older, and she couldn't go in the men's room. And to get a plate of food, you had to stay in line. And you couldn't get two plates. But she couldn't [get him to stay in line]. By this time she was just about crazy. They had put her out of the special needs unit at one place. Then they put 'em in a hospital. Then they sent them to this special needs

unit. Then they pulled them again. I don't know where they went. I lost track of them. It was the most horrible thing. I thought she was gonna crack up, I really did. But nobody was helping her.

Some shelters were able to offer much-needed services such as on-site nurses for middle-of-the-night emergencies, childcare services, and private spaces such as unused offices for mothers who had recently given birth and for adults with disabled children or ageing parents.

Parents staying with host families faced other difficulties. Parenting in a house with multiple families, all ages and little space and privacy, was challenging and evacuee parents often worried that they had overstayed their welcome. Shashi, Kanwal and their two children stayed for over 4 weeks with Kanwal's parents and other extended family members. Shashi was deeply grateful for the care and help that her in-laws offered, but she also commented on the difficulties associated with living in someone else's home for a long period of time:

> I think the hard part was the conflict of parenting styles, just like anybody who goes and lives with their in-laws, whether it's my parents or his parents.... So my husband would tell them, 'No, I think we really want it this way and we really need to talk about it.' One day we all said, 'This is the way it's gonna be.' And then everybody kind of redefined their roles and started kind of letting us do the parenting part.

Another childcare issue concerns non-evacuee parents in locations with large evacuee populations, many of whom had work responsibilities that forced them to be absent a great deal. For example, mothers in Lafayette—not evacuees—who were nurses, disaster crisis workers or probation and parole officers, had added responsibilities and were gone for long periods from their children during the evacuation period. Day-care workers explained that they could tell this was difficult for their children.

Family Uncertainties

Parenting in 'normal' times is challenging, while parenting during and after a catastrophic event can be emotionally and financially over-whelming. Sometimes parents did not have the coping skills or energy in such a draining and exhausting crisis to deal effectively with children. Parents who returned to New Orleans soon after the storm had to prepare their children for a very different and uncertain life. Christie, an African–American married mother of two young children, described her anxiety upon returning to her home:

> But even though I have a home to go back to, things are not the same. Because now, all my family members are spreaded out. So in a sense, I'm fighting with, 'I don't want to go home. It's not home no more.' You're talking about my mama, who lived there sixty years, my aunt, who lived there seventy-something, it's like not home any more. So I'm really uncomfortable with going to that house. It's like, everything is so different. So even when they get back, I have to deal with that. Things are different now. You know, we don't have the family, we don't have the same neighbors.... It's almost easier to be here than to actually go back.

Mothers, in particular, expressed concerns related to health issues, contaminated and toxic environments, safe and adequate schools, job prospects and the work opportunities for their partners or ex-partners. Shashi worried about what New Orleans would be like for her children:

> But is our little park going to survive? The park is a disaster. City Park is gone. The carousel is a disaster. Everything's a disaster over there. How is that going to survive? Is the aquarium going to survive? Is the children's museum going to be there? And all those places may physically be there, but is the funding for those places gonna be there? Because if all this population is gone, how are they gonna keep up? ... And then in our own house, I'm so afraid to even touch the soil. I don't know what's been seeping into it.

Conflicts between mothers and fathers also became more common and more pronounced, which has been found in other disasters (Erikson 1976; Fothergill 2004), often due to the strain of making decisions daily about their futures and their children's well-being. Child custody was an additional source of conflict when one parent but not the other returned to the Gulf Coast. Parents with stable, mutually acceptable custody arrangements before the storm found themselves having to renegotiate arrangements, often with conflict and painful outcomes, and courts seemed at a loss about how to settle custody conflicts (Clementson 2006).

Recommendations for Supporting Mothers and Fathers Following Disasters

As these families attempt to put their lives back together, it is imperative that we learn from their experiences, so that the needs of parents are adequately addressed during the rebuilding process and in future disasters. Based on our research, we offer the following recommendations for supporting mothers and fathers following disasters.

Respect and Utilise Mothers' Roles as Decision Makers

Our research demonstrates that mothers, regardless of their race, class or marital status, are often the sole decision makers when it comes to deciding if and when to evacuate, where to go and how long to stay. Mothers take these decisions very seriously, and often seek out information from the media, the internet, family and friends and many other sources. As emergency managers and risk communication experts continue to grapple with the question of how to get individuals and households to prepare for disaster and to heed evacuation warnings, we recommend that they work to ensure that messages reach mothers of all backgrounds. Indeed, gender and disaster scholars have long recognised the central role that women play in disaster preparedness and response efforts (Enarson and Morrow 1997; Enarson et al. 2006; Fothergill 1996), and our work further supports this.

Encourage the Involvement of Fathers in Disaster Planning and Response Activities

Gendered analyses of men's experiences and roles in disasters are lacking (Enarson et al. 2006). Some earlier research focused on their roles in disaster response organisations and other public sphere activities, but not within the family context. While fathers spend more time with their children now than 30 years ago, there has been no meaningful cultural shift, due in part to workplace policies, the gender gap in earnings and traditional views of masculinity (Wall and Arnold 2007). Our study shows men were not simply 'absent' and some even took on important parenting responsibilities, but women remained the primary caregivers. In disaster settings, we believe there are many benefits for fathers' parenting role to be acknowledged, encouraged, normalised and supported. Indeed, taking care of children in disasters should be 'shared work among social equals', which implies changes of ideology, policy and parental behaviour (Hays 1996: 176–77). We recommend that both researchers and policy makers explore the roles of fathers in disasters in order to understand how to more genuinely involve fathers in disaster planning and response activities.

Acknowledge Familial Conflict and Provide Support for Stressed Parents

Mothers and fathers have struggled to cope with the loss of home and material possessions, financial hardships, the separation of family members, increased childcare demands and decreased levels of social and familial support during an incredibly difficult time. Higher levels of stress and more frequent conflicts between mothers and fathers are one result. Previous post-disaster research has demonstrated that these conflicts may escalate and ultimately lead to increased rates of domestic violence (Enarson 1999; Fothergill 1999; Morrow 1997). Although none of our interviewees reported that they or their children had become the victims of family violence following Katrina, many spoke of intensely stressful situations, which is cause for concern. Thus, we recommend that communities and organisations plan in advance to make sure domestic violence services such as hotlines and safe sheltering options are readily available in a disaster aftermath.

Recognise the Contributions of Advocates for Evacuees and their Children

Cancian et al. (2002) argue that it is a myth that taking care of children can and should be done solely by families, especially mothers. They posit that there are a broad range of people and institutions that can, should and contribute to providing care for children and youth. They also argue against the myth that all parents have equal access to the re-sources necessary for raising children because, in reality, inequality has profound impacts on children and their caregivers. All this is true, and magnified in intensity, during times of disaster.

Community volunteers, disaster recovery coordinators, religious leaders and other child advocates were crucial in providing care and support for evacuees and their children. This was particularly true in the case of low-income, African–American single mothers who occupied disadvantaged positions in society before the storm and were figuratively and literally 'left behind' in the floodwaters (also see Jones-DeWeever and Hartmann 2006). With the support and encouragement of these advocates, we observed these mothers begin the process of recovery. The involvement of advocates who are willing to listen to and respect evacuees, and who have resources and community connections to assist parents with finding adequate schools for their children, housing and work, can make all the difference as disaster survivors begin to rebuild their lives in new environments.

Provide Quality and Affordable Childcare for Evacuees

Expensive, low-quality or unreliable childcare causes many issues for parents during non-disaster times, and in the post-Katrina environment in Louisiana, lack of childcare had reached a crisis state after the storm (Reckdahl 2007). Parents who do not have access to safe, reliable and affordable childcare are more likely to miss work and may lose their jobs, further exacerbating the loss and financial turmoil caused by disaster. In the past, research on disasters has found that a lack of childcare can hinder both family and community recovery (Enarson 2001; Fothergill 2004).

Access to quality childcare was out of reach for many families in Louisiana prior to the 2005 hurricane season. The problems of inadequate space in childcare centres, the cost of care, the lack of trained childcare providers and transportation challenges were exacerbated by the 2005 hurricane season, when Louisiana lost hundreds of childcare facilities (Agenda for Children 2006). To begin addressing this childcare crisis, the restoration of all forms of childcare, including family day care, must be made a priority in the post-Katrina planning and rebuilding process. Moreover, childcare providers need to be more appropriately and adequately compensated for the essential services that they provide.

According to an Agenda for Children (2006) report, the mean wage for a childcare worker in Louisiana is US$ 6.55 an hour, the lowest in the nation. Until childcare workers are better compensated, childcare centres are made a priority in the reconstruction, and the importance of family day-care is acknowledged, families will not be able to return to the Gulf Coast and make a viable living.

Secure Appropriate Shelter Accommodations for Families with Special Needs

Historically, public shelters have been mostly underused during times of disaster (Fischer 1998). This was not the case in Hurricane Katrina. The unique social impacts caused by the widespread flooding and total evacuation of the city of New Orleans created an unprecedented need for the long-term sheltering of evacuees who were bused or flown to shelters throughout the Gulf Coast and to many other regions across the United States (Nigg et al. 2006). Among the more than 100,000 evacuees who spent time in 'official' shelters (that is, those facilities that were pre-identified and/or run by the American Red Cross) and 'unofficial' shelters (that is, those facilities opened hastily in the aftermath of Katrina, often in churches, schools or community centres), were an untold number of children with special physical and mental health needs (Abramson and Garfield 2006). Life in shelters is especially difficult for families with children or ageing parents with special needs. While the lack of privacy and cramped facilities are always problematic in mass shelters, they can actually further threaten the health and well-being of the most physically and emotionally vulnerable groups. We recommend that representatives for disabled and ageing populations be better integrated into local emergency planning activities, to ensure that special needs populations are adequately served during times of disaster.

Conclusion

In the days and weeks following Hurricane Katrina's landfall, people across the United States and around the world watched in horror at the images of devastation being broadcast from the Gulf Coast.

Although the physical destruction, psychological damage and mass displacement caused by Hurricane Katrina were unprecedented in United State's history, the unfortunate reality is that more large-scale catastrophes will continue to confront this nation and other nations around the world. We hope this examination of the complicated and gendered nature of parenting in the aftermath of disaster contributes to a better understanding of the challenges facing mothers and fathers, and to renewed efforts to reduce vulnerability and promote the recovery of parents and children alike.

Acknowledgements

We are indebted to the people in Louisiana who welcomed us into their lives and generously shared their experiences with us. We would also like to thank Jennifer Tobin-Gurley and Megan Underhill for their assistance with data collection and John Barnshaw for feedback on an earlier draft of this chapter. Elaine Enarson's editorial guidance helped shape the ideas that appear in print here, which is gratefully acknowledged. This work was supported by the Natural Hazards Centre and the National Science Foundation Quick Response Research Program, the University of Vermont College of Arts and Sciences Dean's Fund and the Colorado State University College of Liberal Arts Professional Development Fund. This chapter is a revised and abbreviated version of an article that originally appeared in the *National Women's Studies Association Journal*, 20(3): 69–105. We would like to thank Johns Hopkins University Press for permission to reprint the article.

References

Abramson, D. and R. Garfield. 2006. *On the Edge: Children and Families Displaced by Hurricanes Katrina and Rita Face a Looming Medical and Mental Health Crisis*. A Report of the Louisiana Child and Family Health Study. New York: National Center for Disaster Preparedness and Operation Assist, Columbia University Mailman School of Public Health.

Agenda for Children. 2006. *Louisiana KIDS COUNT*. Special Report on Childcare. New Orleans: Agenda for Children.

Alway, J., L. L. Belgrave and K. J. Smith. 1998. 'Back to Normal: Gender and Disaster', *Symbolic Interaction*, 21(2): 175–95.

Bateman, J. M. and B. Edwards. 2002. 'Gender and Evacuation: A Closer Look at Why Women Are More Likely to Evacuate for Hurricanes', *Natural Hazards Review*, 3(3): 107–17.

Cancian, F. M., D. Kurz, A. S. London, R. Reviere and M. C. Tuominen. 2002. *Childcare and Inequality: Rethinking Carework for Children and Youth*. New York: Routledge.

Clementson, L. 2006. 'Torn by Storm, Families Tangle Anew on Custody', *The New York Times*, 16 April.

Cutter, S. L., C. T. Emrich, J. T. Mitchell, B. J. Boruff, M. Gall, M. C. Schmidtlein, C. G. Burton and G. Melton. 2006. 'The Long Road Home: Race, Class and Recovery from Hurricane Katrina', *Environment*, 48(2): 8–20.

Dash, N. and H. Gladwin. 2007. 'Evacuation Decision Making and Behavioral Responses: Individual and Household', *Natural Hazards Review*, 8(3): 69–77.

Enarson, E. 1999. 'Violence against Women in Disasters: A Study of Domestic Violence Programs in the U.S. and Canada', *Violence against Women*, 5(7): 742–68.

———. 2000. '"We Will Make Meaning Out Of This": Women's Cultural Responses to the Red River Valley Flood', *International Journal of Mass Emergencies and Disasters*, 18(1): 39–62.

———. 2001. 'What Women Do: Gendered Labor in the Red River Valley Flood', *Environmental Hazards*, 3(1): 1–18.

Enarson, E. and M. Fordham. 2004. 'Lines that Divide, Ties that Bind: Race, Class, and Gender in Women's Flood Recovery in the U.S. and U.K.', *Australian Journal of Emergency Management*, 15(4): 43–52.

Enarson, E., A. Fothergill and L. Peek. 2006. 'Gender and Disaster: Foundations and Directions', in H. Rodriguez, E. L. Quarantelli and R. R. Dynes (eds), *Handbook of Disaster Research*, pp. 130–46. New York: Springer.

Enarson, E. and B. Morrow. 1997. 'A Gendered Perspective: The Voices of Women', in W. G. Peacock, B. H. Morrow and H. Gladwin (eds), *Hurricane Andrew: Ethnicity, Gender, and the Sociology of Disasters*, pp. 116–40. New York: Routledge.

Enarson, E. and J. Scanlon. 1999. 'Gender Patterns in Flood Evacuation: A Case Study of Couples in Canada's Red River Valley', *Applied Behavioral Science Review*, 7(2): 103–25.

Erikson, K. T. 1976. *Everything in Its Path: Destruction of Community in the Buffalo Creek Flood*. New York: Simon & Schuster.

Fischer H.W. III. 1998. *Response to Disaster: Fact versus Fiction and its Perpetuation*. Lanham, MA: University Press of America.

Fothergill, A. 1996. 'Gender, Risk and Disaster', *International Journal of Mass Emergencies and Disasters*, 14(1): 33–56.

———. 1999. 'An Exploratory Study of Woman Battering in the Grand Forks Flood Disaster', *International Journal of Mass Emergencies and Disasters*, 17(1): 79–98.

———. 2004. *Heads above Water: Gender, Class, and Family in the Grand Forks Flood*. Albany: State University of New York Press.

Fothergill, A. and L. Peek. 2006. 'Surviving Catastrophe: A Study of Children in Hurricane Katrina', in Natural Hazard Center (ed.), *Learning from Catastrophe: Quick Response Research in the Wake of Hurricane Katrina*, pp. 97–130. Boulder, CO: Institute of Behavioral Science, University of Colorado.

Gladwin, H. and W. G. Peacock. 1997. 'Warning and Evacuation: A Night for Hard Houses', in W. G. Peacock, B. H. Morrow and H. Gladwin (eds), *Hurricane Andrew: Ethnicity, Gender, and the Sociology of Disasters*, pp. 52–74. New York: Routledge.

Hays, S. 1996. *The Cultural Contradictions of Motherhood*. New Haven, CT: Yale University Press.

Jones-DeWeever, A. A. and H. Hartmann. 2006. 'Abandoned before the Storms: The Glaring Disaster of Gender, Race, and Class Disparities in the Gulf', in C. Hartman and G. D. Squires (eds), *There Is no Such Thing as a Natural Disaster: Race, Class, and Hurricane Katrina*, pp. 85–101. New York: Routledge.

Kaiser Family Foundation. 2007. *Giving Voice to the People of New Orleans: The Kaiser Post-Katrina Baseline Survey*. Washington, DC: The Henry J. Kaiser Family Foundation.

Morrow, B. H. 1997. 'Stretching the Bonds: The Families of Andrew', in W. G. Peacock, B. H. Morrow and H. Gladwin (eds), *Hurricane Andrew: Ethnicity, Gender, and the Sociology of Disasters*, pp. 141–70. New York: Routledge.

Morrow, B. H. and E. Enarson. 1996. 'Hurricane Andrew through Women's Eyes: Issues and Recommendations', *International Journal of Mass Emergencies and Disasters*, 14(1): 1–22.

Moser, C. with O. Antezana. 2001. *Social Protection Policy and Practice in Bolivia: Its Implications for Bolivia's Poverty Reduction Strategy Paper (PRSP)*. Working Paper 156. London: Overseas Development Institute.

Nigg, J. M., J. Barnshaw and M. R. Torres. 2006. 'Hurricane Katrina and the Flooding of New Orleans: Emergent Issues in Sheltering and Temporary Housing', *The Annals of the American Academy of Political and Social Science*, 604(1): 113–28.

Peek, L. and A. Fothergill. 2006. *Reconstructing Childhood: An Exploratory Study of Children in Hurricane Katrina*. Quick Response Report 186. Boulder, CO: Natural Hazards Research and Applications Information Center, University of Colorado. Available online at http://www.colorado.edu/hazards/research/qr/qr186/qr186.pdf (Accessed on 24 July 2007).

Reckdahl, K. 2007. 'Crisis in Child Care: The Extreme Shortage Strains Local Families and the Economy', *The Times-Picayune*, 14 May.

Scanlon, J. 1998. 'The Perspective of Gender: A Missing Element in Disaster Response', in E. Enarson and B. H. Morrow (eds), *The Gendered Terrain of Disaster: Through Women's Eyes*, pp. 45–54. Greenwood, CT: Praeger.

Wall, G. and S. Arnold. 2007. 'How Involved Is Involved Fathering? An Exploration of the Contemporary Culture of Fatherhood', *Gender and Society*, 21(4): 508–27.

White House. 2006. *The Federal Response to Hurricane Katrina: Lessons Learned*. Washington, DC: White House. Available online at: http://library.stmarytx.edu/acadlib/edocs/katrinawh.pdf (Accessed on 8 June 2009).

10

Women in the Great Hanshin Earthquake

———•✦•———

Reiko Masai, Lisa Kuzunishi and Tamiyo Kondo

The Great Hanshin-Awaji Earthquake was the largest post-war earthquake, causing severe damage in a densely populated urban area and claiming 6,434 lives and injuring more than 43,000 people (Hyogo Prefecture 2002). One of the main characteristics of the Great Hanshin Earthquake was the major housing damage that led directly to the deaths of many people. More than 110,000 buildings collapsed completely and were burned by fire (Table 10.1). Most of the deaths were caused by the collapse of buildings, especially old wooden houses built according to outdated building standards. The majority of victims were elderly people, most of whom were socially weak. At the time of the quake, 14,951 households within Kobe City limits were dependent on welfare. Of this total, 3,619 (24.2 per cent) suffered either total or partial collapse of their homes. This percentage is more than double the overall number of households (10.7 per cent) in Kobe City that had homes that either totally or partially collapsed (Matsuhara 2000).

At first glance, it appeared as though most people in the Hanshin-Awaji region were equally affected by the devastation of the quake. But gender inequality surfaced in the aftermath of the magnitude 7.2 earthquake,

Table 10.1 Damage from the Great Hanshin Earthquake in Hyogo Prefecture

	Number of dwellings	Number of households
Total	257,127	444,900
Full collapse/burned	116,674	187,040
Partial collapse/burned	140,453	257,860

Source: Hyogo Prefectural Government. 1999. *Damage Caused by the Great Hanshin-Awaji Earthquake and the Current Status of Reconstruction. 1999 Consular Summit* (available in Japanese). Hyogo Prefectural Government.

when women's rights were disrespected and women suffered more severe and lasting consequences. Japan's equal opportunity law was proven ineffective in the face of the disaster. Women faced discrimination in shelters, at home, at workplaces and even in the media in the aftermath of the quake. The death toll reflected that women were still more vulnerable and disadvantaged than men in Japanese society, with 1,000 more female casualties than male.

This discussion of the earthquake from the perspective of women is based on gender analysis of women and their housing in the area, policy analysis and original data gathered through the activities of the Women's Net Kobe in the Great Hanshin Earthquake. We begin with the gender issues raised by women survivors and then move to a close consideration of evacuation, shelter and pre- and post-disaster housing conditions as key factors increasing the vulnerability of women to this event.

Women's Net Kobe Hotline: Listening to Women

Women's Net Kobe is a citizen's organisation established in 1992 to promote equal opportunity and protect women's rights, including the hosting and operation of a telephone hotline for women. In March 1995, the Women's Net Kobe also hosted a gathering for women to share sorrow and anger after experiencing the disaster. For the next 2 years, the network continued hosting seminars to support women and mothers with infants. The following discussion is based on inputs from participating women.

Mass media accounts highlighted the expectation of disciplined victims, reporting how Japanese earthquake victims remained orderly without causing any violence or chaos. But this ignored the issues of which women confided to hotline workers as they shouldered the burden of care after the earthquake. In the following section, we report on these concerns before moving to a case study of housing issues facing single mothers. Women make up more than half of Japan's 17 million part-timers and non-regular workers as of 2007, and the employment rate for women was no better at the time of the earthquake in 1995. Devastated companies first let go of part-time workers and the firms foresaw slowdown in business performances and needed to conduct cost-reduction measures. Mothers with toddlers and young children had no choice but to take a leave from work because day-care centres and kindergartens were suspended. It did not take too long for companies to fire such women. At Japanese workplaces, complete insurance is not always provided unless workers have full-time contract employment. Most women, who are on part-time or non-regular contracts, had insufficient social or employment insurance, even after their dismissals. Some groups, including the government offices, opened up labour consultation services after the quake, and they received more than 1,000 cases of labour-related problems within half a month.

In addition to lack of financial security from their employers, women were disadvantaged due to the difference in pay scale between men and women. This inequality emerged in post-disaster Kobe and further exacerbated the problems faced by women. The average income of single-mother families has been estimated as 30 per cent of the national average, much lower than for single-father families. After the earthquake, the government provided subsidies to help the victims regain economic independence. Only men were eligible for government subsidies because Japan only recognises men as proper heads of households. Women who acted as heads of households were told they were not eligible recipients. Some filed a lawsuit and won.

Health and safety concerns arose immediately. Lack of necessary information and health care contributed to post-quake confusion, especially for pregnant mothers and those with newborn babies. Many women suffered cystitis partly because they refrained from using unsanitary toilets or sharing the same portable toilets with men. Vaginitis was also a health problem commonly seen among women due to lack of sanitary napkin supplies. Women were overburdened. Some husbands abandoned their families to join the reconstruction efforts at their companies, choosing to live in hotel rooms close to their offices to avoid the burden of commuting via disrupted railway services. In the meantime, wives were left at home with limited resources and expected to rebuild their lives alone, in addition to routine household chores and the care of out-of-school children and aged in-laws to take care for.

While more than 300,000 people were displaced in the Hanshin region, women told hotline workers about rape in unsafe post-quake neighbourhoods and violence in their own homes. Broken street lights created dark corners and collapsed buildings prompted crimes. Such an environment resulted in more rapes and other sexual assaults on women. Lawyers and health care providers received emergency calls related to sexual violence, but many others went unreported in part because victims were encouraged to remain silent. Some remained mute because they had no other place to live other than the same shelter. Sixty per cent of the hotline calls concerned spousal abuse.

In such an environment, many women felt fatigued, anxious and stressed, with a sense of loneliness. Forced to bear responsibilities alone while their rights were violated, women felt distressed. Unfortunately, some women took out their stress on their children through abuse.

Case Study of Post-disaster Housing: Single-mother Families

This was the context in which women sought safe housing for themselves and their families. In the following section, we will examine housing displacement and government responses to it, housing conditions for women in ordinary times, especially for single mothers and the impact of governmental housing assistance programmes on single women.

Impacts and Government Responses

People who lost their housing left their homes and evacuated to local public schools and public buildings which were pre-designated as shelters or moved in with relatives or friends. At its peak, a week after earthquake, the number of evacuees in Kobe City was over 310,000 throughout the Hyogo Prefecture, and the number of shelters reached 1,153. School buildings overflowed with people and there was no privacy. The state of evacuation lasted upto 6 months. Citizens tended not to leave their neighbourhoods and evacuation shelters, when compared with other countries, because they feared moving to less secure neighbourhoods and losing access to information regarding public assistance or other pertinent information disseminated by local governments. This caused congestion and deteriorating living environments in evacuation shelters, making it particularly hard for the elderly and women with babies and infants to stay in the shelters.

Six months after the earthquake, some citizens moved into the 48,300 temporary housing units, mainly constructed in suburban areas where retail businesses and public transportation are poor. These areas were chosen because the local government had to secure land to construct public housings in the urban area. This temporary housing arrangement was intended to end by September 1998, however, it continued to 2000.

By January 1999, the Hyogo Prefecture provided 125,000 units of public housing to replace temporary housing. According to Hyogo Prefecture Government Survey (2003), of the tenants who lived in public housing, approximately 50 per cent of residents who entered disaster reconstruction public housing programme lived within 3 km of their former residential areas. The local government came to be regarded highly for providing a large amount of high-quality, low rent housing units for people who lost their housing in the disaster. However, the problems of public housing included a concentration of elderly people, standardised high-rise and high-density housing designs and the disintegration of communities formed in temporary housing (Hinokidani 2005). Also, more than 560 tenants died alone in their public housing units by 2005 (Nigata-Nipo Online), most of them middle-aged men. The local government had to send life-support advisors to public housing to provide information, counselling and support for people.

The main problem of the housing assistance programme was that it was a 'single-track' housing restoration assistance programme: evacuation shelters to temporary housing to public housing. People who were not eligible for this housing assistance programme were left to self-help efforts to reconstruct their housing. As for the housing assistance programme, the local government did provide housing as a physical unit, but victims suffered the loss of what they really wanted—to restore their lives, jobs and housing in their neighbourhoods.

Pre-quake Housing Conditions for Single Mothers

Housing conditions in ordinary times are closely connected to the housing damage suffered in a disaster. For example, many real estate agencies were reluctant to lease decent apartments to families without a responsible male, and due to their financial status women seldom owned houses and could only afford to live in old, wooden-structured houses. These are highly vulnerable to disasters and led directly to a higher death rate among women in the Great Hanshin Earthquake, in which 80 per cent of deaths were caused by the housing damage. According to the fire department report, 1,000 more women died than men (Hyogo Prefectural Police Department 1996). The details of these statistics have not been examined; however, the media and activists have insisted that the low economic status of women relegated them to lower quality housing and many women's houses were damaged by the earthquake.

From 1967 to 2003, the number of single-mother households has more than doubled, reaching 1,225,400 in 2003. Single-mother households, in particular, belong to the poorest group of all households. Their income is one-third of average households and over 50 per cent of them live below the poverty line. Under the profit-oriented housing provision, it is hard for low-income people to secure affordable housing. The owner occupation rate of single mothers (20.6 per cent) is about one-third of the average rate (Ministry of Health, Labor and Welfare 2003). Compared with average households, the rate of single-mother households living above the minimum housing standard is lower, and their housing expenses are much higher. This group lives in the lowest quality of private rental housing (Kuzunishi 2005b).

Few single-mother households receive welfare, which contributes to their quality of housing. The rental assistance limit for welfare recipients is US$ 500 per month, which would probably allow for housing of lower quality. In general, there is a high rate of welfare recipients living in public housing (Matsubara 1996). Though half of all single-mother households meet the criteria of welfare recipients, only 10 per cent of single-mother households are on welfare because of governmental budget cuts (Ministry of Health, Labor and Welfare 2003). Another reason why single mothers are not recipients of governmental financial assistance is because they want to avoid the stigma of welfare. As a result, some single mothers probably pay equal or less than US$ 500 per month on rent.

There are three kinds of housing assistance for single-mother households in Japan. The first is accommodation intended for emergency, transitional or temporary housing. Most of these accommodations are old and the living space is narrow. Moreover, there is reported discrimination against the residents based on the stigma of single motherhood. The rate of occupation for this accommodation, designed to assist single mothers, was only 1.6 per cent in 2003 (Ministry of Health, Labor and Welfare 2003).

The second kind of housing assistance is in the form of loans. Loans are available for purchasing and renovating housing and to prepare for moving, but it is difficult for single mothers to get these loans because of strict criteria. Moreover, single mothers avoid applying for these loans because they are incapable of repaying them. According to the national single-parent households survey, about 17 per cent of all single-mother households have used this loan system (Ministry of Health, Labor and Welfare 2003). The third form is public housing. The need for public housing for single mothers is very high; however, this need is unmet due to short supply. More specifically, there are many vacancies in inconvenient locations but few in convenient locations. Single mothers have specific needs that must be met in their neighbourhoods. Although approximately 70 per cent of single-mother households move out of their marital housing after divorce, most of them avoid making their children transfer to another school and wish to remain close to their relatives (Kuzunishi 2006). The need to remain in the same neighbourhood is heightened if children are in preschool, as there is a chronic shortage of these facilities in Japan. Unfortunately, there is little public housing that meets these limited requirements.

In addition, public housing cannot address immediate or sudden housing needs. Most single-mother households need to secure stable housing before or right after divorce (Kuzunishi 2005a); however, public housing requires time between application and entrance. Because of this, single-mother households tend to live in lower quality private rental housing or return to the homes of their relatives if possible.

Post-quake Housing Conditions for Single Mothers

In the Great Hanshin-Awaji Earthquake, 80 per cent of single mothers' houses were damaged. Although these are the only available data on single mothers' housing damage levels for the entire Hyogo Prefecture, there are some statistical data for Takarazuka, a city located within Hyogo Prefecture. The data for Takarazuka show that housing damage levels of single-mother households were higher than those of average households, and compared with welfare recipients, the single mothers' rate of completely damaged housing was lower but the rate of half damaged housing was higher. The higher rates of damage faced by single-mother households can be attributed to the lower cost housing that they occupy (Table 10.2).

Table 10.2   Comparative Housing Damage Levels in Takarazuka City (single-mother household)

	Number of households	Completely damaged	Half damaged
Single-mother households	760	95 (12.5%)	205 (27.0%)
Welfare recipients	440	82 (18.6%)	70 (15.9%)
Average households	73,120	5.920 (8.1%)	14,079 (19.3%)

Source: Adapted from Matsubara, Y. 1996. 'Great Hanshin Earthquake and Single Mother Households in Takarazuka City', *Journal of Hyogo Administrative Policy and Association*, Vol. 1 (available in Japanese).

For single-mother households in poverty, any crisis makes it difficult to reconstruct their lives. From 1985 to 1996, their rate of housing rentals decreased and their rate of living with relatives increased. In Takarazuka, only 40 per cent of single mothers whose houses were completely damaged used the temporary housing. A year after the earthquake, only 1.8 per cent of these women were living in temporary housing (Hyogo Prefecture Welfare Department 1997). It is probable that many single-mother households evacuated to their relatives' house right after the earthquake. Although the government gave single-mother households high priority to enter the temporary housing, why did many single-mother households not enter the temporary housing?

There are two main reasons for why single mothers avoided entering the temporary housing. First, as mentioned earlier, single-mother households have specific needs that made them remain in former neighbourhoods. Temporary housing was generally constructed in inconvenient areas, which prevented them from moving there. Second, the unstable situations after the earthquake made single mothers keep working. After the earthquake, 80 per cent of single-mother households kept working at former work place even though the income was not enough (Hyogo Prefectural

Government 1999). Single-mother households could not leave their children in temporary housing alone while they were at work, and there was shortage of preschools because many of them were damaged. For these reasons, single-mother households were less likely to be in temporary housing.

It was not easy for victims to enter public housing because there was a lot of competition. Although the rate of public housing has increased from 1996 to 2004, the need for disaster reconstruction public housing was high. In addition, it was hard for single-mother households to move from their former neighbourhoods, even though the distances between former residential areas and disaster reconstruction public housing areas were reduced more substantially than for temporary housing, as indicated in the previous chapter. Even though the distance was not as far, it was still hard for single mothers to commute. Single mothers tend to be part-time workers (Hyogo Prefectural Government 1999) and usually they cannot afford the transportation fee, so most of them commute to work by bicycle (Kuzunishi 2005b). Many victims, including single-mother households, who were reluctant to move into public housing could not receive any governmental housing assistance (Table 10.3).

Final Considerations: The Need for Gender Equality in Post-disaster Housing

Twelve years after the Great Hanshin Earthquake, women's needs continued to receive little attention. Then, in the 2007 Nigata-Chuetsu Earthquake, national and local governments for the first time investigated women's shelter and housing needs. This led to new arrangements such as setting aside a tent for women to breastfeed and care for infants. New approaches such as extending government support to privately owned houses during reconstruction are under consideration. Yet the disaster housing assistance programme remains particularly inadequate for the single-mother households. What is needed are programmes that enable and empower women and men equally as they seek to use their capacities and rebuild living, jobs and housing in their prior neighbourhoods. Listening to the gender issues confided by women to Women's Net Kobe is essential. We must learn from single mothers how to shape more equitable government housing recovery programmes in disasters.

Table 10.3 Post-earthquake Housing for Single-mother Households

	Temporary housing	Moved (same city)	Moved out of city	Moved out of prefecture	Did not move	Total
Completely damaged	15 (39.5%)	15 (39.5%)	1 (2.6%)	1 (2.6%)	6 (15.8%)	38 (100%)
Half damaged	17 (19.5%)	5 (5.7%)	3 (3.4%)	1 (1.1%)	61 (70.1%)	87 (100%)
Partly damaged	0 (0%)	3 (1%)	1 (0%)	2 (1.0%)	196 (97.0%)	56 (100%)
No damage	0 (0%)	0 (0%)	0 (0%)	60 (15.7%)	263 (68.7%)	383 (100%)
Total	32 (8.4%)	23 (6.0%)	5 (1.3%)	60 (15.7%)	263 (68.7%)	383 (100%)

Source: Adapted from Matsubara, Y. 1995. 'Great Hanshin Earthquake and Single Mother Households in Takarazuka City', *Journal of Hyogo Administrative Policy and Association*, Vol. 1 (available in Japanese).

References

Hinokidani, E. 2005. *An Evaluation Report on Disaster Reconstruction Public Housing in Great Hanshin Earthquake: 10 Years Evaluation Report of Hyogo Prefecture Government*, pp. 376–415 (available in Japanese). Hyogo Prefectural Government.

Hyogo Prefecture. 2002. *Casualty and Injured Person in Hanshin-Awaji Earthquake* (available in Japanese). Hyogo Prefectural Government.

Hyogo Prefecture Government. 1999. *Damage Caused by the Great Hanshin-Awaji Earthquake and the Current Status of Reconstruction. 1999 Consular Summit* (available in Japanese). Hyogo Prefectural Government.

Hyogo Prefecture Government. 2003. *A Survey of Disaster Reconstruction Public Housing Project* (available in Japanese). Hyogo Prefectural Government.

Hyogo Prefecture Police Department. 1996. *The Report of Police Operation—Struggle with an Earthquake Directly above its Epicenter*, p. 110 (available in Japanese). Hyogo Prefectural Government.

Hyogo Prefecture Welfare Department. 1997. *Single Mother Survey 1996*. Hyogo Prefectural Government.

Kuzunishi, L. 2005a. 'A Study on Insecure Habitation of Single Mother Households', *Journal of Architecture and Planning*, 588: 147–52 (available in Japanese).

———. 2005b. 'Quality Level of Housing and Housing Expense of Single Mother Households: An Investigation of Case in Osaka Prefecture and Osaka City', *Journal of Housing Research Foundation*, 32: 261–70 (available in Japanese).

———. 2006. 'Fundamental Study of Housing Situation of Single Mother Households: Periodical Change of Housing Tenure and Factor', *Journal of Architecture and Planning*, 599: 127–34 (available in Japanese).

Matsuhara, I. 2000. *Care for Most Vulnerable to Disaster*. Assessment Reports of the Global Assessment of Earthquake Countermeasures, Hyogo Prefecture Government Committee for Global Assessment of Earthquake Countermeasures (available in Japanese).

Matsubara, Y. 1996. 'Great Hanshin Earthquake and Single Mother Households in Takarazuka City', *Journal of Hyogo Administrative Policy and Association*, Vol. 1 (available in Japanese).

Ministry of Health, Labor and Welfare. 2003. *Survey of Single Mother Households and Other Households*. Tokyo: Ministry of Health, Labor and Welfare (available in Japanese).

———. 2005. *Data on Causality and Injured Person in Hyogo-Nanbu Jishin*. Tokyo: Ministry of Health, Labor and Welfare (available in Japanese).

Nigata-Nipo Online. 'Public Housing After Disaster.' Available online at http://www.niigata-nippo.co.jp/rensai/n51/n51h8k2m1.html (Accessed on 5 June 2005).

Women's Net Kobe. 2005. *Saigai to Josei (Disasters and Women)* (available in Japanese).

———. 2007. *Women Talk about the Great Hanshin Earthquake* (available in Japanese). Available online at: http://homepage2.nifty.com/bousai/eng/index.html (Accessed on 24 June 2009).

11

Victims of Earthquake and Patriarchy: The 2005 Pakistan Earthquake

———•✦•———

Azra Talat Sayeed

The 8 October 2005 earthquake which hit various areas of the North Western Frontier Province (NWFP) of Pakistan and a vast area in Azad Jammu and Kashmir (AJK) will remain in the memories of the people of Pakistan and AJK for life. The earthquake measured 7.6 on the Richter scale and took thousands of lives instantaneously. Officially, 86,000 people died from the earthquake, but the figure is considered to be low. At the peak of the relief efforts, some 350,000 people were rendered homeless. Thousands of children have been orphaned.

This chapter develops a critique of the relief and rehabilitation services which were offered by the Pakistani state in the aftermath of the Pakistan Earthquake 2005 using a social justice and feminist framework. I base my observations on the relief and rehabilitation services offered by the organisation for which I work, Roots for Equity, as well as a study conducted by Roots in collaboration with Asia Pacific Forum on Women, Law and Development (APWLD 2005). The discussion is presented in a highly personalised tone to counteract the invisibility of women's experience and give weight and texture to general issues. There is merit in moving from the abstract to the concrete as I strive to do later in recounting and analysing women's experiences.

The relief efforts offered in Pakistan can only be understood in the context of the Pakistani state. I argue later that the abuses which women faced at the hands of the state and society as a result of the earthquake cannot be seen as aberrations but must be linked to those they face on a daily basis: they are one in the same. Human rights violations, especially of women's rights, were simply accentuated because of the sudden and acute nature of the disaster that struck with such force.

Pakistan, The Elite State

Pakistan is a semi-feudal state with a strong military presence that has ruled the country for more than half of its 60 years. These two characteristics of the state provide ample grounds for the human rights violations in Pakistan, which are indeed many. There is a sharp class divide with a feudal elite owning vast agricultural lands and other productive resources. Although no reliable statistics are available, it is considered that 90 per cent of farmers in the country are small or landless. A study in the 1970s (White 1974) reported the concentration of wealth in the hands of just 22 families which has resulted in the misuse and abuse of power.

Certainly, the patriarchal norms and practices of the country have tenacious historical roots. Many of the nation's most extreme religious practices are the legacy of General Zia who fostered the Afghan Mujahideen with support from the United States in order to defeat Soviet forces in Afghanistan. Along with the Mujahideen, many *madrassas* were allowed to flourish which created a culture in which women were shrouded in *chaddars* and veils. Previously, shrouded girls and women were an oddity, especially in the urban areas of the country. Even during the Presidency of General Musharraf's so called 'moderate enlightenment era', women who chose not to wear the veil were still careful to adhere to a more conservative style of dress in public spaces.

Women's Everyday Lives and Human Rights in Pakistan

Pakistan ranks near the bottom (100 out of 102 countries) on the Gender Development Index (GDI). In Pakistan, women comprise only 48 per cent of the population. This statistic immediately portrays the situation as around the world, with few exceptions, there are more women than men. Male preference in this highly patriarchal society is considered the cause. Many baby girls do not survive their first few years of life due to neglect by parents who fail to provide them with adequate nutrition and medical care. Cultural norms dictate that women belong inside the house and their public appearance is viewed with disfavour. Women who are employed in paid work are accorded lower social status than other women who appear to respect the patriarchal norm of preserving the 'sanctity of homes' in their roles as housewives.

The right to choose a husband is almost non-existent, with girls brought up to be submissive to their parent's wishes in choosing a life partner for them. According to a country briefing paper by the Asian Development Bank, 'About 23 per cent of females between the age of 15 and 19 are married, compared with 5 per cent of the male population in the same age group' (Asian Development Bank 2000). Divorce rates remain very low giving further testimony to the fact that this highly patriarchal society provides little space to a woman to seek life outside the 'protection' of her husband.

The Pakistani state has never spent more than 5 per cent of its GDP on health and education together. The lack of spending on health by the state has horrendous implications for women. It was reported that 30,000 women die during delivery each year. According to the 1998 census, only 32.5 per cent of females were literate as compared to 56.5 per cent of males. The situation is starkly worse for women in rural areas. As reported by the Asian Development Bank (2000):

> Gender disparities in educational attainment are even greater in the rural areas. Only 3 per cent of rural 12-year-old girls continued in school, compared with 18 per cent of boys. Fewer than 1 per cent of girls remained in school in the 14-year-old age group compared with 7 per cent of boys.... Out of the 172 professional colleges in 1996–97, only 10 exist exclusively for women.

Although by Constitution as well as by the Islamic Shariah, women have rights of inheritance, social norms in clear violation of this right deny girls, especially in rural Pakistan, land entitlement deeds. When women do have property entitlements, it is widely known that this is generally controlled by their spouses. Nonetheless, peasant women play a major role in all forms of agricultural production. Women peasants are responsible for taking care of livestock, and for harvesting food and cash crops such as wheat, rice and cotton. But this vast female agricultural labour force rarely has control over their own earnings. The urban population of women is also economically active (for example, Ferdoos unpublished; Kazi and Raza 1991).

Violations against Women's Rights in the Aftermath

In this backdrop, the practices adopted by the state and other agencies providing relief brought to light both old and new human rights violations against women. In the following section, I shall consider how poorly the lives of girls and women were protected or valued in different sectors and stages of response and reconstruction.

Women Blaming

Listening to women recount their experiences, one has to say that perhaps the most hurtful violation could be the blame attributed to women. It was suggested that the earthquake itself was not a natural calamity but brought on by the 'sins of women'. The earthquake-affected areas were rife with the stories of the immoral character of women, as this vignette illustrates. Once, as our group was travelling to a remote community, our driver reported quite casually that the earthquake was the result of women's sins for he had heard that eight naked women had been recovered from a collapsed building in Muzaffarabad. Another group of women in the NWFP reported that 'People blame us for the tragedy. If our moral practices had been better this would not have happened.' According to this group of young women, 'It is terrible enough to have survived the earthquake, to face the huge loss of family and friends, and possessions; on top of that to feel guilty for all that is being said about our "sins" drives us to despair.'

An extreme situation was reported by one woman who on the day of the earthquake had delivered her baby on the way side. The woman now lived alone in a tent with her four children. Her abusive husband had deserted her before the earthquake because his brother had made him believe that she was of immoral character. In actuality, he had been making amoral advances to her. When she had not complied with his demands, he had made allegations against her to her husband. She remarked that 'people are saying that this disaster had occurred because of women's sins including not observing *purdah*' (wearing the veil). 'Has God created us women just to bear these catastrophes?' She was afraid that if people came to know that she did not have a male 'protector' she would be laying herself open to further abuse so at night, before going to bed, she would stitch the tent flap with a needle. She could not really sleep restfully out of fear, a remark heard from scores of women we met and worked with during our relief and rehabilitation efforts.

Tent Village Conditions

Immediately after the earthquake, thousands of tent villages came into being. Those managed by the Pakistani government were classified as 'organised tent villages', whereas those being managed by various non-governmental organisations (NGOs) were termed 'spontaneous'.

The quality of life in the tent villages was poor in reality. Living quarters were cramped, with no privacy available to family units, and especially for women; with people living in close proximity, illness was a constant threat. Women also mentioned the dark stuffy environment of the tents and their feeling of suffocation as they were forced to remain inside for long hours. In one instance, we found that a woman had tied her 4-year-old son to the bed because she did not want him to go out and play in the mud which would require washing and drying clothes in frigid weather. However harsh her measures may seem, she was protecting her child to the best of her ability.

A majority of expectant mothers delivered their babies in the tents. A Cuban doctor running a medical unit in a tent village in NWFP remarked that most of the time pregnant women were brought to her only when their condition had deteriorated and the family had no recourse but to bring the suffering woman to the medical unit. According to her, husbands or other male household members were not allowing women to seek medical aid.

Again it needs to be emphasised that the lack or scarcity of medical care which was provided to women was the norm long before the earthquake. In Pakistan, women rarely deliver babies with medical facilities.

Male attitudes are further supported by the poor quality of public health care service for the poor and lack of a good transport system which would allow easy access to health care facilities.

Women in many tent villages reported the lack of separate bathrooms for men and women. In one case, a woman reported that six families were using one bathroom. That in itself would have been a very difficult experience for a woman during pregnancy and in the postpartum period. One woman, who had five children already and was 8 months pregnant, was suffering from nausea and mentioned that she could not go to the washrooms in the day time due to their filthy condition. She would only go early in the morning close to sunrise when it was the cleanest.

Accessing Relief and Distribution Systems

Patriarchal norms in Pakistani society have shaped a culture in which women are not used to functioning in the public sphere and find it difficult to voice their concerns, problems and preferences publicly. This worked to the detriment of women-friendly relief assistance.

Neighbourhood committees had been created for distribution of aid. However, in none of the areas visited did we find women included as part of these neighbourhood committees. Distribution of aid was not even-handed; class dynamics and connections to the Armed Forces were certainly a major factor in determining the quantity and quality of aid being received. In many devastated areas of NWFP and AJK, aid had been provided through aerial drops. It was difficult for women, especially widows, to access rations distributed through helicopters as they did not have men who could join the fray, fighting for the dry rations being thrown in packets. Other women stated that they were ashamed to stand in a receiving line to access aid or that they had young infants to look after.

Housing Compensation

The government announced compensation policies for various categories of losses. For the loss of a house, a total of Rs 175,000 (approximately US$ 2,900) was to be distributed in three instalments. These compensatory cheques for the loss of a home were being given to only married men or sons.

One response to these policies was a large number of marriages. False documents were made to claim that these marriages had actually taken place before the earthquake in order to access housing compensation. Many young boys were being married hurriedly to older women, and older men to young girls; young girls were also being married off quickly due to security concerns of girls, especially in the tent villages. With polygamy accepted under Islam, young boys would retain the right to marry again, perhaps to more compatible partners, whereas women would be forced to abide with disaster-impelled decisions in which they had been given no choice.

Death Compensation

For the loss of a family member, Rs 100,000 (approximately US$ 1,670) was available, but again patriarchal norms resulted in many unfair practices. For example, in one case, a compensatory cheque for Rs 100,000 for the death of woman was claimed by her son, who was married and had been living apart from his mother for some time; her unmarried daughter in her late teens moved in with her sister after her mother's death in the earthquake. Like other young unmarried women, she had no space legally or culturally to claim her share in the compensation. Further, compensatory cheques were transferred to banks, generally to accounts of male household members; women often did not really know how much money they had received or have their own bank accounts.

In some cases, young widows received compensation and then returned to their parent's home, leaving behind an elderly mother-in-law who may also not have any other means of economic survival. These women were blamed for forsaking their in-laws though they had few alternative sources of support. Young widows who did remain with their in-laws found the men in the family in control of their death compensation cheques.

The future of young widows, many in their 20s with several children, is an issue of great social concern created by the earthquake. In a society which does not readily accept a second marriage for women, especially if she has children from a previous husband, it is unclear how the government is going to help create space for a safe and productive life for these women.

Medical Concerns and Compensation

Many women in the tent villages had lost not only their husbands but also their children and suffered physical injuries along with tremendous loss of livelihood and assets such as their houses, household goods, clothing and livestock. Few communities have experienced and evolved the capacity to cope with suffering of this magnitude, ranging from the physical to the emotional, and all at the same time. The trauma experienced by women in particular cannot readily be understood without sensitivity to gender relations. However, judgemental attitudes, arrogance, inefficiency and the excessive burden of work in a crisis situation were evident in much of the relief work delivered by the government. There was also no doubt that class-based arrogance and brutality were also factors as is usually the case.

Interviews with a number of NGO personnel who had been helping at the various tent villages echoed the accounts we heard of criminal neglect and hard-heartedness. According to an Oxfam employee in NWFP, who had been serving as a medical aid before he joined Oxfam, women were being discharged from hospitals right after the earthquake. These women had been brought to hospitals in the chaos in the aftermath of the devastation; however, once treated they were forced to leave though many had no relatives with them having been evacuated by helicopters. It was not uncommon that neither the women nor the hospital staff could clearly identify home villages or reach family members when telephone numbers were available. Nonetheless, women were asked to leave.

Safety Concerns

There was a general sense of fear about possible abduction of women and children. We heard about an outsider, a woman, who appeared to have come to assist but one day disappeared with the two teenage girls she had taken with her, ostensibly to shop for clothes. There were many rumours about women, and especially young girls, who had disappeared from tents. Some were being blamed directly for 'running away' while others were supposed to have been abducted. We heard from women that in some cases their men folk were unwilling to go to work as they did not feel safe about leaving their wives alone in the tents. Generally, the tent authorities did not verify such information as they of course would be held accountable for lax security. Women constantly voiced concerns about sexual assault. A widely reported case in point was the rape of a young woman, who had been airlifted from the earthquake area to a hospital in another city, by a doctor. The family was not pursuing the case to protect their 'honour' but it was widely known. A group of women we met cited other examples from their own area, where men from areas outside of Kashmir and in some cases outside of Pakistan had come knocking on doors in the daytime, pretending to sell goods. The women feared that these men were instead gauging who was home and their real purpose was to kidnap young girls rather than sell merchandise.

In tent villages, a major critical concern on women's minds was their short and long-term physical safety and security. A huge number of women had no inkling of where they might be living in the future and this weighed heavily on their minds. Many complained about the lack of doors in the tents and worried constantly about being molested. They mentioned their reluctance to use washrooms at night, as this involved walking some distance and they were afraid.

Conclusion

The many individual cases cited here make a larger point which is the gross neglect of the government. It is imperative that equitable policies be clearly formulated for affected people with acute needs, so many of whom are girls and women, and then these 'vulnerable groups' be informed about what this special status signifies. Further, the intended policies must be effectively and fairly implemented.

It is now nearly 4 years since the Pakistan Earthquake of 2005. The immediate disaster conditions have passed and many agencies providing aid have left. The life of the people is taking on a modicum of normality but this thin veneer hides very deep wounds that are far from healed. I would just like to take a few lines at the end of this chapter to remember those mothers who came to tell us of the daughter they lost—how beautiful they were, how loving, how quick. For them the disaster is never going to be over. Nor is it over for women who have lost their husbands and believe that they cannot look after themselves and their children—even as they do.

One hopes that in societies like ours in Pakistan, measures will be taken to ensure that means are created for women to build a life of dignity for themselves in the wake of this event. The essential conclusion is that one can only bring about a society just by demanding and promoting this in 'normal' times and not in response to disasters.

References

Asia Pacific Forum on Women, Law and Development (APWLD). 2005. *Earthquake Aftermath: Violations of Women's Human Rights Pakistan*. Available online at http://www.apwld.org/publication.htm (Accessed on 23 June 2009).

Asian Development Bank. 2000. *Country Briefing Paper—Women in Pakistan. Situational Analysis of Pakistan—An Overview*. Available online at http://www.adb.org/Documents.Books/Country_Briefing_Papers/Women in Pakistan/chap_01 (Accessed on 23 June 2009).

Ferdoos, A. Unpublished. *Social Status of Rural and Urban Working Women in Pakistan: A Comparative Study*. Dissertation submitted to Universität Osnabrück in 2005. Available online at http://deposit.ddb.de/cgibin/dokserv?idn=980210313&dok_var=d1&dok_ext=pdf&filename=980210313.pdf (Accessed on 6 November 2008).

Kazi, S. and B. Raza. 1991. 'Pakistan Female Urban Employment', *Pakistan Development Review*, 30(4): 733–40.

White, L. 1974. *Industrial Concentration and Economic Power in Pakistan*. Princeton, NJ: Princeton University Press.

12

'A Part of Me Had Left': Learning from Women Farmers in Canada about Disaster Stress

————— • ✦ • —————

Simone Reinsch

In May 2003, a 6-year-old cow was diagnosed with bovine spongiform encephalitis (BSE) in the Canadian province of Alberta. BSE is a fatal degenerative disease that affects the central nervous system of cattle, thought to be caused by the recycling of animal protein in ruminant feeds (Labrecque and Charlebois 2005). The linkage between BSE and Cretzfeldt–Jacob disease (the human variant of the illness) led to human food consumption safety concerns. Public outcry ignited an industry-wide crisis whereby Canadian beef and cattle exports abruptly ceased. As a result, the selling price of Canadian beef dwindled (Labrecque and Charlebois 2005).

Three years into the long-term crisis, farm women described BSE as 'hitting' and 'striking', inferring sudden and unexpected onset; this, in turn, led to gendered and other disruptions of everyday life at the individual, family, farm and community level. Women worried and bore the emotional symptoms of the farm family's economic stress, reporting a myriad of emotions such as guilt, anger, worry and hopelessness. As indicated in this chapter, these emotional states worsened as a result of their perceived lack of voice and social power as women in a male-dominated culture and economy.

Farm women from across the world suffer from stress during their everyday life existence (Dreary et al. 1997; Walker and Walker 1987) with higher rates of reported stress symptom levels among Canadian, American and European farm women as compared to male farmers (Dreary et al. 1997; Walker and Walker 1987). The gender dimensions of disaster-related stress have been well documented in post-disaster studies (Ollenburger and Tobin 1998). In the health management literature, American women have been described as the symptom bearer of their family's health (Stein 1982) but this phenomenon has not before been described in the Canadian literature.

This chapter uses a community health perspective to analyse data from an ethnographic study of the BSE crisis in rural Manitoba. The research explored how farm women conceptualised their stress experiences during the rapid onset and long-lasting BSE disaster. This is a disaster triggered not by a biological hazard or epidemic but by the trade barriers imposed and subsequent health, social and economic effects on farming families already coping with the stress of drought and other challenges to the agricultural economy and rural way of life. I begin with a profile of Canadian farm women and discussion of the research design, followed by a description of the disaster event and its impacts. The coping and resiliency building strategies used by BSE-affected women farmers are then explored in some depth. The chapter concludes with some policy considerations.

Canadian Farm Women

The exact number of farm women in Canada cannot readily be determined. Statistics Canada (2005) reports the number of female farm operators, but fails to account for those women who do not label themselves as farm operators and/or farmers but do share these roles on a daily basis. Bearing in mind this limitation, today's Canadian farm women are likely to be between the ages of 35 and 54 (Statistics Canada 2006), married with children, have off-farm employment, have a high level of education in comparison to their spouse and be less likely than in the past to participate in rural women's networking organisations

(Statistics Canada 1999). Canadian rural and farm women define health as an important priority in life and rate their health as very good to excellent (Kubik and Moore 2001; Roberts and Falk 2002) in spite of being more at risk to die from motor vehicle accidents and diseases such as cancer and diabetes (PWHCE 2003). Farm and rural women also experience a higher incidence of isolation, poverty and unemployment as compared to their urban counterparts (PWHCE 2003). In keeping with women's caregiving/nurturing roles, they continue to prioritise the needs of the farm and families, thereby potentially sacrificing their own health (Kubik and Moore 2001). Fewer social supports (resulting from rural depopulation), gender role overload (van de Vorst 2002), heavy workload (Kubik and Moore 2001), farm familial expectations (Gerrard 2000), the hazardous farming environment (Guilfoyle 1992), cyclic economic farming woes (van de Vorst 2002), ineffective government policies (Lind 1995; Meyer and Lobao 2003) and regionalisation of health services may be factors affecting women's resilience to meet the challenges of everyday life on the farm (Kubik and Moore 2001; Roberts and Falk 2002).

Research Design

Socialist feminist theory recognises women as 'expert knowers' of their everyday and dual (oppressed and dominant) cultural realities (Ardovini-Brooker 2002). With this perspective, I designed a qualitative mini-ethnographic design that gave women the opportunity to express how they thought, behaved and believed about their stress experiences within their social, political, economic, ethnic and gender context (Campbell and Wasco 2000). Face-to-face interviews were conducted with a purposive sample of eight farm women identified through snowball sampling. The women who participated in the study all resided on family owned land in south-western Manitoba, were married with children, ranged in age from 39 to 62 years, had varied educational preparation, lived on beef and/or mixed (beef/grain) farms that had been severely affected by the BSE crisis. Six of the eight women had off-farm employment.

Five sources of data collection strategies were utilised to ensure triangulation: interview transcripts, photographs, demographic questionnaire, reflexive field notes and a windshield survey of the geographic region. I particularly rely in this chapter on data gleaned through the photovoice method, which is a participatory research strategy that used visual imagery (photographs) as a means of depicting the insider viewpoint at a specific moment in time, and can potentially help convey meaning to experiences that are often difficult to express with language (Wang and Burris 1997). I employed this strategy at two points: as part of the initial interview, I provided disposable cameras to my respondents with the request that they document stress factors in their lives; later, the women led our discussion of stress based on the photographs they had taken. During the interviews women cried, punched the table, used sarcasm and screamed. Participating in the research interviews, it was often said, provided them their only opportunity to speak openly without fear, recrimination and judgement.

Insights into Farm Women's Disaster Stress

Quantitative measurement of farm stress in previous studies may neither capture the culturally defined essence of farm women's everyday experiences nor capture their emotional responses to agricultural disasters such as BSE. The interviews conducted revealed how gender power, family roles and the gendered economics of Canadian farms contributed to the BSE-related stress of women farmers.

Patriarchy and Farm Women's Disaster Stress

Fordham (1998) suggests that women in patriarchal societies tend to be at a greater risk of being socially, economically and politically disadvantaged in disasters. As such, their everyday vulnerability cannot be separated from their disaster vulnerability. The farm women interviewed recognised the traditionally male-dominated value system, the gendered division of labour and the invisible nature of their own work contributions (Gerrard 2000; McGhee 1983). As such, farm women felt that, in order to sustain the farm, they had to relinquish control (decision making and autonomy) to male authority, which was not always easy. This farmer wanted only some understanding: 'If he could even understand a little bit and think that my opinion even mattered out here on the farm.' Instead, men tended to consult women about menial decisions which made women feel belittled. The token consultation was not enough:

When you stand back and look at the big picture there are some decisions that he's made, that I certainly didn't agree with, but I also felt that I didn't have any influence over them. He's always smart enough to come and ask me, but, then, I truly believe that he just makes his own decision.... Why don't you ask me something important?

Ideologically, a 'good farm woman' should 'be extremely supportive of her husband, never say a bad word about him, like, you know he's just a wonderful guy and we're gonna do what he wants to do'. Unbending faith in her husband's ability to act in the family's best interest is expected, but this sample of women farmers tended not to have faith and trust in their spouse and in the farm's capacity to provide for the family. They questioned their mate's attachment to the farm, authority and decision making. Within the context of BSE, farm women also had difficulty with the farm/farmer dominance over individual and familial needs. One woman's life priorities were larger than farm survival: 'It's not whether the farm survives this [BSE], or the rain, it is the worry of looking after my children and still being a good parent and giving [to them].'

The farm home is also the focal point of the farm operation, and while women were counted on to meet the expectations of their gendered roles in the home, they were kept out of the business of farming. BSE created a sense of hopelessness that women's current and future needs would be met and they did not feel they had a voice. As a result, women had the perception of being out of control and vulnerable to the effects of BSE. Folkman (1984) suggests that beliefs of control and commitment are influential in the appraisal of stress and subsequent coping.

Family, Community and Farm Women's Disaster Stress

Canadian farm women's connection to their home during BSE is very similar to the sentiments expressed by Scottish women affected by flooding (Fordham 1998). In both cases, there is a symbolic relationship: in the same way that the farm is the farmer, the home is the farmer's wife. The intrusion of BSE was felt within women's most private domain and many spoke with sadness and hopelessness about their homes in the wake of the BSE disaster.

Many of these farming women had an acute awareness that the farm could not provide the things that they considered important. Some questioned the whole notion of the farming way of live and its future.

Women felt that their current needs were not being met and were doubtful that their future needs would be fulfilled. As a whole, they often felt misunderstood by their spouse, for example, in relation to their housing needs.

Asked to photograph stress factors in their lives, all women took photographs of their homes in various states of disrepair and renovation. The state of disrepair of women's housing was not caused directly by BSE nor did they experience evacuation from their homes during the disaster. However, BSE did cause women to reflect and recognise that there might never be enough money to deal with their housing issues. The home was considered women's domain and as such did not receive priority on the farm:

> We could built a house and pay cash, we would not need a mortgage. I just cannot talk him into it. In fact, I don't even try to talk him into it anymore. For some reason, there has to be so much money in the bank, in case of BSE and a drought comes. It is just really frustrating to me because as a woman's point of view, a house is really important ... people are going to judge us by the outside of the house and that causes me a lot of stress.

Women's parenting, off-farm work and spousal roles were also adversely affected. At the family level, farm women as nurturers and caregivers placed much emphasis on the importance of their family's well-being. During the BSE disaster, women's concern grew for their children's immediate and future emotional, behavioural and physical well-being. They volunteered that they could see 'which farm families are struggling and which ones aren't by the behaviour of the kids in the hallways ... they're acting out in the hallway'. In particular, women were concerned about the impacts of the emotional spillover of economic strains on their spouses. As one woman explained, she worried that 'we are like the slaves working the land, and everyone is suffering', and another that the farm was 'sucking my husband dry'.

Farm women are culturally designated as the mainstay of the family who strives to maintain the farming way of life, rear the next generation of farmers and leave their own farm to their own children. But in light of BSE, when women felt that the family farm could 'not make any money' and was an increasingly stressful way of life, they began to redefine what it meant to be a 'good mother' as they could not encourage their children to stay on the farm. This group of women farmers also felt that they were no longer willing to sacrifice the well-being of the family to ensure the farm's survival. Although deeply rooted in generational expectations, women did not have the same qualms of selling the farm to ensure the family's survival as their husbands did.

Women also readily acknowledged changes at the community-level that increased vulnerability and undermined solidarity. Although rural communities tend to be supportive and neighbourly, during BSE more individualistic values surfaced. Survival (defined as 'not losing the farm') led farm families to isolate themselves from each other: 'Sometimes it is easier not to know what is happening to your neighbor'. Women farmers also felt stress due to lack of understanding in nearby urban areas of the nature of farming and the BSE crisis. The media's inaccurate portrayal and sensational representations of the problems faced by people who farm were also hurtful.

Gendered Farm Economics and Farm Women's Disaster Stress

The farm women interviewed did not view themselves as experts of anything. However, the interviews revealed that as a group they had specific knowledge of the economic, social and political forces that had impacted their lives at an individual, family, farm and community-level during BSE. The potential economic impacts of disaster are often overlooked by the general public, policy makers and subsequently by governments (Tierney et al. 2001). Regarding farm stress, economic, social and political factors identified have been found to be major contributory factors as well as gender roles.

The economics of family farming exacerbated farm women's stress. Prosperity was not their farming goal, but they sought the security to pay their bills like everybody else, as this woman explained:

> In farming, you maybe bought some equipment the year before, relying on the money from your calves to pay your bills. When you get no money for your calves because the border's closed, you can't pay your bills and bill collectors start phoning and they have absolutely no compassion.

Farmers are known to be 'asset wealthy but cash strapped' because the nature of farming requires profit reinvestment into the farm. When BSE struck, income dropped while costs increased as farmers held stock back awaiting a stronger market. There was difficulty in placing food on the table for their families and servicing their debt.

Knowing how severely BSE had compromised the farm's economic feasibility, the women in this study felt powerless to influence the dramatic economic changes brought on by BSE. It is well documented that 'economic forces clearly play a role in determining both disaster losses and what is done to deal with them' (Tierney et al. 2001: 220). They also felt left out of important farm and family decisions, as this woman complains: 'And it used to really frustrate me that I wasn't more part of those conversations because why would you think that I wouldn't understand or if I couldn't understand or why wouldn't you [husband] take the time to explain?'

Situational factors, where a person has no control may be interpreted as a threat or harm (Lazarus and Folkman 1984), are clearly a concern in a declining economy: 'We can't continue the way we are and keep losing forty thousand dollars a year, we just cannot.' Historically, farms, farm women and their families have endured periods of severe economic downturns as part of Canadian farming.

Approximately 3 years after the BSE crisis, the study participants faced and dealt with economic hardships in ways that the literature had suggested they might: they altered their spending habits, worked harder, reduced their leisure time and kept going at all costs. Women's disaster-induced stress experiences were compounded by what they perceived as ineffective and unsupportive agricultural government policies. These Canadian women felt that the government mismanaged border closures, and missed opportunities to become less dependent on the US government policies in light of BSE were particularly distressing for women. Hence, their confidence in the government's effectiveness in dealing with BSE was severely compromised, leading to feelings that their own government was 'asleep at the wheel', 'being pretty wussy' and 'being pushed around by the Americans'. Compounding this was the powerlessness they felt at their inability to influence policy at the micro- and macro-levels: 'They [governments] are turning farmers into welfare people, because they can't make enough money at what they are doing to pay their bills and you know just be like everybody else.'

Although BSE was labelled as a disaster in the Canadian popular press, emergency relief provisions for other kinds of disaster such as floods or severe storms were not in place or were deemed irrelevant, for example, the opportunity to increase farming loan loads. As a result, the people who farm were left with little support, as these women explained:

When [BSE] came we found that we had to go to the bank, a lending institution and take out loans twice through the year. And you know money has to be paid back. There are outstanding payments on the tractors, and all sorts of stuff that need to be paid for and if we could sell some of these blessed animals we could do that.

Farm Women's Coping Strategies and Resilience

While massages were tempting (but we need to deal with the root causes), and some women felt they would 'rather not know', or 'let go of silly dreams' in order to cope during BSE, for the most part the eight women reported more effective coping strategies. This finding was consistent with the work done by Meyer and Lobao (2003) who found that traditional coping methods (denial, support seeking, comparing oneself to others, having a plan and hoping for a miracle) exacerbated stress when dealing with macro-level agricultural changes. While differences existed among the eight with respect to physical and behavioural manifestations of stress, all shared the sense of emotional upheaval and loss: 'The kid part of me, the part of me that enjoyed life has left. A part of me has left and I don't think it is ever coming back.'

In part, the effects of BSE were mitigated by many previous experiences of farming adversity. While lessons were often hard to learn, with each experience women felt more resilient, as indicated by one woman's comment: 'Like I've learned over the years how to cope. So just as time goes on, I just find different ways that worked for me, might not work for everybody else. Coping is just evolving.' Another woman felt that adversity 'made me stronger', while a third explained that setting boundaries for 'what I would do and not do' made her feel in control. Women characterised 'coming together' as a couple helped them cope and described spouses that support them 'in every way he can'. However, this was not the case for six out of the eight women interviewed. One woman described her husband's lack of support this way: 'I guess a part of that has been snubbed out because of lack of his support, and I've lost interest in the things that I love ... because he does not appreciate it, so why bother'.

Women without spousal support have developed their own support system. Informal supports such as women's group where 'a bunch of women gather who live in the community and then of course you talk farming together' may be helpful. Women farmers preferred friends outside the immediate vicinity in order to protect their confidentiality and anonymity or to keep their 'dirty laundry at home'. Some saw community building as the key: 'I would like to see more strength within to bring us together as a common [place] almost like a religion that the community might build itself.'

Women strongly felt that psychosocial services should be delivered by 'women who are involved in it up to their necks because they are the only ones that can understand'. These services should also be provided face to face 'by someone outside the community'. Finding solutions for one woman meant that 'farmers have to start rowing forward in the same direction' to obtain their goals, while another stressed that public education was required 'to get those stressors on the table and make people aware of them'. All felt that help was required for the male farmer searching for 'practical solutions', including those provided by the regional agricultural representatives, and an end to government policies perceived as 'chronic and debilitating'.

Framework for Change

A population health promotion model emphasises that population health may be achieved by applying principles of social justice and equity, and encouraging community and societal participation in caring for all. This is the recommended framework for change strategies mitigating the stress experienced by the farm women interviewed here and others around the nation. Political will is needed to address underlying health determinants (socio-cultural, political and economic) contributing to how disasters are created and defined.

To begin to identify and mitigate the root causes of farm women's stress to creeping disasters such as BSE, empowerment and community development are key. Empowerment in this context means to enhance farm women's position, power and opportunities in farming. Petterson and Solbakken (1998) suggest that improvement of the quality of women farmers' everyday lives can best be achieved through collaboration, part-nerships, mutual respect, trust, equality of worth and a focus on women strengths and capacities. These essential values and assumptions underlie all empowerment strategies. Community development is a strategy to facilitate a community's effort to establish its goals and take steps to achieve positive change (Haugh and Mildon 2004). It is a strategy that 'gives the power of the few to the many' (Gerrard 1998: 208). Lassiter (1992) suggests that community development is essential in dealing with complex rural health issues.

Farm women's testimony illustrates that the lived experiences of BSE disaster-induced stress is a complex health issue that may result in further devastation of the culture of the farming family and rural community. Gerrard (1998) suggests that community development provides a fresh new way of addressing people's needs within their own social context resulting in building resiliency. In turn, resiliency can transform victims into change agents within their families and communities.

Conclusion

This study indicates that BSE-affected farm women feel voiceless, invisible and unable to exercise control over key aspects of their lives in a male-dominated value system. It is essential for women's voices to be heard which, in the context of a pluralistic model of public policy (Skogstad 2005), means women must organise. Participation in rural women's organisations has been found to be especially beneficial for women because they provide informal supports (Bushy 1990; Leipert 1999; PWHCE 2003). Women's groups may have the opportunity to help re-define and re-conceptualise the farm family stress experience, and in doing so help generate new policy options to respond to this and future crises. Farm women's groups must have the knowledge to influence change. As such, women's groups must form strong networks and also connect with male-dominated agricultural organisations to present a united voice. In the long run, better representation of the farm woman's voice at the policy table will help guide a 'bottom-up' approach to policy decisions and disaster definitions.

BSE did not cause women's oppression. BSE provided a climate for women to reflect on their everyday lived experiences to discover the meanings of their lives. Women carried on with the hope that one day life would get better and it can. The farm women of Manitoba are skilled, resourceful and motivated. They can and should be heard: 'I'm a big person, but the harder I work the better I feel.'

Acknowledgements

I would like to acknowledge the eight farm women who shared their stories with me and Dr Elaine Enarson for her editing proficiencies and insights into the world of disaster and gender. A special thanks to Prairie Women's Health Centre of Excellence (PWHCE) and the University of Manitoba, Graduate Faculty for their financial support.

References

Ardovini-Brooker, J. 2002. 'Feminist Epistemology: The Foundation Feminist Research and its Distinction from Traditional Research', *Advancing Women in Leadership*. Available online at http://www.advancingwomen.com/awl/spring2002ARDOV-CG. HTM (Accessed on 3 June 2005).

Bushy, A. 1990. 'Rural U.S. Women Traditions and Transitions Affecting Health Care', *Health Care for Women International*, 11(4): 503–13.

Campbell, R. and S. M. Wasco. 2000. 'Feminist Approaches to Social Sciences: Epistemological and Methodological Tenets', *American Journal of Community Psychology*, 28(6): 773–91.

Dreary, I. J., J. Willock and M. McGregor. 1997. 'Stress in Farming', *Stress Medicine*, 13(2): 131–36.

Fordham, M. H. 1998. 'Making Women Visible in Disasters: Problematising the Private Domain', *Disasters*, 22(2): 126–43.

Folkman, S. 1984. 'Personal Control and Stress and Coping Processes: A Theoretical Analysis', *Journal of Personality and Social Psychology*, 46(4): 839–52.

Gerrard, N. 1998. 'Community Development: A New Model for Dealing with Farm Stress' in *Doing Health Promotion Research: The Science of Action*. Calgary, AB: University of Calgary, Health Promotion Research Group.

———. 2000. *What Doesn't Kill You Makes You Stronger: Determinants of Stress Resiliency in Rural People in Saskatchewan*. Saskatoon Health District.

Guilfoyle, J. 1992. 'Hazards of Farming', *Canadian Family Physician*, 38(9): 2044–52.

Haugh, E. B. and B. Mildon. 2004. 'Practice Settings, Roles, and Functions', in L. Stamler and L. Liu (eds), *Community Health Nursing: A Canadian Perspective*, pp. 55–71. Toronto, ON: Pearson Prentice Hall.

Kubik, W. and R. Moore. 2001. *Women's Diverse Roles in the Farm Economy and the Consequences for Their Health, Well-being, and Quality of Life*. Available online at http://www.campioncollege.sk.ca/news/pdf (Accessed on 26 January 2004).

Labrecque, J., and S. Charlebois. 2005. *A Conceptual Comparative Analysis between the British and the Canadian Mad Cow Crisis*. Available online at http://www.lfamg,org/ conferences/2005conference/Papers&Discussions/1162_Paper_Final.pdf (Accessed on 19 June 2006).

Lassiter, P. G. 1992. 'A Community Development Perspective for Rural Nursing', *Family Community Health*, 14(4): 29–39.

Lazarus, R. S. and S. Folkman. 1984. *Stress, Appraisal, and Coping*. New York: Springer.

Leipert, B. 1999. 'Women's Health and the Practice of Public Health Nurses in Northern British Columbia', *Public Health Nursing*, 16(4): 280–89.

Lind, C. 1995. 'Powerlessness, Community and the Environment: When the System Farms the Farmer', in C. Lind (ed.), *Something's Wrong Somewhere—Globalization, Community Tend the Moral Economy of Farm Stress*, pp. 69–86. Halifax, NS: Fernwood Publishing.

McGhee, M. 1983. *The Changing Scene: Women in Rural Life*. Toronto, ON: Ontario Ministry of Agriculture and Food.

Meyer, K. and L. Lobao. 2003. 'Economic Hardship, Religion and Mental Health during the Midwestern Farm Crisis', *Journal of Rural Studies*, 19(2): 139–55.

Ollenburger, Jane and Graham Tobin. 1998. 'Women and Post-disaster Stress', in Elaine Enarson and Betty Hearn Morrow (eds), *The Gendered Terrain of Disaster: Through Women's Eyes*, pp. 95–108. Westport, CT: Greenwood Publications.

Petterson, L. T. and H. Solbakken. 1998. 'Empowerment as a Strategy for Change for Farm Women in Western Industrialized Countries', *Sociologia Ruralis*, 38(3): 318–33.

Prairie Women's Health Centre of Excellence (PWHCE). 2003. *Summary Report. Rural, Remote and Northern Women's Health*. Winnipeg: PWHCE.

Roberts, J. and M. Falk. 2002. *Women and Health: Experiences in a Rural Regional Health Authority*. Available online at http://www.pwhce.ca/pdf (Accessed on 11 February 2004).

Skogstad, G. 2005. Policy Networks and Policy Communities: Conceptual Evolution and Governing Realities. Available online at http://www.cpsa acsp.ca/papers-2005/ Skogstad.pdf (Accessed on 11 May 2006).

Statistics Canada. 1999. *For Farm Women, Agriculture Is Just the Beginning*. Available online at http://www.statcan.ca/english/kits/agric/work.htm (Accessed on 16 August 2005).

———. 2005. *Farm Population, by Provinces (2001 Censuses of Agriculture and Population)*. Available online at http://www.statcan.ca/english/Pgdb/agrc42h.htm (Accessed on 3 March 2005).

———. 2006. 'Farm Operators by Sex and Age, by Province (2001 and 2006 Census of Agriculture)'. Available online at http://www40.statcan.gc.ca/l01/cst01/agrc18a-eng. htm (Accessed on 19 June 2009).

Stein, H. F. 1982. 'The Annual Cycle and the Cultural Nexus of Health Care Behaviour among Oklahoma Wheat Farming Families', *Culture, Medicine and Psychiatry*, 6(1): 81–89.

Tierney, K. J., M. K. Lindell and R. W. Perry. 2001. 'The Wider Context: Societal Factors Influencing Emergency Management Policy and Practice', in Kathleen J. Tierney, Michael Lindell and Ronal W. Perry (eds) *Facing the Unexpected: Disaster Preparedness and Response in the United States*, pp. 199–241. Washington, DC: Joseph Henry Press.

van de Vorst, C. 2002. *Making Ends Meet. Farm Women's Work in Manitoba*. Winnipeg, MB: University of Manitoba Press.

Walker, L. S. and J. L. Walker. 1987. 'Stressors and Symptoms Predictive of Distress in Farmers', *Family Relations*, 36(4): 374–78.

Wang, C. and M. A. Burris. 1997. 'Photovoice: Concepts, Methodology and Use for Participatory Needs Assessment', *Health Education and Behavior*, 25(3): 369–87.

13

Supporting Women and Men on the Front Lines of Biological Disaster

————•✦•————

Tracey L. O'Sullivan and Carol A. Amaratunga

In 2003, the world became acutely aware of our global vulnerability when Severe Acute Respiratory Syndrome (SARS), spread across the globe. According to the World Health Organization, SARS infected over 8,000 people worldwide and caused more than 900 deaths. The global outbreak was contained by the relentless dedication of health professionals, who worked in challenging conditions to ensure the safety of the public.

In Canada, 438 probable SARS cases were detected, of which 25 were confirmed. Forty-three per cent of them were health care workers who became infected as a result of occupational exposure. Forty-three people in Canada died from SARS, three of whom were health care workers (two nurses and one physician). Patients who survived experienced high morbidity, many with long-term physical and psychological ailments, including respiratory difficulties and post-traumatic stress. The number of infections and deaths was higher in China (5,327; 349, respectively), Hong Kong (1,755; 299) and Taiwan (346; 37). Singapore reported similar numbers to those reported in Canada, with 238 infections and 33 deaths.

One of the key lessons learnt from SARS collectively was that nations were not prepared for a large-scale, global health-epidemic. SARS occurred on a rapid time frame, which separates it from other types of bio-disasters, such as slow-moving pandemics like HIV/AIDS. While SARS was largely contained within health care facilities, these organisational communities were on the brink of collapsing, with a burnt out workforce and few reserves to draw on (Campbell 2006). In Canada, the health care system, which had faced numerous fiscal and human resource cuts through the previous decade, began the fight against SARS short-staffed, with alarmingly few health care workers trained in infection control measures. The situation worsened as the outbreak went on and more staff were unavailable to work, due to illness and quarantine restrictions. This was due in some part to the nature of gendered, hierarchical organisations in health care and many of the front line workers are women and mothers.

Gender and Public Health Response Systems

Public safety depends on this commitment and willingness to serve, and in Canada approximately 80 per cent of health care workers are women. In nursing, the largest segment of the health care sector, 95 per cent are women (CIHI 2005). Women are also the majority of unpaid caregivers in Canada (Armstrong and Kits in Grant et al. 2004) and are increasingly being recognised as important members of the first response community, especially in relation to surge capacity. It is important, therefore, to better understand the gender and psychosocial dimensions of disaster management, risk assessment and recovery.

Some barriers that health professionals and emergency relief volunteers face include transportation to work while under work quarantine, coping with the psychological stressors presented in a bio-event, managing fatigue and uncomfortable working conditions and complying with quarantine and other infection control procedures. Gendered family arrangements and living conditions impact the capacity and will of professional responders and emergency relief workers to respond; for example, single parents working part-time in several health care organisations, health care providers with young children who may be the primary caregivers for their own ailing parents, an ambulance driver with young children whose spouse who works full-time, any health care worker or emergency services personnel who happens to be pregnant or is trying to become pregnant at the time of a bio-disaster, or a married couple with young children, both of whom are first responders.

As was demonstrated in the SARS outbreak, many nurses faced numerous challenges stemming from work–family role conflict, based on their personal and social networks and roles and work. These sources of conflict interact to form unique challenges at the personal, family and organisational levels. The Registered Nurses' Association of Ontario (RNAO) in its report following the SARS outbreak in Toronto (2003) stated that this public health crisis highlighted the resilience and strength of health care workers working at point of care, as well as in administrative roles. The results of the inquiry showed that the 'response to SARS exhausted individual nurses and tested the very limits of their professional commitment' (RNAO 2003: 5).

The personal and collective resilience of health care professionals, which enable them to perform their duties, are key determinants of whether emergency plans and protocols will be carried out as planned when bio-events and other disasters occur. Unfortunately, in hierarchical organisations, such as health care, where information does not always trickle down to the front line care providers, many employees are unaware of their organisations' preparedness plans (O'Sullivan et al. 2008) and so unable to assess how their concerns as women and men, mothers and fathers, are to be addressed.

Health Care Workers Managing Social Contamination

Public health care workers and other first responders literally put their lives on the line during bio-events and other types of disasters. During SARS, health care workers were stigmatised by the public as possible vectors for transmission. Ellacott (2003) reflected on her profession in the context of the SARS outbreak: 'Nurses are praised for what we do, but shunned because we do it. I live in the paradox of being a hero and a pariah at the same time.'

There were many other challenges for the women and men on the front lines of this health crisis. One of the critical infection control directives imposed by the Ministry of Health in Ontario during the SARS crisis was that health care workers were restricted to working in only one health care facility during the outbreak. This presented considerable financial strain for many health professionals, particularly many nurses, for whom working for multiple employers is a necessity to ensure adequate family income. For a single parent, many of whom are women, this restriction has serious implications for family sustainability if enforced over several months.

Some health care providers faced termination of day-care arrangements, as a result of the concerns of other parents fearful about potential transmission of SARS from the children of health care workers (O'Sullivan et al. 2009). This presented considerable strain for parents who were desperately needed at work, relied on the income for their livelihood, were single parents or those who had to comply with quarantine restrictions.

Public and particularly family attitudes exert a tremendous influence on the emotional health of responders. The following statement by a nurse (Yassi et al. 2004: 65) reiterates this pressure:

> My son-in-law was angry (that I was working) but you just reassure them that you're taking a shower and you're taking all the precautions. And my boyfriend was the same way. You make sure that you wear that stuff and take all the safety precautions because he didn't want me getting sick. I think we were more at ease, but our family members were definitely upset.

Supporting Responders in Health Care Settings: The Need for Gender Sensitivity

Social support is paramount to buffering the negative impact of stress and enhancing resiliency (Jones-DeWeever 2007). In bio-events involving infectious agents, provision of social support becomes more complex, with the heightened risk of transmission. This is an important consideration when planning for biological emergencies, such as pandemic influenza or bio-terrorist incidents. Further, research has established that psychosocial recovery is delayed when disasters are seen as toxic or contaminating, or in which blame can be attributed. The 'corrosive community' that emerges undermines community solidarity and social networks of support (Erikson 1995; Freudenberg 1997).

Conclusion

At the end of the day, health care workers must make important and tough decisions about how and where they will dedicate their time and energy. Female front line responders in particular must often choose to be with their family members or on the job during disasters. Planning and preparedness planning which recognises and acknowledges the dual roles, for example, the family and work responsibilities, of both male and female responders, can help ensure a fully prepared and dedicated workforce. The psychosocial and gendered aspects of disasters necessitate careful advanced planning to ensure that all workers are provided with adequate protections and equity within the workplace.

Bio-event disasters require prompt, prolonged responses from a variety of disciplines, whether they occur from intentional acts of aggression, or naturally from organisms in the environment. Bio-terrorist attacks using the United States postal service in 2001 and the global outbreaks of SARS in 2003 brought attention to the critical role of health care workers in sustaining public safety. The onus is on decision makers to ensure proper supports are in place to protect the health care workforce, upon whom the public relies on to respond. Due to gender segregation in health occupations, this demands gender-based analysis and gender sensitivity in emergency management. When planning for bio-event or other types of disasters, it is essential to consider the need for gender-sensitive instrumental, informational and emotional support mechanisms that are required by first responders. More research is also needed to understand how social support is mobilised and maintained in infectious health emergencies, again with a close focus on gender in order to accurately reflect and respond to the realities of today's families and contemporary health care institutions.

References

Armstrong, P. and O. Kits. 2004. 'One Hundred Years of Caregiving', in K. R. Grant, C. A. Amaratunga, P. Armstrong, M. Boscoe, A. Pederson and K. Wilson (eds), *Caring for/Caring about: Women, Home, Care and Unpaid Caregiving*, pp. 45–73. Aurora, Ontario: Garamond Press.

Campbell, A. 2006. *Spring of Fear, Volume 1: The SARS Commission Executive Summary.* Available online at http://www.health.gov.on.ca/english/public/pub/ministry_reports/campbell06/online_rep/index.html (Accessed on 19 June 2009).

Canadian Institute for Health Information (CIHI). 2005. *Health Care in Canada*. Ottawa, ON: Canadian Institute for Health Information.

Ellacott, K. 2003. 'Behind the Mask', *Canadian Nurse*, 99(7): 12–16.

Erikson, K. 1995. *A New Species of Trouble: The Human Experience of Modern Disasters*. New York: W.W. Norton.

Freudenberg, W. 1997. 'Contamination, Corrosion and the Social Order: An Overview', *Current Sociology*, 45(3): 19–39.

Jones-DeWeever, A. A. 2007. *Women in the Wake of the Storm: Examining Post-Katrina Realities of the Women of New Orleans and the Gulf Coast*. Institute for Women's Policy Research. Available online at http://www.iwpr.org/pdf/D481.pdf (Accessed on 19 June 2009).

O'Sullivan, T. L., D. Dow, M. C. Turner, L. Lemyre, W. Corneil, D. Krewski, K. P. Phillips and C. A. Amaratunga. 2008. 'Disaster and Emergency Management: Canadian Nurses' Perceptions of Preparedness on Hospital Front Lines', *Prehospital and Disaster Medicine*, 23(3): s11–s18.

O'Sullivan, T. L., C. A. Amaratunga, K. P. Phillips, W. Corneil, E. O'Connor, L. Lemyre and D. Dow. 2009. 'If Schools Are Closed, Who Will Watch Our Kids? … Family Caregiving and Other Sources of Role Conflict among Nurses during Large Scale Outbreaks', *Prehospital and Disaster Medicine*, 2(4):195–210.

Registered Nurses' Association of Ontario (RNAO). 2003. 'SARS Unmasked: Celebrating Resilience, Exposing Vulnerability', A report on the Nursing Experience with SARS in Ontario presented to the Commission to Investigate the Introduction and Spread of SARS in Ontario Public Hearing on 29 September. Available online at http://www.rnao.org/Page.asp?PageID=122&ContentID=1685&SiteNodeID=401&BL_ExpandID= (Accessed on 19 June 2009).

Yassi, A., E. Bryce, D. Moore, R. Janssen, R. Copes, K. Bartlett et al. 2004. *Protecting the Face of Health Care Workers: Knowledge Gaps and Research Priorities for Effective Protection against Occupationally-acquired Respiratory Infectious Diseases*. Toronto: The Change Foundation.

PART THREE

Women's Organised Initiatives

The seven chapters of this part take us through some of the grass-roots level initiatives across continents in organising women as active agents of change in both post- and pre-disaster situations.

Maureen Fordham presents a case study on what women and girls did to reduce the risks of disasters in the Central American nation of El Salvador. The study demonstrates how women joining together could significantly change their lives and reduce the risk of disasters of the community. Different groups of women accomplished this in different ways: some organised around disaster management and then progressed to development issues, others started with development and used that as the basis of organising around disaster risk reduction, while still others worked on both disaster and development from the start. This suggests that gender mainstreaming in disaster risk reduction can be achieved differently according to the contexts, resources and ingenuity of the people.

Ayse Yonder with Sengül Akçar and Prema Gopalan recount the experiences of SSP of India (*Swayam Shikshan Prayog*, meaning learning from one's own and others' experiences) and KEDV of Turkey (*Kadin Emegini Degerlendirme Vakfi* meaning the foundation for the support for women's work) following earthquakes in Latur and Marmara. Both SSP and KEDV used peer learning exchanges among local women's groups as a capacity building strategy and demonstrated how post-disaster situations can be opportunities to empower grass-roots women, build more resilient communities and initiate long-term social change and development.

Francie Lund and Tony Vaux in their chapter 'Work-Focused Responses to Disasters: India's Self Employed Women's Association' 'point out that SEWA's response to disaster situations has developed from its long experience of working with women in the informal sector and in the array of other services it has built—childcare, health services, the SEWA bank and an integrated insurance scheme—all of which are called into play when disaster strikes. SEWA's innovative interventions in many disasters highlight that, for poorer people, the central issue of disaster response is livelihood and, for women, an additional central issue is the care of their children and dependants. SEWA has successfully demonstrated that poor working women should not be seen as merely victims but as powerful agents for overcoming disaster.

Leigh Brownhill traces the roots of Kenya's post-election humanitarian disaster and analyses the role women played in organising the resistance movement for peace—from the Green Belt Movement in the 1970s to Freedom Corner hunger strike of 1992 and more recently the Kenyan Women's Consultation Group on the Current Crisis in Kenya. Peace here is more than the absence of violence—it is to facilitate the provision of 'food, shelter, health and education for all', which in turn requires that everyone has secure access to the necessities of life, including a healthy environment. The movement 'wields the power of subsistence, that is, the day-to-day power to keep people alive', which includes feeding and sheltering people as well as keeping alive the will to resist injustice and nurturing the networks within which to organise peaceful resistance and social transformation. Women are at the forefront of this movement.

Sarah Fisher explores the factors that contributed to the increased incidence of violence against girls and women in Sri Lanka following the Indian Ocean tsunami of December 2004. Reports of rape, gang-rape and sexual abuse occurring in the initial hours and days of the crisis quickly emerged in the media. Although media coverage of incidents ceased after the immediate aftermath, the violence did not. Violence against women, and in particular domestic violence, continued in the camps and temporary shelters housing the displaced well beyond the initial emergency phase of the disaster. Sri Lankan women's organisations were quick to intervene in the crisis and to respond to the reports of violence and played a fundamental role in the promotion of gender sensitive disaster management, seeking to address the gendered inequalities underlying women's disaster vulnerabilities.

Judith Soares and Audrey Y. Mullings narrate the important role played by women following the volcanic eruptions in Montserrat in 1995, which demonstrated the strength, patience, perseverance and resilience of Caribbean women, who saw the need and voluntarily brought their wherewithal to take a centre stage in the crisis situation. The part played by them spontaneously without any advance preparations only highlights that the women must be fully integrated into all disaster management plans, programmes and policies as effective agents of change, and they must be fully trained in the theory, practice and technical aspects of disaster management in order to enhance their capacity to realise their full potential. The ability of women to lead in situations of crisis and to re-build in instances of devastation must be recognised and respected for, as one woman stated, 'a we run tings'.

In the last chapter of the part, Adélia de Melo Branco reports on a qualitative study of rural and urban women affected by drought in the state of Pernambuco, located in Northeast Brazil, challenging the myth that women are passive spectators in disasters. The women affected by drought involved themselves in mitigation activities and political mobilisation, which caught the attention of the government for designing programmes for their capacities and needs.

14

'We Can Make Things Better for Each Other': Women and Girls Organise to Reduce Disasters in Central America

————— • ✦ • —————

Maureen Fordham

We used to live in a very uncomfortable way, now we are free. Now we are organized.

—Yuola Health, and Water and Sanitation
Committees, Pequeña Inglaterra

Introduction

When considering disaster risk reduction, it is understandable that people focus on managing disasters and the hazards themselves. However, a focus on the development linkages is becoming increasingly common (UNDP 2004) and of particular value when considering the situation of women. Women are frequent contributors to community-based development projects and activities, encouraged in part by the insistence of donors that they should have an equal role. For example, Canadian International

Development Agency (CIDA) lists equality between women and men as one of its priorities, identifies it as a global issue and a cross-cutting theme throughout Canada's development cooperation programming. The donor expectation that gender equality issues will be mainstreamed throughout programmes and projects helps overcome any local resistance. While gender equality within global development initiatives has clearly gained recognition, it has not yet been universally realised. However, in the disaster management or risk reduction field, gender equality issues are even less visible, despite significant individual examples (Disaster Watch [www.disasterwatch.net]; Gender and Disaster Network [www. gdnonline.org]; see UNISDR 2007).

Disaster Management and Risk Reduction

The typical model of disaster management is dominated by a masculine culture. Women are poorly represented in both formal and informal structures and organisations, despite the fact that women carry much of the burden of responsibility for post-disaster reconstruction at the domestic/household level. In many community-based organisations, women make up the majority of the members: although, again, fewer are in positions of authority. Children are even less visible in disasters. While generally recognised as a vulnerable group requiring particular attention, their specific needs are still often misunderstood or overlooked (Fordham and Ketteridge 1995). More commonly in recent years, children may be recognised as requiring information but they are rarely involved in decision making or action.

The case study used for this chapter focuses primarily on women and girls, but also considers boys and men, in communities in El Salvador visited as part of an ongoing collaboration (since 2004) with Plan International, an international children's and community development non-governmental organisation (NGO). Before discussing this work in more detail, it is necessary to examine briefly the context of El Salvador.

Background to El Salvador: A Case Study

In terms of Human Development, El Salvador is ranked 101 out of 177 countries listed in the 2006 Human Development Report (HDR 2006), which places it in the middle income economies. However, major contributors to its economy are the remittances from migrants to the United States. This was calculated as US$ 2.5 billion in 2004, equivalent to more than 16 per cent of El Salvador's gross domestic product (UNDP and the Government of El Salvador 2005). In terms of gender disparities, the problems related to the indices used (that is, gender-related development index [GDI] and gender empowerment measure [GEM], see HDR 2006: 279–80) mask a clear understanding of its position. It is ranked 76 out of 136 in terms of GDI and 48 out of 75 on GEM. On a widely used measure of income distribution, with 0 and 100 representing perfect equality and inequality, respectively, El Salvador has a value of 52.4.

None of these measures properly represent the considerable inequality in the country: the majority of Salvadorans live in poverty, without access to social services, and, as a result of neo-liberal structural adjustment policies, women bear a disproportionate burden of the deprivation. El Salvador is prone to a number of putatively 'natural' (but socially produced) hazards including earthquakes, floods, droughts, storms, landslides, volcanic eruptions and environmental degradation. It is also subject to social hazards, which include the prevalence of youth gangs. In addition, it is still dealing with the aftermath of a 12-year (1980–92) civil war in which 75,000 people died, 8,000 disappeared and 1 million were displaced (Silber 2004: 562).

Of interest in the context of this chapter is the large number of women who were actively involved in the civil war. More than 30 per cent of the Frente Faribundo Martí de Liberación Nacional (FMLN) combatants were women. However, unlike other left-wing movements in Central America, gender equality was not included in the FMLN political platform and in the post-war settlements and FMLN women did not receive the same entitlements as the men. Nevertheless, following on from political activism during the war, 'Salvadoran women continue to be highly organized at all levels of society' (WomenWarPeace.org).

While in the discussion later an earthquake or a hurricane or a war may be regarded as the triggers of destruction, the people's vulnerability is rooted in structural inequalities embedded within national and international socio-economic systems. It has been said many times before that disasters are unresolved problems of development. Thus, the context must be disaster and development. Some disasters will always happen, and so response and relief provision will remain important, but they should not be the first, the main or the only thing we think of. Increasingly, attention has turned from disaster response to disaster risk reduction initiatives. Furthermore, approaches are being refined to recognise that disaster 'victims' must be seen as members of many (overlapping) social groups and initiatives must be tailored, not only to their needs but also to their rights (Enarson and Fordham 2001). A person's experience of a disaster should not be made worse because they fall into a specific social group—because they are female, black, elderly, or of a lower social class or caste, with a disability, or a mixture of these. However, too often, for those who fall into a social group that is marginalised within the dominant society, we find that their needs are not met, their rights are not recognised and that they have fewer opportunities to contribute actively or professionally to managing a disaster or reducing its future risk.

In the context of this chapter, it is pertinent to ask: how often do women and children play an *active* role in disaster risk reduction initiatives? The following case study is of interest because it attempts to integrate a range of social groups and types of risk.

Integrated Risk Reduction in the Context of Disaster and Development

The model for the integrated, community-based risk reduction measures discussed later is a project plan entitled 'Youth Participation in Disaster Prevention, 2001–2004'. This was subsequently followed up with other initiatives based on this model, for example, with a project funded by the UK Department For International Development entitled 'Children and Young People at the Centre of Disaster Risk Reduction' which began in January 2006. The original project, supported by the CIDA, had three target components: health, environment and disaster. Its objectives were to increase the capacity of children, youth and communities to respond to disasters, through preparation and mitigation; to increase the knowledge and capacity of participating organisations and to integrate gender equality and youth participation and thus to strengthen disaster preparedness policies. Plan worked in partnership with the El Salvador Red Cross, the NGO CATIE (Centre for Tropical Agriculture Research and Education) and the Ministry of Health. In summary, the project achieved the following (Plan El Salvador 2004):

1. The formation and training of community emergency committees (325 women and 290 men).
2. Disaster prevention training for 23 schools.
3. The preparation of 30 community emergency plans in communities and schools.
4. The organisation and training of 30 youth groups (320 girls and 305 boys) in mitigation and preparedness for emergencies.

In late 2004, the evaluation showed that 80 per cent of school and community committees carried out a range of activities, including emergency drills, sanitation campaigns and mosquito eradication. As the figures show, girls and women were well represented on the committees.

Methodology

In 2006, I undertook a series of visits/revisits to these communities specifically to research gender issues during and after Hurricane Stan (which hit El Salvador and other countries within the region in October 2005). The research on which this chapter is based included interviews with staff from Plan and other international NGOs and field visits to assess Plan projects and programmes in El Salvador (November 2004 and February/March 2006), Vietnam, the Philippines and Thailand (March 2005) and Sierra Leone (April 2005). These field visits included meetings with communities (including children), UN in-country agencies, other international and other NGOs and local government. This chapter discusses just the El Salvador work, which included visits to 17 communities in five departments. In the following section, I present some of the findings from the fieldwork, using people's own words (in translation) to illustrate the value of social organisation in reducing disaster risk, and the strong links between disaster and development. In the account that follows, only first names are provided.

Empirical Results

In all these communities, there are chronic health problems linked to a lack, or a contamination, of potable water and sanitation services.

Earthquakes, storms and landslides result in further deterioration of these services and a cyclical process of decline. The earthquake and storm hazards wreak such damage because of the level of environmental destruction (for example, steep hillsides cleared of native vegetation and replanted as coffee plantations) which can, in turn, be attributed to the workings of national and international political economic structures and processes. Inequalities arising from Salvadoran social structures and power systems only worsen the situation in which violence, particularly against women, is an everyday reality and youth are tempted to seek respect through membership in youth gangs. Here are some of the ways local people, women in particular, have confronted some of these disasters and development challenges.

In San Alfonso, Municipality of Tamanique, where many of the families settled in 1989 after being displaced by the civil war, Hurricane Stan destroyed their water supply and sanitation. As Marta shared:

> We went through some very bad worries in Stan and we're still living through them. The river is a risk here. Right now it looks harmless but the river is a traitor. The latrines collapsed, houses were damaged, we don't have drinking water and have chronic diseases. Right now we have a child in the hospital. (Marta, Community Leader)

One of the mothers says:

> The problem is the water. It is contaminated and we don't have any other choice. Even if we wash the well it's not enough. We don't have water to wash—it's too contaminated. We have to go to the river to wash our clothes, far from here and have to pay transportation. It was a problem before but we treated the water with chlorine; after Stan it became untreatable. It became very bad. For us it really hurts to see our children so badly affected and we can't do anything because we are so poor and have no resources. Our situation is heartbreaking. Here we had women who lost their jobs washing and ironing for others because they had to stay at home and tend their children. The employers didn't understand. Three days of not showing up for work is cause for termination. People said, 'I don't care about the job, I don't want to lose my children.'

During my visit, I saw evidence of skin infections on children and also met the tearful mother of a hospitalised child. I also saw—and smelt—the condition of the water pumped from one of the wells. Furthermore, the impacts of flooding are made worse by the beaten mud floors in most of the houses. These are development issues. Typically, as the last part of the previous quotation emphasises, women are forced to choose between their reproductive role and their economic role when employers fail to understand the extended demands that disasters place on women.

Although feelings of helplessness have been expressed here, in fact, the community has organised and made many attempts to reduce the vulnerability of its members. At the time of visiting, they were working on a proposal to gain external funding for a water project and, since Hurricane Stan, they have constructed a risk map which combines both health and environmental data:

> After the storm we worked on our map so now we know the risk areas. We are monitoring the river. In case of evacuation we know how to evacuate safely. Pins show where kids are with severe malnutrition. Blue pins are for pregnant women. Yellow pins are normal weight. Red pins are severe malnutrition. Because of the storm, children lost weight because their families couldn't work and feed them and also the children got sick and lost weight. This map was made by the nutritional counsellors. We know the water will come down the hill. So this area becomes isolated and we couldn't go to the mill to grind the corn for the tortillas. (Community Woman)

Of particular interest in this community is that, first, under the leadership of the women, they have organised to deal with the risks they face. Second, they have not organised around disasters but in order to address food and nutrition issues. It makes more sense to organise on the basis of what people recognise as everyday, pressing risks, rather than on the basis of the risk of a disaster which, by comparison, may be a distant threat. It is the process of organising that is important; the focus of the organisation is secondary:

> In Mitch we were not organized ... we were like crazy bees after the beehive is shaken ... after Mitch we learned to get organized. Now in Storm Stan we have that experience and all houses were evacuated in time.

> In spite of what we have gone through we are better organized. When we have an emergency we know we can count on each other. We have various committees—support, sanitation, emergency—here in San Alfonso. We know what our goal is and our purpose. (Marta, Community Leader)

As long as one of the committees survives it will help in future disasters, which is the lesson learned from the next community, Pequeña Inglaterra (Little England). This is a community built from bare ground by and for some of those who lost their homes in the two earthquakes of 2001, which occurred exactly one month apart (in January, 7.6 magnitude, and in February, 6.6 magnitude) and killed more than 1,100 people. A quarter of the country's population (1.5 million people) was affected. The municipality provided the land for the new community, Plan provided materials and technical support and local people provided the labour. A generous donation from an English donor was the reason local people chose the name Little England. This was an exercise in social engineering on a grand scale. Those first residents in Pequeña Inglaterra came from a number of different earthquake-affected parts and so a new 'community' had to be developed in a new location. This was an exercise that was being carried out in other new, post-earthquake communities, but it seemed to work better here than elsewhere:

> There has been trouble in other communities—the president of one community was killed. Those people have a different [kind of] community. They have electricity but don't have a community. (Yuola)

> Thank goodness we don't have bad people here. We don't have youth gangs here because the young people got trained and know how to avoid dangers. They know they don't have to join gangs. They know better than that. (Rosario)

From the start, Pequeña Inglaterra was managed by various committees, helped and facilitated by Plan. In 2002, Plan helped the community to identify their priorities and prepare a community development plan, which involved the setting up of committees in which women, children and youth were active members. Because water and sanitation were two of the main priorities, a health committee was formed, whose members were trained by Plan in water and sanitation management, proper use of compost latrines, basic hygiene practices and community monitoring and evaluation. As a result of the success of the health committee, several other such committees were formed.

There is general acceptance by the community for such groups to be responsible for specific issues, but there is also a work overload for some of those with leadership skills. A field visit in 2004 showed that all the committees were still in operation but that some were struggling. By 2006, only the Waste Management Committee was running. However, while some committees have not survived, the organised collective behaviour remains:

The emergency committee has disintegrated. It's a challenge that we have. [However] The community committee was ready to respond to the emergency and we took care of each other and provided shelter to those in most need … The greatest disaster of the storm Stan was the result of poor management of waste. The garbage blocked the sewage system—so much garbage all over the streets. If we managed the garbage better the danger would have been better. Especially in the rivers in the rural areas—people just throw the garbage and that's what made the storm worse. It's a struggle we have. (Rosa, Waste Management Committee)

I think we have matured as a community. We have lived things in our own skin. Remember it was the earthquake of 2001 is the reason we are here. We have lived it in our own skin. When the storm happened we took it calmly. In my case we walked around the community to see the families and thank God there were no casualties or losses but around 8 families had difficulty. They were near that street where if it rains a lot it becomes a river and they lived near. (Ruben, President of the Waste Management Committee and member of the Asociación para el Desarollo de la Comunidad [ADESCO]).

These testimonies show the ways in which some of those trained are making the link between not only development issues (waste management) and disasters, but also the way organisation around any focus can help reduce vulnerability.

Apart from the contributions to community-level development and vulnerability reduction, organising can have significant personal benefits such as increase in levels of confidence and self-respect. Women community members gained strength and self-esteem through being active members of community-based emergency preparedness committees:

The other day when I went to another village and I was invited to speak about our committee and I did. Now I feel comfortable speaking in front of people. I learned to have my own ideas. (Community Woman)

Marisol reveals a problem experienced by several women, some of whom had difficulties convincing their partners of the importance of the work which demanded their absence from home:

Maybe we women are not used to share our experiences but I am going to dare to share. I have a problem; my husband is not keen on me attending committee meetings and I have problems going out to assess damages but I delivered food aid in Hurricane Stan. We cooked for families and we gained strength in doing good. In Hurricane Stan I was doing home visits to my neighbours despite mud going up to my knees but I realized we had to save them. We understood that we are important in a committee. Sometimes women don't know about our strength. In emergencies we have the opportunity to test ourself and become not 'just women'. It was us women who dared to go in the canyons, going after the victims. It was us women who took the elderly out of the house. (Marisol, La Laguna Municipal Civil Protection Committee in Chalatanango Province)

Importantly, even older women—a recognised group who are often seen as most vulnerable and given the least opportunities to be active—have a significant role in these committees:

As soon as I joined this project I began learning. I am an old woman but still able to learn! (Christina, Emergency Preparedness Committee, El Portillo)

I am grateful for the opportunity Plan gives women. Nobody cared about women. I am grateful for being considered a valuable human being. I felt important and as a woman I can say that was very important and I was being treated in a different way. I know from the Bible it says men and women are equal but it is not that way. ('Ana Lucía' in Petapa)

During training drills, women learned to recognise new strengths in themselves; the training programmes also became social events and opportunities for enjoyment.

I didn't know I was able to carry someone that was wounded. I had to carry a man. I didn't know I could do it. I was doing first aid, caring for the wounds and I was a part of it and effective. (Older woman in Petapa)

I think I am one of the oldest people here and I remember having fun in the drill. I was full of energy and I felt youthful. (Older woman in Petapa)

But it is the contribution of young women which is particularly novel in Plan's approach. As in the adult committees, there is a significant female presence. Women work together with men and girls with boys. As outlined before, in several communities, youth emergency preparedness brigades or committees have been set up. They have been trained by the Red Cross in basic first aid and have developed warning systems. They know where the vulnerable people are in the communities, which are often scattered across the hillsides; they know who will be in difficulty and have a system for reaching them to warn of dangers. They have prepared their own risk maps showing those areas that are particularly vulnerable. They are an articulate group of young people who are confident in their role and committed to community action.

Cindy, the President of the Santo Tomás School Emergency Risk Management Committee, and two fellow students are credited with rescuing a woman and her child from a house where the husband/father refused to leave.

> We saw a child was at risk. We begged them to leave the house. (Cindy, Emergency Risk Management Committee)

A landslide buried the 7-year-old child to his shoulders but the committee members pulled him out. The house later collapsed. These young people also organised the emergency shelter:

> We ran the shelter for one and a half months. 23 families and 30 children were sheltered here. We took turns, we had shifts. The boys came to sleep over. The girls stayed in the day. We organized events for the children because they were afraid. Things we didn't know, for the next emergency we will know them. We organized the shelter—this we learned through experience. Others were surprised that the youth were organizing the shelter. Our mums—were surprised! Things they didn't dare to do—we were doing them! (Cindy, Emergency Risk Management Committee)

Although the examples presented here show women and girls in an active role, they still reflect rather more typical gender role expectations and cultural norms. For instance, in the previous example, the girls were not allowed to stay out over night in the shelters. It underlines how females are at risk of sexual violence and also the boundaries of what is deemed appropriate behaviour for girls. When members of the School Emergency Preparedness Brigade in San Isidro talk of their experiences in Hurricane Stan, it is clear that the girls are still more protected:

> During the storm, my brother and me—we're both members of the committee—and I wasn't allowed to go out but my brother represented me. My mum said I should do house things—that was needed too. I wanted to go out because I wanted to participate but parents are more careful with girls. (Marie Belle)

And the boys are still expected to be strong:

> My experience was I was scared. I am the only man in the house. When we went to my house I realized it was all destroyed. I hugged my mum and told her that this will pass if God allows it to happen. I tried to conceal my feelings before others because they wanted strength from me. So we supported each other, trying to keep each other cheerful but I felt sad. Right now I feel good. I was a part of the situation. I helped. (Carlos)

Training in gender and children's rights has helped all members of these communities to learn new ways to work together and respect each other. The committees operate from a rights perspective and attitudes can change with experience. Delilah, a young girl from El Portillo, says:

> Boys like to play with boys but now boys and girls are working together and the boys realize it is ok to work with girls.

This sentiment was echoed in several locations where women and men and girls and boys benefited from training programmes that integrated development and disaster initiatives with rights-based approaches to community organisation, in order to facilitate the broadest possible models of cooperation. Not all the communities visited had developed to the same level, but within each one, there was at least a stated commitment to inclusivity. More longitudinal studies are necessary, however, to explore the extent to which these project-led initiatives result in sustained changes in power relations and vulnerability reduction.

Conclusions and Recommendations

> We are grateful to those who have trained us to be courageous and face dangers with less fear. We have realized instead of making things worse we can make things better for each other. (Rosario, Waste Management and Water Board, Pequeña Inglaterra)

The communities studied for this research benefited from a rights-based approach to development and disaster risk reduction, which cut across many of the usual divisions, most specifically those of gender and age. These examples indicate how, when women join together, it can change their lives and also the lives of others. Communities in El Salvador were made safer by community organisation for disaster and development. Some women initially organised themselves around disaster management, and then progressed to development issues; others did it in reverse, starting with development as the basis of organising around disaster risk reduction while some communities worked on both disaster and development from the outset. There is no single right way to achieve safer communities. These communities have few resources other than their members' own knowledge, labour and commitment to cooperative working practices. Such resources helped them save lives during Hurricane

Stan and now they also help them deal with the everyday risks faced by marginalised communities and social groups. All have been strengthened by the process.

It must be said that there can be risks in this kind of community-based approach. Communities are exclusionary as much as they are inclusionary, despite the way the term 'community' is invariably represented as wholly positive and beneficial. Community-based approaches can build social capital but one group's gain may be at the expense of another's loss (Fordham 2006; Woolcock and Narayan 2000). We must examine disaster risk reduction through a gender-sensitive development lens and be alert for the ways in which gender stereotypes and gendered power relations at every scale interfere with equal rights for women and men, girls and boys, to meet their specific needs during and after disasters, and in disaster risk reduction generally. The previous examples suggest one model that has made a contribution to community safety in the El Salvadoran context and, it is hoped, will have value for others elsewhere.

Acknowledgements

The empirical work on which this chapter is based was originally funded by Plan International as part of a study entitled: 'Developing Plan's Capacity to Assist Communities and Children to Prepare for and Respond to Disasters'. Thanks must go to Plan El Salvador for their continuing support for this research. Finally, a special thanks to Patricia Morales for her particular contributions over the years.

References

CIDA (Canadian International Development Agency). *Equality between Women and Men.* Available online at http://www.acdi-cida.gc.ca/CIDAWEB/acdicida.nsf/En/JUD-31192610-JXF (Accessed on 25 July 2007).

Disaster Watch. Available online at www.disasterwatch.net (Accessed on 25 July 2007).

Enarson, E. and M. Fordham. 2001. 'From Women's Needs to Women's Rights in Disasters', *Environmental Hazards*, 3(3–4): 133–36.

Fordham, M. 2006. 'Disaster and Development Research and Practice: A Necessary Eclecticism', in Havidan Rodriguez, E. L. Quarantelli and Russell Dynes (eds), *Handbook of Disaster Research*, pp. 335–46. New York: Kluwer Academic/Plenum Publishers.

Fordham, M. and A-M. Ketteridge. 1995. 'Flood Disasters—Dividing the Community', Paper presented at the Emergency Planning 1995 Conference, Lancaster, UK, 2–6 July.

Gender and Disaster Network (GDN). Available online at www.gdnonline.org (Accessed on 25 July 2007).

HDR. 2006. *Human Development Report.* Available online at http://hdr.undp.org/hdr2006/pdfs/report/HDR06-complete.pdf (Accessed on 11 August 2009).

Plan El Salvador. 2004. *Consultants' Evaluation of the Project 'Youth Participation in Disaster Prevention'.* Plan El Salvador.

Silber, Irina Carlota. 2004. 'Mothers/Fighters/Citizens: Violence and Disillusionment in Post-War El Salvador', *Gender & History,* 16(3): 561–87.

UNDP. 2004. *Reducing Disaster Risk: A Challenge for Development.* New York: United Nations Development Programme Bureau of Crisis Prevention and Recovery.

UNDP and the Government of El Salvador. 2005. *Una Mirada al Nuevo Nosotros: El Impacto de las Migraciones* (in English, 'A Glance at the "New Us": The Impact of Migration'). The fourth National Human Development Report published by the United Nations Development Programme (UNDP) and the Government of El Salvador.

UNISDR. 2007. *Gender Perspective: Working Together for Disaster Risk Reduction: Good Practices and Lessons Learned.* United Nations International Strategy for Disaster Reduction.

WomenWarPeace.org. Available online at http://www.womenwarpeace.org/elsalvador/elsalvador.htm (Accessed on 25 July 2007).

Woolcock, M. and D. Narayan. 2000. 'Social Capital: Implications for Development Theory, Research, and Policy', *The World Bank Research Observer,* 15(2): 225–49.

15

Women's Participation in Disaster Relief and Recovery

——— •✦• ———

Ayse Yonder with Sengül Akçar and Prema Gopalan

As devastating as natural disasters are, they can become focal points, leading to improved future development. Post-disaster recovery can be seen as an opportunity to channel and leverage investments to upgrade the living standards of the poor, to enable the most marginalised to participate and to establish dialogue mechanisms between affected citizens and government to build accountability. In other words, it can apply principles of sustainable development to communities and regions that are likely to remain at high risk of future disasters.

During the relief phase, an infusion of funds and technical assistance often flows to the area, conventional rules and practices are questioned and previously excluded groups—such as ethnic minorities and poor women—are informally involved and take on new roles. Disasters can literally push women out of the confines of their homes and neighbourhoods and lead them to take on non-traditional roles in the name of ensuring their families' survival and well-being. In many post-disaster recovery situations, women have been active in rebuilding their communities. Field reports confirm that women take the initiative in calling grass-roots community meetings and organising disaster-response coalitions (Enarson and Morrow 1998). They outnumber men in the leadership and membership of emergent grass-roots groups working on disaster issues (Enarson 2000; Fothergill 1998). Those communities with pre-existing strong organisations and/or women's groups are able to respond quickly and reduce the amount of damage when disasters strike (Delaney and Shrader 2000). Even in marginalised communities, natural disasters such as floods and hurricanes have inspired women living in extreme poverty to take action and organise their own self-help initiatives (Enarson 2004).

Yet far more information is needed to bring about a shift in disaster response and investment towards poor communities and the women struggling to reorganise daily lives within them. To date, few in-depth case studies have documented multi-year development-oriented disaster responses organised by women's groups over an extended period. Little is known about practical ways of supporting and sustaining women's long-term participation for a 3–6 year period in communities' emergency relief, recovery and hazard reduction initiatives. The following case studies address this gap and describe how groups of local women from Maharashtra and Gujarat in India and the Marmara region in Turkey organised once the earthquakes struck to secure housing, livelihood activities and basic services. The case studies examine how NGOs can support and sustain grass-roots women's involvement from post-disaster recovery to long-term development, and the role government policies play in facilitating or impeding women's involvement.

Women's Organisations and Earthquake Recovery in Turkey and India

Swayam Shikshan Prayog (SSP, translated as 'learning from one's own and others' experiences') in India and the *Kadin Emegini Degerlendirme Vakfi* (KEDV, translated as 'The Foundation for the Support of Women's Work') in Turkey are two non-profit organisations founded in the 1980s, each with more than 15 years of experience working with women and poor communities. Both organisations grew out of social movements in their countries and focused on helping women organise economic activities and participate in local development. Although SSP is primarily rural and KEDV is focused on urban areas, they share a participatory approach to working with women as facilitators and resource partners. They leverage funds, identify innovative grass-roots practice and teach methods that allow women's groups to organise, plan and implement long-term initiatives and lead community-to-community learning exchanges. They partner with local authorities and government officials to persuade them to establish formal protocols that recognise and provide resources for women's involvement. They are committed to networking and sharing their experiences with other community-based women's groups elsewhere as a means for improving their own programmes and pressing for policy change through advocacy and dialogue with major policy-makers and funding agencies to create opportunities for poor women locally, nationally and globally.

The two organisations became acquainted in 1996 when they participated in the United Nations Habitat Conference in Istanbul. Both are members of the Grassroots Organizations Operating Together in Sisterhood (GROOTS) International network, a global network established in 1989, by autonomous locally focused grass-roots women's organisations and NGOs working in poor communities around the world. They came together again in 1999 when SSP hosted a GROOTS exchange in India, enabling KEDV leaders to see how the women's groups organised after the Maharashtra earthquake. This exposure was invaluable when an earthquake struck Turkey later the same year, and it intensified bonds and direct collaboration between the two organisations.

Although SSP and KEDV used different entry points to help women participate in the post-disaster recovery processes, both groups saw disaster response as an opportunity for instituting positive change in the long-term development of poor and working-class communities. The case studies in this chapter present women's experiences with earthquake recovery in chronological order.

Women's Work through SSP in India

India is one of the most disaster-prone regions in the world. Floods, cyclones, droughts and earthquakes hit South Asia every year, causing substantial human and material losses. About 57 per cent of India is prone to earthquakes (Parasuraman and Unnikrishnan 2000). On 30 September

1993, an earthquake with a magnitude of 6.3 on Richter scale hit the Latur and Osmanabad districts in the Marathwadi region of Maharashtra state, affecting 1,500 villages 69 of which were totally destroyed. Official figures placed the death toll near 8,000 and the number of those injured as 16,000. More than 200,000 houses were seriously damaged. Eight years later, another earthquake with a magnitude of 8.0 hit the Bhuj district in neighbouring Gujarat state on 26 January 2001, disrupting lives in more than 620,000 households in cities and villages and resulting in the deaths of more than 20,000 people.

The 5 year rehabilitation programme was launched by the Government of Maharashtra with the support of World Bank, estimated to cost US$ 216 million, as one of the largest in the country's history (Martin 2003). The government decided to relocate the villages hit hardest by the earthquake to new settlements. For 1,300 villages that were partially damaged, the government launched the Repair and Strengthening (R&S) programme to rehabilitate as many damaged houses as possible. The R&S programme was designed as a homeowner-driven, self-help initiative that offered each affected family a grant of Rs 17,000 (US$ 425) towards the repair of their dwellings to be paid in stages.

From the outset, the programme had problems. Access to information, technical support and coordination were major obstacles. By giving subsidies for repair work to individual homeowners rather than to community groups, the programme encouraged patronage, competition and corruption. The appointment of more than 1,000 government engineers to oversee and expedite reconstruction compounded the situation. Many engineers demanded bribes to provide homeowners with the certification they needed to qualify for additional payments and a majority of them were unwilling to share information, train homeowners or resolve problems. Although 'people-friendly' policies and community participation were intended to be innovative aspects of this programme, neither the World Bank nor the government transferred decision-making power or resources in a manner that enabled village committees to function. Gender concerns were also missing from the reconstruction and community participation strategies. As tremors continued for a year after the quake, people were frustrated and mistrustful of the reconstruction process, the R&S programme was coming to a standstill and the government's credibility was at stake.

In late 1994, the state Government of Maharashtra appointed the NGO SSP, which works to build the capacities of rural women's groups to access and manage development resources and participate in decision making, as its consultant, in order to insure community participation in the R&S programme in 300 Latur and Osmanabad villages. This assignment required SSP to balance its role as an advisor to the state with its identity as an NGO committed to transferring decision-making power to local communities and especially to women. The time pressure required SSP to find practical and innovative ways for the residents of 300 villages to learn, cooperate and apply new technology and construction techniques rapidly.

Women Rebuilding their Communities: Mahila Mandals as Agents of Change

SSP started out by creating a picture of the problems and the potential through interviews, village mapping and rapid appraisal techniques. The government authorities clearly lacked a common view of how to implement the programme. Village officials and homeowners lacked not only basic information but also opportunities to discuss and evaluate what was happening. In response, SSP adopted two strategies: training government officials to disseminate information and facilitate bureaucratic processes and identifying community groups that could catalyse and engage local residents.

The latter task led SSP to decide to revive and reorient the government-established women's groups (*mahila mandals*) as community agents for involving households in the R&S programme. Through a large-scale publicity campaign (pamphlets and newspaper and radio advertisements), meetings were organised with 500 women's groups throughout the two affected districts. From this discussion, the idea emerged that women's groups would nominate members to work as official village information and communication assistants (*samvad sahayaks*). To formalise these positions, SSP negotiated with the government so that the state, not SSP, would pay the *samvad sahayaks*, formally recognising the *mahila mandals* as the official interface between the communities and the government administration. Between April 1996 and March 1998, 300 *samvad sahayaks* were appointed in as many villages.

In a mistrustful, deadline-driven and initially hostile environment, the women's groups had to prove that they could inform, motivate and supervise local homeowners. To prepare them for this assignment, SSP provided hands-on leadership training and taught basic safe construction techniques to more than 1,000 village women appointed by the *mahila mandals*. (Larger teams of women were created to support 300 women officially named by the government.) The women's groups organised themselves into teams first to map and survey households in their villages and then worked to ensure that people knew how to access and use their entitlements and understood and could supervise the use of earthquake-safe features, as well as appropriate technology and local resources in construction. They also worked to involve women in planning and designing their houses and interacted with government agencies on behalf of their communities.

As the women began to assume visible leadership positions, the women's groups faced dual and persistent challenges both to empower themselves and to build consensus among village residents and officials. In order to counter social hostility by men (family members, village leaders, engineers, bankers and masons) and promote public responsiveness, SSP adopted a range of simple strategies to help women in their new public roles. Women organised themselves to work in a team, never alone; to speak with everyone in the village, regardless of caste, age or gender to publicly foster an open, inclusive, approach to support local village assemblies (*gram sabhas*), to function as informed, proactive, problem-solving bodies and to speak frankly and directly about problems.

The groups held informal meetings in village lanes to bring women (especially those from poor and lower caste families) out of their homes to discuss their concerns about the R&S process. They also used biweekly (fortnightly) village council meetings and assemblies to share information about aid to homeowners and the progress of the programme and to register how shortages and similar problems were blocking house repairs. When confronting hostility or corruption, teams of women would approach households or officials and speak directly, no matter how high-up in the hierarchy the problem occurred.

As women's intention to improve the situation became clear and officials were forced to act, resistance lessened and cooperation grew. Even masons and engineers became open to adapting the design of houses to include features that women householders considered priorities. Villagers became more active, donating labour, buying materials with their own funds and advancing payment to hire masons and labourers, as they were engaged as homeowners rather than as victims or beneficiaries of aid.

Meanwhile, SSP established 'leading villages' with a team of engineers and expert masons to demonstrate the safest, most user-friendly construction methods. Women's groups as well as local masons received training in earthquake-safe techniques and combining these with the design features that women had requested. These leading villages proved to be an effective means for connecting women's groups across communities as teams of leaders routinely journeyed back and forth to learn first hand how to apply new building processes. Exposure to one village's success energised others. Soon, groups of homeowners began to build houses collectively, sharing costs and designs and jointly dealing with the engineers and supervision of masons and other labourers and recycling materials from their traditional houses.

Interacting with Village, Block and District Governments

To keep the repair process on track, women's groups organised community women to participate in village assemblies and prepared them to describe the problems of their households to local leaders (*gram panchayat* members) so that the leaders would be forced to respond with collective solutions. In several villages where local governments previously had not conducted village assemblies, women's groups pressured local leaders to do so. Women used these assemblies as public platforms for demanding changes in procedures and government accountability, and for pressuring influential local men, including bankers, to support them. Early in the reconstruction process, women's groups had begun to meet with senior district government officials to report formally on village problems and decisions. Over time, they persuaded block and district officials to attend village assemblies regularly to share information and make decisions together with affected families.

The dramatic increase in women's interaction with engineers and government officials and participation in village assemblies produced many benefits. Women helped to expose and reduce local corruption and to promote greater public disclosure of information and investments. They set an example by publicly displaying progress charts, reviewing the goals and outcomes of meetings and convening public dialogues between bureaucrats and affected homeowners. The collaborations women promoted also saved money, advanced public safety and produced restored houses that included features that reduced women's domestic work and improved living conditions.

As local women gained a reputation as resource providers and problem solvers, social relations also changed. Working together across caste lines became more acceptable and traditional discrimination was reduced. Officials became responsive and proactive in addressing problems and complaints, and they trusted women's information. Community support for women's greater participation, both within and outside of the family, helped strengthen women's political identity. Within two years, women stood for local *panchayat* elections, with the support of their groups, to advance the community development they had started.

Building and Managing Public Centres

As the R&S programme wound down the local women's groups and SSP recognised the need to take practical steps to ensure that women stayed active in public life. In conversations with SSP, the women outlined their desire to secure independent public centres that they could manage and control. They envisioned these as permanent 'public homes' that women's groups from five to nine nearby villages could share and operate as information, training and resource centres. They knew that if they had their own space, they would not have to negotiate with men for access to public meeting spaces or confine their activities to their homes.

The women's information centres, *Mahila Mahiti Kendras* (MMK), required group ingenuity to start and quickly multiplied across the two districts by the replicating the same learning by observing and applying methods that SSP had fostered. As women's demand for information centres grew, SSP arrived at a formula by which local women's groups would identify and negotiate for the necessary land, provide the labour and some of the materials and raise funds locally. In turn, SSP would match a part of the funds collected for construction and provide training in construction techniques.

Since the Maharashtrian earthquake rehabilitation programme officially came to a close, the women's groups have sustained a high degree of activism in local development projects and in local governance. In Belwadi, where poor families were frequently keeping their children, particularly girls, out of school, the savings and credit groups began supporting an education campaign that provided girls with loans for bus fare, books and school uniforms. By the end of the campaign, all the girls in the village were attending school. The women's group in Kajala collaborates with local council members on community sanitation and other development projects. Throughout the village, signs remind residents to keep the village clean. A common washing area and a garden of medicinal herbs have been established. Residents claim that cleaning up the village resulted in a significant reduction in the incidence of malaria.

Women's Work through The Foundation for the Support of Women's Work (KEDV) in Turkey

Turkey is at high risk for earthquakes, which account for the majority of damage caused by natural disasters (UNCHS 2000). More than 90 per cent of the country's total surface area is at seismic risk. Two earthquakes, rated as 7.4 and 7.2 on Richter scale, which hit the Marmara region on 17 August and 12 November 1999, were the strongest ever experienced in Turkey. They occurred in the most densely urbanised and industrialised region of the country, located adjacent to the Istanbul Metropolitan Area, where 23 per cent of the country's population and 47 per cent of Turkey's gross national product were concentrated and affected. According to official figures, more than 18,000 people died and about 48,900 were injured. About 100,000 housing units were destroyed and 250,000 units received serious to moderate damage. Estimates of economic damage ranged from US$ 5 to 6.5 billion.

In the few hours that followed the first earthquake on 17 August, volunteers and donations started to flow into the area. Even if uncoordinated and inexperienced, volunteers and local people performed most of the immediate rescue work. Government and international rescue teams arrived 72 hours later. By that time, volunteers had accounted for most of the 10,000 people who were pulled out of the rubble; professional teams rescued only about 500 more. Despite a second earthquake that devastated the region 86 days later, the government—supported by an outpouring of international assistance—was able to rebuild the basic infrastructure and provide temporary accommodation for about 800,000 in 121 tent cities. Within 4 to 9 months, about 42,000 prefabricated temporary housing units were completed with support from NGOs and the private sector.

Although the speed with which the prefabricated houses were constructed was admirable, the size, quality and location of the temporary housing proved controversial. No attention was paid to the livelihood needs of the poor, particularly to those of women, so that many families refused to leave their tents because leaving would cause them to lose their food aid and they would have to move far from their sources of income. Rent inflation and evictions in the region drove more poor families to seek shelter in the temporary housing settlements. Even though the majority of small businesses were destroyed and lay-offs of workers continued to contribute to widespread unemployment in the area, the reconstruction programme ignored replacement infrastructure for small businesses. The government chose to focus on brick and mortar solutions and use recovery aid to construct large-scale permanent housing. Furthermore, the housing programme targeted only homeowners; hence many households did not qualify for housing support from the government as they were tenants or without clear legal tenure. Ultimately, a large proportion of the latter group were stranded in temporary housing settlements that were scheduled to be evacuated and shut down immediately after completion of government-sponsored housing units at the end of 2003.

The majority of the homeowners who applied for government assistance (96 per cent) were qualified to receive it. They could choose to either receive credit for reconstruction or apply it towards new permanent housing built by the government. Many families with alternative options took the subsidy and left the area, but the majority of displaced people stayed and sought shelter, first in tent cities and later in the temporary prefabricated housing settlements. While for some homeowners, this plan was an opportunity to improve the quality of their housing or recover some portion of their life-savings, for others, especially for retired people, the government housing repayment plan was burdensome.

On 1 June 2000, the Ministry of Public Works and Housing began construction of 40,000 housing units financed by the Ministry, World Bank and European Council Development Bank credits and private donations. Again, the public did not have the opportunity to participate in decisions about the location, design or construction of these settlements, or about the terms of the repayment scheme. Many of the new settlements were to be located on prime agricultural land and far from city centres. The Ministry's sample survey to determine the types of housing and a few token public meetings held in connection with World Bank financed housing was largely public relations strategies to gain support for predetermined plans. There was public outcry over the selection of developers for government-sponsored construction of permanent housing as some of them were being sued for malpractice and for causing loss of life.

Women Organise Relief in the Tent Cities

Members of KEDV, an NGO established in 1986 by women with grass-roots backgrounds striving to support poor women's community organising, became involved in disaster-relief and recovery efforts right after the earthquake, working as volunteers. First, the staff helped organise a group of volunteers to provide emergency aid, collaborating with the union of local shipyard owners to respond to requests for help from devastated towns. After observing the chaotic conditions in the area, KEDV stopped distributing food and supplies in a few weeks to provide safe and secure community spaces for women and children. Women could play a key role in the relief and recovery process, but to do so they needed a place to come together, share information and offer mutual support. Life had to return to normal as quickly as possible so that they would not become disaster victims dependent on outside aid.

KEDV first met with local women, NGOs and government officials to determine the most appropriate sites for the new centres in tent cities, seeking campsites that accommodated the largest number of poor families, with cooperative camp administrators and sites that might be sustained for the longest periods of time. KEDV's ongoing partnership with the Social Services and Child Protection Administration (SHÇEK) and a protocol signed with its regional administration helped to quicken the bureaucratic procedures for obtaining access to space. Four new tents were bought to be used as women's centres, and SHÇEK provided some tents for children, mobile toilets and cabins for storage and office/dormitory space for staff. Additional shipping containers donated by private companies were converted into rooms for childcare. Thus, within 2 weeks, the first four Women and Children Centers were set up in the makeshift world of tent cities in Izmit, Golcuk and Adapazari provinces. Within days, local women appropriated the tents as 'public living rooms' and work spaces. They cooked, received guests, made new friends, held support group sessions, discussed the relief programmes, met with journalists, organised exchange visits to Istanbul and started making plans for the future. Soon the tents were housing several income-earning schemes, a priority for women.

In late fall, KEDV was able to negotiate a contract with the Ministry of Tourism to produce toys at the centres. According to the protocol, 300 women produced 750 dolls each week; KEDV coordinated the production activities and the ministry purchased and marketed the dolls. Over a 5 month period, the 300 women who participated in the project produced more than 10,000 dolls and shared earnings of approximately US$ 11,000. Beyond generating much needed income, this project introduced most of the women to the collective production process, helped them to get to know each other better and plan future collective initiatives. It also served as a practical way for most women to overcome the trauma resulting from the disruption of their lives.

In the meantime, KEDV was able to secure funding from NOVIB (Oxfam, The Netherlands) and the American Jewish World Service to set up eight Women and Children Centers in the temporary housing settlements under construction. Their construction required another round of meetings with officials and several site visits to firstly identify settlements with the largest number of poor families, and second, sites that would stay around the longest and located close to the existing centres. Since at this point the authorities were familiar with KEDV's work, securing space was easier, and construction of the centres began in some of the largest settlements in the three provinces.

Women and Children Centres in Temporary Housing Settlements

The move from tent cities to prefabricated temporary settlements marked the transition from the relief to the recovery phase of the post-disaster intervention. Because humanitarian relief efforts were no longer needed, most of the local and international NGOs began to leave the earthquake area. The cooperative attitude that had existed between the public and the NGOs during the relief phase eroded. Only those NGOs with resources and a long-term mission continued to work in the area during recovery and reconstruction.

The women who had moved into temporary prefabricated housing settlements in winter again found themselves isolated. This was at least the second time that the women had to move after they had lost their homes. Separated from their neighbours and friends in tent cities, the women had to look for ways to improve their situation. Living conditions in the overcrowded, hastily built prefabricated housing units were difficult. The settlements suffered from frequent infrastructure problems, lacked basic social services and the barrack-style layout of buildings provided no informal gathering spaces for women. Along with widespread unemployment, social problems (including alcoholism and domestic violence) began to escalate. Tension grew, first, among homeowners who qualified for government housing credits and renters who did not; and second, between residents and the settlement administrations as a result of constant infrastructure problems, favouritism in the allocation of larger units, and so on.

Within this context, the Women and Children Centers became the only source of community information and services in the settlements. As the initial shock of the disaster wore off, the women began to focus on their long-term economic and housing needs. Employment and income generation became a critical concern. As the doll-making project ended, KEDV involved some groups of women in the production of toys and educational materials, while other groups developed their own products, such as household items and candles. The women organised teams to sell their products to local merchants, secured downtown stores from municipalities and succeeded in obtaining stalls at two national chain department stores. With funding and technical assistance from CIDA and the Vancouver-based International Center for Sustainable Cities, several women learned to make recycled paper, while others took up the non-traditional skill of carpentry. Two of the centres set up their own woodworking workshops where the women made wooden toys and screens for windows and doors, which were in great demand in the settlements. They also explored ways to partner with local institutions to enhance their skills.

Another major concern that preoccupied women was earthquake-safe housing. A summer visit from SSP members from India helped women envision what they could accomplish. By late summer, with KEDV staff, they organised weekly community meetings on housing issues, attended by hundreds of women, and even a few men. At each centre, a core group of determined women began to meet regularly to discuss strategy and take action. They selected two women as community-outreach workers to organise and facilitate meetings, take notes, disseminate information and arrange for meetings with local authorities. The groups also began going door to door to collect information on the status of fellow residents in terms of their housing subsidies, livelihood concerns and settlement-related problems. The women mapped facilities and resources at their settlements and other information they gathered (vacant units, tenant households, families with young children and/or disabled persons, and so on). This information, which the government did not have, provided the women with an asset they could use in negotiations with the government and made them feel empowered.

Three women from each centre attended biweekly (fortnightly) regional coordination meetings with KEDV staff to discuss their progress, findings, obstacles, strategies and next steps, and identified local experts (lawyers, engineers and developers) to invite to the centres to explain basic rules for safe construction and issues related to eligibility for government programmes. They strategised about the order in which to visit the local agencies and authorities and prepared questions to ask that they divided up among themselves, so that everyone would have a chance to talk during the meeting. Each group organised visits to local agencies and the construction sites of the new permanent housing being built by the Ministry of Construction and Resettlement. When one group discovered construction errors in new permanent housing blocks in their district, the women grew increasingly concerned about the government's selection of developers, the fact that no public agency was prepared to take responsibility for establishing safe building and repair standards, and the fragmented information they received at World Bank meetings. Over time, the women began developing their own sense of credibility and standards for evaluating the government's accountability. They warned their peers from other centres to be vigilant and to keep good records. Meanwhile, because the government programme did not address their housing needs, groups of tenant women began exploring and developing their own housing cooperatives linked to savings groups.

As women experienced the benefits of acting together as a group, the centres reached out to collaborate more with each other and going to meetings with local authorities together. They exchanged the names and numbers of experts and officials who were helpful, and groups farther along in the process began to help others, participating in their weekly meetings and sharing information, experiences and strategies. At the same time, attitudes within local households started to change and become more supportive of women's activities.

Group discussions of shared-concerns encouraged the women to push so that their priorities related to housing, social services and livelihoods would appear on the local agenda. Recognising that this would be a long-term process, the importance of staying together and sustaining their centres became clear. They began to take the necessary steps to establish a formal identity as autonomous women's groups, so that they could continue their negotiations with authorities and access resources on their own. With support from legal experts and KEDV, the women explored different organisational formats and decided on cooperatives as the most suitable structure for their needs and purposes.

Meanwhile, a 6 year protocol signed between KEDV and SHÇEK in 2001 allowed grass-roots women's groups, beyond the emergency conditions of the disaster region, to set up and govern their own community childcare centres without having to hire an expert administrator. Therefore, this protocol was also an important step towards mainstreaming the establishment of community-run childcare centres throughout Turkey that would be monitored and assessed by KEDV and SHÇEK to develop proposals for legislation to disseminate the model. By early 2003, six of the eight Women and Children Centres were consolidated as autonomous service–production cooperatives.

Also by 2003, housing cooperatives were established by about 200 women from the three provinces, who began looking for funding and negotiating with the authorities for allocation of land for their cooperatives, an effort that required vigilance and ongoing negotiations with authorities. Moreover, small groups of leaders participated in regional and international peer exchanges in Bulgaria, India and South-east Turkey, and more recently in Bam, Iran. These meetings gave women confidence to act as grass-roots experts on micro-finance schemes, housing processes, information gathering and on the establishment and operation of Women and Children Centers.

Sharing Skills and Experience across Borders

Women's groups that participate in emergency relief, resettlement and reconstruction efforts following a natural disaster acquire significant knowledge and expertise that can greatly benefit communities that subsequently experience similar crises. When mechanisms are established for promoting the transfer of this knowledge from community to community, poor women are enabled to come out of their homes and form groups to assess their situation, organise and participate in decisions and programmes that shape their immediate and long-term futures. When disasters strike, the opportunities to decrease women's marginalisation arise early on, when norms of social control and male-dominated family structures are temporarily disrupted and weakened by the chaos that ensues. If affected women can meet and benefit from the experiences of other women who have managed to deal successfully with disaster-related issues, much valuable time can be saved and mistakes avoided. The aftermath of the earthquake in Gujarat in 2001 is one example where local women benefited from the help of their peers from Maharashtra and from the experiences of the Turkish women from the Marmara region.

A powerful earthquake struck the Indian state of Gujarat in late January 2001, leaving nearly a million families homeless. The Kutch region, accounted for 90 per cent of all deaths and almost an equal share of all destroyed assets. The Kutch region had 'high levels of social and economic vulnerability and fragility even in "normal" times' (Martin 2003: 14). A tardy government response required survivors to mobilise relief and recovery efforts on their own, and a number of Gujarati women quickly sprang into action, summoning doctors, pulling children from the debris and rescuing animals. Nevertheless, their initiatives were largely invisible.

SSP worked with local and external NGOs such as Anandi, Hum and Oxfam India to build women's capacities and create livelihood activities. Collaborating with the Society for the Promotion of Area Resource Centres, SSP offered solidarity by soliciting corporate, international and relief agency money to help affected communities organise themselves. Pushed by the women's collectives in Maharashtra, SSP staff travelled with experienced leaders from these groups across the villages of Gujarat to determine how their post-disaster experience could be useful. Within several months, they were providing support to community initiatives in more than 200 Gujarati villages in Jamnagar, Kutch and Rajkot districts in collaboration with several NGOs and SSP partnered district administration.

SSP started out by supporting community-to-community exchanges between leaders from Maharashtra savings and credit federations and affected women in three Gujarati districts. The exchanges enabled experienced women leaders to help their neighbours analyse their own situation and decide upon effective actions that could be taken. For example, they helped Gujarati women map the degree of damage the earthquake caused and shared stories of how they had coped and organised themselves to improve their living and working conditions. This gave Gujarati women, more confined by caste and religious barriers than their visiting sisters, a vision of how they could justify participating in community recovery and work together across social differences.

Soon, the government, armed with more than US$ 300 million from the Asian Development Bank and the World Bank, moved in to repair and strengthen more than 700,000 houses, construct dwellings for the homeless and rebuild core infrastructure. Stalled entitlement applications, bribe taking and faulty repair and reconstruction processes repeated themselves in earthquake-devastated villages across Gujarat, replaying the Maharashtrian experience. When experienced grass-roots leaders visited their struggling peers, they urged them to determine who was taking bribes, where bottlenecks existed in accessing entitlements and repair materials and to decide how they would confront these problems collectively and sustain their action.

One year after the earthquake, women leaders from the Marathwadi (India) and Marmara (Turkey) regions, coordinated by SSP, met with Gujarati women to help them evaluate whether the recovery programme was meeting their needs. At a public meeting with local officials, they listened as Gujarati women described how the scarcity of water and other development challenges in this drought-prone, conservative region, were interfering with the repair and reconstruction process.

Adapting Empowerment Strategies

Despite their widespread poverty, the Gujarat villages where SSP worked had no active savings and credit groups. Initially, the Gujarati women resisted the idea of forming such groups, claiming they were uneducated and would not know how to operate as a group or handle money; some anticipated that men would forbid them to participate. However, after repeated visits, meetings and study tours to observe the savings and credit groups in Latur and Osmanabad, the Gujarati women agreed that they could start the process of saving and lending together. For every step, the Gujarati women took out of their homes, their appreciation grew for how the Maharashtrian women had created tools to make their groups a permanent part of public life and development processes in their villages. From their numerous exchange visits, they soon became curious about the 'whys' and 'hows' of building—from repairing and strengthening their homes to constructing the MMK. SSP helped train Gujarati women in construction methods once households were able to gain access to their payments. Although women's restricted mobility shaped the ways in which they participated, nevertheless, Gujarati women used the information and training they had received to become involved. Numerous village women worked in construction and supervised the masons to make sure that they were incorporating earthquake-safe features in the construction.

To establish MMKs, women organised the work into five committees: a water committee responsible for ensuring that water is available for construction; a purchasing committee responsible for checking the prices and quality of construction materials before buying them; a materials committee responsible for keeping records of the materials coming in, the amount used and for informing the purchasing committee when more materials are needed; an accounts committee responsible for recording the amounts spent daily on construction and a supervisory committee responsible for the overseeing construction, recording the masons' work and all other daily construction activities and ensuring that masons use appropriate, earthquake-safe building techniques.

Participating women have been eloquent in expressing how these processes have helped them learn to plan, solve problems and negotiate and monitor planning and construction. A MMK in a village, be it in Maharashtra or in Gujarat, symbolises an important milestone in the learning process of local women. These multi-purpose centres house the activities of women's groups from as many as fifteen surrounding villages and testify to the ability of women working collectively to acquire land, mobilise labour, materials and monies and to build and manage new community structures. Moreover, when women's groups can establish their own building, with their name on it, they acquire new status in their village.

Conclusions and Recommendations

The case studies of the SSP and KEDV experience highlight how post-disaster situations can be opportunities to empower women at the grass-roots level, build more resilient communities and initiate long-term social change and development. They also suggest principles of effective NGO practice for how to partner with affected women's groups, capture the momentum in the region early to integrate women's participation in post-disaster efforts and scale up and sustain their energy over the cycle of relief to reconstruction.

In India, SSP began by negotiating with the government to secure the appointment of women as communication intermediaries, placing them at the centre of reconstruction processes. The women's groups underwent training to take on this role. Over time, women acquired the confidence and skills to become community development inter-mediaries, monitoring basic services, voicing women's priorities in their communities, initiating local development projects and facilitating dialogues between their communities and government officials. Training of public agency staff concerning community and women's participation was also critical in ensuring the success of this process. As a result, 250,000 households were involved in earthquake-safe construction in Gujarat and Latur. As 4,000 women and families took loans, 1,200 women started businesses, and livelihoods and assets were stabilised. Communities organised for long-term development. Today, more than 800 women's groups work on health, education, water and sanitation in their communities.

In Turkey, KEDV used a different entry point for women's partici-pation. It began by creating public spaces for women and their children as a way to legitimise and sustain women's participation in the public sphere and to rebuild disrupted community networks. The Women and Children Centers provided women's groups a place to meet, organise, learn new skills to start individual and collective businesses and gather and share information on the reconstruction process. The centres also gave women's groups legitimacy in their dialogue and negotiations with officials. Since the beginning of the relief phase, over 10,000 women and their children have participated in various activities at the centres. Women's groups, organised as independent service and production cooperatives, assumed control of the centres, started numerous savings and credits groups and collective and individual businesses and more than 100 women organised around tenant housing cooperatives to seek a solution to their housing problems.

Both SSP and KEDV used peer learning exchanges among local women's groups as a capacity-building strategy. This approach promoted the rapid expansion of effective practice and demonstrated that women can function at the grass-roots level as technical assistants to one another. An unexpected outcome is the eagerness and effectiveness of women's groups to provide support and guidance to other women's groups in areas experiencing disasters.

Some Lessons Learnt

The case studies underscore the conventional attitudinal and operational approaches to post-disaster programming that must be overcome to support women's grass-roots organisations' initiatives. Some of these are derived from the tension between emergency and development approaches; others are related to biases about gender roles and professional expertise.

First, despite the lip service paid to disaster reduction and sustainable development, policy makers often fail to realise that post-disaster efforts are, in fact, development interventions that should reflect principles of participation and sustainability. Short-term disaster-response programming favours technical responses that favour outside professionals' involvement over the priorities, skills and knowledge of affected citizens. Standardised, top–down, bricks-and-mortar type government programmes ignore the complexity of the communities' needs in rebuilding their lives and livelihoods.

Second, even when the importance of local communities' participation is recognised, often no clear agreement exists about what this participation should entail in relation to the roles of the different stakeholders and the lack of communication and coordination wastes a sizeable share of the resources flowing into the area. International aid efforts, concentrated on emergency relief, frequently foster dependency, competition and corruption.

Third, relief and recovery efforts ignore the gender-specific impacts of disasters and generally target male-headed households as the primary claimants for support. This approach ignores women's dramatically increased burden to keep their families and communities together, the income-generating roles women do and must play and their joint claim on family assets. These biases substantially undermine prospects for household and community recovery.

Fourth, there are widespread misconceptions about women's groups at the grass-roots level as being small-scale, passive and low tech, despite considerable evidence to the contrary (Batliwala 2001). The case studies indicate that grass-roots efforts can, if supported, rapidly mobilise a critical mass of actors. Women can acquire non-traditional skills and take on information-giving roles often considered to be the male domain, overcome male opposition and scepticism, and take on active leadership to rebuild their communities. Reducing the economic vulnerability of women and of their families is a key mitigation measure that reduces potential losses from future disasters.

Lessons learned from the case studies also include a set of good practice principles that could redirect post-disaster programming towards gender-equitable, community development opportunities. First, donors and international emergency aid agencies must broaden accountability measures for aid to reward efforts that reduce social vulnerabilities and foster participatory local development. Guidelines to distribute resources more evenly across the stages of relief to recovery should include holding the powerful relief industry accountable. Distribution and procurement policies should encourage innovative local approaches that recognise the pivotal role that women's groups can play throughout the recovery process. Second, policy and programme designers must establish specific monitoring mechanisms to ensure that women can access resources, participate publicly in planning and decision making, organise and build their capacities to sustain their involvement through the recovery and development processes. Third, the case studies suggest two cornerstones for good programming: creating formal spaces where women's groups can organise to participate in post-disaster efforts and formally allocating resources and roles to groups of affected women to ensure that they can (a) access entitlements in a way that reduces the prevailing gender and class/caste biases; (b) participate in government and donor planning processes to design social, livelihood and housing support services that reduce the household and public work burden of poor women; (c) have equal access to public platforms for ongoing dialogue, negotiations and feedback; (d) collect and disseminate information and (e) claim recognition for their accomplishments and knowledge, and in turn, be resourced to advise their peers in other affected communities when similar disasters strike.

The case studies also suggest that institutional frameworks are crucial in helping to achieve the large-scale participation of women. The state government of Maharashtra was persuaded to make formal spaces available for women's participation available in reconstruction efforts, and it also supported long-term development efforts at the district level. Coupled with the Indian quota system for women's representation in village governments, and the existence of government anti-poverty programmes designed to help rural women, Maharashtrian women's groups were able to organise effectively and at a much larger scale than in Turkey where there were no similar programmes.

Finally, given the significant obstacles to applying a development and gender equity approach to post-disaster investments and programming, the case studies also imply that women's groups in affected communities (and supporting NGOs) benefit from joining networks that connect their experience, publicly highlight their results and link them to key institutions to advocate for policy and programme change.

Acknowledgements

This chapter is a revised version of the pamphlet of the same title produced by the Sustainable Environment and Ecological Development Society. For more information on the partners and activities GROOTS and Disaster Watch, see http://www.groots.org and http://www.disasterwatch.net/index.html.

References

Batliwala, Srilatha. 2001. *Remarks made at the Grassroots Women's International Academy at Habitat +5, New York*. Available online at http://www.groots.org (Accessed on 5 January 2005).

Delaney, Patricia L. and Elizabeth Shrader. 2000. *Gender and Post-disaster Reconstruction: The Case of Hurricane Mitch in Honduras and Nicaragua*. Decision review draft. Washington, DC: LCSPG/LAC Gender Team, The World Bank.

Enarson, Elaine. 2000. 'Gender and Natural Disasters', Employment Working Paper 1. International Labor Organization (ILO) Recovery and Reconstruction Department. Geneva: ILO.

———. 2004. *Making Risky Environments Safer: Women Building Sustainable and Disaster Resilient Communities*. Available online at http://www.un.org/womenwatch/daw/public/w2000.html (Accessed on 24 August 2005).

Enarson, Elaine and Betty Hearn Morrow (eds). 1998. *The Gendered Terrain of Disaster: Through Women's Eyes*. Westport, CT: Praeger.

Fothergill, A. 1998. 'The Neglect of Gender in Disaster Work: An Overview of the Literature', in Elaine Enarson and Betty Hearn Morrow (eds), *The Gendered Terrain of Disaster: Through Women's Eyes*, pp. 11–26. Westport, CT: Praeger.

Martin, Max. 2003. *Women Builders: Breaking Barriers in Earthquake-torn Villages.* Bangalore: Books for Change.

Parasuraman, S. and P. V. Unnikrishnan (eds). 2000. *India Disasters Report.* New Delhi: Oxford University Press.

United Nations Commission on Human Settlements (UNCHS). 2000. *Habitat +5 Draft Report for Turkey.* United Nations Commission on Human Settlements.

16

Work-focused Responses to Disasters: India's Self Employed Women's Association

————•✦•————

Francie Lund and Tony Vaux

Introduction

The Self Employed Women's Association (SEWA) of India was born out of poorer women's need for secure work. SEWA was founded in 1972 by lawyer Ela Bhatt, who was the head of the women's wing of the Textile Labour Association. With a membership of over 690,000 workers in 2004 (Chen et al. 2006: 7), it is now well-known for its Gandhian principle of self-reliance and comprehensive approach to development. SEWA's members are all working women, who may be self-employed or informal wage workers who generally earn less and are in more precarious work than men. From the start SEWA focused on averting the kinds of crises that were a 'normal' part of members' everyday working lives. Its central focus was security because that was what such workers lacked. In its more than 30 years of experience, it has also learnt about responding to more widespread crises. Gujarat state, where the majority of SEWA's members live and work, has been assailed by a variety of disasters in recent decades—droughts, cyclones, earthquake. In the devastating Gujarat earthquake of January 2001 nearly 20,000 people were killed, of whom more women than men constituted the total number of dead.

The purpose of this chapter is to present SEWA's distinctive approach to responding to crisis. We argue that poor working women perceive disaster in a different way from the external agencies—governments and international organisations—who usually lead the response to crisis. For poorer people, the central issue of disaster response is livelihood. For women, an additional central issue is the care of their children and dependants. The responses made by SEWA to women affected by drought and then earthquake demonstrate their position that women are not victims but powerful agents for overcoming disaster and rebuilding more sustainable livelihoods.

SEWA Resources for Disaster Responses

SEWA is a trade union as well as a set of cooperatives, and has built a range of services which help members to secure their livelihoods. There are more than 100 cooperatives—producing, marketing and service cooperatives. Health and childcare services are managed through these cooperatives. Other types of organisations built by SEWA provide support in particular sectors, such as the Gujarat Mahila Housing SEWA Trust, SEWA Gram Mahila Haat, which promotes local marketing and Banascraft, which is a craft retail outlet. The Trade Facilitation Centre focuses on global marketing and trade issues.

In order to achieve economic self-reliance for its members, SEWA has built institutions and programmes that insure against risk or help mitigate disasters when they occur. One of the largest and oldest of these is the SEWA Bank (Shree Mahila SEWA Sahakari Bank Limited), started in 1974. It is run by professional managers; SEWA members, as well as the staff, sit on the board, and the bank is recognised by the Reserve Bank of India. It has borrowing and lending facilities, and its hours of opening and style of operation are geared to the needs of its customers. The bank is key to the existence and growth of SEWA's Integrated Insurance Scheme called Vimo SEWA (see Chatterjee and Ranson 2003; Dayal 2001; ILO 2001; Jhabvala and Subrahmanya 2000). Starting in 1977 in partnership with a private insurance firm, members were offered access to simple life insurance. In 1992, the scheme was upgraded to an integrated insurance scheme, including a health insurance component and an assets insurance component. By 2005, Vimo SEWA had more than 100,000 members.

Some of the confidence of SEWA members in responding to disasters arose from having savings and insurance policies that protected them against the most immediate problems. There was a rapid release of savings to those who wanted to withdraw them, and most insurance claims were also settled rapidly. Insured members who had lost their houses received only a modest amount (under US$ 100). The amount was small because poorer people can only afford small premiums, but it was a cash input at a time when they might otherwise starve. Other people now began to appreciate the value of savings and insurance. Following the 2001 earthquake, SEWA experienced a huge increase in membership especially in Kutch and Surendranagar, mostly linked to savings and insurance activities.

Focusing on Work and Employment

The main area where SEWA promotes a different view in disaster response is in the importance of employment. Gender is not 'about women' but concerns the unequal allocation of power and resources between men and women at home, in the labour market and in all aspects of daily life. SEWA's values, activities and plans involve women as workers, with a right to self-reliance and full human dignity.

In the normal course of its work, SEWA is guided by eleven questions for its own assessment of its performance. All these questions apply also to and guide its response to disasters (Box 16.1).

Often it is not the immediate destruction caused by disaster that most affects poor people, as they have few possessions to lose. It is the loss of employment that strikes them most deeply. For example, when Ahmedabad was affected by severe floods in 2001, poorer people living in the gullies found their homes were under 2 or 3 feet of water. Aid agencies focused on the damage to houses. Rajiben, a paper picker, saw the problem differently:

> The slums were flooded and many of the houses collapsed. But the real crisis for us was that we had no work. Because of the flood all the garbage was wet .... With SEWA we approached the Municipality and got them to agree to

Box 16.1	SEWA's Eleven Assessment Questions

1. Employment—have our members obtained more employment?
2. Income—has their income increased?
3. Ownership—do they have more assets in their own name?
4. Nutrition—are they (and their families) better nourished?
5. Health care—do they (and their families) have better access to health care?
6. Housing—do they have improved or more secure housing?
7. Childcare—do they have access to childcare, if needed?
8. Organised strength—has the organisational strength of our members increased?
9. Leadership—have more and stronger leaders emerged from our membership?
10. Self-reliance—have they become more self-reliant both individually and collectively?
11. Education—has the education of our members (and their children) improved?

Source: Chen, M., N. Mirani and M. Parikh. 2005. *Towards Economic Freedom: The Impact of SEWA.* Ahmedabad: Self-Employed Women's Association (SEWA).

pay us to clean up our own locality … (Rajiben Parmar, paper picker, *SEWA Annual General Meeting 2002*)

As one can note from the quote, the importance of employment is frequently emphasised in poor people's own accounts of their problems. They also show how other services, such as health, savings, childcare services and housing, are a route to a return to secure work. Many SEWA members became ill after the floods; the SEWA medical team was not seen simply as a health service but as a way of bringing better health so that people could get back to work and be self-reliant again. Also, members did not perceive savings as a way only to procure consumer goods, but as a protection against the times when there might be no work.

The Responsibility for and Right to Compensation

A priority for SEWA has been to change the way that influential external agents such as government and international organisations define disasters and strategic responses to disasters. A starting point is to raise awareness that many so-called 'natural disasters' are foreseeable events, with risks that can be anticipated—and that poorer people cannot alone bear the responsibility for responding to these events.

After the cyclones, SEWA sought to establish a government responsibility to compensate people affected by major disasters, in such a
case where the events are foreseeable and the risks arise from the use of
cheap labour. This followed a similar case made over many years about
people living in the flood-prone slums of Ahmedabad. Given that no
other affordable land and housing are available, poorer people have no
choice but to live in areas which are likely to be flooded. SEWA argued
that government had a responsibility to help when disaster struck,
and that this was not charity but a right. It argued that government
should compensate people not only for their direct losses but also for
the lost income and time taken in rebuilding their homes.

SEWA made a similar case with the drought of 2000. Poorer people
suffered the worst consequences of the drought, but it was the people
who were better off who were more responsible for causing it. Industries
and commercial farmers had pumped huge amounts of water from the
underground reserves. The water table had fallen and in some places salt
water from the sea had then entered the aquifers. The shallow wells of
poorer people went dry. As wealthier farmers with bore wells extracted
more, the water table sank lower and lower.

Thus, one important part of SEWA's overall strategy is to identify
the dynamics of poverty and inequality that lead to the worst effects of
disasters which are nearly always being felt by poorer people, especially
by women.

SEWA's Approach to Earthquake Relief

Just 3 days after the 2001 earthquake, SEWA began distributing materials
to its craft embroidery members. As Gouriben from Bakhutra village
said:

> After the earthquake we sat in a group of about twenty people. Even at night
> we wanted to be together. The embroidery work really supported us. Then we
> made a committee for the village and it took over all the reconstruction. But
> I would like to emphasise that it was our embroidery work that was crucial.
> Every ten days we would get paid. Through that we gained our confidence and
> now we have been able to rebuild our lives. (Vaux and Lund 2003: 279)

SEWA mobilised groups of members in decentralised Spearhead
Teams to take responsibility for particular areas or tasks. In craft

embroidery, there were teams for procurement, production, distribution and marketing as well as support teams for payment, accounting, record keeping and reporting. The concept of these Spearhead Teams, developed during the drought response, was used as the basis for faster expansion that followed the earthquake (Vaux et al. 2001).

SEWA's Renana Jhabvala described at the 2002 Annual General Meeting how important it was that the organisation already had a presence in the area and how quickly it introduced the focus on work:

> Members were already there so they mobilised. Structures were already there. The child centre could start acting as a channel. SEWA could easily set up village committees to respond. There was also a channel to the outside world. And the picture we gave was accurate because of having organisation in the village.... People outside know that food and water are needed. But what comes out of experience is that people need work. They want to get back on their feet. (SEWA 2003)

A noticeable feature of the earthquake response in 2001 was the assertiveness of SEWA members, based on their experience in responding to the cyclones and drought. Immediately after the earthquake, they began travelling around their own villages and nearby areas, and in many cases themselves became leaders of the whole community. In the most devastated areas, people were stunned, and unable to do anything for days. Typically villagers gathered in a single place, afraid to return to their homes. Continued aftershocks added to their sense of fear and insecurity. SEWA members encouraged them to tell their stories of what had happened. They identified people who needed special help and then got them active in making food for the others or collecting wood. In a short training in Ahmedabad just a few days after the earthquake, members learnt more about ways to respond to the emotional consequences of shock. This response to the psychosocial trauma, and preparedness to deal with it, is almost certainly related to the fact that SEWA is a woman's organisation.

Few external agencies had arrived in India so soon after the earthquake, and it would be a further week before they organised relief programmes. SEWA, on the other hand, started early to move from relief to rehabilitation. The return to work led to a requirement for childcare centres so that mothers could have time for the embroidery. These provided not only basic schooling for children but also a range of other activities including monthly weight checking of children, medical check-ups immunisation, mothers' meetings, training for teachers on child development and a place for meetings of all the teachers from the area (SEWA 2001).

Nearly a million houses had collapsed, and household items and clothes were buried in the rubble. For many of SEWA's members, the problem was that they had nowhere to work, nowhere to keep their remaining belongings and nowhere safe for their children. Outside agencies imagined that the need was for 'shelter'. However, no rain was expected for many months and people could keep warm with blankets. The real problem was that they needed a secure base where they could keep children and property. They could not move away from the rubble and needed to keep an eye on their vulnerable children. Their gendered roles and responsibilities determined this awareness of need. The tents and plastic sheets supplied by aid agencies did not really meet this need.

Similarly, when it came to reconstruction, outside agencies designed houses for living purposes only, rather than as places where work, particularly women's work, commonly takes place as well. They devised plans based on urban housing projects, the houses took many months to design and build, and very few were constructed within a year of the earthquake. What was needed was a basic, temporary structure, with four walls, a solid roof and a door that could be locked. The materials could be distributed easily, and when permanent housing solutions were found these could be recycled. If donor agencies had understood this need, far more of these shelters could have been constructed.

It was in the response to the earthquake that SEWA realised most clearly that the ideas generated by its members were different from those of others, especially the external professional agencies. The international agencies preferred to run their own programmes rather than support local agencies, and if they gave money to a local organisation it was according to their own plans and ideas. They treated SEWA as a contractor, expecting the organisation to implement their ideas and write reports in the way they dictated. Most seriously, the international organisations showed little interest in building long-term capacity or reducing vulnerability in the future. At least for the first few months, they focused almost entirely on relief, and some of them never addressed issues of livelihood or recovery at all. Some decided to finish their operations within just a few weeks of the earthquake. The British government's Department for International Development, for example, had set itself a target of spending £10 million within 3 months. On such a timescale, it was impossible to support the kind of programme that SEWA members wanted.

SEWA's view is that the nearer the source of assistance is to the person in need, the more reliable that source of assistance. The typical faults of the international response have been documented elsewhere (Vaux et al. 2001). International agencies failed to link up with and support local organisations, and they relied instead on formal 'needs assessments' conducted by survey. These were generally superficial and often only amounted to a short tour of the area by foreign staff. By contrast, SEWA argues that the accuracy and precision of its response arose because it was already working in the disaster area, and enjoyed relationships of trust with the local people.

SEWA Links Disaster Response to Sustainable Development

One typical government response to scarcity or to disaster is to offer minimal wages on special relief works in the affected areas. Typically, this means clearing the roadsides and digging water-collection pits. Wages paid to the workers may be cut by petty corruption, and the conditions at the worksite are typically very poor. Children are exposed to the blazing heat, perhaps close to a busy road without any supervision. Few of the structures are maintained afterwards and it has been common for labourers to work on the same (failed) project time after time.

In the case of the drought in 2000, SEWA felt that the assistance offered by government could be improved to enhance the skills that its members already had. They suggested to government that instead of digging pits, people could do craftwork, using the traditional skills for which the area was famous. This might enable them to train younger women and develop their skills in marketing. Instead of a battle for survival, the drought could become an opportunity to escape from vulnerability.

SEWA then thought even more broadly. It realised that the root of the problem was not a sudden rain failure; it was the long-term neglect of the interests of the poor in marginal areas. SEWA drew the conclusion that it must work with government to prepare for such events. From 2000 onwards, it began to press government to set up a long-term Livelihood Security Fund that could be mobilised in the early stages of a disaster with minimum delay. It asked for permanent community-based fodder banks to tide cattle owners from periods of plenty to periods of scarcity. And the organisation argued for government to tackle the root causes of the problem by long-term disaster mitigation measures.

It is instructive to look at the details of these longer term proposals to government, all of which were identified by the poorer women members. They recommended a fodder security programme, employment around water conservation, roof rainwater harvesting for every house, the regular supply of water by tankers, better communications for remote villages, plantations for drought prevention with diversification of plants, mobile fair price shops, artisan training, craft activity as a form of drought relief and the necessary inclusion of health and childcare in drought relief.

SEWA's strongest conclusion from the drought work was that disaster relief should be integrated into longer term perspectives of disaster mitigation and prevention. Underpinning all of SEWA's strategic thinking, however, is the knowledge of the importance of organisation of the poorer workers themselves, in order to promote self-reliance:

> SEWA members and organisers strongly believe that it is not solely the responsibility of the government to respond to the immediate needs of the people in a time of crisis. Community-based organisations that involve the key participation of the local people should also be involved in disaster interventions and prevention measures. Because the lives of members are deeply affected they should be active in the planning process. A partnership between grassroots organisations like SEWA and the government are the most effective approach to ensuring sustainable intervention measures that meet the needs of rural communities. (SEWA n.d.: 34)

In the drought and earthquake responses, SEWA worked jointly with government to respond to the drought and the earthquake, for example, by helping officials assess damage and implement drought relief programmes through craftwork. It has also sought to influence the government's relief and rehabilitation policies. At the state level, it was appointed as a member of the Advisory Committee on the Gujarat State Disaster Management Authority. At the national level, it sits on a number of committees including those dealing with rural development, microcredit, environment and water.

Thus, SEWA members are active in representing their own interests in engaging with the wider policy environment. Over the long term, and for other organisations, it must become normal practice that poorer workers create and claim space on national and international platforms. For their part, organisations of informal workers need to strengthen themselves to become strong negotiating partners who are able to effectively represent their own interests.

One strategy used by SEWA is to consistently document its experiences and views so that they are visible to the international community. Another is to engage in well-publicised international debates about issues such as poverty and trade policies and programmes. Some of these policies will have certain predictable effects on poorer people and will reduce their ability to be economically independent. Examples are as follows:

1. International trade agreements which lead to massive retrenchments in certain industries, especially those in which poorer people predominate.
2. International 'development' agreements (for example, the construction of large dams) which will lead to the displacement and destruction of livelihoods of thousands of people.
3. Situations where governments collaborate with the private sector in allowing the labour regulations on safe working conditions to lapse, or to erode, leading to uncontrolled and hazardous working environments even for formal workers.
4. Macro-economic policies which result in a reduction of public spending on education or on the public health sector.

Such economic policies, while not defined as 'disasters', are disastrous for the poor. SEWA activities challenge these policies and highlight the central role of work in the lives of poor women. This promotes risk reduction as surely as their more evident relief and recovery activities in the aftermath of disasters.

Conclusion

SEWA is an organisation focused on women and run by women and its policies reflect the views of poor working women. It has taken some 30 years to build itself, learning from its weaknesses and developing its strengths. It tries to balance the need for long-term self-reliance with the availability of external assistance; it is wary especially of externally imposed plans that do not lead to long-term security for its members.

People's organisations need to represent themselves on commissions, committees and task forces in order to influence the development of pro-poor disaster policies, as well as general policies on the labour market and on social protection. They are experts in understanding disaster and they can be experts in response.

In the case of disaster, organisations that have already been present in affected areas have built structures and networks through which disaster agencies can work. Authentic people's organisations are not there to work for disaster agencies; the latter should seek out ways to assist people's organisations. An immediate start of surveying to assess damage is essential, and the people affected by disaster should play a central and leading role in this. The reconstruction of housing is also an immediate need, but depending on the circumstances, housing needs are simple: for a secure and safe space for storing assets, privacy, the safety of children and for working. Childcare is likewise an immediate and pressing need and can be a medium for the provision of other services such as nutrition, health services, immunisation and for holding general community meetings. Poorer people's own savings and insurance policies, too, when made prior to disaster can be central in enabling people to get back to work. In addition to increased membership, the Gujarat earthquake sparked a steep rise in the demand for savings and insurance facilities, the demand came from non-members who had witnessed SEWA members drawing down their often small assets in the crisis.

We have indicated that SEWA's view of disasters is different from that of many other actors, notably professional international aid agencies. Characteristics of the SEWA approach are its focus on issues of self-esteem and capacity building; it is good at communication; it emphasises emotional support and it is strategically sophisticated. The dominant model, on the other hand, tends to focus on immediate needs, materials and finances, 'results' rather than capacity building and the present rather than the future. The poor are perhaps consulted, but are not usually involved in management. Certainly, the dominant view tends to attract the resources because those in power favour it and may indeed be appropriate where a simple search and rescue response is needed.

Crisis can be turned to opportunity if people are organised, and that opportunity can be the beginning of building more secure and sustainable futures. SEWA's experience demonstrates that the empowerment of poorer people, and especially of poorer women, is an essential first step.

Acknowledgements

We thank the *Journal of Human Development* for permission to reprint this revised version of Vaux and Lund (2003). Initially prepared for the Commission on Human Security, we draw on the reflections of SEWA members at their 2002 Annual General Meeting in Ahmedabad and on Tony Vaux's interviews with SEWA members and others about the SEWA response to the 2001 earthquake (Vaux 2002). We thank Reema Nanavaty, head of SEWA's rural operations, for general guidance and detailed comments on the various drafts of this chapter. We have also drawn on and acknowledge the pioneering work of Mihir Bhatt of India's Disaster Mitigation Institute.

Bibliography

Bhatt, M. 2001. 'Integrating Disaster Mitigation with Social Security', in R. Jhabvala and R. K. A. Subrahmanya (eds), *The Unorganised Sector—Work Security and Social Protection*, pp. 172–79. New Delhi: Sage Publications.

Chatterjee, M. and K. Ranson. 2003. 'Livelihood Security through Community-based Health Insurance in India', in L. Chen, J. Leaning and V. Narasimhan (eds), *Global Health Challenges for Human Security*, pp. 277–300. Cambridge: Asia Center, Harvard University.

Chen, M., N. Mirani and M. Parikh. 2005. *Towards Economic Freedom: The Impact of SEWA*. Ahmedabad: Self-Employed Women's Association (SEWA).

———. 2006. *Self-employed Women: A Profile of SEWA's Membership*. Ahmedabad: Self-Employed Women's Association (SEWA).

Dayal, M. (ed.). 2001. *Towards Securer Lives—SEWA's Social Security Programme*. Delhi: Ravi Dayal.

ILO. 2001. *Women Organizing for Social Protection: The Self-employed Women's Association's Integrated Insurance Scheme, India*. Geneva: International Labour Office.

Jhabvala, R. and R. K. A. Subrahmanya (eds). 2000. *The Unorganised Sector—Work Security and Social Protection*. New Delhi: Sage Publications.

SEWA. n.d. *SEWA Fights Drought—A Documentation on Drought 2000*. Ahmedabad: SEWA.

———. 2001. *SEWA Annual Report 2000*. Ahmedabad: SEWA.

———. 2003. *SEWA Annual General Meeting 2002*. Ahmedabad: SEWA.

Vaux, T. 2002. *Disaster and Vulnerability—SEWA's Response to the Earthquake in Gujarat*. Ahmedabad: AIDMI/SEWA.

Vaux, T. et al. 2001. *Independent Evaluation: The DEC Response to the Earthquake in India* (Three Volumes). Ahmedabad: All India Disaster Mitigation Institute (AIDMI).

Vaux, T. and F. Lund. 2003. 'Working Women and Security: SEWA's Response to Crisis', *Journal of Human Development*, 4(2): 265–87.

17

A Climate for Change: Humanitarian Disaster and the Movement for the Commons in Kenya

————•✦•————

Leigh Brownhill

Introduction: Kenya's Humanitarian Disasters

Poverty in Kenya is a *chronic humanitarian disaster* and its most vicious expression is hunger. One-third of Kenyan children under the age of five are malnourished. In many cases, chronic hunger leads to stunted growth and development. As cobblers' children go barefoot, so in this country of farmers do children go hungry.

The 2007 election disaster was an acute expression of this deeper disaster which sees some 15,000,000 people with insecure tenure in rural areas, whittling away at the 'free' fuel and fodder of the forest; and crowded into slums, measuring living space 'by the handkerchief' (Kaara 3 February 2008). On 2 January 2008, Kenya's President Mwai Kibaki termed the post-election crisis in Kenya a 'humanitarian disaster'. Between 28 December 2007 and the end of February 2008, some 1,500 people were killed and 500,000 people were evicted from their homes.

Those chased from their homes crowded into police station compounds, churches, mosques, schools as well as beside roads, at the edge of forests and on the corners of relatives' small rural plots. The post-2007 election chaos in Kenya was especially disastrous for women. Nairobi doctors, who treated some 500 rape survivors within the first weeks after the election, said that 95 per cent were gang-raped. Scores of women were feared to have been infected with HIV (Mwai 2008).

Women were also key peacemakers. In Kibera, in early January 2008, 200 women joined together across party and ethnic lines to march through the Nairobi slum calling for peace and reconciliation (Kumba 2008). A coalition of women's organisations formed the Kenyan Women's Consultation Group on the Current Crisis in Kenya. In a petition to mediators Kofi Annan, Graca Machel and Benjamin Mkapa, the women drew attention to the fact that during the crisis 'Kenyan women have been at the forefront in community peace building and mediation efforts in the North Rift and other areas'. They recommended, among other steps, comprehensive constitutional reforms that would 'ensure equitable distribution of national resources, gender equality, affirmative action, equal rights for minorities and persons with disabilities including rights to political participation' (Kenyan Women's Consultation Group on the Current Crisis in Kenya 2008).

A Kenyan politician, who in January 2008 led healing circles at a camp for internally displaced people in the Rift Valley, asked the women attendees when they felt they were 'at peace'. The refugees answered that they had peace 'when they are able to provide food, shelter and health to their families, including being able to educate their children' (Ringera 2008). These are among the hundreds of peace initiatives that ordinary Kenyans have launched in early 2008. Behind these initiatives are thousands of long-standing, multi-ethnic, social, cultural, economic, spiritual and political organisations, both formal and informal, founded by women.

Peace is more than the absence of violence. To restore peace is to facilitate the provision of 'food, shelter, health and education' for all, which in turn requires that everyone has secure access to the necessities of life, including a healthy environment. Rooted among the networks of Kenya's 23,000 women's groups are two key social forces that constitute what I call here a 'commoners' movement'. One major source of women's organising in Kenya is the Green Belt Movement. Though founded in 1977 by Wangari Maathai, the Green Belt Movement really took off after the United Nations Women's Conference in Nairobi in 1985. Tree planting was taken up by thousands of Kenya's women's groups, which also entered into wider discussions and actions in five areas: food security, civic education, voter registration, the negative impacts of petrochemical-based agriculture on health and environment and the dangers of genetically modified seeds. The second key social force within the commoners' movement consists of thousands of registered and unregistered citizens' groups that took up issues such as human rights, democracy and debt relief in the 1980s, 1990s and 2000s (Turner and Brownhill 2001). Many of these organisations first came together at the Freedom Corner women's hunger strike of 1992, to which we turn later. Freedom Corner was a critical point of genesis for the commoners' movement as a whole (Brownhill and Turner 2002).

We now turn to a detailed consideration of these two major forces that will help us to assess the power of this commoners' movement to address Kenya's immediate election disaster as well as the country's hunger problem.

Tree Planting for Peace and Climate Justice

Perhaps the most prominent acknowledgement of the wide-ranging humanitarian benefits of the Green Belt Movement's ecological work was when the Nobel Peace Prize was awarded to Wangari Maathai in 2004. In describing their decision, the Norwegian Nobel Committee stated that:

> Peace on earth depends on our ability to secure our living environment. Maathai stands at the front of the fight to promote ecologically viable social, economic and cultural development in Kenya and in Africa. She has taken a holistic approach to sustainable development that embraces democracy, human rights and women's rights in particular. (Norwegian Nobel Committee 2004).

The Nobel Committee recognised that Maathai did not work alone. It is the hundreds of thousands of Kenyan women engaged in Green Belt Movement activities who together constitute what the Nobel Committee rightfully termed 'the best forces in Africa to promote peace and good living conditions'.

The World Bank presented numerous challenges to women's tree planting and environmental initiatives. Beginning in 1980 the Bank encouraged the conversion of food farms to export cash crop plantations in Kenya with development policies, programmes, research, grants and loans. The more that men planted coffee, tea, sugar, flowers and cotton, the less food women were able to produce. In Kenya by the late 1980s, starvation and malnutrition had become endemic. Farmers' focus on export cash crops meant removing land, water and labour from locally defined farming. It also meant more deforestation, agrochemical inputs, soil-compacting tractors, land clearances and depletion, and pollution of water systems. In this way, Kenya's chronic hunger problem has been deeply entwined with ongoing ecological crises. As chronic hunger and climate change competed to devastate East Africa in the 1990s, farmers acted to defend and extend local food production and marketing by strengthening women's groups' focus on farming and local food trade. Central to women farmers' promotion of food farming for local consumption has been the effort to stop deforestation. Farm women's reforestation efforts were bolstered by the activities of the Green Belt Movement.

When women planted trees, they also strengthened their claims to the land. Green Belt ventures further laid the groundwork for the expression of a renewed form of women's power: the power to heal the eroded, compacted and chemically damaged soil. Tree planting and associated activities were adopted by hundreds of women's groups, many of which continued to engage in other types of activities such as merry-go-rounds, or collective savings groups, shared work on each others' farms and collective care for common resources. By creatively combining several of the most pressing needs of Kenya's peasants, the Green Belt Movement engaged hundreds of thousands of rural Kenyan women in expanding and defending their rights to control and protect land on which, by the new millennium, they had planted some 20 million trees.

The subsistence uses of the land that peasant women farmers pursued were, however, direct challenges to local and foreign businessmen who wished to buy forests and clear, 'develop' or sell the land. The cash cropping and other forms of industrial development that ensue, such as carbon trading, have very high opportunity costs, especially in human terms. In Kenya, as in many other locations in Africa, those displaced by industrial development search elsewhere for land on which to secure a livelihood.

As Kenyan women engage in reforestation, they shift agricultural practice towards indigenous bio-diverse and mixed farming systems. Women's reforestation practices and subsistence food production demonstrate an ecologically positive agriculture capable of reversing local climate change and serving the needs of all. This realisation emanates from a collective culture of commoning that is in opposition to the neo-colonial culture of international exploitation and environmental destruction.

Twenty Years at Freedom Corner: Women and the Commoners' Movement

Women engaged in Green Belt Movement activities are integrated into and lend their ecological perspectives to the larger 'commoners' movement. This movement includes organisations promoting, among other goals, constitutional change, land rights for all and subsistence-oriented farming systems focused on self-provisioning, food sovereignty and regional trade. Kenya's commoners' movement, so constituted, embraces peaceful coexistence based not within the existing lop-sided property rights system, but within a newly minted constitutional framework of 'inclusive, comprehensive, participatory democracy' that prioritises the rights of every citizen to the necessities of life, or to 'the commons'. (Kaara 17 January 2008).

The many citizens' initiatives that make up the commoners' movement emerged in fledgling form in 1992 during a women's hunger strike at 'Freedom Corner'. On the morning of 28 February 1992, 12 women, including Wahu Kaara and Wangari Maathai, petitioned Kenya's Attorney General Amos Wako and demanded that he release the political prisoners, hundreds of whom languished in jail. The 12 women went across the street and sat down on blankets at Freedom Corner, in Uhuru Park, at one of Nairobi's busiest intersections, vowing to starve themselves until he acted.

By the fourth day of the hunger strike, 3 March 1992, 10,000 people had gathered from all over Nairobi to join and support the women. President Moi sent in the police. Hundreds of policemen and General

Service Unit soldiers descended on the protesters in the park through clouds of tear gas. Ruth Wangari wa Thungu threw off her clothes and ran towards the police (First Woman 29 May 1996). Her dramatic action, the power of which is rooted in women's capacity to give birth, stopped the police in their tracks. They walked away without shooting. With her daring action, Ruth Wangari established the Mothers of Freedom Corner for the mothers of a whole generation of Kenyans: her nakedness announced that, as a mother, she would rather die than sit idly while her children suffered under the boot of dictatorship.

Each of the women had come to demonstrate on behalf of her own son, husband or brother. But they also came, as hunger striker Wahu Kaara remembers, 'for all Kenyans' because 'we were all in a big prison known as "Kenya"' (Kaara 3 February 2008). By nightfall the police had cleared the park. Within 24 hours, without telephones or broadcast media, all the hunger strikers had reconvened at the All Saints Cathedral adjacent to Uhuru Park. The women were joined by dozens of young people who kept vigil with them. A full year after beginning their protest at Freedom Corner, the women ended their vigil as they had secured the release of 51 political prisoners.

The Freedom Corner hunger strike was an historical turning point for the democracy movement in Kenya. It was the first time in many years that Kenyans were able to come together as one, across every kind of divide, to publically say 'no' to dictatorship and 'yes' to democracy. At its core, the struggle for democracy in Kenya in the 1990s was, as it remains today, a struggle for land. Moi was considered 'undemocratic' not only because he had for so long outlawed all political parties other than the ruling party, KANU. Moi was undemocratic because the policies of KANU denied and overrode the demands and interests of the majority of citizens. It was in the context of citizens' dispossession, hunger and alienation, and corporations' increasing wealth and power, that Kenya's democracy movement gathered force.

The comprehensive, inclusive, participatory democracy that was articulated by thousands at Freedom Corner in 1992 required a whole new legal constitution. In the years that followed, social movement actors worked with politicians to draft one. Mwai Kibaki was elected the president of Kenya in December 2002 on the promise that he would enact a new constitution within 100 days of his inauguration. By March 2004, every chapter of what became known as the 'Wanjiku Constitution' was passed by a two-thirds majority of the government-appointed Constitutional Conference. The Wanjiku Constitution brought the needs and demands of the landless into the legal framework governing the society as a whole. It abolished the colonial system of government-appointed 'chiefs.' It included provisions for the devolution or shift to the bottom of power by establishing local community committees with the power to decide on development priorities in their area. The 10 members of the committees were to be elected and three seats were reserved for women. The Wanjiku draft extended protections of women's rights to inherit land. It specified that Parliament had the power to decide on the acceptance of any loans from external sources. Ultimately, Kibaki rejected the Wanjiku Constitution and extended agreements giving the United States full access to military sites in Kenya (Volman 2008). It is within this shrinking democratic space characterised by increased police powers that the election disaster of December 2007 took place. After two decades of concerted struggle, Kenyan commoners have strengthened their skills, experience, networks and global connections. All these are needed to pull Kenya out of the deep chasm into which it was thrown on 27 December 2007.

Commoners, the Constitution and the Climate for Change for Women

Land and resources, and decision-making power over these common goods, lie at the heart of the twin Kenyan crises. The underlying cause of Kenya's hunger problem and election violence is extreme inequality leading to commoners' lack of secure access to the resources required for life. Until there are fundamental shifts in land and resource use and the support of all is undertaken, hunger will persist and election violence will likely occur again. Will Kenya's parliamentarians introduce the comprehensive changes that are so desperately required?

As the Green Belt Movement has long addressed the climate and environment issues facing *all Kenyans* (and indeed all humanity), so has the wider commoners' movement long discussed and put into practice the social and economic relations of cooperation. To generalise, the good work of Kenya's environmentalists and commoners would also depend upon policies reorienting land use away from flowers and pineapples and towards bio-diverse reforestation and local food farming, along with the redemption of urban ecological spaces, including residential villages (slums) and common resources like Nairobi's rivers. Answers to some of Kenya's toughest problems can already be found within the women-led commoners' movement.

The 2007 election crisis has had one positive outcome and that is the opportunity for the formulation of a new constitution that truly addresses all Kenyans' needs. This 'constitutional moment' is the 'climate for change' of my title. While Kofi Annan has been praised for his part in formulating a peace deal, ordinary Kenyan women also deserve credit. It is in large part due to social movements led by women, for peace, human rights, democracy and the environment, that the 2-month-long conflict in Kenya turned to law making instead of war.

Kenya's commoners' movements wield the power of subsistence, that is, the day-to-day power to keep people alive. This includes feeding and sheltering people as well as offering spiritual uplift, keeping alive the will to resist injustice and nurturing the networks within which to organise peaceful resistance and social transformation. They have the powers of protest and the tactics of land occupations and general strikes. And they are well prepared to employ the tools of constitutional change in order to extinguish, once and for all, the flames of election violence, of hunger and of looming ecological disaster.

As this chapter has shown, Kenyan women are well organised, well versed in the debates and well prepared to help re-envision and re-organise the use of resources—or the commons—in ways that meet the needs of all.

References

Brownhill, Leigh and Terisa E. Turner. 2002. 'Subsistence Trade Versus World Trade: Gendered Class Struggle in Kenya 1992–2002', *Canadian Woman Studies/Les Cahiers de la Femme*, Special Double Issue, *Women, Globalization and International Trade*, Vols 21/22(4/1): 169–77.

First Woman. Interview with Ruth Wangari wa Thungu, Nairobi, 29 May 1996.

Kaara, Wahu, Interviewed by Leigh Brownhill, by telephone, 17 January 2008.

Kaara, Wahu, Interviewed by Leigh Brownhill and Terisa E. Turner, Ottawa, 3 February 2008.

Kenyan Women's Consultation Group on the Current Crisis in Kenya. 2008. 'Women's Memorandum to the Mediation Team', released 25 January 2008, republished in *Pambazuka News*, Issue 340, 30 January.

Kumba, Samwel. 2008. 'Kibera Women in Campaign to Restore Peace', *Daily Nation*, 20 January.

Mwai, Elizabeth. 2008. '1000 New HIV Infections', *The Standard Online*, 29 January.

Norwegian Nobel Committee. 2004. *Nobel Peace Prize 2004*. Press release, Oslo, 8 October. Available online at http://nobelprize.org/nobel_prizes/peace/laureates/2004/press.html (Accessed on 1 February 2008).

Ringera, Karambu. 2008. 'The Heart of the Kenya Violence and Peace', *Pambazuka News*, Issue 341, 31 January.

Turner, Terisa E. and Leigh Brownhill. 2001. 'African Jubilee: Mau Mau Resurgence and the Fight for Fertility in Kenya', *Canadian Journal of Development Studies*, Special Issue, 'Gender, Feminism and the Civil Commons', No. XXII, pp. 1037–88.

Volman, Daniel. 2008. 'U.S. Military Activities in Kenya', *Bulletin of the Association of Concerned Africa Scholars*, 5 January. Available online at http://www.concernedafricascholars.org/080110_volman.php (Accessed on 1 February 2008).

18

Sri Lankan Women's Organisations Responding to Post-tsunami Violence

———•✦•———

Sarah Fisher

This chapter describes some of the initiatives undertaken by Sri Lankan women's organisations to respond to and reduce the risk of violence against women following the 2004 South Asian tsunami crisis. These findings provide insight into the important roles that women's organisations can play in addressing violence against women and linking post-disaster recovery to more equitable long-term development. Previous research shows that violence against women tends to increase in the aftermath of natural disasters and women are known to 'play a vital role in disaster reduction (prevention, mitigation and preparedness), response and recovery' (United Nations Commission on the Status of Women 2002: 12). Yet few studies have examined the exact ways that women organise to mitigate the impacts of gender-based violence (GBV) following disaster.

I begin by exploring some of the factors that help explain the increased risk of violence against women in natural disaster situations and discuss examples of organisational responses. In the next section, the wider study on which my discussion is based is introduced. Following discussion of the initial responses by Sri Lankan women's groups to the tsunami, I discuss a number of activity types undertaken by women's organisations in response to disaster-related violence and consider changes needed to strengthen their capacity to respond to future disasters.

Violence against Women during Disasters and Community Responses

Women's vulnerability to violence is perhaps one of the lesser known and studied gendered impacts of disaster but there is evidence to show that levels of domestic and sexual violence increase during natural disaster situations. Studies of multiple disasters in the developed world, mostly the United States and Canada, have found strong indications of increased domestic violence in disaster-affected communities (Dobson 1994; Enarson 1999a, 1999b; Enarson and Fordham 2001; Enarson and Morrow 1997; Fothergill 1999; Morrow and Enarson 1996). Although detailed research on the phenomena from the developing world is scarce, increases in domestic abuse and other forms of GBV have been observed following natural disasters in countries of the South. These countries include Bangladesh (Kafi 1992 as cited in Ariyabandu and Wickramasinghe 2003), the Philippines (Delica 1998) and Nicaragua (Delaney and Shrader 2000; Solorzano and Montoya 2000).

Many factors may account for the increased likelihood of violence against women in the aftermath of disasters. The trauma, loss and stress caused by disasters are considerable. Several authors note that men are more likely to express anger and emotional suffering destructively through socially dysfunctional behaviours such as alcoholism, aggression and violence (Delaney and Shrader 2000; Wiest et al. 1994). Frustrations and uncertainties associated with economic hardships and struggles to replace housing, jobs and possessions have been found to increase tensions and stress within relationships, sometimes leading to conflict and violence (Enarson 1999a, 1999b). Women's vulnerability to abuse is exacerbated by social dislocation and loss of traditional community support and protection mechanisms (Ariyabandu and Wickramasinghe 2003; Byrne and Baden 1995; Wiest et al. 1994). Isolated or overcrowded post-disaster environments and temporary accommodation centres leave women and children at greater risk of abuse from male inhabitants, including family members. Poorly designed, gender-insensitive interventions increase the likelihood of violence, for example, by leaving women vulnerable to assault when accessing basic facilities such as bathing areas or when carrying out daily tasks, including water collection (Dugan et al. 2000; UNHCR 2003).

Little research has examined community and humanitarian agency responses to disaster-related violence against women. Several studies from North America have addressed preparedness and response to post-disaster violence by communities and pre-established domestic violence organisations. A study by Wilson et al. (1998) exploring perceptions of post-disaster violence in several disaster-affected communities in the United States found that organisational awareness and responses to violence were dependent on community sensitivity to the incidence of domestic violence prior to the disaster. Organisations that had previously defined violence as a problem and provided counselling and shelter services continued to respond in this way following disaster. A study of domestic violence programmes in the United States and Canada by Enarson (1999a) reported that programmes most severely hit by disasters faced increased demand for services while experiencing declining resources. This was also a finding of Fothergill's (1999) enquiry into community responses to violence against women following a United States flood. Enarson (1999a) found that despite low levels of disaster preparedness, shelters responded resourcefully to the greater workload, continuing whatever services possible and undertaking new initiatives related to violence or other pressing needs.

Research focusing on violence against women during disaster highlights the importance of service provision to ensure the safety of women and demonstrates the crucial role that domestic violence organisations play in articulating and meeting the needs of vulnerable women (Enarson 1999a; Fothergill 1999). Gender and disaster literature shows that women and community-based women's organisations display great strength and resilience in coping with natural disasters, and that women's collective mobilisation and relief efforts at the community level are essential for responding to local needs and promoting effective disaster management strategies (Akçar 2001; Ariyabandu 2000; Delaney and Shrader 2000; Pan-American Health Organization 1998). Yet despite this, the active and diverse roles that women and their social networks play in post-disaster response are often overlooked and women are instead viewed as helpless victims. This results in underutilisation of the skills and capacities of women, coupled with the neglect of their specific needs and vulnerabilities (Delaney and Shrader 2000; Scanlon 1998; United Nations Division for the Advancement of Women 2004).

Sri Lanka Case Study

The research presented in this chapter was undertaken as part of a wider study examining the incidence of violence against women in tsunami-affected areas of Sri Lanka and the role of humanitarian organisations in preventing and responding to this violence. Research was conducted in Sri Lanka at multiple locations within the three most affected provinces over a period of three months, beginning approximately four months after the tsunami. The findings therefore reflect the circumstances for the first seven months of the disaster only. Future publications are forthcoming in which the incidence of post-tsunami violence against women and the response of international humanitarian organisations will be examined.

Qualitative data were collected through semi-structured interviews with respondents identified and selected purposely due to their involvement in tsunami-related GBV initiatives. Respondents included staff members from women's and community organisations, non-governmental organisations (NGOs), and international agencies and feminist activists. Additional material was obtained through conducting monitoring work and attending inter-agency meetings on behalf of the Women's Division of the Disaster Relief Monitoring Unit of the Sri Lankan Human Rights Commission. This work permitted observations in displaced settings and conversations with disaster-affected women and men, including camp managers. Select secondary sources complement this research, including documents provided by humanitarian agencies and media reports verified by primary informants and checked for consistency with findings.

Initial Responses to Violence by Women's Groups

The tsunami that hit multiple South Asian countries on 26 December 2004 devastated entire costal areas of Sri Lanka. One of the gendered impacts of the tsunami in Sri Lanka was the increased vulnerability of girls and women to violence (Fisher forthcoming). Reports of rape, gang-rape and sexual abuse occurring in the initial hours and days of the crisis quickly emerged in the media. They included that of a woman pulled from the waves then raped by her 'rescuer' (Senayake 2005), and the sexual assault of a young woman by her grandfather in a makeshift relief centre sheltering the homeless (Associated Press 2005). Although media coverage of incidents ceased after the immediate aftermath, the violence did not. Violence against women, in particular domestic violence, continued in the camps and temporary shelters housing the displaced well beyond the initial emergency phase of the disaster (Fisher forthcoming).

Sri Lankan women's organisations were quick to intervene in the crisis and respond to reports of violence against women. They mobilised funds and distributed essential items, including items for women overlooked by other relief agencies such as sanitary towels and underwear. Visiting relief centres and speaking with members of affected communities they listened to women about their concerns, identified pressing needs and offered support and assistance to state and non-governmental agencies to help ensure that needs were met.

During the first weeks of the crisis, a collective of over 60 women's organisations including groups from each of the tsunami-affected districts formed the Coalition for Assisting Tsunami Affected Women (CATAW). CATAW established a fund to finance the work of its member organisations to protect and promote the rights of women in post-tsunami reconstruction and rehabilitation and strengthen community-based women's initiatives (IWRAW-AP 2005). Soon after the tsunami, CATAW members visited affected regions on fact-finding missions and investigated safety issues for women. In press releases highlighting concerns, CATAW confirmed 'incidents of rape, gang-rape, molestation and physical abuse of women and girls' (CATAW 2005a: 18) and reported a lack of security provision in camps (CATAW 2005b: 20). Demands for preventative action and recommendations to ensure the safety of women were made. These included the establishment of a monitoring body and mechanisms to receive, investigate and respond to reports of abuse, and the issuing of gender-sensitive guidelines to security forces and camp officials (CATAW 2005a, 2005b). CATAW's exposure of incidents so early in the crisis was critical for raising awareness of the potential for tsunami-related violence and focusing attention on the issue. This was a catalyst for some preventative measures, including the deployment of police and army personnel to camps for security provision.

Women's groups also made efforts to improve the conditions in camps that were creating environments in which women and girls were susceptible to sexual harassment and abuse. Advocacy initiatives appealed for gender-sensitive facilities to prevent invasions of women's privacy and reduce the risk of sexual attacks. These included separate, covered bathing areas and latrines, adequate lighting and attention to the location and layout of temporary accommodation centres and spacing of facilities. In some cases, women's organisations covered bathing and changing areas themselves. Many groups called for adherence to minimum standards for humanitarian intervention and appealed to agencies to incorporate violence-prevention methods into interventions. In addition to consciousness raising about safety issues, women's groups increased awareness of the overall specific and diverse needs of women, such as those of single, pregnant and breastfeeding women, as well as those of other disadvantaged and less-visible groups.

Women's Initiatives to Prevent and Respond to Violence

Throughout the rehabilitation and reconstruction process, women's groups undertook diverse measures and approaches to respond to disaster-related violence. The women's organisations found to be working on programmes directly related to post-disaster violence tended to be those carrying out violence-related work prior to the tsunami. So while some initiatives were specific to the disaster situation, others were linked to pre-existing programmes.

Monitoring, research and information gathering and dissemination were activities in which women's organisations played a significant role. Surveys and needs assessments by women's groups supplied gender-disaggregated data lacking from governmental assessments, providing findings on gendered impacts, needs and rights violations. This identified gaps in assistance and formed an evidence base to inform advocacy initiatives and policy and programme development. A number of these initiatives were financed or commissioned by UN agencies and fed into wider programmes.

District and local level alliances and networks of women's organisations were formed in several areas, in addition to the national coalition CATAW. The most prominent of these was the Women's Coalition for

Disaster Management (WCDM) in Batticaloa, Eastern Province. The coalition consisted of a group of women's organisations with a strong background of gender and human rights activism, including perhaps the most vibrant Sri Lankan feminist organisation, Suriya Women's Development Centre. International and governmental agencies were also represented on the coalition and a 'Gender Watch' network was formed consisting of WCDM members, female representatives and local action groups initiated in tsunami-displaced communities. Gender Watch met weekly to monitor and address inadequacies and abuses of women's rights in the relief and reconstruction process. Issues, incidents and remedial action points were documented in Gender Watch reports, in which violence against women was a reoccurring theme. Resultant action included provision of legal aid and support to access police and health services, intervention by local groups in response to violations by a government officer and preventative measures and assistance to protect children and women at risk of abuse (WCDM 2005).

Advocacy interventions and liaison with agencies and service providers played a significant part of the response by women's organisations to post-tsunami violence. These efforts sought to increase awareness of protection needs and promote the mainstreaming of safety and other gender-specific concerns throughout reconstruction programmes. In this regard, the WCDM and Gender Watch were very effective. The coalition issued memoranda to the government and district operational committee setting out specific demands and policy recommendations. Local groups and representatives played an integral part of the coalition, identifying concerns for redress. For example, insensitive distribution of relief was identified as exacerbating conflict between partners because men were selling excess items to purchase alcohol. In response, the coalition carried out initiatives to sensitise agencies, officials and camp managers to the gendered implications of aid distribution and the necessity of prior needs assessments and responsible distribution methods (WCDM 2005). Other women's groups also acted to reduce the impacts of alcohol consumption. The Affected Women's Forum campaigned against illicit alcohol sales, successfully lobbying local government to prohibit the sale of alcohol inside camps.

Multi-sectoral GBV networks developed reporting and referral systems for the prevention and management of violence and collectively provided essential support services. Several networks of this kind were initiated prior to the tsunami, mostly by international agencies, which continued this work in the post-tsunami context. In Batticaloa, the WCDM worked with a pre-existing network called the 'Gender Based Violence Taskforce' comprising international agencies, local organisations, government officials and service providers, such as health professionals and lawyers. The taskforce maintained a database of incidents managed as part of the Gender Watch meetings. Some months after the tsunami, a Violence Against Women sub-committee of the WCDM was formed to establish response mechanisms.

Case work and crisis intervention were undertaken by women's organisations with the experience of violence against women work, as well as by GBV networks. Several groups of this kind were identified and found to be carrying out their usual services including legal aid and counselling, as well as new, violence and non-violence-related activities. This included Women in Need (WIN), a well-established national violence against women organisation which had several offices in tsunami-affected areas. In Sri Lanka, there is a drastic shortage of trained counsellors and psychosocial workers (CARE International 2004); yet, following the tsunami, there was a great need to address the psychosocial needs of the affected communities. Women's organisations with this expertise played an important role in meeting demands for trauma counselling, through both direct provision of psychosocial care services and mutual and self-help support strategies.

Facilitation and capacity building of women's groups and committees, and sometimes men's groups, played a great part of psychosocial work. Many organisations initiated groups of this kind to provide forums for women to come together to share grievances and support one another. Some organisations incorporated rights-based education programmes, seeking to increase women's ability to tackle violations by increasing their knowledge and awareness of their rights. Men's and women's groups played a major role in WIN's community work. Prominent community members were trained in leadership and communication skills to enable them to establish groups. Beginning with discussion of problems, goals and ideas, these groups encouraged affected communities to work together proactively to resolve common problems. Like the action groups of 'Gender Watch', in collaboration with WIN, these groups monitored and responded to incidents of violence and other concerns.

Provision of capacity-building training to key agencies and service providers, such as police, security forces, governmental officers and camp leaders, was another widespread approach. This often consisted of 'gender sensitisation' or humanitarian law and protection training, in which GBV was a component. Some of these schemes were already underway prior to the tsunami, yet the need for this work was demonstrated by the behaviour of police and security officers assigned to camps. Having received no specific training or instructions relating to the management of GBV, they saw their role as primarily one of maintaining discipline and were reluctant to intervene in instances of abuse (CATAW 2005b). The common view in Sri Lanka that domestic violence is a 'personal' or 'family' matter prevails among the police and other key service providers (Wijayatilake and Gunaratne 1999), making capacity-building and sensitisation programmes all the more necessary.

Community-based campaigning and awareness-raising initiatives were undertaken by women's organisations to promote long-term behavioural change and challenge harmful and dominant social attitudes contributing to violence. This work was often combined with women's and men's groups in camps. Discussions were facilitated on issues of concern, and to avoid stigmatising these sessions the issue was broached sensitively, for example, through discussion of 'healthy relationships'. Other issues of focus with men's groups were increased alcohol consumption, through 'health promotion' programmes, and child protection issues, through 'good parenting' initiatives.

Innovative social and recreational activities were employed within campaigning and awareness work to break the silence on violence against women. Street theatre, songs and other activities portrayed anti-violence messages to prompt thought and discussion. These creative and resourceful initiatives seized the opportunities awarded by camp life, where large numbers of people were living together with much free time, and entertainment and leisure-based activities generated great interest. These were excellent techniques for reaching the whole community to encourage engagement with GBV and underlying gender inequality issues. The WCDM used the occasion of International Women's Day to increase recognition of the impacts of the tsunami upon women. In a positive manner, celebrations were organised involving artwork, poetry and performances which emphasised the importance of working together in solidarity to equitably rebuild the community.

Media-based campaigning and awareness raising were conducted by the organisation Women and Media Collective. Investigative journalism, posters and radio and TV programmes encouraged gender-sensitive discourse and drew attention to the diverse roles of women in post-tsunami recovery. Rights-based notices placed in newspapers stated: 'Women are key in the process of Sustainable Reconstruction and Rehabilitation—Let women's voices be heard!' Particular attention was paid to women's safety, highlighting the need for prevention of violence and harassment and the inclusion of reproductive health services in reconstruction plans.

Programmes to create and restore women's livelihoods sought to alleviate women's economic marginalisation within the relief process which increased women's dependence on men and vulnerability to violence and exploitation (Fisher forthcoming). In the South, WIN ran a 'women's empowerment project'. Economically disadvantaged women at particular risk of violence were targeted, including women who had lost their families or were experiencing domestic abuse. The programme included a focus on livelihoods and education and also benefited tsunami-affected women living outside of camps who were neglected by governmental assistance and relief distribution channels.

Long-term programmes to provide safe places for women were in the initial stages of development funded by international agencies. These included the establishment of 'women's centres' to provide women affected by or at risk of violence with shelter, holistic treatment and support, and also to serve as meeting places for women. Furthermore, two centres being established by the Association of War Affected Women would support vocational training and income generation activities.

Increasing Women's Participation in Post-disaster Reconstruction

In addition to specific activities undertaken in response to post-disaster violence, women's groups helped to focus attention on GBV and other gender-specific needs by helping to increase the participation of disaster-affected women in recovery. Women's lack of representation in the relief and reconstruction process was a significant concern (Fisher forthcoming). Recognising this as a considerable barrier to gender-sensitive disaster response, women's groups were highly active in promoting inclusive dialogue and gender balanced participation on disaster reconstruction governance structures at local, district and national levels.

Locally, women's membership of camp management committees was severely limited and designated camp managers were predominantly male, meaning that commonly little regard was paid to issues adversely affecting women. Women's organisations therefore lobbied for and facilitated women's representation on camp management committees and at meetings involving humanitarian agencies, state officials and service providers.

Advocacy work also sought to positively influence state and non-governmental agencies. Women's groups organised or fed into multi-sectoral meetings and forums, bringing issues of concern to light in the public arena, providing feedback on policies and offering solutions. Several women's organisations participated in international networks to facilitate information sharing and solidarity with other tsunami-affected countries.

Discussion and Conclusions

These findings from Sri Lanka demonstrate that activism by women's organisations and community-based groups is instrumental to the response to violence against women in the aftermath of natural disasters and other gendered impacts of disaster. From the very first days of the tsunami crisis, the women's movement in Sri Lanka was at the forefront of highlighting the threat of violence against women and gender bias within the relief and reconstruction process. Without women's groups voicing inadequacies and securing a greater role for women in post-disaster recovery, the needs of women and other marginalised groups would have been further neglected. Women's groups showed considerable energy and dedication to rebuilding communities in a way that was responsive to the inequalities on which women's vulnerabilities were based. Their ability to mobilise and foster the strength and endurance of tsunami-affected women for this purpose showed that grass-roots women's organisations are key 'agents of social change' (United Nations Division for the Advancement of Women 2004).

The complex causes of violence against women and factors which increase its likelihood in disaster situations necessitate a wide range of approaches to prevent violence and support those affected by abuse. This was reflected in the variety of initiatives undertaken by women's organisations in response to post-tsunami violence against women. Some of these activities were a continuation of pre-disaster work and others were new initiatives. These findings are consistent with Enarson's (1999a) study of domestic violence programmes in the United States and Canada which shows similarities in the type of anti-violence activities undertaken by women's groups following disaster. Some programmes by Sri Lankan women's groups responded to women's immediate or practical needs for protection. Others attended to women's long-term, strategic needs which cannot be addressed in isolation from violence against women.

The existence of pre-established domestic violence organisations has been shown to be a significant resource driving a community's response to post-disaster violence (Enarson 1999a; Wilson et al. 1998). This was the case in Sri Lanka. For in the South, where there were fewer prominent women's groups and pre-established violence against women programmes (in comparison with the North and East), there were fewer post-tsunami violence initiatives and less overall activism and coordination between women's groups. Experienced and well-established women's groups therefore play an essential role in managing violence in disaster situations and in the overall mobilisation of disaster-struck women and communities. The contextual knowledge and vital understanding of community power relations that local grass-roots organisations have suggests these groups are most able to identify and respond to their community's needs and priorities and to reach those in most need. This is particularly the case in relation to GBV and other culturally sensitive issues. Humanitarian agencies must therefore provide greater assistance and resources to community-based organisations and work more closely with them in all stages of programme development. This should include granting local organisations a greater role in policy identification and formulation. Working in this way is critical for ensuring meaningful local engagement and increasing accountability.

Women's organisations are able to command the greatest visibility and have most impact when they work collectively pooling skills, expertise and resources. This was seen in the broad alliances at the national level with CATAW, and at the district level with the WCDM. The WCDM presents an excellent collaborative model, linking rights-based advocacy work with direct action, rallying, alerting and supporting other humanitarian organisations, service providers and local groups to work together. Coalitions of local and international NGOs offer opportunities for building the capacity of member organisations through the coordination of activities, formation of linkages between actors, and sharing of skills and knowledge (de Alwis and Hyndman 2002). Alliances and cooperative movements such as these are important for the strengthening of civil society and the social networks that are necessary for the promotion of a culture of socially responsible disaster prevention and management. Coalitions should therefore be encouraged and assisted as part of capacity-building programmes in disaster-prone areas.

Violence against women services can be lacking in disaster-affected communities and a significant number of programmes by women's groups sought to increase local capacity to meet the needs of women affected by violence. The inter-agency structures in which women's organisations played an important role are examples of invaluable coordinated approaches necessary to build the long-term commitment and capabilities of state institutions and local service providers to holistically manage GBV. Similarly, the women's centres being established offer sustainable systems of support which have the potential to reduce the impacts of violence against women in times of disaster and otherwise.

Capacity-building work undertaken with disaster-struck women and communities offers the greatest possibilities for women's advancement and reducing women's vulnerability to future disasters. The full and equal participation of women in the planning and implementation of disaster programmes is essential for gender-sensitive disaster management (United Nations Inter-Agency Standing Committee 2006) and where there were active women's organisations in Sri Lanka they played a key role in promoting this. Women's groups not only focused on women's exclusion from established structures within the reconstruction process but also created increased opportunities and alternative spaces for women to assert needs and remedy issues neglected by the relief process. These initiatives brought new opportunities for the tsunami-affected women that women's organisations were able to reach. For many of these women, increased involvement in local governance activities and the process of engaging with agencies, government officials and other community members was an empowering experience. It was the chance to develop new skills and confidence which may bring lasting benefits to themselves and their communities.

For these reasons, disasters can be seen to offer opportunities for transformation of gendered inequalities and power relations (for example,

Delaney and Shrader 2000). To ensure that this prospect is seized and to prevent women from instead being disempowered by post-disaster reconstruction, disaster recovery programmes must support opportunities for women to organise and provide leadership. Sri Lankan women's organisations helped to mitigate post-disaster violence against women and integrated long-term, structural considerations into their response. In doing so they used the disaster to address the low status of women underlying women's vulnerability to violence and other gendered disaster vulnerabilities.

Women's groups play a fundamental role in post-disaster response and are a vital asset for the promotion of sustainable, gender-sensitive disaster management which supports longer term development and gender equity. Greater recognition must be granted to women's organisation for this role. Viewing women as capable stakeholders is necessary to transcend the view of women as passive victims of disasters, which could generate increased support and investments to advance the work of women's organisations. This would allow women's groups to reach larger numbers of disaster-affected women and to rebuild more equitable communities with greater capacity to withstand the impacts of future disasters.

Acknowledgements

This research was undertaken as part of a dissertation submitted to the University of Leeds, UK, for an M.A. in International Studies. The author is extremely grateful for a grant provided by the EU-funded Asia Link Project 'Gender, Development and Public Policy in the Asian Context' between the University of Leeds, UK, and the Asian Institute for Technology in Bangkok, Thailand. Special thanks for all those who participated in this study.

References

Akçar, S. 2001. *Grassroots Women's Collectives—Roles in Post-disaster Effort: Potential for Sustainable Partnership and Good Governance (Lessons Learned from the Marmara Earthquake in Turkey).* Paper prepared for the United Nations Division for the Advancement of Women, International Strategy for Disaster Reduction, Expert Group Meeting on Environmental Management and the Mitigation of Natural Disasters: A Gender Perspective, Ankara, Turkey, 6–9 November. Available online at http://www.un.org/womenwatch/daw/csw/env_manage/documents/EP11-2001Nov07.pdf (Accessed on 5 July 2007).

Ariyabandu, M. 2000. *Impact of Hazards on Women and Children: Situation in South Asia*. Intermediate Technology Development Group. Paper Presented at 'Reaching Women and Children in Disasters' Laboratory for Social and Behavioural Research, Florida International University, June 2000. Colombo, Sri Lanka: ITDG South Asia. Available online at http://gdnonline.org/resources/ariyabandu_paper.doc (Accessed on 20 June 2005).

Ariyabandu, M. and M. Wickramasinghe. 2003. *Gender Dimensions in Disaster Management—A Guide for South Asia*. Colombo, Sri Lanka: ITDG South Asia.

Associated Press. 2005. 'Fears of Rape Haunt Women in Lankan Tsunami Relief Camps', *Lanka Newspapers*. Available online at http://www.lankanewspapers.com/news/2005/1/151.html (Accessed on 5 February 2005).

Byrne, B. and S. Baden. 1995. *Gender Emergencies and Humanitarian Assistance*. Bridge Report Number 33, Commissioned by the WID Desk, European Commission, Directorate General for Development. Sussex, UK: Institute of Development Studies. Available online at http://www.bridge.ids.ac.uk/dgb4.html (Accessed on 1 September 2005).

CARE International. 2004. *Towards a Rights-based Approach to Ending Gender-based Violence—A Batticaloa Perspective*. Policy and Networking Report 2004, Gender-Based Violence Project CARE East, Batticaloa, Sri Lanka.

CATAW. 2005a. 'Women's Groups Appeal for an Inclusive Framework for Disaster Response', (Press Release, 1 January), *Options*, 3(6): 18–19.

———. 2005b. 'Gender Specific Issues Relating to Post-tsunami Displacement' (Press Release, 15 January), *Options*, 3(6): 19–22.

Delaney, P. L. and E. Shrader. 2000. *Gender and Post-disaster Reconstruction: The Case of Hurricane Mitch in Honduras and Nicaragua*. World Bank Draft Report. Available online at http://www.gdnonline.org/resources/reviewdraft.doc (Accessed on 11 June 2006).

Delica, Z. G. 1998. 'Balancing Vulnerability and Capacity: Women and Children in the Philippines', in E. Enarson and B. H. Morrow (eds), *The Gendered Terrain of Disaster: Through Women's Eyes*, pp. 225–31. Westport, CT: Praeger Publishers.

de Alwis, M. and J. Hyndman. 2002. *Capacity-Building in Conflict Zones: A Feminist Analysis of Humanitarian Assistance in Sri Lanka*. Colombo, Sri Lanka: ICES.

Dobson, N. 1994. 'From Under the Mud-Pack: Women and the Charleville Floods', *Australian Journal of Emergency Management*, 9(2): 11–13.

Dugan, J., C. J. Fowler and P. A. Bolton. 2000. 'Assessing the Opportunity for Sexual Violence against Women and Children in Refugee Camps', *The Journal of Humanitarian Assistance*. Available online at http://www.jha.ac/articles/a060.htm (Accessed on 7 February 2005).

Enarson, E. 1999a. 'Violence against Women in Disasters: A Study of Domestic Violence Programs in the United States and Canada', *Violence Against Women*, 5(7): 742–68.

———. 1999b. 'Women and Housing Issues in Two U.S. Disasters: Hurricane Andrew and the Red River Valley Flood', *International Journal of Mass Emergencies and Disasters*, 17(1): 39–63.

Enarson, E. and M. Fordham. 2001. 'Lines that Divide, Ties that Bind: Race, Class, and Gender in Women's Flood Recovery in the US and UK', *Australian Journal of Emergency Management*, 15(4): 43–52.

Enarson, E. and B. H. Morrow. 1997. 'A Gendered Perspective: The Voices of Women', in W. G. Peacock, B. H. Morrow and H. Gladwin (eds), *Hurricane Andrew: Ethnicity, Gender and the Sociology of Disasters*, pp. 116–40. London: Routledge.

Fisher, S. Forthcoming. 'Violence against Women and Natural Disasters: Findings from Post-tsunami Sri Lanka', *Violence Against Women*.

Fothergill, A. 1999. 'An Exploratory Study of Woman Battering in the Grand Forks Flood Disaster: Implications for Community Responses and Policies', *International Journal of Mass Emergencies and Disasters*, 17(1): 79–98.

International Women's Rights Action Watch Asia Pacific (IWRAW-AP). 2005. *Appeal to Support a Women's Fund Set up by the Coalition for Assisting Tsunami Affected Women (CATAW) in Sri Lanka*. Available online at http://www.iwraw-ap.org/womens_fund. htm (Accessed on 17 February 2005).

Morrow, B. H. and E. Enarson. 1996. 'Hurricane Andrew through Women's Eyes: Issues and Recommendations', *International Journal of Mass Emergencies and Disasters*, 14(1): 5–22.

Pan-American Health Organization. 1998. 'The Role of Women in Disasters', *Disaster Preparedness and Mitigation*. Available online at http://nzdl.sadl.uleth.ca/cgi-bin/ library (Accessed on 25 June 2005).

Scanlon, J. 1998. 'The Perspective of Gender: A Missing Element in Disaster Response', in E. Enarson and B. H. Morrow (eds), *The Gendered Terrain of Disaster: Through Women's Eyes*, pp. 225–31. Westport, CT: Praeger Publishers.

Senayake, S. 2005. 'Tsunami Survivor's Life Scarred by Rape', *C News*. Available online at http://cnews.canoe.ca/CNEWS/World/Tsunami/2005/01/07/826059-ap.html (Accessed on 5 February 2005).

Solorzano, I. and O. Montoya. 2000. 'Men against Marital Violence: A Nicaraguan Campaign', *ID21 Insights*, Issue 35. Available online at http://www.id21.org/insights/ insights35/insights-iss35-art05.html (Accessed on 4 February 2005).

UNHCR. 2003. *Sexual and Gender-based Violence against Refugees, Guidelines for Prevention and Response*. Available online at http://www.unhcr.org/3f696bcc4.html (Accessed on 10 August 2009).

United Nations Commission on the Status of Women. 2002. *Report on the Forty-Sixth Session, 4–15 and 25 March 2002*. Economic and Social Council Official Records, 2002 Supplement No. 7, E/2002/27-E/CN.6/2002/13. Available online at http://daccessdds.un.org/doc/UNDOC/GEN/N02/397/04/PDF/N0239704. pdf?OpenElement (Accessed on 22 July 2007).

United Nations Division for the Advancement of Women. 2004. *Women 2000 and Beyond: Making Risky Environments Safer—Women Building Sustainable and Disaster-Resilient Environments*. Available online at http://www.un.org/womenwatch/daw/public/ w2000-natdisasters-e.pdf (Accessed on 22 July 2007).

United Nations Inter-Agency Standing Committee. 2006. *Women, Girls, Boys and Men: Different Needs—Equal Opportunities: Gender Handbook in Humanitarian Action*.

Available online at http://ochaonline.un.org/HumanitarianIssues/GenderEquality/ KeyDocuments/IASCGenderHandbook/tabid/1384/language/en-US/Default.aspx (Accessed on 10 August 2009).

Women's Coalition for Disaster Management (WCDM). 2005. *Gender Watch*, No. 1–6. Batticaloa, Sri Lanka: WCDM.

Wiest, R. E., J. S. P. Mocellin and D. T. Motsisi. 1994. *The Needs of Women in Disasters and Emergencies*. Report prepared for the United Nations Development Program, Disaster Management Training Program, and the Office of the United Nations Disaster Relief Coordinator. Winnipeg, Canada: The University of Manitoba, Disaster Research Institute. Available online at http://www.radixonline.org/resources/women-in-disaster-emergency.pdf (Accessed on 10 August 2009).

Wijayatilake, K. and C. Gunaratne. 1999. *Monitoring Progress on the Elimination of Discrimination against and the Achievement of Equality for Women: Sri Lanka Report on Domestic Violence*. Colombo, Sri Lanka: Centre for Women's Research.

Wilson, J., B. D. Phillips and D. M. Neal. 1998. 'Domestic Violence after Disaster', in E. Enarson and B. H. Morrow (eds), *The Gendered Terrain of Disaster: Through Women's Eyes*, pp. 225–31. Westport, CT: Praeger Publishers.

19

'A We Run Tings':
Women Rebuilding Montserrat

————— • ✦ • —————

Judith Soares and Audrey Y. Mullings

Though some of the most vulnerable in times of natural disasters, women must be seen as agents of change and subjects of history rather than victims of natural disasters and objects of history. This is very well demonstrated in the case of Montserrat where the lives of Montserratians were disrupted in July 1995 when volcanic activity altered the physical and social landscape of their country. The Soufriere hills volcano had awakened from its long slumber and, as it yawned and stretched, it embraced the capital town of Plymouth and its environs with its deadly fiery tentacles. This occurrence meant displacement, trauma and fear for all Montserratians who had to respond to a crisis and a natural disaster for which they were not fully psychologically and practically prepared.

It also meant preparations for evacuation, relocation, psychosocial counselling, re-knitting of communities and the rebuilding of the structures of civil and political societies. In this, women were in the forefront of managing the crisis and rehabilitating the country. One observer noted, 'women were critical during the crisis and women are critical in the rehabilitation process' (Meade 1998). Another recalled, 'our men were more scared than the women, [they] were more nervous, they were cowering' (Cassell-Sealy 1998). So when the crisis came, 'it was the women who had to find a way' (Francis 1998).

Generally, the role of women in disaster management and rehabilitation has gone underestimated, under-recognised and under-researched. Essentially, women are seen as wedded to traditional tasks related to their reproductive role and, therefore, deemed unable to undertake activities such as technical and managerial roles associated with disaster management. It is both important and necessary to examine women's role or potential contribution before, during and after a natural disaster. The case of Montserrat demonstrates that they are critical to the survival of the family, the community and the country. Any disaster management programme which does not focus on women's role and their contribution to strengthening local and national response capabilities will be less than effective. As Tuitt (1998) observed, 'in any emergency situation, women are critical, there is no way of getting around them and if you don't have them, then you will have a disaster'.

With this in mind, this chapter, based predominantly on primary research, will address the central role women played and continue to play in preserving their families, re-knitting their communities and rebuilding Montserrat. We chose an unconventional narrative voice that highlights specific contributions made by women who are personally identified, in this way bringing them to life and countering the overly generalised account of 'women's roles in disaster'.

Women Are Not Victims

Women play a significant role in directing and influencing human activity, thought, action and events. In doing so, women are also creating history. Nonetheless, the prevailing image of women in instances of natural disasters, and their exclusion from the disaster cycle can and does effectively limit their contribution and participation in disaster management.

Within Caribbean societies, the subordination of women has been ideologically conceived and practically expressed as integral to the 'natural order' of social and political arrangements. The dissemination of this ideology is sustained through civil society's material and institutional structures of the church, school, the media and other social and political 'private bodies' through which male dominance is exercised. It is this ideology which renders women's participation in and contribution to the life of societal development invisible. In this strand of thought and action, women are not seen as active participants involved centrally in the process of social and productive life, though in the Caribbean approximately half of all households are headed by women, and they are active in all dimensions of natural disasters.

In disaster management, this is exemplified by the Caribbean Disaster Emergency Response Agency (CDERA) which, since its inception in 1991, has never addressed the role of women in emergency response situations or programmes for vulnerability reduction. In no aspect of the disaster management cycle is the role of women considered, despite the fact that women's issues have been taking centre stage both regionally and internationally since the 1970s, the UN Decade for Women. This is not surprising since the leadership of CDERA and its participating states is ideologically rooted in the (mis)conception and practice of male superiority and women's inferiority. Therefore, the recognition of women, as a distinct social group, is not accommodated and so their needs are not adequately met when disasters strike. Pastizzi-Ferencic Dunja (1997) notes:

> [We] should start questioning the resurgency of old patriarchal values in emergency situations. Even in this passive approach, women's needs are not entirely met, such as their health and psychological needs, not to mention their traditional but neglected role in food distribution. The still prevailing image of women as victims only poses formidable barriers to the most efficient use of female talents and full and equal participation of women in disaster management and economic rehabilitation.

Hence, women are usually portrayed as hapless, helpless victims as can be evidenced in the media images of despairing women and their children standing helplessly among the ruins caused by cyclone flooding in Bangladesh, the rubble of an earthquake in Mexico or simply holding a malnourished child in drought-struck Ethiopia. This image of women is far from the reality as Tuitt (1998) cites in the case of Montserrat:

> Women were vital and critical during the crisis. They did play a pivotal role. They interacted more with the public. They were better able to do shelter management than men. They played a critical role in the evacuation process,

in providing food and taking care of the elderly and the disabled. They worked with the men who were preparing shelters. It was total team effort.

Furthermore, 'women in Montserrat have ... never been victims ... they are the ones who borrow money ... and ... build houses.' Montserratian women do feel that they had to provide leadership in rehabilitating their country:

> Because traditionally women are the ones who are at the forefront, we have to use our strength to assist in the rebuilding. We have been given this role whether by mistake or design. We are in leadership positions. We need to find ... new ways to bring together women in the rebuilding process whether through women's groups, co-ops or the church. We need to come together and plan strategically for the development of our country. (Francis 1998)

Women Take the Lead

Preparedness and Awareness

In the preparedness phase, women laid the groundwork for any necessary evacuation and relocation of families or even whole communities. For example, in Long Ground, a small village at the foot of the volcano, a district disaster committee of five women and four men were responsible for preparing the community for and executing the evacuation, and providing information to the Emergency Operation Centre (EOC) which is activated when a crisis exists. Preparing for evacuation called for an intimate knowledge of the community and involved activities such as ensuring that bags were packed with essentials and locating the emergency centre; knowing the social composition of the village and where all residents lived to identify any missing persons in the evacuation; knowing where the disabled and elderly lived to ensure they would be the first to be evacuated; preparing a community profile for the EOC and providing a breakdown of all the women, men and children in the community with the location of their homes. Though the Committee was headed by a man, women had more intimate knowledge of the village and had the responsibility for sensitising community members, through house-to-house visits, on the need for planning and preparing for the impending disaster.

At the start of the crisis, the National Coordinator, Juliet Brade, an information officer, functioned at a time when public interest in disaster management was at a low level, and this area of social responsibility was not given high priority by government. Brade, therefore, worked virtually single-handedly to sensitise the public of the necessity and importance of disaster management as she maintained her determination to keep a national disaster programme alive and in full public view. With Montserrat's critical link with CDERA, Brade was responsible for national disaster operations, ensuring that all district disaster committees were set up and functioning effectively, that all arrangements for shelter management were in place, that shelters were being efficiently run and that relief operations benefited all the dislocated.

Information specialist, and manager of the local radio station, Rose Willock, was critical to holding the country together to allow the people to weather the crisis. Willock, a graduate of the Caribbean Institute for Media and Communication, received training at the British Broadcasting Corporation and was a pioneer in the area of disaster communication. Her main concern was how to use information as a point of mobilisation, as a means of social cohesion, an instrument of calm and relaxation, a medium for reflection and sharing and a channel for the elevation of spirits. During the crisis, she effectively managed information through Radio Montserrat, the focal point for information dissemination. Through her own initiative, Willock introduced and hosted special discussion programmes to broaden the country's information base on disaster management and related issues, to build morale, counsel people by encouraging them to talk through their experiences and to raise spirits and hope. Some of these programmes included 'Tuff Talk', a call-in programme on social issues; 'The Golden Years', a one-hour educational programme which targeted the elderly and engaged them on issues of health, nutrition, culture and entertainment and a two-way children's programme on the dynamics of the volcanic eruption and how it affected them. On 'black-out' day, the day the country was covered with ash, she was alone at the radio station. All others had fled.

In the supporting field of science, Deputy Chief Scientist, Jill Norton, worked alongside other women scientists to provide the necessary information for national decision makers and planners for more effective response actions and information dissemination.

Emergency Response

During the crisis, women provided food for local consumption, worked voluntarily in the evacuation process and in shelters as managers and hands, coordinated the flow of information and were involved in relief tracking. They kept children in a state of readiness for school and led the way in persuading government to reopen schools or to build new ones as a priority. They also opened a laundromat to alleviate laundry woes and kept commercial enterprises open for business.

Spiritually, the churchwomen got involved in social work among the dislocated and the invaded. Chief among them was Methodist cleric, Joan Meade, who used the pulpit to give spiritual and psychological sustenance to her congregation. Notably, the men ministers had left the island: 'they jumped ship, they were not staying and fighting with the people' (Francis 1998). Women, sensitive to their added responsibilities, formed support groups to give each other spiritual succour, mental strength and psychological support. With respect to the latter, for example, psychologist Carol Tuitt collaborated with the Montserratian Christian Council and the local Red Cross to conduct stress management workshops for some 120 shelter managers, householders and teachers to prepare them to give better quality guidance to their constituents by helping to reduce anxiety and encouraging them to face their reality calmly and with a clear mind.

Florence Daley, Mary Cooper and Marjorie Joseph, all retired nurses, gave special attention to care of the elderly. Having volunteered her services to the EOC, Daley took charge of the various shelters for the elderly, where she was instrumental in developing interactive seniors' programmes. These involved making handicraft items, creating and tending kitchen gardens and entertainment and cultural activities. The three nurses lobbied for the establishment of a single facility where all senior citizens could be accommodated and cared for under one roof, culminating in the establishment of the Golden Agers Home and a day-care facility which provided living quarters for 50 persons, most of whose families had migrated. Lystra Osbourne, businesswoman, wife, mother as well as head of the Red Cross, provided support for both able-bodied and persons with disabilities in preparedness, evacuation, relocation and relief.

Caribbean women have a long history of leading at the national level in the public administration sector and Angela Greenaway, Economist and Director of Development, is an example. Described as one of the 'most powerful persons' in Montserrat, she is responsible for all personnel matters relating to contracts, coordinating all aid projects and oversees the development of the country. She sits on the Emergency Operations Group which implements the decisions of the Emergency Policy Group within which no other women are present. She was, therefore, critical to the management of the crisis and the rebuilding process. In fact, Greenaway is the key link between the Montserratian government and the British government in terms of the provisions of external aid and decisions about its use.

Rebuilding Spirits and Livelihoods

Family therapist and counsellor Clarice Barnes, first worked for the PALS Support Group, a collection of women across classes and occupation who met monthly to confer on coping methods and mechanisms and to share in group counselling. She also conducted 'street counselling' and provided the same services through the telephone and Radio Montserrat. Through these methods, she was able to reach a wider audience, experiencing loss and separation. Barnes' work was critical to crisis prevention, a necessary component of disaster mitigation and response.

Women on the Move (WOM) is a women's cooperative enterprise which emerged on the ruins of the Harris/Streatham Women's Cooperative (HSWC), a vibrant rural-based group that offered skills training in areas of sewing, fashion designing, tie-dying, baking, making preserves and block making. The group ended with the eruption of the volcano. Consequently, there was mass out-migration of women and their families. Some went into shelters, others went abroad. After the demise of the HSWC, dauntless Juliana Meade, Cooperative Officer, Ministry of Agriculture, took the initiative to assist women in shelters by organising them in cooperatives similar to those of HSWC. This meant that those unskilled women who had never had a chance to get training would now be exposed to acquiring useful skills.

It was because of her concern for the future of women and a realisation that learning, training and investment was a continuous process and was now more critical to the development of the country, that in February 1998, WOM was born. Based on the notion that women could assist in meaningfully rebuilding Montserrat only if they could rebuild themselves and their families, WOM comprised 'women from all walks of life.' Organised with a non-hierarchical structure, WOM offered training in sewing, handicrafts, tie-dying, making preserves and computer studies, as well as a Teacher of Teachers programme for a multiplier effect. For some women, WOM meetings were social events which assisted in easing their depression, helping them to cope with their losses and the psychosocial trauma they experienced and continue to experience. This is a new area in disaster management which is still under-researched and in which the women of Montserrat were trailblazers. The psychosocial aspect of disaster management is also critical since the women who comprised the shelter population, and the 'new' communities such as Davy Hill, where WOM is active, were thrown together from various communities. For them, building a new community spirit was important for social integration and social cohesion. Their intention was to create 'a new woman', not just by providing disaster-affected women with marketable skills but also by promoting self-confidence and encouraging new relationships with their men and their society.

WOM was locating women, as a distinct social group, at the centre of the national development process in the aftermath of the volcanic eruptions, urgently addressing the need to rebuild community spirit. In Davy Hill, also, the 75-member *Emerald Gems Cheerleading Group*, organised by 24-year-old Fiona Meade, was an attempt to lay the groundwork for developing activities for young women and girls.

At a time when all financial institutions in the country were not lending money as freely as before, Coop Credit Union Manager Roslyn Cassell-Sealy paved the way for new loans which were accessed mainly by women, most of whom were unmarried. For Cassell-Sealy, access to productive assets and financial capital are even more necessary now to build the backbone sectors of agriculture and small business. She operates on the belief that the financial dimension is indispensable to independence and sustained development. She believes in women:

> Women can rebuild communities on a number of levels: spiritually, developing a community spirit, making communities habitable, disciplining our children, reviving Montserratian pride, reviving our culture, taking back our country

from Britain so that we can control our own lives and, most of all, nurturing our men, teaching them to be men again and building their confidence so that they can take on their role in society. (Cassell-Sealy 1998)

Under her leadership, the credit union adopted the nearby community Davy Hill, where she sought to implement an environmental project to create green spaces in the community. The participatory 'Greening of Davy Hill' project encouraged beautification and also good neighbourliness with a view to creating a cohesive community in a spirit of kinship.

Local businesswoman and farmer Theresa Cassell-Silcott was among those who decided not to leave Montserrat, but to stay and contribute to the rebuilding process. With her husband, she operates the Grand View Bed and Breakfast guest house, based on healthy living through natural foods and herbs, many grown in her 'bush garden' of local herbs known for their medicinal and nutritional value. John Silcott, a broadcast engineer, sees in his wife the resilience of the Montserratian woman as she operated virtually on her own during the crisis, organising the four-member family and their community of Foxes Bay for evacuation and relocation:

During the crisis, she was mostly on her own because I was hardly at home. She was on her own with three children ... we would not have come this far if she wasn't behind the business. She runs the business, cultivates the food ... and it was her idea to set up the bed and breakfast, it was her design.... She decided to rebuild Montserrat for those people coming to the island: government personnel, business people, professionals, workers and tourists. She is an example of the resilience of our women. She is contributing to part of a process of rebuilding Montserrat. (Silcott 1998)

Theresa Cassell-Silcott (1998) also served on several committees appointed with the role of articulating a national 'Sustainable Development Plan', helping to establish a new farmers' cooperative to enhance the social, educational and economic well-being of farm families. Women organising in agricultural producers' organisations is not out of keeping with the general agricultural development in the Caribbean as women do play a major role in agriculture. In Montserrat, over 50 per cent of the country's agricultural labour force is comprised of women, who continued to be the major producers of food in the post-volcano period. During the crisis, farmers did not abdicate their responsibility and many of the 19 farmers who were killed in the 25 June 1996 tragedy were women reaping the harvest.

Conclusion

The case of Montserrat clearly demonstrates that there is, indeed, the need for a holistic approach to disaster management with women located at the centre, alongside men, and not at the margin, with full integration into existing systems. This means that women must be fully included in all disaster management plans, programmes and policies. As effective agents of change, women must be fully trained in the theory, practice and technical aspects of disaster management in order to realise their full potential.

The case of Montserrat shows, and as one woman stated, 'a we run tings'. The ability of women to lead in situations of crisis and to rebuild in instances of devastation must be recognised and respected. In Caribbean societies, women are usually given credit only for their role in family life and the exceptional training in leadership, organisational and survival skills that this provides in times of crisis is overlooked. This case of women in Montserrat shows the strength, patience, perseverance and resilience of Caribbean women. These women saw the need and voluntarily brought their life experience and skills to give direction during a period when their country Montserrat faced its greatest need ever.

Acknowledgements

I would like to thank the following persons who so willingly gave of their time to share their knowledge and experiences with me in the period I spent in Montserrat: Clarice Barnes, Roslyn Cassell-Sealy, Theresa Cassell-Silcott, Sarita Francis, Angela Greenaway, Delene Lynch-Mason, A. Mullings and G. Noel (1998), Juliana Meade, John Silcott, John Skerrit, Horatio Tuitt and Rose Willock. I am also grateful to all other women and men who shared their views with me.

References

Cassell-Sealy, Roslyn. Manager, Coop Credit Union, Montserrat, Interviewed 26 October 1998.
Cassell-Silcott, Theresa, Interviewed 27 October 1998.

Dunja, Pastizzi-Ferencic. 1997. 'Disaster Management, Women: An Asset or Liability?' *DHA News*, No. 22, April/May. Available online at http://www.reliefweb.int/ocha_o/pub/dhanews/issue22/assetor.html (Accessed on 13 October 2007).

Francis, Sarita. Acting Permanent Secretary, Ministry of Agriculture, Montserrat, Interviewed 27 October 1998.

Meade, Fiona, Interviewed October 1998.

Meade, Juliana. Cooperative Officer Ministry of Agriculture, Montserrat, Interviewed 27 October 1998.

Mullings, A. and G. Noel. 1998. 'The Role of Women in Disaster Management', *UNDRO News*, September/October.

Silcott, John, Interviewed 28 October 1998.

Tuitt, Lt. Horatio, Deputy Head, Emergency Department, Montserrat, Interviewed 27 October 1998.

20

Women Responding to Drought in Brazil

———— • ✦ • ————

Adélia de Melo Branco

The drought is ugly, it brings hunger and sadness for us. For days the pan has nothing to cook. Besides that we see our families split. We had to send two of our daughters to engage in domestic work in Petrolina and a son to São Paulo so that we would not starve. The worst is that we stay here wondering how they are doing there. I stayed with my old man (husband) and the small children. I tell you, we did not starve to death because they sent money. (Rita, 40 years old)

I have only one daughter. In the drought my husband goes away and I stay here with her. During the drought my parents helped me and I was able to get some money to buy food from the corn husk crafts I made in the women's group, but this was only at the beginning; after that, the situation got worse. (Rosa, a 27-year-old group member)

Before I was home, hiding. I was ashamed of everything, never opened my mouth when there were many people together. I did not know anything. Now I learned how to talk, I am not ashamed, nor do I fear to open my mouth. Now it is hard for me to stay quiet. Now I feel I belong to the struggle. (Rosa, a 27-year-old group member)

The notion of vulnerability of women has often led to the belief that women are passive beings in a disaster situation. The main objective of this discussion is to demystify this notion by examining the drought hazard in north-east Brazil. In this qualitative study of rural and urban women affected by drought, I find that as a result of ineffective mitigation, response and recovery measures which ignore women's needs, women develop their own responses, the most important of which are migration and mobilisation in action groups. The discussion will show that women's invisibility in society is culturally constructed and that once women engage in effective responses they have the opportunity to assert themselves and mitigate the social impacts of disaster in their lives. In times of crises, therefore, women become agents of change rather than objects of change, and turn their vulnerabilities into capacities. Acknowledgement of the strength and initiative of women renders them visible in the society at large and points to the limitation of policies which do not address women's needs. The engagement of those women in migration and mobilisation in rural action groups demonstrates that they are by no means passive and destitute of power. Their behaviour challenges patriarchy and makes them visible. This could not take place, however, if they did not have the support of non-governmental organisations (NGOs) and Rural Labourers Union. Political mobilisation is an important step for women to become visible and grass-roots organisations play an important role in supporting women's mobilisation.

Understanding Drought in Brazil

In contrast to sudden-onset disasters, such as floods and hurricanes, which often have a dramatic impact on the population, drought is a slow-onset disaster which occurs cyclically (Branco 1995; Winchester 1992). Natural hazards such as droughts cannot be treated as the result of natural and physical forces solely, but as the result of a combination of socio-economic and political forces (Cuny 1983; Maskrey 1989, 1993; Rogge 1992; Wiest et al. 1994; Wilches-Chaux 1993). This is clearly apparent from the fact that a disaster usually does not equally affect a population as a whole but rather tends to affect the most vulnerable more profoundly.

Droughts cannot be seen as isolated, local or regional phenomenon and should be understood within the context of globalisation. The social and political nature of the drought and its relation to the globalisation of the economy are clearly demonstrated in the context of the Brazilian north-east. Whereas there is in the semi-arid north-east Brazil, a developed irrigated area devoted to the production of fruits and vegetables for export, there is also a drought-prone area which is characterised by severe poverty, located in the same region. The population of this poverty-stricken and drought-prone area serves as a labour reserve to the irrigated, developed and wealthy semi-arid area. The drought which affects the Brazilian north-east semi-arid region should therefore be understood in the context of the globalisation of the economy.

The lack of political will to address the root causes of the drought, combined with a variety of socio-economic and physical factors, are responsible for the perpetuation of the drought in north-east Brazil. The nature and magnitude of drought disasters in the north-east are primarily the combined result of lack of rain or irregular rainfall and the character of agricultural production organisation, particularly the distribution of landholdings (Andrade 1985; Coelho 1985). A highly skewed distribution of land has characterised the region since colonial times and up until the present there has not been an effective solution to the problem by the government (Branco 2000).

The Brazilian government has also historically implemented short-term emergency measures focused on infrastructure, instead of long-term measures with sustainable development goals. Among the mitigation measures implemented are short-term employment for the construction of dams, wells and reservoirs. The number of persons who apply for the work available through this short-term employment is higher each year and the number of jobs available is not enough to absorb all of those in need. This reflects a worsening of the problem year after year. These governmental measures have been of a palliative nature, actually increasing the vulnerability of the population. The government has not implemented mitigation measures for long-term solutions based on education, raising awareness and active participation of the population in decision making.

An accurate account of the drought phenomenon cannot be given unless consideration is given to the role of all sectors of society, including women. Unless this is done, sustainable development planning which would bring long-term solutions to the drought problem cannot be put in place. For instance, in the case of short-term drought-related jobs, the majority of those hired were men until the most recent droughts (1989–93 and 1998–99). Priority was given to men because they were considered by policy makers to be the heads of their households (Branco 2000).

This ignored the fact that in many cases women become heads of their households when their husbands or partners migrate during the drought. The Rural Labourers Union and NGOs pressured the government to increase the number of women employed as well as to increase the number of workers per family (Branco 2000).

In the absence of formal or governmental mitigation measures, the population tend to develop their own measures and to reduce their level of vulnerability. This is especially the case of women in north-east Brazil, as their needs are not properly considered in policies to mitigate the effects of drought. Women, therefore, have had to develop their own mitigation measures. These are discussed in the following sections.

My observations are based on a research undertaken in the 1990s with migrant and non-migrant women. Four different categories of women comprised the population studied: young migrant women who migrate unaccompanied to the city and engage in the domestic service sector; middle-aged and elderly women who have migrated to the city along with their close family members and who engage in irrigated agricultural labour; young as well as elderly return migrant women who have settled back in their place of origin and participate in a rural women's action group and women who never left their place of origin despite the drought hazard who have been dealing with the drought on a permanent basis and who also participate in a rural women's action group. Fieldwork was done in the semi-arid region of the state of Pernambuco located in north-east Brazil.

The Social Construction of the Vulnerabilities and Capacities of Women

In order to understand the role of women in face of the drought, it is important to understand their vulnerabilities and capacities. Vulnerability refers to the conditions determined by the physical, social and environmental factors or processes which increase the susceptibility of an individual or community to the impact of hazards. The concept of vulnerability becomes clearer when consideration is given to capacities (UNISDR 2004). Capacity is a combination of all the strengths and resources available at the individual or community, society and organisational level that can reduce the level of risk or the effects of a disaster.

Capacity may include physical, institutional, social or economic means as well as skilled persons and collective attributes such as leadership and management (UNISDR 2004). Women's capacities are, in many instances, undermined due to their invisibility.

The vulnerability of women should be understood to be cultural and organisational rather than biological or physiological (Wiest et al. 1994). The subordination of women is closely related to the notion of their vulnerability since it is embedded in the culture of the society concerned. This is intrinsically linked to the fact that the social structure of most societies formally relegates women to inferiority and dependency, increasing their vulnerability (Wiest et al. 1994). Studies have shown, however, that the actual performance of women in production and distribution differs significantly from gender ideology and role stereotypes in most societies (Branco 2000; Wiest et al. 1994). Such a view clearly shows that the vulnerability of women, in many societies, including the Brazilian north-east, is culturally constructed and increased by gender ideology and stereotypes which are also largely responsible for the undermining of those women's power and capacities (Branco 1995; Ramalho 1995). This ideology, along with the fact that women's contribution is primarily restricted to the domestic sphere, serves to perpetuate the invisibility of women in the larger society, including government policy making (Branco 2000).

These factors have led to the assumption that rural women have a low self-esteem and often feel inferior to men. Their subservient behaviour towards men hinders them from participating in unions or groups devoted to the political mobilisation of rural workers. This is especially the case of rural women who are highly isolated.

Women's Responses: Migration and Political Mobilisation

Women are far from being a homogeneous group in any society but vary with regard to age, marital status and life situations. In Brazil, where migration is an important way for women to mitigate the worst effects of the drought, migrant women are mainly young and single women who engage in rural–urban migration to work as domestic servants. Older women also migrate with their husbands and children and engage in domestic services or in agricultural work in the irrigated fields. Two groups of women, then, remain in the countryside: married women whose husbands and sons and/or daughters migrate and older migrant women who have returned to their villages.

Women's political mobilisation can be a result of responding to drought as well as an important precondition for action. Changing women's attitudes and behaviour can be seen as a challenge and entails changes in a variety of sectors related to the patriarchal model, including men's attitudes. Change is not easy, especially when women are not aware of the importance of political mobilisation. The hardships women have to face are compounded for those with new roles as heads of their households due to the drought-related migration of their husbands and can also be a major step towards changing women's attitudes. Local NGOs in the region often support women's daily struggle to cope with the drought. As a result, women assert themselves and engage in measures to decrease their vulnerability and fulfil the needs of their households. This is especially the case of women who stay in the countryside during droughts.

Migration Strategies

The invisibility of women in the drought context in north-east Brazil is such that it is often thought that rural–urban migration during droughts involves only men. This is far from the case and significant differences exist in the patterns of male and female migration during drought. Rural women, especially, face a difficult situation as there are no drought policies which specifically target them.

Women who migrate to urban centres in search for jobs send remittances to those who stay in the countryside. In the case of migrant men, although they promise to send remittances home, women very commonly experience that they never do. A further disadvantage is that sometimes the migrant men constitute another family in their place of destination. The wives who stay in their place of origin are usually referred to as 'widows of the drought' (Portella et al. 1999).

Decisions about the migration of family members are undertaken at the household level. Women play a very important role as they are usually the ones who make the final decision about the migration of daughters, sons and husbands, demonstrating their power as decision makers at the domestic level. Young women are sent to the city so that their fathers can remain working in the rural areas with the help from the remittances sent by their daughters. Rural women also have an easier time than men finding employment in cities since they usually work as domestic servants. In the case of north-east Brazil, women are also preferred for the work on irrigated agricultural labour in the production of fruits and vegetables for export. Workers usually reside in peri-urban areas close to the irrigated properties and commute to work on a daily basis.

Rural women migrants encounter a new world of experience in the city and many who work as agricultural workers on irrigated land soon join the Rural Labourers Union. Besides sending remittances to those who remain in the countryside, migrant women also stimulate the migration of other members of their family to the city. According to migrant women, life in their place of destination provides them with a cash income and with the opportunity to learn about their rights as women workers. These migrant women are not willing to return to their place of origin. They usually mention that life in the countryside was more difficult. Besides not having employment, they had to walk long distances in search for water during drought periods. Despite having to work very hard and, in many cases, facing separation from their husbands, these women prefer to remain in their place of destination as they say they face less discrimination there.

However, it must be said that life in the city is far from being a paradise. Sometimes tension increases between married migrant women and their husbands. Marriages often break up in the case of women who migrate with their husbands and children, as men who were the primary providers at their place of origin feel their authority threatened as a result of their unemployed condition in the city. Alcohol abuse and violence can follow.

Political Strategies

The situation of the women who stay in the countryside and take on the headship of their households in the absence of their husbands is very different from that of migrant women. As mentioned, most rural women have low self-esteem and are subordinated to men at society-level. It is therefore not easy to raise awareness about their rights as agricultural workers. Recognising that very few rural workers participated, the Rural Labourers Union in the early 1980s reached out to rural women and formed women's groups.

The underlying basis for the formation of these women's action groups was initially not directed towards the specific needs of women, but towards the involvement of women in the political agenda of the Rural Labourers Union. The idea was initially not well accepted by the majority of rural women workers as they did not understand the reason why it would be important to form women's groups to realise the agenda of the Rural Labourers Union. As the number of women increased and women were incorporated into the union's struggle, the role of women's groups became clearer. The basic idea was the need for a higher participation of rural women in all aspects of society, to increase their engagement in the struggle for better conditions of life, to raise their awareness of the exploitation of their labour and of how drought was affecting their lives.

Meetings were usually once a month. Each of the participants contributed with food and after the meeting, they had a collective meal. The meetings included discussions on workers' rights, the role and importance of the union to advocate for the labourers and the rights of women agricultural workers to retire. Through these discussions, women became aware not only of the political implications of the drought which affects their lives directly but also of the implications and exploitation of wage labourers outside the drought-prone area. Women, therefore, achieved an understanding of the reality to which they were never exposed before (Branco 2000).

After a few months, women's action groups gained the support of ecumenical grass-roots organisations and NGOs. During severe droughts, attention in the Union and women's groups turned to income-generation projects in order to complement the family income of women. It is interesting to note that the income-generating activities in which women engaged were traditionally women's activities, but since they were performed collectively within the domain of the women's action group, they were now acknowledged as important activities. Women engaged in the production of crafts made with corn husks when those were available. With the support of NGOs, women had access to funds and bought sewing machines and material to produce clothes, embroidery and handcrafts such as crochet work. From an external threat, the drought became the centrepiece of the women's group since it allowed expression of shared pain and misery which united the women. For those involved, the Union represents much more than an opportunity to earn income as they earn an insignificant amount of profit, but the gain is large when considering increased awareness of the importance of women uniting to fight the drought.

The women's action group has brought not only material benefits to its members but also awareness about their stand as women workers and their rights. Such awareness is acquired by women as they learn about the conditions of life of women workers in other regions and their rights as subsistence agricultural workers. Women's participation in this learning process places their own life experiences in a broader perspective. Furthermore, by participating in the group, women have the opportunity to share their problems with their fellow women and to receive support in times of need. This is seen not only in the political discussions but also in women's collective income-generating activities.

It is undeniable that the decision of women to join the action group can be a difficult one. As women decide to participate, they go through changes. The changes involve breaking out from the domestic sphere and entering into the public sphere. In most cases, men in their lives initially disapprove of the entrance of women into the group and women have to renegotiate their decision in the domestic domain. Renegotiations of relationships also take place between women and the other rural village members. Women's action group members are seen as different and indeed they do grow as women, as workers, as wives and as mothers when they join the group.

The women's group of the Rural Labourers Union has clearly been an important vehicle for the women involved. It entails a transformation of everyday life for women who had previously been secluded within the domestic domain and isolated from other women. Through the action group, women attempt to mitigate the drought both by earning income and by reconceiving their sense of themselves as women. The entrance of women into the action group signals their entry into the public sphere of the rural patriarchal society and hence challenges patriarchy itself. In some cases, the attitudes of men too change as they become supportive of the group after seeing the practical results during the drought.

Windows of Opportunity for Change

Migration continues to be a dominant mitigation response of the local population to the drought as it has for many years. Although rural–urban migration takes place in normal drought years, it increases considerably during severe drought periods as employers in irrigated semi-arid areas take advantage of the dire straits of rural workers afflicted by the drought. Migration is a response to drought used by both women and men. Though their place of destination offers a series of advantages for migrant women, including access to employment and to the Rural Labourers Union, the transformation of women's lives is only partial as they face new forms of exploitation as they are absorbed into urban capitalist labour markets.

The research conducted on rural women's efforts to cope with drought and mitigate its economic and social impacts has also demonstrated the important role played by NGOs such as the Rural Labourers Union. These organisations have been focusing not only on the needs of the local population, in general, but also on the needs of women themselves. Migrant women have benefited from awareness through the Rural Labourers Union, which provides them with a learning process about their conditions as workers and also about the political and economic nature of the drought. Among rural women and returning migrants, the support of grass-roots organisations and organisations such as the Rural Labourers Union has been very significant. Through the formation of women's action groups, women affected by drought have learnt about the nature of the government's response to drought and about their own lives as workers and women in a patriarchal and capitalist world system. Mobilisation of rural women in action groups decreases their vulnerability as they gradually become aware of the limitations imposed by the ecosystem, the political and economic nature of the drought and the limitations of the capitalist labour processes in the absorption of migrant women labour power. Such mobilisation increases women's self-esteem and allows women to demonstrate more explicitly the social power they do indeed have.

The drought experiences of the migrant and non-migrant women under consideration are very distinct. Nevertheless, all women respond to the drought situation and attempt to change the limitations it imposes on their everyday lives and the lives of their family members. The changes women go through in their mobilisation in rural action groups and rural–urban migration challenge patriarchy in both the city and the countryside. This leads to important changes not only for the women involved but also for the men and for the society more generally. Awareness raising is an important avenue for women to challenge patriarchy.

Implications

Through this discussion I hope to have demonstrated the important role women play and to have demystified the notion of women as powerless and passive beings in disasters. I hope to have demonstrated that disaster mitigation should move away from emphasis on emergency measures to incorporate long-term development planning. In order for this to be accomplished, governments should not only support but also work closely with NGOs, religious grass-roots organisations, neighbourhood associations and labour unions, so that appropriate and effective measures can be implemented. These organisations work closely with populations affected by disasters, seeing people at the grass-roots level as a resource. By working along with grass-roots organisations, the local population can be involved in planning and implementing disaster mitigation. Empowerment of the population at the grass-roots level through awareness raising should not be considered as a threat to governmental action, but an important condition for development to take place. This may require breaking away from old political and economic oligarchies and turning towards the implementation of a model which incorporates the needs of a majority of people and that is based on people's participation.

The incorporation of women in disaster research and in policy making is a crucial step in the development of realistic and effective measures to promote long-term sustainable development planning in the region. Future research in this area should not only give attention to women but also investigate how women can be incorporated into the planning process to address their needs. Disaster mitigation efforts geared to long-term regional development are essential and can only be achieved if women and men participate actively in development planning projects.

Acknowledgements

The research was funded by CIDA and International Development Research Centre as part of an international cooperation project on disaster management between Canada and Brazil. Dr Raymond Wiest gave considerable contribution to the study as did Mr Jan van Wonderen.

References

Andrade, M. C. 1985. *A Seca: Realidade e Mito* (The Drought: Reality and Myth). Pernambuco: Editora ASA.

Branco, A. M. 1995. 'Organizadas para Sobrevivir: El Caso de Un Grupo de Mujeres del Sertão del Araripe' (Organized to Survive: The Case of a Group of Women in Sertão de Araripe), *Desastres y Sociedad*, Vol. 3 (Julio–Diciembre, 5). Lima: La Red.

———. 2000. *Women of the Drought: Struggle and Visibility in Face of a Disaster Situation.* João Pessoa: Editora Universitária.

Coelho, J. 1985. *As Secas do Nordeste e a Industria das Secas* (The Droughts in Northeastern Brazil and the Industry of the Drought). Petrópolis: Editora Vozes.

Cuny, F. 1983. *Disasters and Development.* New York: Oxford University Press.

Maskrey, A. 1989. *Disaster Mitigation: A Community Based Approach.* Oxford: Oxfam.

———. (ed.). 1993. *Los Desastres no son Naturales* (The Disasters are not Natural). Lima: La Red/ITDG.

Portella, T. (Coord.), D. Aamot, D. Suassuna, I. Portela and T. Castello Branco. 1999. *Viúvas da Seca* (Widows of the Drought). Recife, Brazil: Edições Rebento/SUDENE/ Tarciana Portella Produções.

Ramalho, D. M. S. 1995. 'Sequía, Migración y Vivienda: Donde Queda la Mujer Invisible?' (Drought, Migration and Habitation: Where are the Invisible Women?), *Desastres y Sociedad*, Julio–Diciembre, no. 5, año 3. Lima: La Red.

Rogge, J. 1992. *Research Agenda on Disaster Mitigation.* Disaster Research Institute: University of Manitoba.

UNISDR. 2004. *Living with Risk: A Global Review of Disaster Reduction Initiatives.* Geneva: UN/ISDR. Available online at www.unisdr.org (Accessed in August 2008).

Wiest, R., J. Mocellin and T. Motsisi. 1994. *The Needs of Women in Disaster and Emergencies.* Disaster Research Institute, University of Manitoba.

Wilches-Chaux, G. 1993. 'La Vulnerabilidad Global' (The Global Vulnerability), in A. Maskrey (ed.), *Los Desastres no son Naturales* (The Disasters are not Natural). Lima: La Red/ITDG.

Winchester, P. 1992. *Power, Choice and Vulnerability: A Case Study in Disaster Management in South India.* London: James and James.

PART FOUR

Gender-sensitive Disaster Risk Reduction

In the final part of the book, we present five chapters on gender-sensitive disaster risk reduction, three of them case studies drawn from the field, and two on action plans and tools for mainstreaming gender in disaster risk reduction, climate change policies and practices and emergency management.

First, Cecilia Castro García and Luisa Emilia Reyes Zúñiga illustrate some of the advances made in Mexico in the generation of institutional capabilities in risk and disaster management, as well as the challenges that still need to be overcome to reduce vulnerabilities in communities at risk and affected by disasters. The authors stress the need for specific governmental measures which should aim at creating greater preventive and response capabilities within a framework of gender equity to ensure the involvement of men as well as women.

Ulrike Röhr, Minu Hemmati and Yianna Lambrou then explore the difficult and hitherto uncovered issues of gender equality in climate change policies and practices. Five critical connections between gender and climate change are studied in the areas of induced human migration, increased civil conflicts, women's health, demographic changes in the North and South and gender-specific consumption patterns. The chapter highlights the need for more research, political support and specific tools and materials for gender mainstreaming in climate change policies and practices. The progress achieved in the areas of awareness, discourse, policy development and women's personal and organisational development are discussed and strategies for the future are suggested.

Chandni Joshi and Mihir R. Bhatt present the experience of UNIFEM in engendering tsunami recovery in Sri Lanka. UNIFEM added value to the recovery process in two key ways: first by promoting the leadership of female survivors in recovery processes and second by protecting and reviving the livelihoods of female tsunami victims in these processes. This could be achieved through three different channels: first enhancing female voices in the existing institutions such as National Committee for Women, second by providing a platform for tsunami-affected women and decision makers to come together to articulate their priorities for the recovery process and finally, by promoting South–South partnership through initiatives focusing on livelihood, mental health and disaster recovery.

Taking a cue from *Words into Action: Implementing the Hyogo Framework for Action*, developed by the International Strategy for Disaster Reduction, Elaine Enarson identifies fifty-seven steps for mainstreaming gender into the five priorities of action of the Hyogo Framework for Action. This would provide very useful guideline to policy makers and practitioners in gender mainstreaming in their respective areas of operation. 'Engaging women and girls fully and equally', she writes, 'is not a luxury that only some countries can afford nor is it a distraction from the main business of disaster risk reduction. The need for action is more urgent than ever before and hence the need for inclusive strategies engaging the resources, capacities and energies of women as well.'

Finally, the part ends with the chapter 'Toolkits for Mainstreaming Gender in Emergency Response' by P. G. Dhar Chakrabarti and Ajinder Walia. The toolkit is presented covering different activities around three different but inter-related aspects of preparedness, response and early recovery. The practical ways of dealing with the issues based on the experiences gained by various organisations around the world have been suggested in the toolkits. This will no doubt be a useful guide for emergency managers.

21

Balancing Gender Vulnerabilities and Capacities in the Framework of Comprehensive Disaster Risk Management: The Case of Mexico

———•✦•———

Cecilia Castro García and Luisa Emilia Reyes Zúñiga

Research initiatives to link the gender equity (GE) approach with disasters or comprehensive disaster risk management (CDRM) in Mexico are scarce, though readers will find these ideas developed in the papers collected in *Desastres Naturales y Vulnerabilidad de las Mujeres en México* (Natural Disasters and the Vulnerabilities of Mexican Women) following a workshop supported by the Instituto Nacional de las Mujeres (National Women's Institute) and the United Nations Development Programme (UNDP) (see Castro and Emilia 2006; also see Castro 2005a, 2005b; Moya et al. n.d.; Reyes 2005, 2006; UNDP 2008). Qualitative case studies of women caught up in the 1995 Colima earthquake (Serrat 2000) and the 1985 Mexico city quake (Arbeláez 1987; De Barbieri and Guzmán 1986; Massolo and Schteingart 1987; Poniatowska 1995; Rabell and Mier y Teran 1986) are also instructive.

We add to the discussion with an institutional review and findings from research in hazard zones across Mexico, demonstrating the efficacy of a new theoretical approach that merges two powerful theoretical lenses—CDRM and GE, including gender and development (GAD). Doing so addresses the entire process of configuration and management of risk through identification of risk scenarios, prevention-mitigation, transference of risk, early warning, intervention during crisis, recovery and reconstruction. The two perspectives complement each other by providing a comprehensive solution to problems with profound structural roots that must be corrected on a personal, collective and institutional level. Both the approaches promote a mainstreaming intervention to modify those conditions that limit and impede more democratic and harmonious human development. Both aim at influencing and transforming those human relations that keep large sectors of population under circumstances of inequity and injustice, favoured directly by the social construction of gender. These relations are also unsustainable both in the natural and in the constructed environments.

The concept of CDRM originated from the environmental sciences and has been nurtured through new interpretations from the perspective of the social sciences, which consider human activity as part of the causality of risks and disasters. It seeks to prevent the causes of risk by modifying and eliminating social, economic, political, cultural, gendered and environmental vulnerabilities, among many others, thus lessening the risk of disasters beyond simply assisting in their harmful and destructive effects. The GE approach, on the other hand, arose from the egalitarian struggles of feminist theorists and activists and more recently has been developed as an integrated and relational approach to gender as a social category that applies to both men and women.

The CDRM and GE approaches are now more frequently used in the academic world but are presented as two separate things in a fragmented fashion. Their institutional implementation, both theoretical and operative, is still incomplete in Mexico since there is no legal mandate to do so. This leads to the challenge of linking and working with both the approaches at the same time, through two-way mainstreaming: that is, including GE in activities linked to CDRM and including the CDRM approach in activities that foster GE. Gender experts will be able to offer more effective proposals by having a conceptual and practical understanding of the problem of risk and disasters, and experts in Civil

Protection and risk management will be able to propose actions that do not perpetuate inequitable gender relations.

Actions and measures for prevention tend to generalise and homogenise all of the nation's diversity into 'people in general', although there is clear evidence that disaster risk owns a gendered face. How is it shaped? How should it be confronted? These questions guide our discussion in the following pages. In the first part of this chapter, Cecilia Castro García shows some of the main advances in Mexico in the generation of institutional capabilities in risk and disaster management, as well as remaining challenges. Luisa Emilia Reyes Zúñiga then offers concrete examples and proposals for the integration of two schools of thought in the intervention on vulnerabilities and capabilities. We focus mainly on prevention and risk mitigation because we believe that the phase of preparation and emergency has been more widely considered than mitigation or identifying the vulnerabilities and capabilities of local men and women.

Institutional Shortcomings and Strengths

Overly general, homogeneous approaches to reducing disaster risk still prevail in Mexico. These are not adapted bio-climatically and culturally to the regions of the Mexican country in which they are to be implemented. Housing is one example, especially in relocations implemented in rural areas; housing projects are hardly or not at all linked with options for work and productive activities that might provide for a more sustainable recovery and help prevent post-event migration, mostly by the men, and desertion of relocation projects by the elderly population. In rural areas, drought and the loss of income and local unemployment may be heightened even more with disasters and their environmental and economic consequences, and so increase the migration of men and women. But migrants confront different disadvantages based on gender differences and other factors. Women and children face sexual exploitation, problems related to illegal work status, job insecurity, sub-employment and lack of local support networks. The destination cities to which they move may have reduced capacities for providing quality services and housing due to the increased demand of the influx of migrants. These factors place migrants once again in conditions of vulnerability in the case of future disasters.

This situation is closely linked to the condition of indigenous communities, most of which have long suffered from governmental neglect.

Political instability, corruption, insecurity and violence by organised crime have fragmented social networks. Mistrust and a reluctance to participate prevail due to political, economic and cultural segregation and discrimination. Thus, socio-organisational vulnerability in the face of disaster risks makes government initiatives for the development of recovery projects and disaster risk prevention even more difficult. In addition, some traditional cultural 'usages and customs' in these indigenous communities reflect strong inequalities in gender relations between men and women leading to women's reduced recovery capacity due to limited educational training, sexual and reproductive health, property rights over the land, status and leadership and other factors.

Exclusionary practices in economic recovery programmes are also evident. For example, in cases of post-disaster recovery in Mexico by the programmes of temporary work offered by the federal and local governments, 70 per cent of the jobs are assigned to men because of the types of work included in this programme are mostly traditional masculine tasks such as clearing rubble from roads and bridges, or as labourers in housing construction (Centro de Información del Programa de Empleo Temporal [CIPET] 2004, 2005). Although the call is open to the entire population, it is mostly attended by men. Not surprisingly, many women do not feel included or assisted by this kind of post-disaster economic recovery programme and their work remains restricted to food preparation or cleaning in temporary shelters.

Further, while the legislative framework and legal apparatus in the field of Mexico's Civil Protection are one of the most advanced in Latin America, legal measures for prevention and mitigation to reduce pre-existing disaster risks have still not been fully adopted by the authorities responsible for Civil Protection. Still needed are stronger institutional relations with those responsible for carrying out urban development and housing, as well as social and economic development. These are some of the limitations that impede the identification and rectification of the causes of multiple vulnerabilities, which continue to proliferate and repeat. For example, while the existence of vulnerable groups is recognised in the 2000–06 National Civil Protection Programme, it is in a neutral way with no specific recognition of either gender or social diversity. Since vulnerabilities are a fundamental part of risk scenarios, any attempt to reduce disaster risks necessarily implies reducing vulnerabilities, both overall and specifically to address gender and social diversity. The participation of the population and its authorities must also be enlisted to reduce the social construction of disaster risks and build disaster risk management capabilities. There is an advance in the diagnostic part of the 2008–12 National Civil Protection Programme: it acknowledges that the gender perspective is missing as well as the need to reduce social vulnerabilities in communities at risk, but the principal action proposed is researching. Thus, the advances in the field are not yet recognised and incorporated into the law.

Despite these shortcomings, strong institutional foundations for an integrated approach can also be identified. Institutes for women at the federal, local state and municipal levels seek the advancement of women. They are contributing—though often in an uneven way—towards the reduction of social vulnerabilities, a fundamental task of risk reduction, in that they fight discrimination, promote women's sexual, reproductive, political and economic rights and strive to improve living and working conditions through legal and policy reform. In conjunction with the UN Development Programme, Mexico, the Instituto Nacional de las Mujeres, or National Institute for Women (INMUJERES) supported action research into practical tools for mainstreaming GE in Civil Protection at different levels in the national and local systems. But there is still the need to incorporate CDRM in its own mandatory actions.

In the field of social development in Mexico, there is a policy of territorial organisation based on decentralisation of functions and resources. Since 2000, it is mandatory for local states to establish funds for intervention in case of disasters derived from natural phenomena. This makes local management of risks and disasters more effective, but at the same time requires greater commitment on the part of the population as well as the authorities to prevent future disasters and reduce present risks. In 2004, a programme co-funded by the federal government was established to support state and municipal efforts in creating hazard atlases. In some cases, these became risk atlases, taking into consideration accumulated and differential vulnerabilities in the territory; however, these still do not include a gender and social diversity perspective.

Other advances in Mexico involve an ongoing process of democratisation. The legal apparatus in Mexico still leaves little margin for citizen's participation. Nevertheless, both the financial agency FONDEN (Fondo de Desastres Naturales, or Natural Disaster Fund) as well as SEDESOL's (Secretaría de Desarrollo Social, or Ministry for Social Development) include mechanisms for disaster prevention that incorporate social practices proven to be successful in recovery and reconstruction efforts. For this reason, they have been integrated into the institutional organisational capability through the formation of social service panels, damage evaluation committees and reconstruction committees. In the latter, which are large collective assemblies, the different government agencies, as well as representatives of disaster victims receive information, participate and make decisions. Through these mechanisms, institutional work becomes more horizontal and participatory for those affected as they can influence the decision-making process and learn about the characteristics of the projects that will come to their aid. These assemblies fulfil the role of a social audit by avoiding or minimising corruption and injustices in assigning aid to disaster victims and preventing the duplication of efforts and financial resources.

Working directly with women and representative leaders of rural and urban communities, especially those who suffer recurrent disasters, has allowed for the generation of synergies that outlast the inevitable changes in administrative authorities. This approach provides greater transparency and continuity of management while at the same time recovers credibility for institutional intervention and for local and national authorities. It has also led to the recognition and appreciation of women leaders, who have at times proven to be more reliable and transparent, more effective, inclusive and equitable in spreading information and assigning support and resources. Women leaders have displayed greater sensibility in visualising complex problems in matters relating to education and health, and have a more evident commitment than that shown by male leaders in their role as representatives of collective interests. It also should be acknowledged that there is prejudice in the idea that male leaders, in contrast, tend to work for their own personal benefit and that of their political parties more than for the benefit of the community (Castro and Emilia 2006: 19).

Challenges in Practice of an Integrated Approach

This section elaborates the outline of an integrated approach utilising the core concepts of both GAD and CDRM theory. In CDRM, the concepts of vulnerabilities and capabilities have been central to guiding the design of public policies in risk reduction. For GAD, practical needs and strategic gender interests have been the key concepts.

The CDRM approach considers capabilities as part of vulnerabilities, in the sense that capabilities themselves do counterbalance the effect in the equation of disaster risk. But since risk prevention requires effective actions, when it comes to gender it becomes imperative not only to separate capabilities from vulnerabilities, clearly determining the assets and needs of specific gendered groups of population, but also, and perhaps more importantly, to detect those strategic points which need to be addressed to diminish the breach of inequity between genders.

We know now that gender differences demand gender differentiated actions, with respect to vulnerabilities as well as in capabilities. But on this point it is also important to emphasise that gender is a relational concept, and thus requires an intervention addressing relational structures: women and men should not be considered in isolation. Every action designed for either gender must bear in mind its relation to the other.

As a starting point in the identification of vulnerabilities and capabilities, it is useful to bear in mind the gendered division of labour. As a result of it, each gender has developed its own set of capabilities (in accordance with those specificities related to their social conditions, for example, age, erotic preference, religion) and suffers from a particular set of vulnerabilities. Traditional roles prevailing today are not a sufficient basis for planning or executing programmatic interventions. As a consequence of certain flexibility in gender roles, new capabilities are already at sight for each gender and also new vulnerabilities. These changes are due to modifications in the social structures, inspired at times more by the harsh demands of contemporary life than a spirit of equality, but nonetheless real.

A closer look to the implications of this demonstrates that gender roles are a starting point—but not the only one—for good interventions to decrease disaster risk. Diminishing the breach between the genders requires that the intervention should go beyond the reduction of vulnerabilities or the strengthening of capabilities resulting from established gender roles. We should aim to the development of new capabilities which by themselves may lead to more equitable social relations. This requires from us a thorough gender analysis to find those strategic points. The question arises: which vulnerabilities and which capabilities? The concepts of practical gender needs and strategic gender interest deepen our understanding of capabilities and vulnerabilities. Although arising from schools of thought close in spirit, neither CDRM nor GE has taken full advantage of the benefit of synthesis (Table 21.1).

Table 21.1 Integrating CDRM and GE

Public policies for GE in CDRM	Women and men's capabilities	Women and men's vulnerabilities
Practical gender needs	Strengthening capabilities due to (and without modifying) traditional roles, or due to the breaking of traditional roles	Diminishing or eliminating vulnerabilities due to (and without modifying) traditional roles or due to the breaking of traditional roles
Strategic gender interests	Strengthening or forging capabilities, aiming to change relational structures of power between genders	Diminishing or eliminating vulnerabilities, aiming to change relational structures of power between genders

Source: Developed by the authors.

Practical Gender Needs Addressing Vulnerabilities and Capabilities

Practical needs arise from roles assigned to genders in a given historical context (Kabeer 1995). Policies oriented to practical needs tend to the fulfilment of pre-assigned statuses, and thus perpetuate and at times deepen inequality between genders. In relation to capabilities and vulnerabilities, the satisfaction of practical needs by a public policy in disaster risk management—whether by strengthening capabilities or diminishing vulnerabilities—will address those which have their origin in traditional roles.

In Mexico, an example of an intervention oriented to a practical need, focused in this case to strengthening capacities developed through traditional gender roles, is to address women for health campaigns to reduce the risk of epidemic infections in rainy seasons. Dengue fever, a disease very common in Mexico, has its vector in a mosquito that lays eggs in accumulated waters in domestic sites. This hazard is increased by the customary habits of poorer men who tend to collect all kind of old metal and tires 'just in case they're needed'. Women traditionally have been in charge of the health of the families, so it is only 'natural' to address them with the recommendation to eliminate these breeding grounds and clean and keep their utensils dry.

Another example to prevent a risk by means of strengthening traditional gendered capacities is to relocate a human settlement to an area in which men can find work, taking into account their role as the providers of their families. In the case of La Nueva Yerbabuena in Colima, sources of jobs for the male population were considered while planning the relocation and new settlement established due to threat posed by Colima's volcano (Volcan de Fuego). This resulted in La Nueva Yerbabuena being placed in a semi-urban location near industries that are mostly in need of male workers.

When considering vulnerability reduction strategies built around practical needs that relate to traditional gender roles to the complexity of roles, it is useful to recall the specific socio-economic environment. To illustrate: Mexican authorities have to deal with a delicate situation arising from a particular vision of poor Mexican men and women. Women especially practice the 'culture of the survivor' as they do not see themselves as human subjects with human rights. They take for granted that their lot in life is to live in scarcity, without any services in houses made mostly of unsuitable materials. Since it is possible that the government, in an attempt to demolish a dangerous settlement, will come to evacuate them with an offer of a proper house, they remain in that situation for years, and, until that time comes, women risk their lives and those of their children. Most of these offers of housing are to be obtained by means of loans in long-term payments, and some are accepted. However, two things have to be said regarding this matter: first, there are not enough accessible governmental credits for all those families at risk. Second, because many of these 'survivors' (at times survivors of real disasters) want these housings to be given for free by the government, due to the fact that they do not want to be subjects of credit for a long period of time (25–30 years), they resist evacuation or relocation and thus they remain under great hazard, hoping their conditions of life functions as a pressure for the government to accept their demand.

An example related to men refers to an intervention for risk prevention in urban environments in the north of the country. In seasons of harvest, young men, mostly indigenous men, are often under the influence of alcohol, homeless or temporary migrants in poor housing and are the most likely to die in the streets due to low temperatures. Wanting to feel like strong men, they are more reluctant to take advantage of a shelter than women. Making their rounds, patrols more frequently bring these young men at high risk into shelter or provide them with blankets and hot beverages.

In the previous examples, traditional roles for women and men are not challenged, although the results of the interventions may lower risk and appear to be radical changes. More can be done, especially with respect to reinforcement and improvement of the social link. The clearest example is La Nueva Yerbabuena, as vulnerability was reduced but work options were limited and poorly paid. Because the inhabitants of La Nueva Yerbabuena were men from the countryside, wages were kept low and the quality of their life was diminished. The intervention, then, was effective in reducing certain vulnerabilities but increased others.

It should be highlighted that gender inequity is not necessarily promoted by challenging traditional gender roles. On the contrary, this may bring new vulnerabilities to both genders, and reduced capabilities, as it does not relate to their usual practices. After all, what is seen as valuable to one gender is not accepted by the other, and there may not be sufficient social support for the practicing of new roles. For instance, economic migration to the United States in Mexico is a serious problem. Pressures to migrate were formerly stronger on men and many women have learned to take charge of their families and enter realms of productive labour previously reserved to men. Women did not find liberation in this way. On the contrary, they are more vulnerable since their new situation does not grant them the same conditions men had when they held these positions. Besides, they are exposed to sexually transmitted diseases—including HIV—when their partners return to home having acquired these STD during their absence. Moreover, in recent years, Mexican women see themselves forced to emigrate as well, facing different challenges and new forms of exploitation. For men as well as for women, there are many vulnerabilities inherent in migration. Migration leaves its mark on local communities as well; land desertification and the breaking of the social bonds are direct consequences. An unfortunate policy for migrants in Mexico in President Vicente Fox's administration was to give migrants maps so that they could cross the country 'in safety', a policy which did not address for women or for men the structural causes of their migration.

Strategic Gender Interests Addressing Vulnerabilities and Capabilities

How to determine what is structural? The concept of strategic gender interests (Kabeer 1995) is of great use when planning an intervention for risk mitigation and prevention geared to sustainable development with GE. Our work needs to be carefully planned according to a full analysis and not be based only or mainly on our own personal notions of gender roles. Strategic gender interests convey the idea of a change in the relational power structures between the genders; thus, we have to be aware of gender social inequities which appear in every aspect of life. Strategic interests relate to the strengthening of autonomy and safety, for both men and women, and ensure the participation of both genders in every area of life. For both genders, the elimination of the gender labour division is a strategic interest, since it limits their access to a full human life.

Women have specific strategic interests: the elimination of institutionalised forms of discrimination, political equality, reproductive options and measures against male violence, sexual exploitation and coercive forms of marriage (Kabeer 1995). Bearing these strategic interests, while also diminishing vulnerabilities and strengthening capabilities in our disaster risk management efforts, is the best way to ensure sustainable development with GE.

Strategic interests are not the same for men and women, and sometimes they are even opposites, but to think in relational structures gives us the opportunity to find creative and inclusive solutions. This is illustrated in the case of an intervention by Mexican authorities designed to strengthening capability in accordance with women's strategic gender interests. During the reconstruction of a community devastated by a flood in Chiapas, women cooked for the men working in the fabrication of bricks. One Friday, these women asked the supervisor if he could lend them the machinery (which belonged to the federal government) to use it for the weekend. They said they had learned how to operate it by watching it while they were cooking, and wanted to produce some materials for the reconstruction of their private houses. In time, the supervisor made sure that they had proper training and managed to get them a loan to acquire the machinery. To this day, they run their own construction material business. The impact of this process is noticeable at a micro-level in the women themselves; at the medium and macro-levels, it was responsible for the placement of a construction industry in a locality at constant risk of disaster risk due to poor quality of construction, and thus created employment options for both women and men.

Capabilities can be strengthened, as before, and vulnerability reduced, in either case with the knowledge of the strategic gender interests of women, taking into consideration the particularities of the social conditions in which they live. The following example demonstrates this. Civil Protection in the state of Chihuahua attempted to reduce the impact of low temperatures in the Tarahumara zone by providing warm clothing for the indigenous population, but with unequal results. Donated garments were distributed to both men and women, and although all Tarahumaras were trying to maintain their traditional costumes, men showed less resistance than women to wearing modern pants or sweaters. Those men who were less willing to wear the donated clothes also wore their traditional cotton pants with an oversized overcoat on top. But the women absolutely refused to wear any of the clothes given to them. Then Civil Protection bought metres of several different warm and thick wool fabrics with traditional patterns. These were distributed among the women along with sufficient materials for them to sew their own traditional costumes, and the intervention was successful. The strategic interest to recognise and strengthen ethnic diversity was addressed and coupled with gender analysis. Women's decisions were taken into account and sustainability took on a broader meaning, strengthening traditional cultural practices that are threatened by the dynamic of social uniformity arising from current economic and social patterns across the nation and region.

In the case of men's strategic interests, it is difficult to identify good practice in Mexico in the field of prevention, whether with respect to strengthening men's capabilities or diminishing their vulnerabilities. It can be said that perhaps the strongest vulnerability for men is their 'overgeneralisation' which in turn fosters women's invisibility; they have still not acknowledged the fact that they own particular conditions as men and therefore their gender specificities are hidden as well. In their desire to represent human kind, they have vanished as a gender. Most policies aimed at prevention are understood as applicable to all and not gender-specific but are actually based on men's experiences, though not in a way that accounts for men's practical needs or strategic interests. Paradoxically, this hinders our efforts to reduce inequities suffered by men. More precise gender analysis and a systematic commitment to include men's strategic interests in planning are needed in order to achieve more democratic, sustainable development that respects differences and advances more equitable relations between the genders. In the end, this will bring more balanced relations between men and women and safer, more equitable conditions of life for men, also.

Final Reflections

Phenomena causing disasters are natural, but disasters are not. Rather, they are social creations and products of a process of indiscriminate development oriented to a globalised and predator market. Therefore, aiming at sustainable development with gender equity can only result in safer environments for all of us. From this perspective, prevention must be at the core of the entire process or 'cycle' of disaster risk management. A mainstreaming of CDRM with a gender approach is needed to fundamentally modify unequal social relations exacerbating risk. Since preventive activities are still incipient, recovery and reconstruction best afford the opportunity, not only to prevent new risks but also to stop and reverse historical processes of social injustice, abuse, gender discrimination and other patterns of oppression and exploitation. Governmental measures should aim at creating greater preventive and response capabilities within a framework of gender equity. This will ensure the involvement needed on the part of men and women in risky communities, which in turn will surely reduce their vulnerabilities in the face of risks and disasters.

Acknowledgements

We owe the reflection regarding the overgeneralisation of men's experience and their vulnerabilities to Andrea Medina, a young Mexican lawyer devoted to the defence of the rights of women.

References

Arbeláez, A. M. 1987. 'Las Costureras', in *Historias para temblar: 19 de Septiembre de 1985*. México: Instituto Nacional de Antropología e Historia.

Castro, Cecilia. 2005a. 'La Inequidad de Género en la Gestión Integral del Riesgo de Desastre. Un Acercamiento', in *Revista Universidad Cristóbal Colón*, Núm. 20, tercera época, año III, Número especial sobre Construcción social del riesgo: desastres, vulnerabilidad y género, Veracruz, México, pp. 21–45 (Electronic version). Available online at http://www.proteccioncivil.gob.mx/upLoad/Publicaciones/especiales/LA01. pdf.

———. 2005b. 'Programa de reconstrucción de vivienda en Veracruz 1999: atención a comunidades en zonas de riesgo. Entrevista a Salomón Orta Vargas, ex Director General del Instituto Veracruzano de Desarrollo Regional', in *Revista Universidad*

Cristóbal Colón, Núm. 20, tercera época, año III, Número especial sobre Construcción social del riesgo: desastres, vulnerabilidad y género, Veracruz, pp. 141–54.

Castro, Cecilia and Reyes Emilia. 2006. *Desastres naturales y vulnerabilidad de las mujeres en México*. México: Instituto Nacional de las Mujeres (INMUJERES), Programa de Naciones Unidas para el Desarrollo (PNUD).

CIPET. 2004 (revised 29 July 2007). 'Centro de Información del Programa de Empleo Temporal, Cuadro sobre el Cierre por Dependencia, para la Secretaría de Desarrollo Social, Sedesol'. Available online at http://www.cipet.gob.mx/CIPET/transparencia/2004/tr2004.cfm.

———. 2005 (revised 29 July 2007). 'Centro de Información del Programa de Empleo Temporal, Cuadro sobre el Cierre por Dependencia, para la Secretaría de Desarrollo Social, Sedesol'. Available online at http://www.cipet.gob.mx/CIPET/transparencia/2005/tr2005.cfm.

De Barbieri, Teresita and Carlota Guzmán. 1986. 'Las Damnificadas y el Empleo', *Revista Mexicana de Sociología*, 48(2): 59–101.

Kabeer, Naila. 1995. *Reversed Realities: Gender Hierarchies in Development Thought*. New York: Verso.

Massolo and Schteingart (Coords.). 1987. *Participación social, reconstrucción y mujer. El sismo de 1985*, 116 pp. México, DF: PIEM, COLMEX-UNICEF.

Moya, Xavier, Orlando Tejada and Alvaro Montero. n.d. (s/f), *Plan Comunitario: Manejo de Riesgos con Equidad*, pp. 23. México: PNUD.

Poniatowska, Elena. 1995. *Nothing, Nobody: The Voices of the Mexico City Earthquake*. Poinatowska (Aurora de Camacho Schimidt, translator). Philadelphia: Temple University Press.

Rabell, Cecilia and Martha Mier y Teran. 1986. 'Los damnificados de los sismos de 1985 en la Ciudad de México', in *Revista Mexicana de Sociología*, 48(2): 3–28.

Reyes, Emilia. 2005. 'Género y desastres humanitarios', in *Revista Universidad Cristóbal Colón*, Núm. 20, tercera época, año III, Número especial sobre Construcción social del riesgo: desastres, vulnerabilidad y género, pp. 47–60. México, Veracruz.

———. 2006. 'Sororidad y solidaridad en el frente de la protección civil: los pactos necesarios entre hombres y mujeres para la gestión integral del riesgo de desastres', in Antología de lecturas para Guía Metodológica, en Castro y Reyes, *Desastres naturales y vulnerabilidad de las mujeres en México*, Instituto Nacional de las Mujeres (INMUJERES), Programa de Naciones Unidas para el Desarrollo (PNUD), México (Electronic version). Available online at http://www.proteccioncivil.gob.mx/upLoad/Publicaciones/especiales/LA04.pdf.

Serrat, Carolina Viñas. 2000. 'Women's Disaster Responsibility and Response to the Colima Earthquake,' in Elaine Enarson and Betty Morrow (eds), *The Gendered Terrain of Disasters: Through Women's Eyes*, pp. 161–72. Miami: IHC, Laboratory for Social and Behavioral Research. Available online at http://www.proteccioncivil.gob.mx/upLoad/Publicaciones/especiales/LA18.pdf.

UNDP. 2008. *Superar la desigualdad, reducir el riesgo. Gestión del riesgo de desastres con equidad de género*. México.

22

Towards Gender Equality in Climate Change Policy: Challenges and Perspectives for the Future

———•✦•———

Ulrike Röhr, Minu Hemmati and Yianna Lambrou

It is increasingly being confirmed by research and acknowledged in the policy debate that climate change will hit the poorest regions of the world most severely, and that the most impoverished social groups will be affected the most. It is also well known that a majority of the world's poor are women, being especially vulnerable due to cultural, religious and economic factors, as well as bearing knowledge of coping and survival strategies under changing environmental conditions. Nevertheless, there is little consideration of gender aspects in the area of adaptation to climate change in existing research or policy debates.

Climate protection and climate change have been rarely addressed as discrete topics from a gender perspective. Gender is most significantly absent from international climate negotiations and regional or national measures to prevent climate change and its implications, and undertake the necessary adaptation measures. Only a few local projects incorporate gender, for example, in vulnerability assessments.

This chapter develops the implications of this gender-blind approach and offers recommendations and strategies for change. We begin by reviewing the background of gender mainstreaming in UN work in this area and identifying five critical connections between gender and climate change. We then consider new directions in research and advocacy and substantive progress made towards gender sensitivity in climate change advocacy and policy development at the international level. Based on this discussion of achievements and constraints, the chapter concludes with three specific strategies for the future.

Gender and Climate Change—Making the Connections in International Policy

The UN has taken an active role in the pursuit of gender equality, and member countries have been formally committed to gender mainstreaming within all the UN's policy and programmes. In 1992, the UN Conference on Environment and Development produced Agenda 21, which recognised women as one of nine Major Groups whose active participation is essential to sustainable development, and the advancement of women is indeed a prerequisite for making sustainable development a reality. The Fourth World Conference on Women in 1995 subsequently adopted the *Beijing Platform for Action*, in which governments agreed to implement gender mainstreaming. Other UN conferences have also acknowledged the importance of adopting a gender-specific approach to implementing policies. Gender equality has been identified as one of the Millennium Development Goals; and it has been designated as a cross-cutting theme for work of the Commission on Sustainable Development, 2002–2017 (Hemmati 2005; Roehr and Hemmati 2008).

Since the UN Conference on Environment and Development 1992, the climate change discourse has been led by the United Nations Framework Convention on Climate Change (UNFCCC). However, despite its status as a UN process, the international climate change negotiation process has failed to adopt a gender-sensitive approach or, in fact, integrate gender aspects in any way in its deliberations and decisions on climate change mitigation and adaptation (Lambrou and Piana 2006). This failure not only causes concern in terms of pursuing gender equity at the international level but also leads to ineffective and inefficient national and international policies and measures that aim to deal with the increasingly more dramatic and extreme impacts of anthropogenic climate change.

Adaptation to Climate Change

Studies have shown that due to gender-based responsibilities and roles, women and men manage natural resources and their environment in different ways (UNEP 2004). Small farmers are especially vulnerable to the impacts of climate change. Men and women farmers possess different knowledge about coping with climate variability. Consequently, any proposed adaptation policies and measures need to be gender sensitive, ensuring that adaptation planning involves both men and women, that the relevant knowledge is taken into account when developing policies and projects and that the measures developed actually benefit those who are supposed to implement them (Roehr and Hemmati 2008).

Mitigation of Climate Change

In general, there is a lack of gender-disaggregated data related to the production of CO_2 emissions as well as the impacts and preferences of mitigation measures. Nevertheless, there are a certain amount of data that point to differences between the sexes, and lead to the assumption that the priorities of women in climate protection may be different from those of men. For example, there is considerable research confirming women's more sensitive risk perception (for example, Finucane et al. 2000), and there is some evidence that they recognise climate change as a more serious problem than men (Grunenberg and Kuckartz 2003). Gender differences are also detectable when it comes to assessing adequate response measures. While men tend to trust technical solutions, women tend to put more emphasis on lifestyle changes and reducing energy consumption (PIK 2000). Decision making in climate change planning and policy is male dominated. Hence, it may not be surprising that climate change policies are more tailored towards traditionally male livelihoods and economic conditions than towards the care economy dominated by women.

It is important to note that women's and men's contributions to climate change differ, especially with regard to their respective CO_2 emissions (Roehr 2007).

Emerging Aspects of Gender and Climate Change

Research recently undertaken on behalf of the United Nations Food and Agriculture Organization (Hemmati and Roehr 2007) has shown that some gender analyses exist in some areas related to climate change and protection such as energy, water, agriculture and disaster management/ risk reduction (as demonstrated in this book). Issue-specific gender and women's networks active in research and advocacy have ensured that such sector analyses are available. However, in most cases, this work remains unconnected to the work and debates on climate change. For example, there is a significant amount of research on gender aspects of agriculture, and some of the existing knowledge (for example, strategies for coping with drought or other changes in weather patterns) can be used to understand the impacts of and potential adaptation measures in response to climate change. However, such analyses have not been taken into account in climate-related policy making, such as negotiating mechanisms for adaptation support. Given that small farmers, who are usually women, produce food and ensure food security for the family, they must be provided with access to information, education and capacity development. They need to have easier access to land, water and other natural resources, in order to continue to ensure food security. Existing institutions and local practices must be evaluated regarding their contribution to climate change adaptation so as to ensure that community and household resources are managed sustainably. By ensuring the equitable access of benefits, vulnerable groups will have greater opportunities for improved livelihoods. Overexploitation of certain resources will be reduced, which in turn can support climate change mitigation measures.

Other critical issues that should be addressed in gender-sensitive research and receive attention of policy makers include the following:

1. Climate change induced migration: Climate change is likely to in-crease human migration and thus exacerbate associated challenges. Soil degradation, water shortages, rising sea levels and increased frequency and severity of extreme weather events, among others, may force people to sell off their assets and migrate when trad-itional coping mechanisms do not suffice. When whole regions are affected, environmental resources can no longer support cur-rent livelihoods, and traditional risk-sharing mechanisms, based on kin and social groups, may not be adequate anymore.

2. Increased conflicts due to climate change: Potential sources of conflict include water, food and fuel, as well as competition for agricultural land, housing, conflict over relief and rebuilding aid after natural disasters, health care and migration. In addition,

climate change may exacerbate inequalities and worsen poverty, thus increasing the potential for conflict, as Osei-Agyemang (2007: 25) describes for the situation in Darfur, Sudan:

> In many developing regions of the world where the balance of peace is barely maintained, imminent climate change events could eventually tip the scales and cause unprecedented social and political catastrophe. (…) In regions of the world where there is little economic development, low Human Development Indices, tenuous infrastructure, and fragile socio-political conditions, the risks and consequences of micro- and macro-climate change events are much greater. Thus, it is imperative to understand what may be described as *socio-climatic* impacts of global warming.

3. The effects of climate change on health: Women's and men's health may not be affected in the same way. Changes in environmental quality (air, water and soil) can impact women and men differently because of biological differences or diverse exposure patterns. Hence, the provision of health services must be gender specific.

4. Demographic change in the global North and population politics in the global South: There is also a growing debate about demographic change in various industrialised countries where decreasing birth rates and extended life expectancy lead to shifts in the population structure. It would be important to learn more about the potential effects on both gender relations and environment. In terms of population growth, Thomas (2007: 2) writes:

> Recent white paper reports have recognized the importance of climate change and population growth as both interacting and contributing to severe deterioration of the world's environment; predicted consequences include conflict, mass migration, water shortage, and food security issues.

5. Gender-specific consumption patterns: Climate change is closely related to consumption as the most prominent human behaviours causing green house gas emissions include energy consumption, transport, (industrial) agriculture and conversion of forests and wildlife habitats into land for various human purposes. Gender-specific consumption patterns differ significantly between the global North and the global South. In the South, questions of survival and poverty are the main focus, whereas in the North an expanding consumer culture has been evident. In the North, environmental degradation is mostly caused by over-consumption;

in the South, poverty narrows the range of behavioural choices and often forces people into environmentally degrading behaviour patterns (Hemmati 2000).

Gender Mainstreaming Strategies

We see three major streams of activity that must be undertaken in science and politics in order to address gender issues in climate change mitigation and adaptation more effectively.

Research

We need an improved knowledge base about the nexus of gender and climate change. Sufficient data and analyses exist confirming that there are gaps in our understanding that must be filled. This can, and indeed should, mainly be done by integrating gender into climate-related research, obtaining gender-disaggregated data and including gender considerations in the analysis of individual and societal behaviour relating to climate. However, specific research taking a women's and gender studies approach also warrants investment, for example, in relation to women's resilience and coping strategies, and questions relating to ownership and control of resources. For example, the environmental degradation process in different ecological regions has not been sufficiently documented to understand the causal relationships between climate change variability and its impacts on men's and women's livelihoods. Existing local strategies must be the starting point for documenting and understanding peoples' coping strategies. These local efforts must be linked with regional and national policies and initiatives aiming to reduce poverty and increase food security, thus ensuring that men and women can sustain themselves, their communities and cultures.

Policies and Political Support

Gender mainstreaming in climate policy depends on having evidence-based knowledge, but also on clearly stated and demonstrated political will. Gender-sensitive policies need to be developed and political leaders and spokespeople from government, civil society, business and research should expressly support these. Gender-relevant knowledge should be made available to the above-mentioned stakeholders, in terms of their own discourse and conveying the message in their own language. Integrating a new issue like gender into the stage of climate policy is a matter of advocacy, and cross-sectoral coalition building, particularly with individuals and organisations interested in social aspects of climate change.

For example, national institutions must understand the close link between the sustainable management of natural resources, food security and poverty reduction as an efficient way of providing the rural population (men as well as women) with tools to respond efficiently to such climate change processes as drought, inundations, plant and animal pests, and so forth. At present, such understanding is low and scattered at best, and appropriate tools are hardly being made available.

Policy support is also needed to develop and strengthen the capacities of rural development institutions and extension staff to understand women's needs alongside men's in the areas of energy, water, agriculture and disaster management, especially with regard to gender-sensitive participatory approaches. Equal access to and control of natural resources are the basis for being able to address unpredictable situations in dealing with climate variability and its effects on people. In order to share information about climate change, gender-sensitive, participatory and multi-stakeholder platforms at the local and provincial level should be initiated and resourced. As local or regional level support of integrated natural resource management is of prime importance, this is especially needed at the local and provincial level. Additionally, potential coping strategies should be developed and shared. Such adaptation measures should be jointly implemented. Starting points for adaptation must always build on existing knowledge and practices of communities and their coping strategies. Any policy must include—not only take account of—the most vulnerable people and also sensitise planners and governments to the existence of local, regional and national networks of gender expertise.

Specific Tools and Materials for Gender Mainstreaming

A variety of tools have been developed for the purpose of gender mainstreaming in policy making as well as implementation and evaluation.

Among them are checklists that help determine possible gender implications of draft environmental policies (FrauenUmweltNetz/LIFE 2004) or reviews of draft policies produced by internal working groups. Fact sheets and brief brochures on gender issues provide summary information, and gender mainstreaming courses can initiate learning as well as intra-organisational discourse on the topics. However, not much is available in the context of climate change. One exception is the vulnerability assessment conducted by CARE Canada (Dazé 2006), which does take a gender-sensitive perspective. Using climate-related examples in mainstreaming materials, directly addressing climate policies in the language of people who work on climate change from a policy or scientific angle, is crucial; it ensures that tools and materials are understandable, accessible and likely to be used to effect change.

Bringing Gender into the Climate Change Discourse

We now turn to a discussion of the state of the art in this ongoing effort to integrate gender into all aspects of the climate change discourse and policy development. First, we consider past achievements that have begun to support gender sensitivity in climate change discourse, especially through international conferences, and then examine factors that we believe are constraining gender sensitivity on the part of women's organisations as well as traditional climate change stakeholders.

Gender issues are rarely addressed in the UN climate change negotiations, even though there was an encouraging start at the First Conference of the Parties (COP) to the UN Framework Convention. An international women's forum 'Solidarity in the Greenhouse' attracted 200 women from twenty-five countries to discuss their views on climate protection. Unfortunately, there was a lack of follow-up. During the following years, gender and women's issues as well as representation of women's organisations were lacking at the COPs. Only 5 years later, at COP6 in The Hague, women's participation got some attention again: various statements in the daily newsletters of the NGO community highlighted the important role of women in the negotiations as they served as key bridge builders between opposing parties. This can be seen as a second starting point, picked up by the following COPs.

The first (and so far only) official mentioning of women is contained in the text of a COP7 Marrakech resolution: Decision FCCC/CP/2001/13/

add.4 (2001) calls for more nominations of women to UNFCCC and Kyoto Protocol bodies. It also tasks the Secretariat with determining the gender composition of these bodies and with bringing their results to the attention of the parties. At the following COPs, several side events on gender and climate change and meetings of gender experts took place, aiming to bring gender aspects to the attention of participants and to discuss strategies towards increasing cooperation and improving lobbying efforts for a stronger integration of gender perspectives into the negotiations and the implementation of outcomes.

A real shift in women's activities was achieved at COP11/COP-MOP1 in 2005 in Montreal. In preparation for the conference, a strategy paper was drafted by genanet/LIFE identifying possible entry points for gender aspects into the climate change debate. Women then engaged in three complementary activities:

1. Raising awareness and disseminating information via an exhibition booth with the theme 'gender—justice—climate', two 'Climate Talk' events, and a statement in plenary.
2. Building women's capacity and joint strategising on gender mainstreaming in climate policy via women's caucus meetings.
3. Developing a future research agenda and initiating a gender and climate change research network via convening a research workshop.

These activities helped kick-start a new era in women's involvement and gender issues in the UNFCCC process. After almost 10 years of discontinuous and uncoordinated participation by women's organisations, the path from COP1 has finally been picked up again. Activities from COP11 were continued at COP12 in Nairobi. Among others, first results of the research review on gender and climate change, undertaken by the authors on behalf of the FAO, were presented and discussed. This report aimed to provide 'hard facts' on gender and climate change for better argumentation and to identify research gaps. COP13 in Bali, Indonesia, is the first time that the hosting ministry has expressed interest involving more women's organisations in the conference and to organising a high-level panel on gender and climate change. In addition, genanet has organised support for women's participation via the UNDP, and other women's organisations from the North (for example, WECF, Women's

Environment and Development Organization [WEDO], MADRE) have also resolved to attend the COP.

Constraints and Resources

Despite these achievements, the majority of climate experts are not yet convinced that integrating gender into climate change policy will make it more efficient and more effective. Most of these experts are natural scientists or economists who give more credit to 'hard facts' than to individual case studies or glaring inequalities. They will need further, preferably quantitative, evidence of gender sensitivity in climate change in order to draw their attention to gender issues. Viewing climate change and climate protection more as a scientific than as a political process, they also tend not to link political goals like social and gender justice to climate-related policy making. As equity issues gain increasing attention in the focus on adaptation in UNFCCC process, it may become easier to include aspects of gender and gender justice in the future.

At the same time, many women's organisations (most of them involved in UN CSD debates) are not familiar with the different process and procedures of the UNFCCC and do not feel comfortable with the debates dominated by technocratic thinking and economic argumentation that lead to disregard of the social aspects of climate change and less attention to the integration of gender aspects.

Another reason for the absence of women's organisations in climate change-related negotiations may be due to the different mechanisms of participation: 'women' are not a separate constituency in the UNFCCC as they are in the UN CSD process, where they are one of the nine major groups. Thus, women have to lobby for the integration of gender aspects not only within parties or governments but also within key constituencies engaged in the climate change discourse including environmental NGOs, business and industry NGOs, research organisations, indigenous peoples and local and regional authorities. Currently, of about 800 NGOs accredited to the UNFCCC as observers, there are only five women's organisations, and of these just one or two participate regularly.

Skutsch (2002) mentions the excellent work done by female negotiators leading to the Kyoto Protocol and discusses why they did not integrate gender aspects: they needed to focus on universal issues in order to have success. She assumes that gender issues might have diverted attention from generalised desired outcomes. This analysis is in line with the perspectives of many negotiators from parties as well as from environmental organisations: 'First we have to mitigate climate change, all the other issues and especially social issues we can deal with afterwards.'

But can this wait until tomorrow if we are not able to integrate the needs, livelihoods and innovative ideas of more than half of the population today? These structural disadvantages in international climate change negotiations do not entirely answer the question why there is so little involvement by women and why there is only marginal integration of gender perspectives at the regional, national or local levels, where traditionally women have had the highest share in planning and decision making. One of the conclusions of our research review on gender and climate change is that women and women's organisations are indeed involved, but not under the label 'climate change'. They are working extensively on gender and energy issues, farming and biodiversity, water-related issues, consumption, transport and of course natural disaster issues. Linking this work with climate change, however, is lacking. Putting the gender aspects of natural disasters, water, energy and so on in the context of climate change will pave the way for including gender perspectives in the wider climate change debate and recognising women's voices in this context.

Women Raise their Voices

Following the extensive media coverage of the latest Intergovernmental Panel on Climate Change (IPCC) Report, 2007, women's organisations became more involved in climate debates and began to raise their voices. For example:

1. On the occasion of the International Women's Day 2007, genanet/ LIFE organised a photo shooting on a market place in Berlin, Germany, with the theme 'Women protect the climate—women demand climate protection'. Photos of women delivering their messages to politicians were taken. These messages clearly state that women want politicians to take stronger actions and that they are willing to contribute, too, by changing their behaviour. The campaign was broadened to the international level for the

G8 Summit that took place in Germany some weeks later. It is now evident that women have strong opinions regarding climate protection; they are willing to formulate these, and they want to be heard.

2. In the United Kingdom, the Women's Environmental Network (WEN) and the National Federation of Women's Institutes (NFWI) carried out a survey that examined women's attitudes towards climate change, actions taken by women to reduce their carbon emissions and the decision-making responsibilities they assume. The findings show 'that climate change is a women's issue, affecting women differently given their different social role and status' (WEN & NFWI 2007: 4). Based, in part, on these findings, a Women's Manifesto on Climate Change has since been elaborated.

3. Women from all over Africa met in Uganda in mid-2007 to discuss gender and climate change in Africa and what to do to engage more women's organisations in the discussions. A network of organisations from the African region working on gender and climate change was established, and strategies and issues for immediate attention were discussed. These include influencing local, national, regional and international policy responses to climate change as well as focusing on biofuels, forestry issues (such as offsets and avoided deforestation), and undertaking local case studies documenting the impacts of climate change on women.

4. The WEDO, based in New York, is aiming to partner with local women's and environmental NGOs in developing countries to advocate for a gender perspective and for increasing women's participation in national responses to climate change, particularly in government adaptation planning. They are also launching a media campaign calling on the US government to engage in global climate change negotiations.

Three Directions for the Future

The previous discussion illustrates progress in the areas of awareness, discourse, policy development and women's personal and organisational involvement. We end by highlighting three new directions to build on these accomplishments.

Broaden the Movement and Join Forces: To create an influential movement demands more coordination. For example, to prepare for the recent UNFCCC COPs, genanet started early to organise and host regular women's caucus meetings and set up a mailing list to disseminate information. This level of coordination is important. Additionally, it would be desirable to hold global strategy meetings with women's organisations and gender experts (for example, every 2 years), with the aim of discussing latest research and recent developments from a gender perspective and strategising about the integration of gender perspectives in climate change negotiations, programmes and measures at all levels. A small step in this direction is the capacity building workshops held prior to the UNFCCC COPS that started with COP13 in 2007 in Bali.

Information and Sensitisation: On gender aspects in climate change must not be limited to the UNFCCC and Kyoto Protocol processes, of course, but should also reach stakeholders at other levels to get more people involved. With a broader and more integrated social movement to mainstream gender concerns into climate change policy and action, more continuous participation in UNFCCC activities, and more visible interventions by and with women, it may well be possible for women's organisations to be recognised as a distinct constituency in future global climate change negotiations.

Create a Coordinating Body: As discussed earlier, there are numerous knowledge gaps about gender and climate change. Nevertheless, in recent years, women's organisations and gender networks were established, mainly from the South, that deal with gender-sensitive approaches in energy, water, agriculture, biodiversity and risk reduction and disaster management. These networks not only coordinate and assemble existing research and knowledge but also dedicate themselves to producing overview compilations of existing knowledge, and advocating the inclusion of gender aspects into policy in international fora and at the national level.

Due to the expertise and resources of these networks, extensive materials aimed at sensitising decision makers have been published, and training and research undertaken. The link to climate change is mostly lacking, but these could provide entry points and a basis for developing positions concerning gender and climate change. Strengthening gender perspectives in climate change policy demands a strong and well-funded network capable of serving as a competence centre that would facilitate discussions, provide regional studies, collect data and support institutions in mainstreaming gender into their climate change activities.

Cooperate within the climate change community: It would be very useful to cooperate with those governments, intergovernmental organisations and NGOs that are aware of gender inequalities and prepared to support gender activities. Particularly, environmental NGOs have often demonstrated even less gender awareness than some of the governments, indicating a need for training and sensitisation. Intergovernmental organisations like UNDP, UNEP and FAO could be supportive by addressing climate change in their gender equality strategies and encouraging other UN organisations, particularly UNFCCC, to address gender aspects as well. Furthermore, we also need 'champions' or leading figures, such as outstanding ministers to spearhead gender mainstreaming in the debate.

In conclusion, it will certainly take more time and more effort to provide substantive data demonstrating that (and how) climate change is a gender issue. This will help to make a significant contribution to influence climate change policies and debates and create more just and more effective climate policies. The time to do so is now. If we are willing, and we join our efforts among many stakeholders committed to gender equality at all levels, we will succeed.

Acknowledgements

We thank our colleagues in this global movement, and invite readers to visit www.gendercc.net.

References

Dazé, A. 2006. *The Reducing Vulnerability to Climate Change (RVCC) Project in Bangladesh: Gender Perspectives*. CARE Canada, RVCC Project.

Finucane, M. L., P. Slovic, C. K. Mertz, J. Flynn and T. A. Satterfield. 2000. 'Gender, Race and Perceived Risk: The "White Male" Effect', *Health, Risk & Society*, 2(2): 159–72.

FrauenUmweltNetz/LIFE. 2004. *Towards Gender Justice in Environmental Policy. Implementing Gender Mainstreaming in Germany*. Frankfurt, Germany: FrauenUmweltNetz/LIFE.

Grunenberg, Heike and Udo Kuckartz. 2003. *Umweltbewusstsein im Wandel*. Ergebnisse der UBA-Studie Umweltbewusstsein in Deutschland 2002. Environmental Consciousness in Flux. Results of the Study of the German Federal Environment Agency, Environmental Consciousness in Germany 2002. German Federal Environment Agency, Opladen.

Hemmati, M. and U. Roehr. 2007. *Gender and Climate Change: Existing Research and Knowledge Gaps*. Unpublished report prepared on behalf of FAO, Berlin.

Hemmati, M. 2000. 'Gender-specific Patterns of Poverty and (Over-) Consumption in Developing and Developed Countries', in E. Jochem, J. Sathaye and Daniel Biulle (eds), *Society, Behavior, and Climate Change Mitigation*. Proceedings of IPCC Expert Group Meeting on Social Scientific Approaches to Climate Change Mitigation, pp. 169–90. Dordrecht, NL: Kluwer Academic Publishers.

———. 2005. *Gender & Climate Change in the North: Issues, Entry Points and Strategies for the Post-2012 Process and Beyond*. Berlin: Genanet/Focal Point Gender Justice and Sustainability.

Lambrou, Y. and G. Piana. 2006. *Gender: The Missing Component of the Response to Climate Change*. Rome, Italy: FAO.

Osei-Agyemang, M. 2007. 'Temperatures Rising. Understanding the Relationships between Climate Change, Conflict', in *Women & Environments International Magazine*, No 74/75, Spring/Summer, pp. 25–27. Women and Gender Studies Institute, New College, University of Toronto, CA.

PIK—Potsdam Institute for Climate Impact Research. 2000. *Weather Impacts on Natural, Social and Economic Systems*. Potsdam.

Roehr, U. and M. Hemmati. 2008. 'Solidarity in the Greenhouse: Gender Equality and Climate Change', in V. Grover (ed.), *Global Warming and Climate Change. Kyoto Ten Years and Still Counting*, pp 779–804. Enfield, USA: Science Publishers.

Roehr, U. 2007. *Gender, Climate Change and Adaptation. Introduction to the Gender Dimensions*. Background paper for the project 'Local Experiences Shape the Adaptation Debate, run by Both Ends'. Available online at http://www.bothends.info/project/project_info.php?Id=50&scr=tp

Skutsch, Margaret. 2002. 'Protocols, Treaties, and Action: The "Climate Change Process" Viewed through Gender Spectacles', in *Gender and Development—Climate Change*, 10(2): 30–39. Oxford: Oxfam.

Thomas, G. 2007. 'Speech delivered at "Population Forum", London, January 2007', in *Population and Sustainability Network* Newsletter, March.

UNEP. 2004. *Women and the Environment*. UNEP Policy Series. Written by Irene Dankelman. Nairobi: UNEP.

WEN & NFWI. 2007. *Getting in the Picture. A Survey of Women's Priorities for Action and Involvement in Tackling Climate Change*. London: WEN & NFWI.

23

Engendering Tsunami Recovery in Sri Lanka: The Role of UNIFEM and its Partners

———•✦•———

Chandni Joshi and Mihir R. Bhatt

The tsunami that hit the countries of the Indian Ocean in December 2004 had a severe impact in Sri Lanka, a country ridden for decades with conflict and poverty. Around 31,000 people were killed and 15,000 were severely injured. Furthermore, 500,000 people were displaced, and the damage to infrastructure was extensive. Nearly 400,000 people were put out of work by the tsunami, and hence it is easy to imagine that daily life in Sri Lanka came to a temporary but damaging halt. Women and children suffered significantly higher casualties than adult men (Christoplos 2006). Challenges were enormous with regard to restarting people's lives. For example, almost 80 per cent of all the fishing boats (about 22,940 vessels) were destroyed by the tsunami. Considering that a vast part of the Sri Lankan population on the coast is employed by the fishing industry, the dimension of the disaster's impact on people's livelihoods is readily apparent.

We take this opportunity to analyse gender issues emerging in the aftermath that specifically affected girls and women, and relate these to interventions by government and by non-governmental organisations

(NGOs) involved in relief and reconstruction efforts. Recognising that many significant initiatives were undertaken, we focus here primarily on reviewing and assessing the model responses of UNIFEM and its partners.

Gender Issues in the Aftermath of the Tsunami

Women and children are in normal times more vulnerable than men to inequalities and violations; in times of disasters, this vulnerability is exacerbated. There are thus generally more casualties of women and children than men during disasters. In the South Asian context, women as survivors are doubly vulnerable, particularly if they have become heads of households or carry the additional burden on behalf of their extended families (Parakrama 2006).

The role of women in disaster response and disaster mitigation stands out remarkably, particularly as women are not only more vulnerable to disasters but also often sidelined and not integrated in the planning and implementation of recovery and rebuilding processes. Women in South Asia tend to be more affected by virtue of their lower economic and social status and tremendous gender discrimination. Besides their physical vulnerability, they have less access to resources and fewer opportunities to be part of decision-making processes or to actively participate in recovery planning. They are overburdened with domestic responsibilities and can be vulnerable to gender-based violence in the context of relief and reconstruction (AIDMI 2005).

Yet, this vulnerability does not render them helpless. In many conflict-ridden countries like Sri Lanka, women have for many years been at the forefront of survival strategies for their families and communities. In disasters, women lead relief at the local level. Women in Sri Lanka assumed critical roles in the response to the tsunami emergency, taking in relatives and children orphaned in the tsunami, offering care and support within camps and shelters for grieving survivors, participating in the distribution of emergency aid and health care services, and taking up leadership roles in organising reconstruction and rehabilitation (UNIFEM 2005).

We briefly review some of the many specific gender concerns that arose for girls and women in the aftermath of the tsunami before turning to the role of women's organisations in response and recovery.

Physical and Sexual Violence

In the wake of the tsunami, many persons were forced to live in what were generally very poor conditions that prevailed in relief camps. These were often not designed with women's needs in mind. There was very little privacy for women, and sanitary systems were not in place that catered to their needs. Additionally, as lighting is poor in the relief camps, women were vulnerable to a variety of physical abuses. Rape, trafficking and violence were not uncommon in camps that were inadequately designed and where provisions for women's needs were not incorporated. Apart from poor conditions in relief camps, increased alcoholism also contributed to an increase in violence against women. In the aftermath of the tsunami, many men used alcohol as a means to deal with the stress, trauma and depression that ensued.

Mental Health

Though both women and men had mental health needs to deal with, the needs of women were particularly acute due to the gender dimensions of the disaster and its effects. The fragility of physical health and safety mentioned earlier added to the women's sense of insecurity. To live in constant danger or constant fear is bad for mental health, so psychosocial needs can be addressed by improving safety in the camps. Pregnant women, especially widowed women who had their babies without their husbands, experienced additional mental health stress which added to the normal strains associated with pregnancy. Women's specific mental health needs must be prioritised and adequately met. If unaddressed, these will have major implications, not only for the central cultural role that women play in caring for all members of the family but also as heads of household, providers and contributors to household and national incomes.

Young Brides and Education

There were increasing concerns about educational opportunities for many young Sri Lankan women. This was because, as the number of women who died in the tsunami vastly outnumbered the number of men who perished, demand increased for eligible brides. This created a situation where increasingly more young women were married to significantly older men. The concerns are twofold: first, this could entail physical, sexual and mental abuse; and second, early marriage diminishes the chances of young women to learn, grow or acquire vocational skills. Once women are married, opportunities to obtain education are reduced, as household responsibilities and family care overtake them. There is a real concern that in the most affected regions, a whole generation of young women will miss any chances of education due to forced early marriages.

Access to Relief Funds

Gender comes very much into play with regard to accessing resources and tsunami relief. Women were disadvantaged at the outset as household allocations were usually distributed in the name of the husband. In cases where women were widowed, the authorities often refused to give her aid, as her husband was not present. This was a very clear example of gender bias and patriarchal socialisation processes and mindsets, which for the most part, are part of policy making. As a result, women were often not able to access the necessary resources and aid to assist their families or themselves.

Lost Employment Opportunities for Women

In Sri Lanka as elsewhere in the tsunami-affected region, there have been severe difficulties for women striving to get back to work, as their liveli-hoods were located in areas which have been destroyed by the tsunami. This is because women were predominantly involved in domestic and cottage industries or were working as uninsured home-based workers, precisely those industries that were hardest hit by the devastation caused by the tsunami. Therefore, the tsunami has had a differential effect on livelihood resources as well.

Organisational Responses to Women

Government of Sri Lanka

One of the institutional responses taken by the Sri Lankan authorities to the 2004 tsunami is the establishment of the Disaster Management

Centre (DMC). The key responsibilities of the DMC are to reduce the country's vulnerability to future disasters and manage post disaster activities (DMC 2005). The DMC responded to the tsunami by:

1. distributing one million information leaflets on floods, cyclones and other disasters in order to educate people;
2. initiating radio- and television-based tsunami education and warning systems and setting up the hierarchy of early warning action procedures and
3. setting up mechanisms to facilitate cooperation among central government, district level government, donors and development agencies.

Selected NGOs

Oxfam has been very active in gender issues in Sri Lanka. Its most important activity has been the production of a briefing note on gender that has since been used as a basis for much of the post-tsunami work on this topic in Sri Lanka. In order to coordinate the issues of gender and gender protection in Sri Lanka, Oxfam has established an organisation called Gender Watch. This is an organisation dedicated to the protection and promotion of issues regarding women in the country and consists of the major NGOs active in tsunami recovery programmes in the tsunami regions as well as some of the largest multilateral organisations undertaking tsunami reconstruction work. It is hoped that this alliance will be able to promote women's issues in Sri Lanka in the post-tsunami environment and support issues of women's security and health in the ongoing.

Action Aid is one of the many international NGOs involved in the relief and recovery process in Sri Lanka. In the wake of the tsunami, they were engaged in meeting the immediate humanitarian needs that appeared and in rebuilding livelihoods. Furthermore, Action Aid also emphasised psychosocial help to assist victims to overcome the post-tsunami trauma, and the importance of getting children back in school as soon as possible. They, too, were mainly concerned about the poorest among the poor in whatever work they were doing as a response to the tsunami. They also had, and still have, an important and interesting involvement in women and the special issues they face. Action Aid worked closely with eleven different local organisations and in close consultation with the Government of Sri Lanka, local administrations, different UN agencies, international NGOs and community-based organisations.

The Sarvodaya Women's Movement (SWM) aims to provide women with opportunity and direction so that they can assume their rightful place in society and realise their aspirations, hopes and strengths. They have several key aims and objectives. First, they aim to realise the contribution of gender to the empowerment of the family and the country's economic development. Second, they wish to empower women by generating awareness among them, and by building capacity through knowledge and increasing responsibility. Third, they aim to bring about the full development of women as mothers, social workers, income generators and spiritual leaders. Importantly, for a country that has been divided by civil war, they make no separation in activities between ethnic or religious group, giving help solely based on need.

After the tsunami, Sarvodaya instituted several activities. In order to enable the community to conduct spiritual activities on behalf of their relatives lost to the waves, Sarvodaya provided spiritual assistance. The organisation gave women materials and financial resources in order to assist them in conducting the *Dhanya*, the religious distribution of funds after a death or tragedy.

With regard to the environment, the organisation concentrated on planting coconut palms and mangroves that were destroyed by the tsunami and which were an important economic asset. As women were paid for this work, the scheme served several purposes: it replaced the natural stock lost to the tsunami, it provided the communities with income and it provided women with temporary employment. With regard to women's health, several activities have been undertaken. These activities include running health clinics for women and children, providing each patient with a medical file, running eye and dental clinics and distribution of spectacles free of charge. Sarvodaya has no reproductive health education programmes despite the increasingly high rates of pre-marital sex and rising teenage pregnancy rates. SWM helped widows and other female victims replace or secure key documents needed to demonstrate residence, documents usually registered in the husband's name. Education on the importance of documentation and how to access it was also undertaken.

Sarvodaya also focused on economic empowerment by facilitating self-employment through provision of finances and relevant trainings, encouragement of business proposals and provision of start-up resources. The focus has been to help women establish businesses and manufacturing products for export.

UNIFEM and its Partners Respond

UNIFEM played a key role in building women's capacities in South Asia, in linking them to policy makers, and providing them a space to voice their needs and priorities (UNIFEM n.d.; UNIFEM 2005). Essentially, the intervention was demand-driven, participatory and rights-based. UNIFEM's work in Sri Lanka, including that with the government, supports an integrated effort towards gender-responsive recovery and reconstruction. Promoting the leadership of women and women's organisation, it focused on reviving livelihoods of tsunami-affected women, supporting them in moving up the value chain of production and in making women's human rights central to tsunami relief, recovery and rehabilitation efforts. UNIFEM offered support early in the post-tsunami period and hosted a relationship-based effort. UNIFEM in Sri Lanka identified some key local partners, which included existing partners, women's groups, the government, the Human Rights Commission, the Ministry of Women's Affairs, the National Committee for Women (NCW), the UN System, NGOs and experts from the region. Key inputs from women's organisations focused on issues ranging from livelihoods to sensitising the media on gender issues and highlighting women's concerns through insights from tsunami-recovering women. It identified the following integrated priorities:

- Identify the specific needs of women, and women-headed households in particular, in the reconstruction effort, and advocate for an adequate response to those needs.
- Support women's organisations in their efforts towards recovery and reconstruction in tsunami-affected areas.
- Ensure that efforts undertaken by the UN system, international NGOs and multilateral and bilateral organisations mainstream the specific needs of women in the reconstruction and rehabilitation phases.

- Build the capacity of UNIFEM's partners to advocate for the full inclusion of women's perspectives into programme design and implementation.

The response to the tsunami in Sri Lanka has focused on adding value to ongoing local and mainstream initiatives, and to activities of civil society and international organisations and local partners. UNIFEM has added value to the recovery process in two key ways: first, by promoting the leadership of female survivors in recovery processes, and second by protecting and reviving the livelihoods of female tsunami victims in these processes. In adding such values, UNIFEM made use of three different channels. First, UNIFEM focused on enhancing existing female voices in Sri Lanka, such as the NCW and the Siyath Foundation and the Centre for Women's Research (CENWOR). UNIFEM brought them together and linked them with the process, facilitating cohesion and synergy in their efforts. It supported the NCW to expand its data collection initiative in relief camps, using the women's agency to collect qualitative data covering 53,613 households. These data were shared at the National Meeting as well as used later by women's groups to advocate for engendering the post-tsunami policies and programmes. Non-traditional employment opportunities for women were promoted; for example, teachers were trained as counsellors and community health workers. Issues related to women's mental health were addressed through a community approach, and this contributed to the building of a cadre of local mental health experts. In short, UNIFEM helped its partners, not only in raising questions but also in facilitating the inclusion of women in the recovery process, and in presenting them with new options around opportunities for work, skills, education and changed roles.

Second, by providing a platform for tsunami-affected women and decision makers to come together, women were able to articulate their priorities for the recovery process. In May 2005, over 150 women survivors of tsunami from all parts of Sri Lanka were brought together to share their experiences with the policy makers. This brought to the fore the leadership roles they had played in rescue operations, as well as key concerns of women which had not been addressed. These included access to land, shelter, privacy and personal security; access to health and education; access to cash and credit; and the exclusion of women, particularly female heads of households, in planning and resource allocations on livelihoods, resettlement, housing and infrastructure development. As a result, senior officials of the government were requested to place before the Development Forum the urgent need to give women's groups access to policy-making bodies, recognising that they were already civil society organisations actively contributing to recovery and relief efforts in the affected communities. UNIFEM and its partners used survey results and survivors to bring voices of the affected women to the forefront, influencing recovery policies. Its influence on the legal framework developed in Sri Lanka is believed to have been significant as women are given deserved recognition as both victims and active recoverers.

Third, UNIFEM promoted South–South partnership and leadership building through initiatives focusing on livelihoods, mental health and disaster recovery. UNIFEM has supported and organised trainings and consultations to strengthen women's voices in disaster risk reduction and recovery. It supported a training entitled 'Disaster Risk Reduction and Transfer in Tsunami Recovery' designed by All India Disaster Mitigation Institute (AIDMI) and jointly conducted by AIDMI and the Social and Human Development Consultants in Galle, Sri Lanka, in October 2006 (AIDMI 2007a). In November 2006 in Islamabad, Pakistan, UNIFEM South Asia, in partnership with the Ministry of Social Welfare and Special Education, Government of Pakistan, organised a one-and-half-day Regional Consultation on Engendering Disaster Management, followed by a 5-day Training of Trainers Workshop on Disaster Risk Reduction and Risk Transfer in Recovery. The Regional Consultation and the Training of Trainers were attended by governmental and NGOs of Sri Lanka, Pakistan and India. Thus, the work that was begun in Sri Lanka was taken to the regional level. Experts from India and Sri Lanka shared their knowledge through a specialised module on engendered risk reduction and disaster management. The Regional Consultation concluded with the Islamabad Declaration (AIDMI 2007b). With the Government of Sri Lanka's Ministry of Child Development and Women Empowerment (MoCDWE), UNIFEM organised a National Meeting on UNIFEM-funded tsunami projects in Sri Lanka. This meeting was held in December 2006 in Sri Lanka to review activities of the local partners in the women's tsunami recovery programme which was coming to a close, to consolidate the gains made and to plan for the future (AIDMI 2007c).

UNIFEM Partnerships

UNIFEM's partners on the ground are a diverse mix of eighteen international, national and local organisations that address specific priority areas or a mix of areas. The partners of UNIFEM are the International Labour Organisation (ILO), the Senior Gender Advisor of the UNRC, AIDMI, the Consortium of Women's Entrepreneurs of India (CWEI), MoCDWE, NCW, Human Rights Commission, Colombo (HRC), the Women and Media Collective (WMC), Siyath Foundation, NGO Management Development Centre, Social and Human Resource Development Consultant (SHRDC), Women's Development Centre (WDC), CENWOR, Damrivi Foundation, Muslim Women's Research and Action Forum (MWRAF), Dammacarini, Women's Development Foundation (WDF) and SAARTHAK.

UNIFEM has played a critical role in enabling these organisations to successfully implement gender-sensitive strategies of relief and rehabilitation. The organisation has been extremely successful in terms of partnering with local organisations in Sri Lanka, becoming involved in actions at the local level and in advocacy at multiple levels, and in clearly demonstrating innovative ways of engendering the tsunami response. It is important to remember that UNIFEM's response to the tsunami in Sri Lanka was a building of its long history of work with women's organisations and networks. UNIFEM came into Sri Lanka at the insistence of its partners (it was new to work on disaster relief) because UNIFEM partners and their network members were among the millions who lost their lives, homes or livelihoods, especially home-based workers. UNIFEM came to Colombo with an open mind, holding consultative processes with government, women's groups, the UN system and affected women to ensure that its relief interventions responded to the urgency of the present and did not recreate the gender inequities of the past. Recognition of the fact that women have different and special recovery needs was at the core of UNIFEM partners' involvement in Sri Lanka. They have worked in both central and marginalised locations such as Galle, Matara, Ampara, as well as in conflict-affected areas. The selection of primarily women's organisations was a key to the success of UNIFEM operations in Sri Lanka at household, project and policy levels.

Assessing the Outcomes of UNIFEM and its Partners

The recognition that women have different and special recovery needs and that gender needs to be central to relief, recovery and rehabilitation efforts was at the core of UNIFEM partners' interventions in Sri Lanka. The main objectives of UNIFEM partners in Sri Lanka were to:

- focus on poor women and support their livelihood recovery;
- strengthen capacities of women and women's organisations to lead the tsunami recovery;
- focus on multilevel interventions and forge cross-sector linkages and partnerships to engender tsunami responses in favour of women and
- promote a culture of safety and protect women's human rights.

To meet the objectives, UNIFEM with its partners implemented a wide range of activities for the tsunami-recovering women of Sri Lanka in the locations that were most affected and neglected, especially in terms of women's concerns. All the projects were implemented between the relief and the rehabilitation phases. Thus, UNIFEM support was valued and considered timely by most of the implementing agencies. Originally designed to be a short term, some projects were extended as the request of the implementing agency.

Engendering tsunami responses at multiple levels takes time. In general, many partners felt that there was insufficient time for them to complete some of the key activities. We review later other conclusions to be drawn about the outcomes of UNIFEM's work and that of its partners in responding to the gender dimensions of the tsunami in Sri Lanka.

It is quite evident from the field visits and desk review that local capacity (even for women) is there and can be used, not only during relief and rehabilitation phases but also in long-term recovery interventions. It is possible to move away from supply driven inputs to the demand side of intervention. UNIFEM partners have successfully demonstrated that women do and can lead the recovery process. Building local partnerships is a creative process. It is complex and slow as well. Short-term inputs have their limitations. UNIFEM should develop a long-term process-oriented strategy for its local partners in Sri Lanka. Similarly, UNIFEM interventions are focused on recovery. However, it is important to assess how, or whether, these do in fact make recovery less risky.

UNIFEM partners have been extremely successful in making women's issues visible in both practice and policy with the Government of Sri Lanka. Women's voices were enabled to be heard by policy makers at the highest levels, including at the Sri Lanka Development Forum. The tsunami-affected women have been supported with resources as well as capacity building inputs. Issues such as women's human rights and protection have been raised, and the authorities and population at large, including media, have been sensitised. Outreach of these partners to local women in and around communities has increased over time. Similarly, these partners have been able to raise awareness about disaster risk reduction, which was reflected during some of the field visits. However, linkages with disaster risk reduction are weak and need to be strengthened.

The work of UNIFEM partners in Sri Lanka is valuable for UNIFEM and others to understand not only how women recover but also how they lead. Thus, expanding some of the activities that integrate pure risk reduction inputs with recovery will be very timely. There is a real possibility of accelerating the speed of tsunami recovery under the leadership of women and women's organisations. They must be backed up with both risk reduction and financial resources. Establishing a local women's cadre for disaster risk reduction is one such possibility. Material support from UNIFEM has been one of the most valuable inputs in strengthening local institutions of women in Sri Lanka.

Gendering the Hyogo Platform for Action: UNIFEM's Model

UNIFEM, with its partners, has played a crucial role in mainstreaming gender issues in tsunami responses. In addition to other reasons suggested earlier, its effectiveness was supported by organisational planning undertaken to help implement the priority areas of the Hyogo Platform for Action from a gender perspective (Table 23.1).

Table 23.1   The Role of UNIFEM in Sri Lanka in Building Women's Resilience to Disasters

Hyogo priorities for action	*Actions by UNIFEM and its partners*
Ensure that DRR is a national and local priority with a strong institutional basis	• Advocating policy reform for example, Bill on Women's Rights, Bill on Domestic Violence, allocation of assistance and property (NCW, HRC, Gender Advisor of the UNRC) • Mainstreaming specific needs of women in disaster in efforts undertaken by the government, the UN system, INGOs and bilateral organisations, for example, training, studies, advocacy for partners and government officials (UNIFEM, MoCDWE, SAARTHAK) • Building capacity of partners to advocate for the full inclusion of women's perspectives in programmes and designs (UNIFEM, MoCDWE, SAARTHAK) • Fostering community awareness and institutionalising community-based risk reduction (NGO DMC, MoCDWE)
Identify, assess and monitor disaster risk	• Conducting needs and risk assessment specific to women and women-headed households (NCW, HRC, SHRDC, SAARTHAK) • Collecting sex-disaggregated data (NCW, HRC, CENWOR, Gender Advisor of the UNRC, SHRDC) • Developing gender-specific indicators on vulnerability and risks (NCW, SHRDC, HRC, Gender Advisor of the UNRC)
Use knowledge, innovation, education to build a culture of safety and resilience	• Advocating gender concerns in policy making fora (UNIFEM, NCW, WMC, HRC) • Engendering media reporting on the tsunami, sensitising media on women's concerns (WMC, UNIFEM, NCW) • Organising DRR awareness and management trainings for women and women-headed organisations (NGO DMC, AIDMI) • Sharing good practices on gender-specific disaster response and mitigation (AIDMI) *(Table 23.1 Continued)*

(Table 23.1 Continued)

Hyogo priorities for action	Actions by UNIFEM and its partners
Reduce underlying risk factors	• Empowering women by supporting their leadership role (NGO DMC)
	• Monitoring and protecting women's human rights (inadequacies in relief, domestic violence, and so on) (HRC, Gender Advisor of the UNRC)
	• Restoring, strengthening and rebuilding women's economic activities for home-based workers, entrepreneurs, teachers, and so on (CWEI, Siyath, MWRAF, Dammacarini, ILO)
	• Reducing vulnerability of women with diversified or alternative income options and livelihood training (CWEI, Siyath, MWRAF, WDF Ampara, ILO)
	• Offering financial recovery schemes (start-up funds) and safety nets for women (Siyath)
	• Training health volunteers (WDC)
	• Providing and training mental health counsellors especially for women, children and families (Damrivi, SAARTHAK)
	• Addressing land-use issues and shared property rights (Gender Advisor of the UNRC)
Strengthen disaster preparedness for effective response	• Advocating for the inclusion of a gender perspective in national and local disaster management and emergency response plans (HRC, Gender Advisor of the UNRC, MoCDWE)
	• Building management capacity of women and women-headed organisations (NGO DMC, MoCDWE, AIDMI)
	• Building community capacity through women organisations, for example, training of trainers (NGO DMC, AIDMI)

Source: UNIFEM. 2006. *Supporting Local Institutions for Tsunami Recovery in Sri Lanka, The United Nations Development Fund for Women.* UNIFEM.

Conclusions

Taking into consideration all gender-sensitive initiatives in Sri Lanka following the tsunami, the following conclusions can be drawn. First, women's recovery is multidimensional, gradual and complex. It requires a long-term approach and continued support from donor agencies. Second, partnership with a diverse range of women's NGOs and the Government of Sri Lanka strengthens recovery and each stakeholder's ability to achieve results. Third, it is apparent that community-based organisations are a critical interface between international resources and the initiatives undertaken by the tens of thousands of local foot soldiers who want to contribute. Fourth, at present women are not being protected from risk and are still exposed to falling back into poverty. This leads to the fifth observation that both domestic and family tensions rise alarmingly at community and household levels. Sixth, reducing feminised poverty in a post-disaster context takes time. Well-targeted recovery inputs, integrated with risk reduction, can accelerate such recovery and bring women out of both poverty and risk. Finally, we conclude that when women's groups are made more central and visible with concrete work and arguments, the risk of excluding the poor and the marginalised is reduced.

Based on these overarching observations, we conclude by offering six specific recommendations for change that can better engender disaster recovery in future:

1. Formulation and promulgation of national policies that make gender concerns central in disaster risk management and response.
2. Generation of sex-disaggregated data that would effectively help address the concerns of women and girls at every stage of the relief and reconstruction effort.
3. Active and strong women representation in disaster risk reduction and recovery planning.
4. Identification of specific needs and vulnerabilities of females, including female-headed households, in order to formulate adequate responses.
5. Supporting women's grass-roots organisations and networks to participate in local decision-making processes so that their perspectives are including in mainstream recovery efforts.
6. Sensitising both women and men on the importance of the inclusion of gender considerations in risk reduction and recovery efforts and the importance of women's voices in such efforts.

References

AIDMI. 2005. 'Tsunami, Gender and Recovery'. *Southasiadisasters.net*, issue 6.
————. 2007a. 'Strengthening Local Capacities to Reduce Disaster Risk in Sri Lanka'. *Southasiadisasters.net*, issue 24.
————. 2007b. 'Engendering Disaster Risk Reduction in Recovery: Profile of a Regional Training'. *Southasiadisasters.net*, issue 27.
————. 2007c. 'Women Reducing Risk after the Tsunami in Sri Lanka'. *Southasiadisasters. net*, issue 28.
Christoplos, C. 2006. *Links between Relief, Rehabilitation and Development in the Tsunami Response*. London: Tsunami Evaluation Coalition.
Disaster Management Centre (DMC). 2005. *Towards a Safer Sri Lanka: A Road Map for Disaster Risk Management*. Available online at http://www.preventionweb.net/files/1745_RoadMapforDisasterRiskManagementVol2.pdf (Accessed on 23 June 2009).
Parakrama, A. 2006. *Impact of the Tsunami Response on Local and National Capacities: Sri Lanka Country Report*. London: Tsunami Evaluation Coalition.
UNIFEM. n.d. *UNIFEM Responds to the Tsunami Tragedy*. Available online at http://www.unifem.org/campaigns/tsunami/page4.html (Accessed on 23 June 2009).
————. 2005. *UNIFEM Responds to the Tsunami Tragedy: One Year Later. A Report Card*. Available online at http://www.unifem.org/campaigns/tsunami/documents/TsunamiReportCard_1yrAnniversary.pdf (Accessed on 23 June 2009).
————. 2006. *Supporting Local Institutions for Tsunami Recovery in Sri Lanka: The United Nations Development Fund for Women*. UNIFEM.

24

Gendering Disaster Risk Reduction: 57 Steps from Words to Action

—————•✦•—————

Elaine Enarson

One quake or eruption or flood at a time, we learn (or do not) how we are manufacturing the great and small catastrophes of our day. Politicians fly back to their comfort zone, relief workers set up off stage to relieve human suffering and journalists file their stories. Soon, scientific, government and academic studies follow with recommendations meant to interrupt the risk production process. The 'lessons learned' mantra implies a process of learning, reflection and change that is widely believed, deeply desired and rarely realised in practice. Time and again, it is instead its particular horror and political context that drive change, and so it was with the Hyogo Framework for Action (HFA).

Meeting in Kobe so soon after the Indian Ocean earthquake and tsunami, the work of the 2005 World Conference on Disaster Risk Reduction had a great sense of urgency. To many, the most pressing need was self-evident: to extend technological advances in forecasting and warning systems to all peoples and marry these with effective community warnings. But the dialogue extends well beyond this: What frameworks or systems could best reduce the risk of avoidable harm in the next decade?

What tools or resources were needed to turn the ship around? How could successes be scaled up and momentum sustained?

If Kobe was the moment for concerted world action, the HFA is the vehicle. With their agreement to the HFA, national signatories committed to an integrated and prevention-based approach closely linked to sustainable and safer development. Woven throughout this important roadmap is the sense that neither governments nor communities alone can make the kind of changes needed to build safer and more sustainable ways of organising our lives in the 21st century. What is not so clear is that men cannot continue to act alone, either. Signing on to the HFA, nations also agreed in principle on this strategic priority for 2005–15: 'A gender perspective should be integrated into all disaster risk management policies, plans and decision-making processes, including those related to risk assessment, early warning, information management, and education and training.' But with few exceptions 'gender' stays put in the introduction.

Knowing how useful concrete examples, specific suggestions, action guides and indicators can be, the International Strategy for Disaster Reduction (ISDR) developed *Words into Action: Implementing the Hyogo Framework for Action*, step-by-step guidelines for realising the five broad goals of the HFA. This document is the basis for this discussion, in which I offer a number of steps to governments and their private and public partners seeking to implement the agreed principle of gender inclusivity.

Implementation: Just Another Wish List?

Government planners, policy analysts, administrators, researchers and other experts may not come readily to the gender perspective. But without the full and equal participation and leadership of girls and women in the eye of the storm, we cannot succeed in the daunting work ahead to reduce risk and respond wisely to disasters when they do occur. Only the most naive confuse guidelines and checklists with the difficult political work of crossing boundaries, bridging gaps, challenging power systems and building partnerships where none are likely or even desired. But it is an article of faith in our field that guidelines can indeed prompt action or at least set standards and goals. Gender is, indeed, a clearly identified 'guiding principle' in *Words into Action* (p. 11):

Gender is a cross-cutting concern requiring attention throughout the planning, implementation and evaluation phases of the activities adopted to implement the *Hyogo Framework for Action*. Toward this end, the need for sex-differentiated data is stressed as is the need to analyse the gender division of labour and power relationships between the sexes as these may impinge on the success or failure of all risk reduction strategies. As gender is a central organising principle in all societies, the daily routines of women and men across and within societies put women and men, girls and boys, differently at risk. While gender concerns in disasters cannot be equated with poverty or the challenges of sole parenting alone, it is evident from past disasters that low-income women and those who are marginalised due to marital status, physical ability, age, social stigma or caste are especially disadvantaged. It must be recognised, too, that gender also shapes the capacities and resources of women and men to minimise harm, adapt to hazards and respond to disasters when they must.

This statement is worth revisiting for, following this introductory statement, *Words into Action* is curiously blind to sex, sexuality, gender and gender relations. When it comes to implementation, *Words into Action* rarely calls directly upon governments to recognise, develop, strengthen and utilise the capacities of high-risk women; to anticipate gender-based risks to the health and well-being of boys and men in disaster recovery; to recognise the significance of the gender division of labour in the public and private spheres of our everyday lives; to address the underlying gender inequalities that both directly and as cross-cutting factors undermine disaster resilience or to simply count heads and impacts in ways that enable gender-based analysis and planning (Box 24.1).

Box 24.1   Five Action Areas of the HFA

Making disaster risk reduction a priority
Identifying, assessing and monitoring risk/enhancing early warning
Increasing awareness, education and training
Reducing risk in key sectors
Strengthening disaster preparedness

Source: UNISDR. 2005. *Hyogo Framework for Action 2005–2015: Building the Resilience of Nations and Communities to Disasters (HFA).* Available online at http://www. unisdr.org/eng/hfa/hfa.htm (Accessed on 22 September 2007)

In the following sections, I take up each of the sub-points raised in the five major lines of action and propose more concrete actions. Most are drawn from workshops on gender and disasters conducted since 1993 (Pakistan, Costa Rica, Australia, Canada, United States) and from the

Ankara meeting organised by the UN Division for the Advancement of Women (Environmental Management and Mitigation of Natural Disasters: A Gender Perspective) in 2001 and the subsequent Gender Equality and Disaster Risk Reduction Workshop in Honolulu in 2004.

I hope and anticipate that the following action steps will inspire much more specific and context-sensitive action planning involving women and men in all aspects of disaster risk reduction. These action steps are largely for 'including women', which is short hand for policy and practice driven by and for both women and men. One hopes that future gender guidelines can focus less on the exclusionary practices and gender inequalities that, at present, put girls and women front and centre in this discussion.

HFA Action Area 1: Making Disaster Risk Reduction a Priority

Four general lines of action are identified to help national governments promote DRR on a priority basis: *(a)* multi-stakeholder dialogue, *(b)* coordination mechanisms, *(c)* strong institutional basis and *(d)* appropriate resources. Decades of hard-won experience in gender mainstreaming suggest that consulting with women early, often and continuously is essential in developing effective development and disaster initiatives. But how?

First, *assess the status quo*: How are women and gender issues currently reflected in existing national DRR systems and approaches? *Conduct a desk review* of gaps and opportunities for bringing women's organisations and the needs and interests of girls and women into the work already underway in this country.

Second, *write a clear gender equity policy* to ensure that the National Platform explicitly recognises the need for women's full and equal participation. It should reflect appreciation of women as decision makers who bring expert knowledge of disaster risk and risk reduction, especially but not exclusively at the household and community levels. *Use gender-specific language* in policy statements and terms of reference and *develop formal mechanisms for including women* as the national platform is developed and resourced. For example, appoint women's representatives from disaster-affected communities or ask women scientists from established national associations to sit or both; recognise the demands on women's resources, energies and time and enable and compensate their participation as fully as possible.

But which women should be involved? *Map women's organisations and networks* in the nation, including development and grass-roots organisations active in high-risk areas. Time and again, it is women at the grass-roots who step up in the wake of disasters; their contribution to monitoring and mitigating known hazards is now well established. Consult with women leaders in and out of government and with gender and development organisations to find and inventory all relevant groups, associations and networks knowledgeable about housing, livelihood, health, the environment, conflict and other contexts within which residents are exposed to hazards and disasters. In the same vein, *seek out credible women leaders* in high-risk and disaster-affected communities, especially to promote mitigation and preparedness; they have connections and knowledge that may well be lacking in government.

Add women's bureaus to the inter-ministerial network to ensure that women with technical and professional skills and those who are active in the areas of family, health, violence, education, employment and the environment can contribute. Too often, these experts are overlooked when key actors and agencies are sought out; to take just one example, women and family ministries must be at the table as it is difficult to overemphasise the significance of family issues in disasters.

Hire gender experts to ensure that all DRR consultations of the National Platform are organised in ways that bring women and men together for dialogue and action planning. *Plan only family friendly events* organised in ways, places and times that make them accessible to women with different abilities and languages, and to all women and men with family responsibilities (Box 24.2).

HFA Action Area 2: Identifying, Assessing and Monitoring Risk and Enhancing Early Warnings

In this area, the current 'roadmap' to risk reduction emphasises the need for: *(a)* useful data and information, *(b)* meaningful risk assessment, *(c)* effective early warning systems and *(d)* effective communication of DRR information and early warnings. This is a critical area for increased gender sensitivity. We fail communities when we fail to reach women with lifesaving information. Further, women's perspectives on hazards, vulnerabilities and capacities can enrich community-based

Box 24.2   National Government Policy for Gender Equity in Emergency
Assistance

Gender Equality and Humanitarian Assistance: A Guide to the Issues is a 29-page
policy document produced by Beth Woroniuk for the Canadian International
Development Agency (CIDA) in 2004. It focuses on capacities as well as
vulnerabilities and men as well as women with sections on what gender-sensitive
humanitarian assistance means, myths and misunderstandings around it,
concrete assessment questions to be asked across sectors and in programme
development, and references to related work.

Source: CIDA website: http://www.cida.gc.ca or http://www.acdi-cida.gc.ca/INET/
IMAGES.NSF/vLUImages/Africa/$file/Guide-Gender.pdf

risk assessments. There is no single 'community' or 'household' to reach
but a mosaic of intersecting households embedded in communities of all
kinds; there is no single 'women's perspective' either, so concerted effort
must be made to engage as broad a range of women as possible.

Are government planners well served by existing information systems?
Do they have the sex- and age-disaggregated data needed for gender-
sensitive disaster risk reduction initiatives? Finding out is a critical first
step. *Assess possible gender bias in local, state and national information
systems.* Gender-based analysis of hazards, capacities, vulnerabilities,
communication systems and early warning systems is not possible without
this fundamental building block.

By *initiating gender and disaster research collaboratives*, government
actors can begin to capture qualitative, community-based insight into
risk communication and warning systems. These can include government
and university partnerships that involve gender and women's studies
units as well women's organisations with research capacities and non-
governmental organisations (NGOs) active in communities at risk. *Fund
gender and disaster researchers* who engage with high-risk communities
in participatory action research. Geographic Information System (GIS)
maps are increasingly a valued tool for local risk assessments, but fall
short if women are under-represented or gender-specific information and
perspectives are not incorporated into the mapping process, so it is also
important to *fund gender-sensitive participatory GIS mapping.*

Words into Action recommends that all risk assessments be based on
updated geophysical data; it is equally significant that governments invest

resources and develop the capacity needed to *mandate updated sex- and age-specific socio-economic data* as an essential planning tool.

Require that developers *consult with gender and communication specialists* when under contract to design risk communication and warning strategies. Similarly, public awareness about risk and effective warnings and warning systems is enhanced when messages are specific and not overly general. Both the message and the media are important; effective use has been made of women's radio shows to increase women's emergency preparedness, for example, and of sporting events attractive to boys and men. *Target and market messages to women and men, respectively*, with attention to age, culture and context.

Similarly, refine risk communications to reach specific groups of women and men. *Evaluate existing risk communication practices for gaps* that may limit the access of high-risk girls and women to information and warnings. Do not reinvent the wheel. Local women's groups or national organisations have expert knowledge about how best to claim the attention of particular groups, for example, mothers or migrant working women or low-income women with disabilities. Governments should require that communication specialists under contract *consult with women's organisations* and gender experts to identify popular education and communication outlets likely to reach target populations of women and men equally before, during and after an emergency.

But it is equally important to recognise that community-based women's groups and networks can themselves serve as information experts conveying information to marginalised populations and, importantly, sharing their knowledge with governmental and non-governmental actors. Knowledge exchange is the linchpin of community preparedness and cannot succeed without building and exchanging women's (as well as men's) diverse points of view. As most community women's groups are under-resourced, they may have the potential but not the capacity to step into this role in a sustained way, so government should *develop well-resourced risk communication partnerships with women's groups in high-risk communities*. Though the important role of women and girls in community education in the family, school and local community is well established by research and frequently observed by practitioners in the field, it is currently an under-utilised resource (Box 24.3).

Source: Gender Perspective: Working Together for Disaster Risk Reduction: Good Practices and Lessons Learned, pp. 43–45. Available on the ISDR website http://www. unisdr.org/eng/about_isdr/isdr-publications/09-gender-good-practices/ gender-good-practices.pdf

HFA Action Area 3: Increasing Awareness, Education and Training

The defining character of the HFA is its focus on increasing awareness at all levels of how hazardous living conditions are made and can be unmade. Towards this end, the HFA roadmap *Words into Action* stresses the need for: *(a)* compilation, dissemination and use of disaster risk reduction information, *(b)* training on risk reduction for key stakeholders, *(c)* mainstreaming risk reduction in education systems and *(d)* comprehensive awareness programmes. As in the discussion earlier, the multifaceted roles of women as family and community educators cannot be over-emphasised.

Which women should be targeted for active participation in governmental outreach? There is no one answer. The first task of gender-sensitive awareness, education and training programmes must be to identify high-risk women who must be reached. Is it women health care providers in rural areas, women raising families alone in urban shanty towns, elders in migrant communities or poor women stigmatised by infection, disability or ethnicity? Local expertise must then be deployed to reach these groups, as in the case of risk communication discussed earlier. Governments can *create gender-balanced awareness planning teams* to make these determinations.

But women are also educators. The experience of Grassroots Organisations Operating Together in Sisterhood International, for example, demonstrates the effectiveness of women-to-women peer training conducted by women's groups with hard-won knowledge of what women and girls need in the aftermath of disasters and how they can organise to mitigate hazards and vulnerabilities before they occur. *Scaling up proven community-driven and women-led awareness programmes* is essential. Community education approaches are essential in order to cultivate long-term relationships and strategies for local awareness and action and are also the essential step to reach women facing literacy and other barriers.

At the post-secondary level, *curricula evaluation teams* can review and assess college and university courses to identify gaps and opportunities for increasing sensitivity to gender in disaster-related courses. This can and should also be done in the case of training and certification programmes. Are nations teaching the most current research findings about women, men and gender in disaster contexts? If not, what is needed? How can this be changed? One approach is to *support at least one women's institution or programme in the nation to develop and operate a full-fledged degree programme in disaster risk reduction.* The benefits of a new generation of girls and women knowledgeable about hazards and disasters far outweigh the costs.

Developing *context-specific gender and disaster training modules* is another approach that can be utilised across institutions and sectors, including planning, development, health studies, social welfare, law, engineering, information technologies and other relevant fields. *Contract with gender and education specialists* to help develop and disseminate these DRR course modules targeting both women and men. For example, engineering, architecture and planning students, male or female, may not know about the roles women have played in constructing seismically resistant housing, but should.

New gender-sensitive educational media created by and for women have proven highly effective, for example, community video created by disaster-affected women to increase awareness of women in other risky environments. Girls as well as adult women can participate in developing and disseminating new ideas about reducing disaster risks if they are supported in this role. *Fund the production of women-led community education materials* and make these widely available.

The organisation as well as the content of trainings is important. As noted with respect to activities of the National Platform, governments should *develop standards for gender-inclusive awareness programming*, ensuring that these are accessible to women and that women are compensated for the extra burden imposed on their time and energy. This is one way of demonstrating commitment to the principles of gender-sensitive risk reduction practice. Similarly, *gender benchmarks and indicators* are needed in risk reduction programming and project planning, with special attention to gender-budgeting and women's active participation in project monitoring and evaluation. How, without asking, will governments learn if their awareness, education and *training dollars* are spent in ways that reach girls and women?

At a different level, government leadership can also promote gender sensitivity in the work of public and private partners with which countries collaborate. *Supporting mentoring programmes and institutional exchanges*, for example, will increase the capacity of all partners to conduct the level of gender analysis required to fully and equally engage girls and boys, women and men in disaster risk reduction. The partners of the National Platform can also *create or support information sharing networks* to increase gender awareness. The Gender and Disaster Sourcebook, for example, is a one-stop resource with international materials on all dimensions of disaster risk reduction. By *linking to the Gender and Disaster Network (GDN)*, these resources can be shared (Box 24.4).

Box 24.4   Gender and Disaster Sourcebook

What is the link between gender equality and disaster risk? What lessons have been learned in the field and through scientific study? How can this knowledge be applied in practice to reduce risk and respond equitably to disaster events? These are the questions an international team of writers set out to answer by compiling materials for this new electronic resource. Click on 'planning and policy frameworks' to access the many practice-based checklists and planning guides prepared by UN agencies, and on 'good practice' for examples of innovative approaches already implemented through women's organisations, governments and non-governmental organisations. The Sourcebook is hosted on the website of the Gender and Disaster Network (http://www.gdnonline.org/), the global virtual network with members working in government, at the community level and in academia.

Source: The 'Gender and Disaster Sourcebook' can be accessed online through the GDN: http://www.gdnonline.org/sourcebook/index.htm

HFA Action Area 4: Reducing Risk in Key Sectors

Making risk reduction a priority, effective risk communication, and education and training all heighten awareness about hazards and disasters; but, at the core of the HFA, is the commitment governments make to taking action to reduce risk in key areas. Those highlighted in the HFA are environmental management, livelihoods and social protection, physical planning, engineering and the financial and economic sectors. Sustainable recovery planning cannot succeed without close attention to how risk is increased and can be decreased in these realms. What is not clearly identified in *Words into Action* is how to build on gender-sensitive practices that reduce risk, though a well-established body of research and practice affirms the effectiveness of gender-sensitive approaches. Implementation of sectoral projects and programmes should be informed by this knowledge (Box 24.5).

Box 24.5   Institutional Support for Gender-sensitive Action Research

Gender in Community Based Disaster Management (CBDM) is a 2-year project spearheaded by the UN Centre for Regional Development that aims to: investigate gender sensitivity in current disaster management strategies and studies; identify policy gaps and bottlenecks; develop action plans and produce and distribute educational materials; and research and programme development in support of gender-sensitive CBDM. With support from the Hyogo Trust Fund Action Research Project, participatory workshops involving government and community members are being conducted in a number of case communities selected in Bangladesh, Nepal, Sri Lanka and Turkey.

Source: UNCRD Hyogo Office website: http://www.hyogo.uncrd.or.jp/cbdm/ cbdm.htm

---

As noted earlier, *building capacity for conducting gender-sensitive disaster risk assessments* is an essential step for capturing and acting upon specific knowledge about hazards, vulnerabilities and capacities in the everyday lives of women and men, boys and girls. Gender-sensitive risk assessments are essential to capture and act on this knowledge in specific contexts. For example, within socio-economic groups, women and girls are generally disadvantaged, and traditional strategies to redress these may not reach them; increasing employment, for example, may not address the root causes of women's poverty. Government-led interventions in this area must also reflect women's vulnerability to environmental hazards and the active roles of girls and women as users and managers of environmental resources. Consult with *women's work associations, unions, producer groups and others* to identify and support traditional or indigenous good practice in environmental resource management and to plan employment-intensive crisis interventions. *Include gender sensitivity as a standard* in funding, implementing, monitoring and evaluating pre- and post-disaster livelihood initiatives as a way to recognise gender as a cross-cutting theme in pro-poor DRR initiatives.

In the area of social protection, it is essential to prioritise the protection of women, girls and boys from gender-based violence in disaster contexts. *Mitigate gender violence* by building pre-disaster relationships with women's groups knowledgeable in this area. Collaborative plans are then possible for specific actions such as community education to increase awareness of the threat of violence in this context and increased dedicated funding to programmes providing prevention and response services. Similarly, government can demonstrate leadership by recognising the role of wives, mothers, daughters and partners as informal 'shock absorbers' in times of disaster. As women are likely than men to depend on state-supported social services such as housing, health and education including childcare and other family supports, *identifying strategies for ensuring social service continuity* through partnership with grass-roots women is a step that increases the disaster resilience of women and women's groups playing key social support roles. Identify and *prioritise the protection of critical social infrastructures,* as well as critical communication or energy infrastructures, including women's spaces, childcare centres, shelters, faith-based places and other community structures that build solidarity and sustain meaningful recovery.

Gender-sensitive risk reduction also means engaging women as housing reconstruction experts, for example, through *increased support to local women's building cooperatives* that train women in safer building techniques, or by helping to develop these. Partnering with women's groups to monitor reconstruction is another strategy that has been trialled and proven effective. Governments can *fund women's development groups knowledgeable about women-led and community-based* evaluation and monitoring roles during reconstruction. Including gender experts on planning teams for reconstruction will help ensure that gender patterns are reflected, for example, differences in women's land rights and tenancy, use of space for home-based production, women's transportation resources and needs and the value of women's spaces for psychosocial support, shared childcare, livelihood projects and other post-disaster activities that can be anticipated. *Consultations with both local experts and women with technical and scientific expertise* are not a luxury or distraction but essential steps to sustainable recovery for all.

With respect to financial planning, by *supporting existing microfinance systems* reaching low-income women, governments also reduce their disaster vulnerability. This is especially so for women in the informal sector but is also a major form of social protection for women operating small businesses around the world. *Provide gender training to economic recovery experts* and ensure that recovery planning groups or teams are gender balanced. *Make women's small businesses a priority in business continuity planning.* Additionally, insurance schemes promoted by women's groups for low-income women should be scaled up.

Disaster risk can certainly also be reduced through an integrated and cross-sectoral approach that engages all relevant government ministries, including those with mandates for promoting gender equity. *Develop personal networks* with women's organisations and advocates actively engaged with promoting the goals of the Convention for the Elimination of Discrimination against Women, for example, or the gender-specific Millennium Development Goals.

Explicit policy for gender-sensitive recovery planning will help guide the work of the National Platform partners. *Established gender benchmarks and indicators* will be needed and can best be developed at the country level to reflect specific conditions. Explicit policy guides are needed linking sustainable development, gender equality and disaster risk reduction at all levels. Ensure that this fundamental principle is reflected in emergency planning for response and recovery to avoid reconstructing vulnerabilities (Box 24.6).

HFA Action Area 5: Strengthening Disaster Preparedness

As expected, the implementation guide for the HFA gives strong support to the concept of preparedness, urging that signatories support: *(a)* activities in support of disaster preparedness, *(b)* assessments of disaster preparedness capacities and mechanisms, and *(c)* strengthen planning and programming for disaster preparedness.

> **Box 24.6   Local Government Working with Women to Reduce Risk in Peru**
>
> Women are building disaster-resilient houses and communities in Peru in an innovated project involving women's community groups and local government. Estrategia, which is a 16-year-old Lima-based NGO supporting women leaders in poor communities, initiated the project, negotiating with local authorities and NGOs to create strategic partnerships that increase the geographic scope of their work and garner financial support. The initiative provided an entry point for women to negotiate with the local government to develop more resilient housing policies for the poor.

Source: Gender Perspective: Working Together for Disaster Risk Reduction: Good Practices and Lessons Learned, pp. 40–42. Available on the ISDR website http://www. unisdr.org/eng/about_isdr/isdr-publications/09-gender-good-practices/ gender-good-practices.pdf

Women's capacity to undertake activities that help them and their families and communities prepare for disastrous events can and must be strengthened. Towards that end, *women's groups active at the local level must be resourced.*

Assist municipalities to compile gender-sensitive risk profiles needed for an integrated and gender-sensitive approach emphasising preparedness and risk reduction. Especially in preparedness plans, it is important that *governments partner with women's groups knowledgeable about high-risk women* and *also engage women with professional and technical experts.*

Make existing resources such as gender-sensitive relief guides available to response agencies but recognise that community members, including girls and women, are always the first (and last) responders. *Revise and disseminate existing tools* to produce context-specific guidelines (Box 24.7).

Organisational cultures and practices historically dominated by men are slow to change and perhaps are slower yet in the field of disaster management. A practical step to promote gender inclusiveness is to *incorporate gender sensitivity into results-based evaluation* systems of disaster preparedness and response. *Adapt personnel policies to reward demonstrated gender sensitivity* in these areas. *Tie funding to effective gender mainstreaming* in emergency preparedness and relief operations by making this a National Platform standard. Governments can create an enabling environment and demonstrate leadership and political will in this area. Equally important, government leaders can strive to the extent feasible to *provide the human and financial resources needed to institutionalise gender-fair policy and practice* in the area of preparedness and relief.

To realise the full spirit of the HFA, government leadership is needed *to promote interpersonal and inter-organisational networks* between girls' and women's organisations and male-dominated emergency organisations. In the short run, potentially life-saving preparedness and relief operations can be made stronger and gender-inclusive sustainable recovery planning can become the norm. In the long run, acting now to build and promote dialogue—women and men at the same table speaking a common language—will leverage the momentum, political will and organisational work cultures needed to sustain a gender-sensitive, community-led and effective disaster risk reduction strategy.

Looking Ahead

At the heart of the HFA is the certain knowledge that safer ways of organising our social life on this dynamic planet can and must be found. Working with both women and men is the catalyst and essential precondition. But there is no one way to do much of anything, certainly not when the challenge is to reverse course and address the driving forces creating the hazards and disasters of the 21st century. No single-minded focus will do—on developing countries only, on women as heroic environmental stewards. Instead, gendering disaster risk reduction is a challenge as complicated as our own personal histories and families and just as difficult to navigate.

Engaging women and girls fully and equally is not a luxury that only some countries can afford nor is it a distraction from the main business of disaster risk reduction. Hard decisions and commitments must be made. Gender mainstreaming disaster risk reduction can be imposed (and ignored) from high or bubble up from below; it can be tolerated or promoted, enabled or starved of resources; it can certainly be championed by men and women but just as easily be disparaged as an external political agenda or cultural imposition and confined to bureaucratic backwaters. At a minimum, effective mainstreaming takes political imagination and leadership, sufficient and appropriate resources, long-term partnerships and sustained attention. It challenges established priorities and power relations and empowers women as decision makers.

A nation state strong in the face of disaster is one that capitalises on the everyday knowledge of its people. It is a country whose leaders know how women and men have historically coped with hazards and disasters, and who appreciate the political, economic and social forces that have especially disempowered girls and women in risky environments. It is a country whose leaders at all levels of government know that their most important stakeholders are the women and men whose lives and futures are most at risk and who reach out to develop, strengthen and sustain community partnerships with women as well as men.

Acknowledgements

Readers should refer to chapters in this edition and to the Gender and Disaster Sourcebook (http://www.gdnonline.org/sourcebook/index.htm) and other resources of the Gender and Disaster Network (www.gdnonline.org) for materials in support of this chapter.

I acknowledge with pleasure the hard work of the many women and men who have elaborated these action steps over the years. I also gratefully acknowledge the contributions of my former colleagues on the ISDR Gender Expert Team to the development of these ideas. Naturally, I do not assume their agreement nor do I represent these ideas as those of the ISDR. I offer these remarks especially to Fouad Bendimerad in appreciation for *Words into Action*.

References

UNISDR. 2005. *Hyogo Framework for Action 2005–2015: Building the Resilience of Nations and Communities to Disasters (HFA)*. Available online at http://www.unisdr.org/eng/hfa/hfa.htm (Accessed on 22 September 2007).

———. 2006. *Words into Action: A Guide for Implementing the Hyogo Framework*. Available online at http://www.unisdr.org/eng/hfa/docs/Words-into-action/Words-Into-Action.pdf (Accessed on 22 September 2007).

25

Toolkit for Mainstreaming Gender in Emergency Response

———— • ✦ • ————

P. G. Dhar Chakrabarti and Ajinder Walia

This chapter offers a toolkit to mainstream gender issues in every aspect of emergency management. The methodology adopted is not to 'reinvent the wheel' but rely on what is prevalent and existing, and to address the special needs of women along with their involvement in the process of responding to an emergency. The comprehensive toolkit has been developed as part of an Emergency Response Framework that would, on the one hand, integrate various aspects of emergency response starting from *ex ante* preparedness for response to the ex-post-disaster response and early recovery and, on the other, link emergency response with the disaster risk reduction and long-term reconstruction. Such a framework would provide a perspective and purposefulness to the specific activities undertaken by various actors. The framework, however, does not mean that emergency response has to take place under a 'unified command', it only highlights the need to link the various activities together so that there is greater clarity in role and functions and there is greater coordination and synergy in response, which is often a casualty in an emergency situation (Figure 25.1). Such a desegregation of activities would enable identification of specific gender mainstreaming efforts required in each sector.

Figure 25.1 Emergency Response Framework

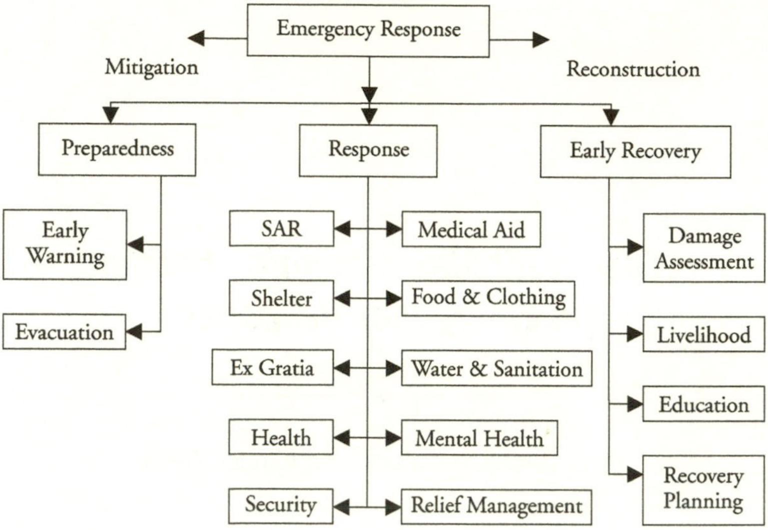

Efficacy of any emergency response is largely determined by the level of disaster preparedness. Strengthening of disaster preparedness is one of the priorities of Hyogo Framework for Action: 2005–2015. Hence, the seeds for mainstreaming gender in emergency response have to be sown while we are still planning for management of any disaster. Pre-disaster planning should meticulously incorporate a gendered focus on every aspect of response which can be implemented during emergency management. The goal can be achieved by ensuring participation of women in pre-disaster planning, incorporating gender concerns in planning for an emergency, developing gender-sensitive standard operating procedures and training the emergency responders in adopting a gender-sensitive approach on the field.

Early Warning

Gender is an important factor in the dissemination of early warning issued during an emergency. In the 1991 Bangladesh cyclone and flood, emergency warnings were given mainly by loudspeaker and word of mouth. In a highly sex-segregated society, warning information was transmitted by the males to the males in public spaces. Women who had comparatively less knowledge about cyclones and were dependent on male decision making, perished, many with their children, waiting for their husbands to return home and take them to safety (Baden et al. 1994) (Table 25.1).

Table 25.1   Toolkit 1: Early Warning

S. No.	Early warning function	Tool
1	Dissemination	• Ensure that warnings are issued at every doorstep of the vulnerable population not only public places • Involve women and men warning dissemination
2	Awareness	• Explain the meaning of warnings to women who may lack the information to understand warning signals • Sensitise women regarding the importance of early warning and the need to adhere early to these

Source: Developed by the authors.

Evacuation

Evacuation is an important decision, taken in the golden hours of an impending a disaster, which would determine the mortality and morbidity rate of the vulnerable population. The vulnerability of women is accentuated during this critical phase as they are constrained by cultural norms that restrict women's freedom of movement in public (Baden et al. 1994). Many women waited for their husbands to return home to take the decision to evacuate, thereby losing precious time that might have saved their lives and those of their children (D'Cunha 1997). The status of women in society generally determines the process of decision making for evacuation. A case study of Afghanistan earthquake in 1993 cited women not evacuating as the cultural practices did not allow them to touch a man other than their husband (Table 25.2).

Search and Rescue

Gender variation in mortality and morbidity vary by disaster type and location. In 1994, twice as many males died in weather-related hazards, such as winter storms, thunderstorms and lightning (US Department of Commerce 1995) as they were the ones who participated in work

Table 25.2 Toolkit 2: Evacuation

S. No.	Evacuation function	Tool
1	Information	• Advise women and men about escape routes • Appoint a nodal officer to coordinate the evacuation of women and children
2	Transportation	• Provide transportation for evacuation of women and children especially for pregnant and lactating mothers
3	Training and sensitisation	• Train the team assisting in evacuation to respond to women reluctant to evacuate due to socio-cultural norms • Sensitise women to make immediate decisions of timely evacuation on their own

Source: Developed by the authors.

and leisure activities and most of these deaths occurred outside home, in vehicles and in the open. However, more females died in the Indian Ocean tsunami as women remained home while men were fishing on the sea (Oxfam 2005). The relationship between gendered use of space and mortality rate has also been noted in other natural disasters in South Asia. In the Afghan earthquake of 1993, more women and girls were killed as they were preparing the evening meal (ALNAP 2005) and during the Latur earthquake in Maharashtra in 1993, fewer men than women died because they happened to be sleeping outdoors because of the warm weather. Moreover, because the gender division of labour kept women in or closer to homes, it was generally women who suffered disproportionately from the collapse of poorly constructed dwellings (Byrne and Baden 1995).

Immediately after a disaster, the search and rescue (SAR) teams arrive on the scene to rescue the disaster survivors. Male-dominated response organisations act on a view of society in which vulnerable women must be supervised or managed by their own men (Scanlon 1996). The International Search and Rescue Advisory Group (INSARAG) has also listed gender restrictions as one of the sensitive issues which has to be considered while carrying out all SAR operations (UNOCHA 2007) (Table 25.3).

Medical Aid

Provision of medical aid and ensuring their accessibility to the affected women are critical areas of concern in emergency management in such societies.

Table 25.3   Toolkit 3: SAR Operations

S. No.	SAR function	Tool
1	Composition of the response force	• Ensure that SAR team includes women too
2	Mapping	• Conduct needs analysis of men and women before initiating a rescue operation • Prepare a checklist of the differential needs of men and women
3	Social inhibitions/cultural practices	• Train the response force to work with women rendered immobile by social practices related to *purdah* system
4	Special vulnerability	• SAR team is trained and fully equipped to rescue and provide first aid to pregnant women • SAR team is trained in rescuing physically and mentally challenged women • One member is trained in sign language

Source: Developed by the authors.

Soon after the Pakistan earthquake in October 2005, newspapers highlighted stories about the need of female doctors in providing medical aid to the women disaster survivors after the devastating earthquake as families were very hesitant to bring the doctors to the tents or to take the women to the medical units as doctors were mostly men (APLWD 2006). Women in certain conservative cultures are not used to talking with strangers, and this has caused many hurdles in getting them needed help, medical and otherwise. They feel shy to come forward with their problems, and medical aid givers have had to make special efforts to reach women (Sayeed 2005) (Table 25.4).

Shelter

Women and children are the primary occupants and tend to spend more time than men in the shelters. Survivors are forced to live in congested relief camps, but through these processes the needs of privacy and care for the more vulnerable group of pregnant, lactating and menstruating women are not adequately taken care of. In the aftermath of 1991 cyclone in Bangladesh, women who are able to reach the temporary shelters found

Table 25.4   Toolkit 4: Medical Aid

S. No.	Medical aid function	Tool
1	Medical services	• Recruit male and female staff to provide medical aid • Set up a private consultation room for women and girls • Female obstetricians and gynaecologists should be included in medical teams servicing camps and affected communities • Address concerns of women feeling too shy or fearful to consulting the medical team
2	Accessibility of services	• Locate health services within walking distance of communities and on safe access roads • Clinics located in close proximity to the relief camp • Make opening times of the clinics convenient for women and children relative to their household duties

Source: Developed by the authors.

them ill-suited to meet gender- and culture-specific needs; in a social context where seclusion is practiced as large number of men and women were crowded together with no respect to privacy for pregnant, lactating and menstruating women (UNEP 1997) (Table 25.5).

Water and Sanitation

Inadequate water and sanitation facilities directly influence the health of the disaster survivors which is a primary concern of the administration. Drinking water had become a 'mirage' after the tsunami as water sources had been salinised (SRED 2006). Women and girls were responsible for childcare and household activities and lack of water and sanitation made them more likely to come into contact with polluted water sources and exposes the entire family to potential health hazards (Mehta 2007). In the tsunami aftermath, in Kanyakumari, India, it was reported that water and sanitation needs of women were compromised to a large extent. There were only ten toilets and ten bathrooms for about 1,225 affected members of the community. The toilets were either too far way or in the midst of the camps. They lacked proper drainage and water facilities and were very unhygienic (SRED 2006) (Table 25.6).

Table 25.5 Toolkit 5: Shelter

S. No.	Shelter function	Tool
1	Design and layout	• Consult both men and women in the design and layout of camps and shelters
		• Mobilise women and men to participate in the location, design and maintenance of water and sanitation facilities
		• Discuss with women how their activities are carried out and what suitable space allocations are needed, including use of activity clocks to identify needs of women/men
		• Strive to relocate widows, adolescent girls and physically and mentally challenged women in temporary shelters which are centrally located
		• Build temporary shelters close to schools and hospitals
		• Ensure that every shelter has an adequate minimum surface area of camp per person
		• Ensure that shelter is friendly to disabled persons
2	Space and location	• Shelter should be in close proximity to water and fuel collection and other activities involving off-site travel
		• Provide a common area for children's play where family members can watch them from the shelter
		• Make adequate arrangements for lighting, particularly in common facilities like toilets
		• Provide adequate material for partitions between families in a temporary shelter
		• Women and girls should not be compelled to share accommodation with men who are not members of their immediate family

Source: Developed by the authors.

Food and Clothing

In a crisis situation, women and girls are more likely to reduce their food intake as a coping strategy in favour of their household members (IASC 2006). Malnutrition of pregnant and breastfeeding women led to malnutrition and morbidity of their children (Solidaritas Perempuan 2006). Hence, effective food security and nutrition strategies require an understanding of the gender dimensions of crises in order to identify and assess sex-specific relief needs. The participation of women in decisions

Table 25.6   Toolkit 6: Water and Sanitation

S. No.	Water and sanitation function	Tool
1	Provision of services	• Ensure that the water sites, distribution mechanisms and maintenance procedures are accessible to women, including those with limited mobility • Ensure that a specific minimum quantity of about 15 litres of water is available per person per day • Involve both women and men in the design and location of toilets • Build three toilets for women for every one toilet built for men • Ensure all users, particularly women and girls, participate in identifying risky hygiene practices and conditions, and that all strive to measurably reduce these • Mark out a private laundering area for undergarments and sanitary clothes • Design communal bathing, washing facilities and washrooms in consultation with women and girls • Target hygiene programmes to fathers as well as mothers and others caring for children • Establish water and sanitation committees in camps that are half women and make them responsible for the maintenance of water and sanitation facilities • Train both women and men in the use and maintenance of water and sanitation facilities
2	Accessibility and location	• Locate water points in areas that are accessible and safe and near the relief camps/temporary shelters • If water is rationed or pumped at specific times, ensure that these are convenient and safe for women and others responsible for collecting water • Facilities should be central, accessible and well lit • Bathing facilities should have doors with locks inside

Source: Developed by the authors.

about how to best implement food security and nutrition programmes is critical to reducing the risks women and girls face in emergency situations (IASC 2005). Another related issue is the abundant but inappropriate clothes that are sent; sometimes such clothes are contrary to the cultural practices of the affected population. For example, in the Kashmir earthquake of 2005, saris were discarded as they are not worn by the women in Kashmir. After the Indian Ocean tsunami, blankets were supplied in large numbers as relief material in Andaman and Nicobar islands, even though weather conditions do not permit their use (Table 25.7).

Health

Studies have reported adverse reproductive health problems following a disaster, including early pregnancy loss, premature delivery, stillbirths, delivery-related complications and infertility. Pregnant and lactating women need pre-natal and post-natal care in the aftermath of a disaster. Social taboos around menstruation norms about appropriate behaviour for women and girls were reported to contribute to health problems in disaster situations. During the 1998 floods in Bangladesh, adolescent girls reported perennial rashes and urinary tract infections because they were not able to wash out menstrual rags properly in private and often had no place to hang the rags to dry, or access clean water. They reported wearing the damp clothes, as they did not have place to dry them (WHO 2003). Finally, the issue of recanalisation of parents who have lost their children in disasters also needs consideration (Table 25.8).

Ex gratia

Payment made by governments to relatives of the deceased are often made to the head of the household which, more often than not, excludes women. In India, after the tsunami, ex gratia payment for the loss of the children was given only to men unless the husband died in tsunami. This resulted in spending of money on alcohol and other things not related to family needs. In Batticaloa, the regional capital of eastern coastal area of Sri Lanka, the authorities recognised only male-headed households, so women whose husbands had died could not claim the money. In Thailand, the government paid twice as much to the families for the funeral expenses of men than for those of women based on the assumption that men are heads of households (APWLD 2006) (Table 25.9).

Table 25.7 Toolkit 7: Food and Clothing

S. No.	Food and clothing function	Tool
1	Distribution	• Conduct a need assessment of men and women before initiating food and nutrition services
		• Distribute food through a sex-balanced team
		• Weight of food packages should be manageable and efficient for women
		• Ensure that each household ration card for free food distribution is issued in the woman's name
		• Distribution should be early in the day to allow the affected community to reach home during daylight
		• Select the time and space of distribution according to women's activities and needs, and encourage the organisation of groups to travel together to and from distribution sites
		• Ensure that women and men actively participate in the design, implementation, monitoring and evaluation of food aid programme and policies
		• Consult women, girls, boys and men to identify areas for improvement
2	Nutrition	• Know the recommended calorie intake disaggregated by sex emphasising infants, young children, pregnant and lactating mothers
		• Ensure access to a range of food material such as cereals, pulses, milk and so on
		• Prepare kits of nutritious food material and safe water disinfectants for pregnant and lactating women
		• Ensure that physically challenged women can access food and develop mechanisms for feeding support, for example, eating utensils
		• Strive to provide breast milk to infants without mothers before encouraging alternative nutritional supplements
		• Include breast milk substitutes in food aid package for families with infants as stress can inhibit lactation
		• Provide packaging that facilitates handling and can be re-used for other domestic activities
3	Clothing	• Ensure that used clothes are avoided
		• Clothes should be appropriate to the climatic conditions and cultural practices, suitable for women, girls, boys and men, and sized according to age
		• Undergarments should be distributed to women only by women

Source: Developed by the authors.

Table 25.8   Toolkit 8: Health

S. No.	Health function	Tool
1	Pregnant and lactating women	• Identify a qualified and experienced person to coordinate maternal health activities • Sensitise the family and others to the special needs of pregnant women, women who have aborted and post-natal needs • Identify health workers with midwifery skills and other health workers among survivors to provide care • Identify women in advanced pregnancy and develop plans for safe delivery and seeking assistance • Give each pregnant woman a home delivery kit as well • Sensitise disaster survivors to danger signs, how to use the delivery kit, location of facilities and also provide care for women who have aborted during the disaster • Provide 24-hour access for complications of pregnancy services • Lactating mothers who have lost their children need medical aid to prevent clotting in their breasts
2	Menstruation	• Distribute sanitary packs at regular intervals • Following initial distribution, consult with women and girls to identify materials most culturally appropriate sanitary supplies • Equip toilets with incinerator for proper disposal
3	Contraception	• Provide adequate provision and easy access to different forms of contraception and to pregnancy tests • Distribute contraceptives and pregnancy tests only through women
4	Recanalisation	• Free recanalisation facility should be made accessible and available to a couple • The couple should be counselled prior to surgery on associated benefits and risks of recanalisation • Surgery decisions should reflect physical age as well as the mental well-being of a woman • Wider counselling of the community is needed on broader terms to encourage consideration of alternatives such as adoption

Source: Developed by the authors.

Table 25.9   Toolkit 9: Ex Gratia Payment

S. No.	Ex gratia function	Tool
1	Payment	• 'Head of the household concept' should not be the criteria • Pay the ex gratia to joint accounts for married couples or make a fixed deposit in the name of a woman to avoid misuse of money by a man, for example, liquor consumption • The ex gratia payment can be coupled with a job for the spouse/relative of the deceased, free education for children and free family medical services, a monthly allowance, and so on
2	Information	• Nominate a male and a female officer in each camp for disseminating clear information about applying for ex gratia payments • Information should be in simple language aiming at both literate and illiterate men and women

Source: Developed by the authors.

Mental Health

Post-disaster studies indicate considerable higher stress among women in disasters (Solomon et al. 1987). This arises from the cumulative effect of family environment, caretaking roles, health, mobility and age. Women may express their emotions by crying, talking about the event, trying to reach out to other in the community, exhibiting physiological reactions such as fainting and numbness, experiencing vague multiple aches and pains as a response to stress and may even sometimes take the role of a caretaker by showing more resilience under difficult circumstances (Sekar et al. 2005) (Table 25.10).

Gender-based Violence

Violence is exacerbated by the disruption of support and protection mechanisms (Ariyabandu and Wickramasinghe 2003). Families and communities are often separated, which results in a further breakdown of community support systems and legal and judicial protection mechanisms

Table 25.10   Toolkit 10: Mental Health

S. No.	Mental health function	Tool
1	Assessment	• Conduct a rapid mental health assessment focusing on women through mental health service providers • Establish a proper referral system for critical cases
2	Psychological reactions	• Sensitise mental health workers about common psychological reactions of women in disasters • Assist women in understanding that these feelings are normal reactions to abnormal situations
3	Counselling	• Ask the mental health workers to establish rapport with the affected women before counselling begins • Allow women to express themselves in an environment where confidentiality is maintained • Mental health service providers should be female and male as women may feel more comfortable sharing their feelings with other women • Adopt a non-judgemental approach assuming that even if they make a mistake, they are not victimised • Adopt a comforting attitude by attending non-verbally, giving feedback on feelings, repeating ideas and allowing silence during the course of counselling • Encourage expression of emotions through anger or tears • Highlight women's personal resources and the courage she has to master her problems
4	Special groups	• Counselling services should be targeted towards special vulnerable groups like widows, women who have had abortions, those subjected to gender-based violence, physically and mentally challenged women, and so on
5	Sustainability	• Help women identify their social support network through family, friends, relatives, neighbourhood, and so on • Train the affected women in providing counselling to other affected members as well

Source: Developed by the authors.

(IASC 2005). Unlike women, men are more likely to repress emotional suffering and express anger and frustrations through destructive means such as drinking and violence (Table 25.11).

Table 25.11   Toolkit 11: Gender-based Violence

S. No.	GBV function	Tool
1	Delivery of services	• Locate the services in close proximity to the shelters • Ensure that services are delivered in day time and well-lit paths are available for evening services • Monitor security and instances of abuse in the distribution point as well as on departure roads • Do not make women and girls depend on men for shelter construction or other services as this may lead to sexual exploitation
2	Provisions of safety and security	• Ensure both male and female police officers patrol camp • Form vigilance committees in each camp consisting of men and women to act as monitoring officers • Develop and disseminate written and verbal safety guidelines against possible violations against women • Train women to raise immediate alarms against violations in the camp sites • Station women police officers to record and address safety complaints made by affected women and monitor women's rights violation • Maintain night security at camps • Train security guards of both sexes to be sensitive to women's apprehensions to encourage women to seek assistance • Ensure that women participate directly in decision making on local security arrangements for the camp community • Restrict the sale of alcohol near disaster-affected area
3	Counselling	• Discuss violence survivors' needs for emotional support and strive to ensure that individuals, groups and organisations available in the community will offer supportive, compassionate, non-judgemental, confidential and respectful assistance • In counselling women subject to violence, adopt a non-judgemental approach, empowering the affected woman to cope in a positive manner through social support, spiritualism and recreation

Source: Developed by the authors.

Relief Management

Relief mechanisms, as are currently practiced, need to look into the specific needs of women (Walia 2006). There is limited representation of women on national and local emergency committees, and their potential as a resource for organised action at all levels of the managerial process has been seriously overlooked (Noel 1990). Therefore, an effective relief management strategy has to be built upon two pillars, namely, addressing the specific needs of women and ensuring their participation and involvement in the management process (Table 25.12).

Table 25.12   Toolkit 12: Relief Management

S. No.	Relief function	Tool
1	Relief camp management	• Develop database disaggregated by age and sex • Nominate both men and women in camp management teams/committees • Encourage women in camp decision making • Ensure that women are not represented by male family members in camp management • Hold meetings on camp management at times for women • Ensure that each camp has a separate enclosure for private needs of pregnant, lactating and menstruation women
2.	Relief supplies	• Design relief kit contents in consultation with both men and women • Include both men and women in distributing aid
3	Information dissemination	• Appoint male and female officers to disseminate information on relief assistance being provided by the government, entitlements, distribution site, date and time of procedures, and so on • Reach out to women as in some cultures they do not participate in public meetings where information is being announced

Source: Developed by the authors.

Education

Disasters often create extremely unbalanced demographics with large numbers of women-headed households, forcing women to take up work outside the home, leaving older daughters to care for siblings and attend other household chores, resulting in increased girl children dropouts (UNESCO 2006). It is critical to establish gender-responsive emergency education programmes early on as these lay the foundations for increased participation of women and girls in emergency programmes in future (Table 25.13).

Table 25.13 Toolkit 13: Education

S. No.	Education function	Tool
1	Physical protection	• Locate schools close to relief camps to control sexual violence against girls
		• Involve community members to ensure safe travel to and from school, particularly for girls
		• Regularly monitor school attendance and perform random follow-up on dropouts
2	Cognitive protection	• Educate girls and boys about reproductive health with emphasis on sanitation and cleanliness in camp life
		• Impart life surviving skills to both girls and boys such as swimming, karate and rope climbing as these may also act as a bulwark in situations of gender-based violence
		• Impart vocational training to girls and boys as they will be useful in their future livelihood
		• School should undertake activities advocating gender sensitisation and equity of both the sexes in every aspect of life through group exercises, bulletin board decorations, drawing and poster competitions, and so on
3	Psychosocial protection	• Encourage and create opportunities for various forms of expression such as art, music, poetry and dance and so on
		• Create opportunities for girls to engage in creative activities, work in groups with peers, play and engage in such physical activities as sports or dance

Source: Developed by the authors.

Damage Assessment

Not only do women sustain direct damages or production losses (housing and means of production) but they also have relatively high opportunity costs because they lose income when they have to apply themselves temporarily to unpaid emergency tasks and an increased amount of unpaid reproductive work, such as caring for their children when schools are closed as they are being used as shelters for disaster survivors. After the El Salvador earthquake in 2001, a research study revealed that the lack of schooling for children affected 60 per cent of urban women's productive activities and 48 per cent of rural women productivities. Even if a woman does not hold a paid job, she may generate household income from a variety of informal sector activities, whether from the backyard economy or from a small home-based business, thus allowing her to combine productive tasks with reproductive ones (ECLAC 2002). But these informal productive and reproductive activities are not included in official national accounts and hence do not get accounted in the damage assessment mechanisms which are operationalised after a disaster (Table 25.14).

Livelihood

Lessons learnt from past disasters suggest that a foregrounding of gender concerns in disaster management should begin by drawing upon the connection between women's social and economic needs and priorities, addressing the root causes of their low status as well as attending to the long-term sustainable development concerns (Mehta 2007).

The construction of permanent shelters and other infrastructure should rely on generating livelihood to the affected populace. The short-term relief programmes started in the aftermath of a disaster should not be 'stand alone programmes' but culminate into sustainable employment for both men and women. After Hurricane Mitch hit Honduras and Nicaragua, many women reported that their husbands were listening to their opinions more than they did prior to Hurricane Mitch. They attributed this change to the 'public' work that they did during the disaster (Delaney and Sharder 2000). Initiatives promoting livelihood regeneration of the women working in the informal sector are needed, for example through vocational training and provision of credit (Table 25.15).

Table 25.14   Toolkit 14: Damage Assessment

S. No.	Damage assessment function	Tool
1	Direct damages	• Assess the financial value of all property owned by both men and women • Cover damages to the house as well as household furnishings and appliances • In case of business, the assessment should include its equipment and machinery, as well as any other productive property owned • In case of backyard economy, assessment should include farm animals, fields and crops • Evaluation should include stocks of goods produced, whether stored at home or nearby
2	Indirect losses	• In case of loss of productive employment outside home, the value of the indirect damage should be obtained by multiplying the days or weeks during which remunerated employment was interrupted by the average unit wage for each level of income • Production losses in small and micro-businesses should be assessed on the basis of temporary interruption
3	Reproductive tasks	• Make a list of common reproductive work activities and quantify the time spent in performing each; if no quantitative data are available, affected women may be consulted or the assumption made that women dedicate at least 8 hours a day to unpaid work • Assign monetary value to the time spent by women on reproductive tasks, for example, the average monthly wage for women could be divided by thrity 8-hour days instead of twenty-two • Determine the new pattern of reproductive activities that women have to perform after a disaster which may increase as women may also now do volunteer work and prepare meals in camps, collect firewood and water as the usual sources have been damaged, care for children whose schools have been closed, purchase goods that require transport along roads in bad state of repair and so on • Calculate the increase in time spent on these tasks by estimating the duration of the abnormal situation created by the disaster and assign a monetary value to it

Source: Developed by the authors.

Table 25.15   Toolkit 15: Livelihood

S. No.	Livelihood function	Tool
1	Livelihood planning	• Involve women and men in planning and implementation of all livelihood programmes • Plan livelihood programmes addressing the common obstacles faced by women in participating • Design programmes based on an assessment of women and men's knowledge, skills and livelihood needs • Design and implement livelihood programmes which would break the gender stereotypes of men and women
2	Training	• Organise vocational trainings for both men and women • Ensure gender balance in the training teams • Skills training should be imparted to support women to consider new areas of income earning activity • Discuss the timing of the training programmes to ensure it is suitable to women • Link vocational trainings with employment initiatives being undertaken in the affected area
3	Credit	• Appoint two nodal officers, one male and one female, to generate awareness about the loans, schemes and subsidies given by the government to initiate livelihood • Ensure easy access to working capital, materials and resources along with technical and marketing assistance for women • Banks, trading and business institutions should be encouraged to create structures for providing special aid and investment advice to small and medium women entrepreneurs • Ensure that the credit institutions target women working in the informal sector
4	Relief programmes	• Assess the appropriateness of food for work, food for training and cash for work programmes, and ensure equal participation of women and men • Arrange crèches for women who have to carry their small children with them for engaging in short-term relief programmes • Provide adequate transportation facilities for women travelling long distances to attend livelihood trainings • Create opportunities for women in development and reconstruction programmes

Source: Developed by the authors.

Recovery Planning

Recovery planning creates opportunity for introducing vulnerability reduction and hazard mitigation measures, and for mainstreaming gender issues in recovery and reconstruction programmes. After the Latur earthquake in 1993, which killed about 10,000 people, women were taught the basic construction techniques used for adapting and strengthening traditional village houses and learn how this type of construction would protect residents from future tremors. They were involved in planning and designing their houses and received training in earthquake-safe techniques along with the local masons (Yonder et al. 2005) (Table 25.16).

Table 25.16   Toolkit 16: Recovery Planning

S. No.	Recovery planning function	Tool
1	Involvement of the community	• Map recovery needs as well as services required by the community with a gender-sensitive approach • Prepare a long-term vision plan and share it with the men and women of the affected community • Organise special interaction sessions with women to receive their inputs, ensuring an environment where they can express themselves freely • Establish specific monitoring mechanisms to ensure that women can access resources and participate publicly in planning and decision making associated with post-disaster recovery
2	Economic recovery	• Ownership of all physical assets including multi-hazard resistant houses reconstructed after disasters should be given in joint names of husband and wife • Employment generation for the affected community should include measures and activities that challenge gender stereotypes • Implement reconstruction and recovery projects involving affected men and women as this will help bolster the local economy and generate confidence
3	Social recovery	• Make special recovery programmes for widows, single mothers, old aged and challenged population • Create formal/public spaces for women where they can meet and organise their participation in post-disaster efforts and future activities

Source: Developed by the authors.

Conclusion

Disasters have differential impacts on men and women. Lack of understanding of these differential impacts of disasters on women by disaster managers not only runs the risk of overlooking obvious and more subtle needs and priorities but can also diminish the efficiency of disaster response. It is expected that the toolkit shall provide useful and practical guides to disaster managers to address to the differential needs of women and facilitate an inclusive, equitable and efficient emergency management system.

Bibliography

ALNAP. 2005. *Unnatural Disasters*. World Watch Paper 158. Washington, DC: Worldwatch Institute.

APWLD [Asia Pacific Forum on Women, Law and Development]. 2006. Guidelines for Gender Sensitive Disaster Management. Available online at http://www.apwld. org/pdf/Edit_Guidelines_small_18-8-2009.pdf (Accessed on 23 September 2009).

ARC International. 2005. *Gender-based Violence Legal Aid: A Participatory Toolkit*. ARC International, GBV in Conflict-Affected Setting.

Ariyabandu, M. and M. Wickramasinghe. 2003. *Gender Dimensions in Disaster Management: A Guide for South Asia*, p. 69. Sri Lanka: ITDG South Asia.

Baden, S., A. M. Goetz, C. Green and M. Guhathakurta. 1994. *Bangladesh Cyclone Response Fails to Meet Women's Needs*, BRIDGE Report No. 26. Background Paper on Gender Issues in Bangladesh. Available online at http://www.ids.ac.uk/bridge/dgb1.html

Bradshaw, S. 2004. *Socio-economic Impacts of Natural Disasters: A Gender Analysis*, Manual prepared for the Economic Commission for Latin America and the Caribbean (ECLAC) and the Women and Development Unit, Santiago Chile. Available online at http://www.eclac.cl/mujer/reuniones/conferencia_regional/manual.pdf

Byrne, B. and S. Baden. 1995. *Gender, Emergencies and Humanitarian Assistance*. Report No. 33 (Commissioned by WID Desk, European Commission, Directorate General for Development) BRIDGE, Institute of Development Studies, Sussex University.

CARE and SEEDS. 2005. *Handbook on Shelter Rehabilitation*. India: Advocacy Unit.

Clinical Management of Rape Survivors. 2005. *Developing Protocols for Use with Refugees and Internally Displaced Persons*, revised edition. WHO, UNHCR. Available online at http://www.who.int/reproductive-health/publications

Cupples, A. 2007. 'Gender and Hurricane Mitch: Reconstructing Subjectivities after Disaster', *Disasters*, 31(2): 155–75.

D'Cunha, J. 1997. 'Engendering Disaster Preparedness and Management', *Asian Disaster Management News*, 3(3): 2–5.

Delaney, P. and E. Shrader. 2000. *Gender and Post-disaster Reconstruction: The Case of Hurricane Mitch in Honduras and Nicaragua*. Report prepared for the World Bank. Available online at www.anglia.ac.uk/geography/gdn

Economic Commission for Latin America and the Caribbean and United Nations (ECLAC). 2002. *The Impact of Disasters on Women, Handbook for Estimating the Socioeconomic and Environmental Effects of Disasters.* Available online at http://www. eclac.org/publicaciones/xml/4/12774/lcmexg5i_VOLUME_IVd.pdf

Enarson, E. 1998. 'Surviving Domestic Violence and Disasters', Research paper prepared for the Freda Centre for Research on Violence against Women and Children, January, p. 4. Available online at http://www.harbour.sfu.ca/freda/reports/dviol.htm

———. 1999. *Gender Aware Disaster Practice: A Self-assessment Tool for Disaster Responding Agencies.* Disaster Preparedness Resources Centre, University of British Columbia.

———. 2000. 'Gender and Natural Disasters', Working Paper No. 1, International Labour Organization, in Focus Programme on Crisis Response and Reconstruction. Available online at http://www.ilo.org/public/english/employment/recon/crisis/publ/wp1.htm

———. 2001. 'Promoting Social Justice in Disaster Reconstruction: Guidelines for Gender-sensitive and Community-based Planning'. Drafted on 13 March 2001 for the Disaster Mitigation Institute of Ahmedabad, Gujarat.

———. 2005. *Sectoral Guidelines for Gender-sensitive Outreach.* Gender and Disaster Network.

FAO and WFP. 2003. 'Passport to Mainstreaming a Gender Perspective in Emergency Programmes, Key Analytical Questions for Designing Gender-Sensitive Humanitarian Interventions'. Available online at www.fao.org/sd/SEAGA

Fordham, M. 1999. 'The Intersection of Gender and Social Class in Disaster: Balancing Resilience and Vulnerability', *International Journal of Mass Emergencies and Disasters,* 17(1): 15–36.

———. 2001. 'Challenging Boundaries: A Gender Perspective on Early Warning in Disaster and Environmental Management'. Background Paper for Expert Group Meeting, Ankara, Turkey, conducted by UNDAW and UNISDR.

Fothergill, A. 1996. 'The Neglect of Gender in Disaster Work: An Overview of Literature', *International Journal of Mass Emergencies and Disasters,* 14(1): 33–56.

Global Fund for Women. 2006. *Caught in the Storm: The Impact of Disasters on Women.*

Gomez, S. 2006. *Guidelines for Gender Sensitive Disaster Management.* Thailand: Asia Pacific Forum on Women, Law and Development.

Inter-Agency Network for Education in Emergencies. 2004. *Minimum Standards for Education in Emergencies, Chronic Crises and Early Reconstruction.* London: INEE.

———. 2006. *Good Practice Guide: Girls' and Women's Education.* Available online at http://www.ineesite.org

Inter-Agency Standing Committee (IASC). 2005. *IASC Guidelines for Gender-based Violence Interventions in Humanitarian Settings. Focusing on Prevention of and Response to Sexual Violence in Emergencies.* Geneva: Inter-Agency Standing Committee Task Force on Gender and Humanitarian Assistance. Available online at http://www. humanitarianinfo.org/iasc/content/products/docs/tfgender_GBVGuidelines 2005.pdf

———. 2006. *Gender Handbook: Different Needs—Equal Opportunities, Gender Handbook in Humanitarian Action.* Available online at http://ochaonline.un.org/AboutOCHA/ GenderEquality/KeyDocuments/IASCGenderHandbook/tabid/1384/Default. aspx

International Federation of Red Cross. *Working with Women in Emergency Relief and Rehabilitation Programmes*. Field Studies Paper No. 2. League of Red Cross and Red Crescent Societies. 1991. Geneva.

International Recovery Platform. 2007. *Learning from Disaster Recovery: Guidance for Decision Makers*. IRP & ISDR. Available online at http://www.recoveryplatform. org/newBook_E/Learning-From-Disaster-Recovery.pdf

League of Red Cross and Red Crescent Societies. 1991. 'Working with Women in Emergency Relief and Rehabilitation Programmes'. Field Studies Paper No. 2. Geneva.

Mehta, M. 2007. *Gender Matters: Lessons for Disaster Risk Reduction in South Asia*. Kathmandu, Nepal: International Centre for Integrated Mountain Development.

Noel. 1990. 'The Role of Women in Health Related Aspects of Emergency Management', *ICN Nursing Review*, 36(6).

O'Brien, P. and Patricia Archison. 1998. 'Gender Differentiation and Aftershock Warning Response,' in Elaine Enarson and Betty Hearn Morrow (eds), *The Gendered Terrain of Disaster: Through Women's Eyes*, pp. 173–80. Westport, CT: Greenwood Publications.

Ollenburger, J. and G. Tobin. 1998. 'Women and Post Disaster Stress', in Elaine Enarson and Betty Hearn Morrow (eds), *The Gendered Terrain of Disaster: Through Women's Eyes*, pp. 95–108. Westport, CT: Greenwood Publications.

Orstad, L. 2001. 'Tools for Change: Emergency Management for Women', United Nations Division for the Advancement of Women and International Strategy for Disaster Reduction, Expert Group Meeting, Ankara, Turkey.

Oxfam. 2004. *A Little Gender Handbook for Emergencies (Or Just Plain Common Sense)*. Humanitarian Department. Available online at http://homepage.oxfam.org.uk/ emergencies/ed_general/scipio/gender_handbook.htm

———. 2005. 'The Tsunami's Impact on Women. Oxfam Briefing Note'. Oxfam International.

Sayeed, A. 2005. 'The Pakistan Earthquake's Impact on Women', *APLWD Forum News*, 18(3), ROOTS for Equity, Pakistan.

Scanlon, J. 1996. 'The Perspective of Gender: A Missing Element in Disaster Response', *Australian Journal of Emergency Response*, 11(4): 2–7.

Sekar, K., S. Bharath, G. Henry and D. Desikan. 2005. *Tsunami Disaster: Psychosocial Care for Women*. Information Manual 4. Bangalore: National Institute of Mental Health and Neurosciences.

Society for Rural Education and Development (SRED). 2006. *Tsunami Aftermath: Violation of Dalit Women's Human Rights in India*.

Solidaritas Perempuan. 2006. *Tsunami Aftermath: Violations of Women's Rights in Nanggroe Aceh*. Indonesia: Darussalam.

Solomon, S. D., E. M. Smith, L. N. Robins and R. L. Fischbach. 1987. 'Social Involvement as a Mediator of Disaster Induced Stress', *Journal of Applied Psychology*, 17(2): 1092–112.

Solorzano, I. and O. Montoya. 2000. 'Men against Marital Violence: A Nicaraguan Campaign', *ID21 Insights*, 35. Available online at http://www.id21.org/insights/ insights35/insights-iss35-art05.html

Sphere Project. 2004. *The Sphere Project Humanitarian Charter and Minimum Standards in Disaster Response*. Available online at http://www.sphereproject.org/ handbookhdbkpdf/hdbkpdf_full.pdf

UNEP. 1997. 'Asian Disaster Management News', Newsletter of the Disaster Management Community in Asia and the Pacific, 3(3).

UNESCO. 2006. *Education in Emergencies: The Gender Implications—Advocacy Brief.* Bangkok, Thailand: UNESCO.

UNFPA. 2004. *Reproductive Health Kits for Crisis.* Available online at www.aidsand emergencies.org/RHKit_manual_en.pdf

———. 2006. *Manual: Inter-Agency Reproductive Health Kits for Crisis Situations.* Available online at http://www.rhrc.org/pdf/rhrkit.pdf

UN-HABITAT. 2003. *Toolkit for Mainstreaming Gender in Un-habitat Field Programmes.*

UNHCR. 2003. *Sexual and Gender-based Violence against Refugees, Returnees and Internally Displaced Persons. Guidelines for Prevention and Response.* Available online at http://www.rhrc.org/pdf/gl_sgbv03.pdf

UNISDR. 2005. *Hyogo Framework for Action 2005–2015: Building the Resilience of Nations and Communities to Disasters.* Available online at www.unisdr.org/wcdr

UNOCHA. 2005. *OCHA Tool Kit Gender Equality: Tools to Support Implementation of OCHA's Policy on Gender Equality.*

———. 2007. *The International Search and Rescue Response Guidelines: Guidelines and Methodology.* The International Search and Rescue Advisory Group, INSARAG. Available online at http://www.reliefweb.int/undac/documents/insarag/guidelines/topics.html

US Department of Commerce, National Weather Service's Office of Meteorology. 1995. *A Summary of Natural Hazard Fatalities for 1994 in the United States.* Washington, DC: US Department of Commerce.

Walia, A. 2006. 'Accessibility and Sensitivity of Disaster Relief Services towards Women', India Disaster Management Congress, New Delhi, November 29–30.

WFP and FAO. 2001. Passport to Mainstreaming a Gender Perspective in Emergency Programmes. Available online at www.fao.org/sd/SEAGA.

Wiest, R. E., J. S. P. Mocellin and D. T. Motsisi. 1994. *The Needs of Women in Disasters and Emergencies.* Report prepared for the United Nations Development Programme, Disaster Management Training Programme and the Office of the United Nations Disaster Relief Coordinator. Winnipeg, Canada: The University of Manitoba Disaster Research Institute. Available online at http://www.radixonline.org/resources/women-in-disaster-emergency.pdf (Accessed on 10 August 2009).

World Health Organization (WHO). 2002. *Gender and Health in Natural Disaster.*

———. 2003. *Mental Health in Emergencies: Psychological and Social Aspects of Health of Populations Exposed to Extreme Stressors.* Available online at http://www.who.int/mental_health/media/en/640/pdf

———. 2005. *Gender Considerations in Disaster Assessment.*

Yonder, A., Sengul Akcar and Prema Gopalan. 2005. *Women's Participation in Disaster Relief and Recovery.* India: SEEDS. Available online at http://www.popcouncil.org/pdfs/seeds/Seeds22.pdf

About the Editors and Contributors

———•✦•———

The Editors

Elaine Enarson is an American disaster sociologist currently working independently in Lyons, Colorado. Her personal experience in Hurricane Andrew sparked extensive work on gender-based vulnerability and capacity, writing from applied and theoretical perspectives on women's human rights, livelihoods, safety, housing, community roles, political mobilisation, family lives, and disaster quilting as well as gender and extreme heat, evacuation and disaster recovery. She has developed a number of gender and disaster training packages for practitioners and a manual for Canadian grass-roots women's groups on emergency preparedness. A founding member of the Gender and Disaster Network (GDN), Elaine was also the lead course developer of a FEMA course on social vulnerability and initiated a grass-roots risk assessment project with women in the Caribbean as well as the online Gender and Disaster Sourcebook. Currently she consults with UN agencies and teaches part-time in her areas of interest. Elaine co-edited *The Gendered Terrain of Disaster: Through Women's Eyes* (1998) and *Women and Katrina: The Gender Dimensions of Disaster Recovery* (forthcoming) and is developing a monograph on these topics in US contexts.

P. G. Dhar Chakrabarti has been both a researcher and a practitioner of development policies and programmes on a wide range of issues. Starting his career as a Lecturer in Calcutta University, he joined the Indian Administrative Service in 1980 and worked on various assignments at local, provincial, national and international levels. During his tenure as Head of Women's Development Wing in the Ministry of Human Resource Development, he was involved with many new initiatives like the Gender Budget, Women's Component Plan and the National Policy on Women's Empowerment. Presently, he is heading both the National Institute of Disaster Management which is the nodal institute of Government of India for research, documentation, training and capacity building on disaster management; and the SAARC Disaster Management Centre which is a regional organisation of the eight South Asian countries. He was nominated by the Secretary General of the United Nations to serve as a Member of the Advisory Group of Central Emergency Response Fund (CERF) of the United Nations. He further worked as a Member of the Expert Group of the UNISDR on Gender and Disaster. He is the editor of two journals he founded—*Disaster and Development* and *Journal of South Asian Disaster Studies*. Widely travelled, he has authored a number of books and contributed papers in journals published from different countries.

The Contributors

Sengül Akçar is Executive Director and Board Member of the Foundation for the Support of Women's Work in Turkey, as well as a civil engineer with an advanced degree in public administration.

Carol A. Amaratunga is the Dean of Applied Research, Justice Institute of British Columbia. Her research interests include gender and disaster management, infectious disease outbreaks, public and community safety.

Cheryl L. Anderson is a certified planner, Director of the Hazards, Climate and Environment Programme, University of Hawaii Social Science Research Institute and affiliate graduate faculty with the Department of Urban and Regional Planning.

Madhavi Malalgoda Ariyabandu is a development researcher with specific focus on the issues of disaster risk, poverty, livelihoods and gender.

Currently, she is South Asia Programme Officer, UN International Strategy for Disaster Reduction, Asia Pacific (UNISDR).

Mihir R. Bhatt is Director of All India Disaster Mitigation Institute based in Ahmedabad, Gujarat.

Sarah Bradshaw is a Principal Lecturer in Development Studies at Middlesex University. She is also a development worker with the British international NGO Progressio and works with Puntos de Enceuntro in Nicaragua.

Adélia de Melo Branco is an anthropologist, author of *Women of the Drought: Struggle and Visibility in Face of a Disaster Situation* and UNIFEM Country Programme Manager in Mozambique.

Leigh Brownhill is completing a post-doctoral fellowship at York University in Toronto. She specialises in analysis of gender, food and social movements, in particular in East Africa. Her book, *Land, Food, Freedom* will be published by Africa World Press.

Sarah Fisher has a background in gender, development and sexual and reproductive and rights and is currently working as a Policy Research Officer for a maternity organisation in the United Kingdom.

Maureen Fordham teaches disaster management at the University of Northumbria in the United Kingdom. She is a founding member of the GDN and manages the GDN website.

Alice Fothergill is the author of *Heads above Water: Gender, Class, and Family in the Grand Forks Flood*. She teaches sociology at the University of Vermont with an interest in family and childhood studies, disasters, gender, inequality and qualitative methods.

Cecilia Castro García is Mexican, urban planner and an independent scholar for local and Federal Government. She is also a plastic artist with exhibitions in México, Japan and New York City.

Prema Gopalan has served as Executive Director of Swayam Shikshan Prayog (SSP) for over 15 years working to support poor rural women in India and to enable their leadership in periods of crisis.

Minu Hemmati is a psychologist working as an independent consultant on multi-stakeholder processes and on gender aspects of climate change and sustainable development.

Rosalind Houghton is currently a Ph.D. candidate at Victoria University of Wellington in New Zealand, researching domestic violence reporting levels after Civil Defence emergencies in New Zealand.

Chandni Joshi is Regional Programme Director of UNIFEM based in Delhi, India.

Tamiyo Kondo is an Associate Professor at Kobe University researching disaster recovery planning and teaching community-based planning and housing policy.

Lisa Kuzunishi is a Ph.D. researcher at Osaka City University and her major subject areas are housing policy for single mother/father households and domestic violence survivors in Japan.

Yianna Lambrou is a sociologist and senior officer at the Gender, Equity and Rural Employment Division of the UN Food and Agriculture Organization in Rome.

Brian Linneker is a Senior Research Fellow in the Department of Geography at Birbeck College, University of London, and a development worker with the British international NGO Progressio.

Francie Lund is at the University of KwaZulu-Natal, Durban, South Africa and is Director of the Social Protection Programme of the global research and advocacy network WIEGO (Women in Informal Employment: Globalizing and Organizing).

Reiko Masai is Chair of the Board of Directors of the non-profit 'Women's Net Kobe' and manages a shelter for domestic violence survivors. She also assisted vulnerable women in the great Hansin Awaji earthquake.

Manjari Mehta is a social anthropologist and independent researcher/ consultant working on social inclusion, poverty and disaster risk reduction issues in the mountain areas of northern India. She lives in Dehradun, Uttarakhand in India.

Prafulla Mishra earned a doctorate in Mangrove Ecology and has worked since the last 16 years on development and humanitarian programmes in India, Sudan, Chad and Ethiopia focusing on livelihoods, gender and humanitarian initiatives. He is now working at Kenya for the IRC.

Helena Molin Valdés is the Deputy Director of the United Nations International Strategy for Disaster Reduction (UNISDR). She worked for eight years with participatory development projects as an architect in Central America before joining the UN Disaster Reduction Field 18 years ago.

Audrey Y. Mullings is a consultant in the disaster risk management programme for the United States of America's Office of Foreign Disaster Assistance (USAID/OFDA) for Latin America and the Caribbean. She has over 20 years of experience in the field of disaster management.

Tracey L. O'Sullivan teaches in the Faculty of Health Sciences at the University of Ottawa, Canada. Her research and publications have focused on personal and occupation stress, coping and resilience with emphasis on caregivers and disaster preparedness.

Lori Peek is an Assistant Professor in the Department of Sociology at Colorado State University. Her research focuses on vulnerable populations in disasters, including religious and ethnic minorities, children and women.

Simone Reinsch graduated from the University of Manitoba with a Master of Nursing degree (2006). Her ongoing passion for bringing rural gendered health issues and inequities to the forefront provided the impetus for her thesis work.

Ulrike Röhr is a sociologist and civil engineer. She works extensively in the area of gender equality and climate change through the international network Gender CC-Women for Climate Justice.

Samia Galal Saad is Professor of Environmental Health at Alexandria University in Egypt, and a senior consultant for gender and environment integration in policies and programmes of UN Organisations.

Azra Talat Sayeed works on trade liberalisation impacts on the working class with emphasis on landless women in the rural sector. She is on the Programme and Management Committee of Asia Pacific Forum on Women Law and Development and is the Executive Director of Roots for Equity and Organisation working on anti-globalisation movement in Pakistan.

Judith Soares is Senior Lecturer and Head, Women and Development Unit, The University of the West Indies.

Tony Vaux worked for Oxfam for 28 years and is now an international development consultant based in the United Kingdom working in the field of conflict analysis, humanitarian policy and human security.

Ajinder Walia is a sociologist currently serving as Assistant Professor at the National Institute of Disaster Management in India working in the areas of gender, community-based disaster preparedness and needs of children in disasters.

Ayse Yonder is a Professor of City and Regional Planning at the Graduate Center for Planning and the Environment, Pratt Institute's School of Architecture in New York, and a member of the Huairou Commission.

Luisa Emilia Reyes Zúñiga is Mexican. She has studied International Relations, English Literature and psychoanalysis. A specialist in gender and development, she collaborates with the NGO Equidad AC in the area of gender budgets.

Index

———— • ✦ • ————

children
  childcare facilities and, 107
  medical treatment and preventive
    care, 94
  safety concerns, 149
  in single-mother households, 139
  as victims of domestic violence, 9
  vulnerabilities during disaster, 115
Child, Youth and Family (CYF), 103, 105
CIDA. *See* Canadian International Development Agency (CIDA)
Civil Co-ordinator for Emergency and
  Reconstruction (CCER), 76
Civil Defence Welfare group, 109
Civil Protection, 278, 279, 286
climate change
  conflicts due to, 292–293
  constraints and resources for developing
    policy for, 298–299
  demographic changes, 293
  directions for future involvement of
    women, 300–302
  effects on health, 293
  emerging aspects of gender and,
    291–294
  gender adaptation to, 291
  gender-based responsibilities and roles
    in, 291
  gender integration into all aspects of
    policy development, 296–298
  gender mainstreaming, 290
  gender-sensitive approach, 290
  gender-specific consumption patterns,
    293–294
  migration due to, 292
  mitigation of, 291
Coalition for Assisting Tsunami Affected
  Women (CATAW), 237
community-based development projects,
  175
community-based disaster assessment, 68
community-based mitigation, in Northern
  India, 67
community-based projects, women participation in, 82

community-driven gender-sensitive
  watershed management, in North-
  western India, 68–69
community mobilisation systems, for
  disaster management, 68
community preparedness, for natural hazards
  in Nepal, 65–67
community resilience, development of,
  64–65
community-to-community learning, 191
Community Vulnerability Profiles, 21
comprehensive disaster risk management
  (CDRM)
  in Mexico, 275, 276
  public policies in risk reduction, 280
Conference of the Parties (COP), 296, 297
'corrosive community,' 168
country-level risk reduction, 60
Cretzfeldt–Jacob disease, 152
CYF. *See* Child, Youth and Family (CYF)
cyclone
  in Bangladesh, 20
  early warning, 338–339
  effect on rural and urban household, 21
  gender issues during, 179
  parenting in aftermath of, 119–123
  physical destruction and economic
    losses, 112
  shelters, 20, 341–342
  women response to, 12

damage assessment, 352–353
Darfur conflict, 29
'decade of disasters,' 41
decision making, women's role in, 54,
  77, 84
disaster assessment, community-based, 68
disaster assistance, economic needs of
  women and men, 81
disaster cycle, influence of biological factors
  on, 9–10
disaster-induced stress, among farm women
  in Canada, 153–162
disaster management
  capacities and resources of women
    in, xv

emergency response, biological aspects in, 10–11
Emergency Response Framework, 337, 338
emergency shelter, for women and children, 341–342
employment
impact of post-disaster stress on, 101
patterns among men and women, 81
empowerment strategies, adaption by women, 205–206
'Engendering Development,' 79
environmental impact assessment (EIA), 95
ethnicity, 6, 70, 327
evacuation, vulnerability of women during, 339

faith-based domestic violence agency, 104
farm women's disaster stress
in Canada, 153–154
coping strategies and resilience, 160–161
empowerment for reducing, 161
family, community and, 156–158
gendered farm economics and, 158–160
patriarchy and, 155–156
stress symptoms among, 153
fathers, role during initial crisis
care work, 118–119
evacuation, 116–117
relocation, 117–118
Federal Emergency Management Agency (FEMA), 116
female-headed households, 81, 84. See also male-headed households
female homicides, due to family violence, 101
flood disasters, 20
flood-related abuse, in New Zealand, 106
Focus Humanitarian Assistance (FHA), 67, 68
'Food for Work' programmes, 82
food security, 292, 343
and nutrition programmes, 344
forest fires. See wild fires
Freedom Corner hunger strike, 172

Frente Faribundo Martí de Liberación Nacional (FMLN), 177

GAD. See gender and development (GAD)
GBV. See gender-based violence (GBV)
GDI. See Gender Development Index (GDI)
GEM. See gender empowerment measure (GEM)
gender
and climate change, 290–291
difference and gender inequalities, 2
difference from sex or sexuality, 1
division of labour during different phases of disaster cycle, 7
factors for men in disaster situations, 8–9
inequalities (see gender inequalities)
perspectives in disasters, 5–11
relations in communities and societies, 5
risk assessment model in Caribbean, 21
roles and relations through reconstruction, 76
roles and relations within households, 83–85
social construction of risk analysis and practice, xv–xvii
sustainable development and, 1
vulnerabilities and capabilities, 282–284
Gender and Climate Change Network, xvi
Gender and Development, xvii
gender and development (GAD), 276, 280
Gender and Disaster Network (GDN), xvi, xvii, 3, 41, 49, 50
Gender and Disaster Sourcebook, xvii
gender-based prejudices, 15
gender-based violence (GBV), 79, 233, 241, 244, 348–350
Gender Based Violence Taskforce, 240
Gender Development Index (GDI)
in El Salvador, 177
of Pakistan, 143
gender discrimination. See gender inequalities

grass-roots women, 203
Green Belt Movement, 172, 225
  climate and environment issues in
    Kenya, 230
  tree planting for peace and climate
    justice in, 226–228
  women and, 228–230
'Greening of Davy Hill' project, 258
G8 Summit, 300
Gujarat Mahila Housing SEWA Trust,
  213

Hanshin-Awaji Earthquake, 54
  case study of post-disaster housing,
    134–139
  characteristic of, 131
  damage caused by, 131
  health and safety concerns, 133
Harris/Streatham Women's Cooperative
  (HSWC), 256
hazard-resilient communities, 65
Honolulu Call to Action, 2, 41, 43,
  46–48
Honolulu workshop recommendations,
  43–44, 46, 48
households
  biological aspects in emergency re-
    sponse of, 10
  female-headed, 8, 14, 21
  gender roles and relations within,
    83–85
  kinds of housing assistance for single-
    mother, 137
  male-headed, 81
  post-earthquake housing for single-
    mother, 140
  rural and urban, 21
  single-headed, 93
HSWC. See Harris/Streatham Women's
  Cooperative (HSWC)
humanitarian disasters, in Kenya, 224–226
human rights
  gendered inequalities and, 7
  violation in Pakistan, 143–145
hurricane. See cyclone
Hurricane Andrew, 14

Hurricane Katrina, 54, 58
  destruction and economic losses caused
    by, 112
  mothers and fathers in initial crisis,
    116–119
  parenting in aftermath of, 119–123
  recommendations for supporting
    mothers and fathers, 124–127
Hurricane Mitch, 11, 14, 21, 54, 75
  mortality rate among men and women,
    12
  risk reduction and opportunity for
    women after, 22–23
  women participation in community-
    based projects, 82
  *The Hyogo Framework for Action 2005–
    2015: Building the Resilience
    of Nations and Communities to
    Disasters*, 18, 24
Hyogo Framework for Action (HFA), 3,
  44, 50, 274, 320, 338
  action area 1, for disaster risk reduction,
    323–324
  action area 2, for identifying, assessing
    and monitoring risk, 324–327
  action area 3, for increasing awareness,
    education and training, 327–329
  action area 4, for reducing risk in key
    sectors, 330–332
  action area 5, for strengthening disaster
    preparedness, 332–334
  action identified to help national gov-
    ernments, 323
  UNIFEM's model for gendering,
    315–317
Hyogo Prefecture, 135, 137
Hyogo Priority Actions, 49

income-generating activities, of women,
  77, 81, 82, 84, 268
Indian Ocean tsunami, xv, 58
  access to relief funds in aftermath of,
    307
  ex gratia payment by government,
    345–348

sanitary and privacy needs, of women during emergency response, 10

SARS. *See* Severe Acute Respiratory Syndrome (SARS)

Sarvodaya Women's Movement (SWM), 309–310

school contingency planning processes, 66

search and rescue, gender variation in mortality and morbidity during, 339–340

Self Employed Women's Association (SEWA), 212
    approach to earthquake relief, 216–219
    disaster response to sustainable development, 219–221
    Integrated Insurance Scheme, 213
    resources for disaster responses, 213–214
    response to disaster situations, 172
    responsibility for and right to compensation, 215–216
    work and employment, 214–215

senior citizens
    emergency shelters for, 104
    'The Golden Years' educational programme on, 254
    survival during tsunami waves, 12

Severe Acute Respiratory Syndrome (SARS), 55, 165, 166
    gender and public health response systems, 166–167
    global outbreaks of, 169
    health care workers during outbreak of, 167–168
    social support for minimising negative impact of stress, 168

SEWA Bank (Shree Mahila SEWA Sahakari Bank Limited), 213

SEWA Gram Mahila Haat, 213

sexual abuse and violence
    during Hanshin-Awaji Earthquake, 134
    influence of biological factors on, 9
    in Kenya, 225
    risk of, 8

role of humanitarian organisations in preventing, 236
    in Sri Lanka, 233

shelter accommodations, for families with special needs, 127

single-headed households, 93

single-mother families
    impacts and government responses to, 134–135
    kinds of housing assistance in Japan, 137
    post-quake housing conditions for, 137–139
    pre-quake housing conditions for, 136

Siyath Foundation, 311

social classes, 6, 178

Social Services and Child Protection Administration (SHÇEK), 199, 203

social vulnerability
    of children, 115
    community level development for reducing, 183
    community responses to, 234
    factors increasing, of women, 132
    of female-headed households, 8, 81, 318
    gender equality and, 42
    of women in disaster, 1
    women's dependence on man and, 242

'Solidarity in the Greenhouse,' 296

Sri Bhuvaneshwari Mahila Ashram (SBMA), 67

Sri Lanka
    access to relief funds, 307
    capacity building of women's groups, 240
    community responses against violence, 234–236
    domestic violence in, 241
    educational opportunities for, 306
    gender issues in aftermath of tsunami in, 305–308
    lost employment opportunities for women in, 307

*W*omen, Gender and Disaster: Global Issues and Initiatives examines gender within the context of disaster risk management. It argues for gender mainstreaming as an effective strategy towards achieving disaster risk reduction and mitigating post-disaster gender disparity. Highlighting that gender inequalities pervade all aspects of life, it analyses the failure to implement inclusive and gender-sensitive approaches to relief and rehabilitation work. While examining positive strategies for change, the collection focuses on women's knowledge, capabilities, leadership and experience in community resource management. The authors emphasize that these strengths in women, which are required for building resilience to hazards and disasters, are frequently overlooked.

This timely book will be extremely useful to policy makers and professionals active in the field of disaster management and to academics and students in gender studies, social work, environmental studies and development studies.

Elaine Enarson is an independent scholar.

P. G. Dhar Chakrabarti was formerly at National Institute of Disaster Management and SAARC Disaster Management Centre.

ISBN 978-93-515-0239-5

SAGE www.sagepublishing.com
Los Angeles | London | New Delhi | Singapore | Washington DC | Melbourne

9 789351 502395

Markov
Processes
and
Potential
Theory

ROBERT M. BLUMENTHAL
AND RONALD K. GETOOR